EARTHING
THE
MYTHS

With good wish,
Daragh Smyth.

For Scota and Ériu, their rivers, hills and plains.

Daragh Smyth is a retired lecturer from the Technological University of Dublin and co-founder of Saor-Ollscoil na hÉireann (The Free University of Ireland). He was in charge of the Erasmus programme at T.U.D., where he taught Irish Cultural Studies to students from Europe, Australia and North America. Smyth has published two books with Irish Academic Press: *A Guide to Irish Mythology* (1996) and *Cú Chulainn: An Iron Age Hero* (2005).

EARTHING
THE
MYTHS

THE MYTHS, LEGENDS AND
EARLY HISTORY OF IRELAND

Daragh Smyth

IRISH ACADEMIC PRESS

First published in 2020 by
Irish Academic Press
10 George's Street
Newbridge
Co. Kildare
Ireland
www.iap.ie

This paperback edition first published 2021
© Daragh Smyth, 2021

9781788551397 (Paper)
9781788551366 (Kindle)
9781788551373 (Epub)
9781788551380 (PDF)

British Library Cataloguing in Publication Data
An entry can be found on request

Library of Congress Cataloging in Publication Data
An entry can be found on request

Typeset in Minion Pro 11/14 pt

Unless otherwise stated, all images are from the author's private collection.
Images on pp. 13, 20, 23, 28, 62, 134, 140, 158, 213, 266, 277, 279, 321, 355
© Alamy Stock Photo.
Front cover: David Lyons / Alamy Stock Photo

CONTENTS

INTRODUCTION

It is my experience in studying our historical and quasi-historical legends, and in the best of all ways, namely by going over the actual ground where they are alleged to have happened, that wherever you are on sure ground there is a remarkable appropriateness between the episodes and the incidents of the tales and their topographical setting. The story told whether actual happenings or a conflation of legends, or a conscious invention, suits the geography and the terrain.

–Henry Morris, First Battle of Magh Tuiredh, *JRSAI*, 1928.

The purpose of this book is to provide a guide to readers who would like to become familiar with those places associated with early Irish history and mythology. In Ireland, the link between place and myth is strong. The hundreds of dolmens and ring forts associated with the love story of Diarmuid and Gráinne, for example, keep this medieval tale alive, just as 'The Cave of the Otherworld' near Tulsk in Co. Roscommon connects us to the earliest rites of *samain*, a festival that is still with us in the shape of Hallowe'en; or there is Glenasmole on the borders of Dublin and Wicklow, where Oisín, the son of Finn mac Cumhail, fell from his horse on his return from *Tír na nÓg*, having set out 300 years previously from Glenbeigh Strand in Co. Kerry.

Like most mythologies, Irish mythology has a *mythos* or a sacred narrative and a *religio*, that which binds members by vows and rules. In the Irish context, the *mythos* is the strongest component and the *religio* is the weakest. This means that pre-Christian Ireland did not have a religion as such, but this apparent absence of structure does not mean that there were no beliefs of a spiritual nature. The island receives its name from Ériu, a goddess whose name has been translated to mean 'regular traveller of the heavens'. Generally, the Irish for Ireland is Éire, and this is the version that you will find on government papers and on all postage stamps. However, most goddesses are to be found in threes, and Ériu shares a triad with Banba and Fódla; Banba represents the warrior aspect of Ireland, while Fódla represents Ireland in the poetic or spiritual sense, and Ériu is the mother goddess who nurtures the island.

The coming of Christianity in the mid-fifth century brought an end to many ancient rites and the mythology surrounding them. Some ancient ceremonies, however, managed to survive quite late, such as those surrounding the inauguration of a king, and many of the stories from prehistory were preserved in manuscripts written by monks in the eleventh enturies. The fruit of their work can be seen today in such works as the *Book* wide-ranging compilation containing *Lebor Gabála Érenn* ('The Book of ...nd the *Táin Bó Cuailigne* ('The Cattle Raid of Cooley'), or the *Book of the Dun Cow* (*Lebor na hUidre*), which also contains a version of the *Táin* as well as many other stories about the central character of Irish myth, Cú Chulainn. Mention must also be made of two later sources: the *Annals of the Four Masters*, a chronicle with entries stretching back to the Deluge (calculated as 2,242 years after creation) written in the seventeenth century and based on previous annals, and the great seminal work by Geoffrey Keating from the same century, *Foras Feasa ar Éirinn*, which retold many of the ancient tales in establishing an approach to Irish history from a native point of view as a counter-balance against Tudor propaganda.

Many of the stories find their genesis during the Iron Age, a time when ash, elm, and oak began to appear in greater numbers. Grass and bracken also increased, as did cereals. Around the Late Iron Age, agriculture was renewed. The Bronze Age artefacts resulting from the copper mines of west Cork, which influenced the Bronze Age throughout Europe, began to be replaced by Iron Age implements, which influenced agriculture and supplied the weaponry which led to the expansion of tribes or clans. This also led to a greater number of tribes seeking territorial expansion throughout the island, and, in prehistory as in history, the dominant tribes and their gods and goddesses took priority in the sagas and legends. The iron fork and the iron axe represent the beginning of expanding agriculture, the depletion of the woods and the onset of the warrior bands which were to become the stuff of sagas and contain the heart-blood of mythic ritual. The Iron Age proper began around 800 BC in Upper Austria with a culture known as the Hallstatt, and the Iron Age culture which influenced Ireland came from Lake Neuchâtel in Switzerland and is known as La Tène. For centuries the La Tène Celts were the dominant people in Europe. The distinctive craft of La Tène culture can be seen in metal, gold and stone artefacts. An example of the latter is represented in the curvilinear artwork on the Turoe Stone which stands in Co. Galway.

It was this period that saw the emergence of enclosed farmsteads in the form of raths or ring forts, also known as *lis* or *liss* or *lios*, which have left a lasting mark on the Irish landscape and have contributed to the names of many places. Despite many being ploughed over or destroyed, an estimated 30,000 still survive throughout the island. They generally have a diameter between 80 and 170 feet; a single bank with a circular ditch is the most usual form. It was under the roofs of these primitive residences that the tales of gods, goddesses, heroes and the Otherworld were first formed, building up to a corpus of myth that, despite all the losses, is still impressive.

A conventional approach is to see these stories as divided into four broad cycles:

- the Mythological Cycle, containing stories about the various peoples that arrived in migratory invasions and is especially concerned with the god-like race of the Tuatha Dé Danann;

- the Ulster Cycle, which recounts sagas about the heroes of the Ulaid, a tribe inhabiting the north-eastern part of the country, including parts of modern north Leinster;
- the Fenian Cycle, a corpus of prose and verse mainly about the exploits of Finn mac Cumhail and his band of warriors, the Fianna.
- the Historical Cycle, containing accounts of both legendary and historical kings such as Cormac mac Airt, Niall of the Nine Hostages, and Brian Bóruma, but most important of all the tale of *Buile Shuibhne* ('The Frenzy of Sweeney').

Of these, it is the Ulster and Fenian cycles that have caught the imagination of writers through the centuries. As in all mythologies, the role of the hero is central. In the Irish pantheon, the most important is Cú Chulainn, the Iron Age hero defending Ulster from the forces of Connacht who was eventually transformed into the spirit of Irish resistance to English rule. He is the main focus of the Ulster Cycle sagas, which also include the great romantic tale of Deirdre and Naoise and 'The Taking of the Hostel of the Two Reds' (*Togail Bruidne Da Derga*). The tales from the Ulster Cycle are based between the forts of Emain Macha, two miles west of the city of Armagh, and Dún Dealgan, less than a mile west from the town of Dundalk. They tell the tales of the last years of the Picts, or Dál nAraide, before they were subsumed into the Gaelic order under the O'Neills in the fourth century.

The Fenian or Ossianic Cycle is set in the reign of Cormac mac Airt, who is said to have reigned in Tara in the third century of the Christian era. From the thirteenth century these tales were translated from the manuscripts and slowly entered our culture through the work of poets and bards, and in time, from the written word evolved from the oral tradition. Many of these works are contained in works known as the Duanaire Finn or the 'Lays of Finn', many of which were written or rewritten in the early seventeenth century and translated into English in the late nineteenth century.

Not all mythological tales fall into any of these categories. There are, for example, those stories of adventure classified under the heading of *imram*, from the Old Irish for 'rowing about' or 'voyaging'. The most famous of these is *Imram Brain*, or 'The Voyage of Bran', telling of a voyage to the Otherworld, which was reached after the voyagers fell over the horizon. This saga is found in the eleventh century manuscript *Lebor na hUidre*, but according to the noted German scholar Kuno Meyer, it was probably written in the seventh or eighth century. A sixth-century *imram* concerns St Brendan from Brandon Creek in present-day Co. Kerry, who did not fall off the edge of the world but instead discovered America. In the late twentieth century, an expedition using a boat similar to Brendan's successfully made it to America and back.

THE DRUIDS

Much of the mythology reflects the pagan religious background of prehistoric Ireland, at the centre of which stood the priestly caste known as the druids. Their origins are open to debate, but some have connected them to the Dravidians from the Indus Valley in India. Their idea of an afterlife was similar to the Hindu doctrine of reincarnation and the Pythagorean idea of metempsychosis. Thus, they believed that the spirit at the time of death passed into another body, possibly that of a different species. An early coloniser of Ireland, Partholón, is said to have arrived with three druids called Fios, Eolus and Fochmarc, meaning intelligence, knowledge and inquiry; all druids were said to possess these attributes.

Druidic influence extended from the Indus Valley across Europe to the British Isles and has been recorded by Greek and Roman historians and chroniclers, including Julius Caesar. Stonehenge in England was a noted druidic centre, as was Pentre Ifan between Cardiff and Fishguard, close to the Pembrokeshire coast in Wales; the latter would also, like Tara, have been a centre for initiation.

In Ireland, Tara, Emain Macha and Uisnech were three druidic centres. On the first day of May, the Hill of Uisnech, regarded as being the centre of Ireland, became a gathering place for the druids, who lit the first sacred fire, from which all others were lit. During excavation at Uisnech, an enormous bed of ashes which had turned the earth red to a depth of some inches was found, thus reinforcing the theory of Uisnech as the centre of a fire cult.

In early times, the functions of the druid and the *file*, or poet, were similar, and both practised magic. One interesting rite was *Imbas forasnai*, 'the manifestation that enlightens', which was used to acquire supernatural knowledge. A tenth-century manuscript by Cormac, the king–bishop of Cashel in Munster, describes it as follows:

> Thus it is done: the poet chews a piece of the flesh of a red pig, or dog or cat, and puts it afterwards on the flag behind the door, and pronounces an incantation on it, and offers it to idol gods, and afterwards calls his idols to him … and pronounces incantations on his two palms, and calls again his idols to him that his sleep may not be disturbed, and he lays his two palms on both his cheeks, and in this manner he falls asleep; and he is watched in order that no one may interrupt or disturb him until everything about which he is engaged is revealed to him.

Dreams have been at the centre of aboriginal cultures from Australia to India to Ireland to North America. Another notable dream rite in Ireland was the *Tarbfes* or the 'Bull-feast', in which a druid, after partaking of the meat of a white bull that had just been killed, would sleep for a number of hours while other druids recited incantations over him. When he awoke, he recounted his dreams, and these would determine the kind of man who would be king. The rite was carried out at Tara, Co. Meath, which was, and to an extent still is, the spiritual centre of Ireland. It continued until the coming of St Patrick.

FOUNDATION MYTHS

Ancient Irish culture had its own highly developed foundation myths, as found especially in *Lebor Gabála* ('The Book of Invasions'), which cites tribes arriving in Ireland, having set out from the Middle East after the Flood: these tribes included the Nemedians, the Fomorians, the Fir Bolg and apparently the Tuatha Dé Danann and the Milesians. Thus, there is a strong biblical tradition in many of the peoples who arrived here. 'And the sons of Noah, that went forth were Shem and Ham and Japheth; and Ham is the father of Canann. These are the three sons of Noah and of them the whole earth was overspread' (Genesis 9: 18, 19). Sharon Paice Macleod, quoting John Carey in his edition of *Lebor Gabála*, writes: 'native Irish lore and biblical and medieval traditions were "stitched together" in a pseudo-history which served many purposes.'

Thus Gaedel Glas, the progenitor of the Gaels, can trace his line back to Noah. These myths, obscure yet persistent, introduced two sets of gods; those of light and those of darkness. The gods of darkness found their origin in Ba'al or Balor, and he was worshipped by the Fomorians as a sun god. The gods of light found their god in Lug, and these people are known as the Tuatha Dé Danann. The progeny of Gaedel Glas, or the Milesians, from Egypt and then Galicia in Spain were also associated with the gods of light, while the Picts, or Dal n'Araide were associated with the gods of darkness; the gods of darkness were mostly goddesses, depicting a people unimpressed by the patriarchal godhead from the desert.

The foundation myth of the Irish Republic although acknowledging the Judeo-Christian god also uses the hero Cú Chulainn to symbolise both the warrior spirit and the ancestral rights of a people.

Whatever or not these myths have any relation to historical fact is a moot point, but what we can say with a large degree of certainty is that the first peoples to carry pre-Christian mythology with them to Ireland were Picts, or in Irish *Cruithin*, the original inhabitants of Britain and Ireland, and named Priteni by Julius Caesar. Due to the Roman invasion they were forced northwards to Scotland, and as the Romans never invaded Ireland, it remained a stronghold for these tribes and for their myths, rites and customs. It also became a haven for one of the last aboriginal tribes of western Europe living in the last habitable island, away from the imperial armies of the Roman Empire and with nothing beyond but the vast and wild Atlantic Ocean. The Picts were so called because they painted their bodies, and the colours they used defined their tribe or status.

Regarding the Milesians, known as 'the sons of Mil Espaine', there is another theory to be considered. Eoin Mac Neill said that their invasion was a medieval creation and for O'Rahilly the 'authoritative' account in the *Lebor Gabála* or 'Book of Invasions' was a 'primitive' story of the invasion. Who was Mil Espaine, 'the soldier from Spain'? Was he Spanish or was he a Roman soldier in a Spanish division of the Roman army? In an article titled 'The true origin of the Sons of Mil' in the 1973 edition of the *Louth Archaeological and Historical Journal*, Michael Neary writes that the Ninth Legion (Hispana) of the Roman army was stationed in York. This legion apparently disappeared and was never heard of again. Neary contends that they joined with the Brigantes of York and then came to Wexford at Inver Slaney where they joined the Brigantes of that region, after which they proceeded to conquer the other tribes of Ireland. They thus became the Gaels, as legend has it that they originally came from Galicia. The Ninth Legion fought and had victories in Africa and

Europe and took the title Hispana after a victory in Spain. If the legion did in fact invade Ireland with the Brigantes, it would have taken place in the early first century AD.

THE *CAILLEACH* AND KINGSHIP

Of all myths, that of sovereignty stands at the core of Irish mythology. It was known as the *banais rigi* or *banfheiss*, meaning 'woman feast or sleeping feast' and tells of the power of the goddess or *ban dea* or *cailleach* in conferring kingship. Unless the goddess conferred sovereignty, the king was not a proper king; the goddess was sovereignty, and only through her could the king claim legitimacy.

> *Atbér-sa fritt, a mac mín:*
> *limas fóit na hair-ríg:*
> *is mé ind ingen seta seng,*
> *flaithius Alban is hÉrend.*

> *I will tell you, gentle boy,*
> *with me the high-kings sleep;*
> *I am the graceful slender girl,*
> *the Sovereignty of Scotland and Ireland.*

Sleeping with the mother goddess, for example, resulted in Lugaid Mac Con of Munster and Niall of the Nine Hostages of Leinster becoming High Kings of Ireland. Reference to this rite is also found in Roman mythology where the Oracle of Delphi prophesies to the Tarquin brothers that he who first 'kissed' his mother would succeed as king prophesied that the conquest of Rome would be achieved by the one who would first 'kiss' his mother.

A function of folklore is to reduce such a myth to a common understanding without diminishing the substance of the meaning. The story is told thus: a young man meets an old woman in a wood and mates with her; she turns into a young woman and confers sovereignty on him. As a result, he becomes a king and is accepted as such. As an old man he is again in a wood where he meets a young woman and mates with her; she turns into an old woman and kills him. Thus, life and death resided with the goddess.

The old woman or hag is also known as the *ban sídh* or 'woman of the mound', and it is in the mounds that the spirits of the dead are said to survive. The term is now more commonly written as the 'banshee'. She is a harbinger of death and appears or is heard before the death of an individual in certain families.

My mother never forgot a verse about the banshee which she heard as a young girl in Wexford; the verse is as follows:

> Hushed be the banshee's cry,
> unearthly sound

wailing one soon to lie,
cold in the ground.

The folklore commission of Ireland recorded many stories concerning the banshee in the 1930s. In the 1970s, a student told me that on his way home to the country from the city he heard a wailing sound as he approached his parents' farmhouse, which made the 'hairs on his head stand up'. When he arrived home, he found that his mother had just passed away.

Thus, the supernatural being known as the *ban sídh* or *cailleach* has the power of life and death over mortals. However, in time the word *cailleach* was used pejoratively to mean 'hag', 'witch', or 'crone'. With the spread of Christianity, pagan Ireland was predictably vilified, as happens in most cases when one mythology takes precedence over another (one possible exception being the relationship between Shintoism and Buddhism in Japan, where both systems have been allowed to flourish).

One powerful symbol of the *cailleach* is the *Síle na Gig* more commonly known as the Sheela na Gig, and this figure may be connected to the sovereignty rite mentioned above. Sheela na Gigs are a group of female stone sculptures found not only in Ireland but also in

FIGURE 1. Sheela na Gig (illustration by Jack Roberts).

Britain and France. The sculpture is a nude figure, represented face on, with legs splayed and with hands placed behind the thighs with fingers opening the vulva. She is generally regarded as a stone fetish that was supposed to give fertility. Some Sheelas have holes in them and these are regarded as part of the rite. There are more than 100 of these sculptures in Britain and Ireland, although there is a disagreement about the exact number. At a later date they were incorporated into the walls of churches and castles as a 'ward against evil'. For a long time, many were confined to the crypt of the National Museum in Dublin, but for the past twenty years they have been put on public display.

SACRED TREES

The main political centres of ancient Ireland were Emain Macha, which could be regarded as the capital of Ulster; Dind Ríg, that of Leinster; Cashel of Munster; and Cruachain of Connacht. The spiritual capital of Ireland was Tara in the ancient province of *Mide* (Meath), which also served as the ceremonial home of the High King. On a more local level, the most important ritual centre was the *bile* or 'sacred and venerated tree'. Under these trees, which could be ash, oak, yew or hawthorn, chiefs were inaugurated, and they were the gathering place for tribal meetings and fairs. Some were cut down as a consequence of the zeal of Christian missionaries, others as a result of intertribal warfare. The influence of the sacred tree was demonstrated by the fact that the greatest insult that could be inflicted on an enemy was the desecration of the tree. For instance, the inauguration tree of the Dál gCais at Magh Adhair, now Moyre, near Tulla, Co. Clare, was, according to the *Annals of the Four Masters*, 'cut after being dug from the earth with its roots' by Maelseachlainn of Meath, King of Tara in 980 AD This date lends credence to the persistence of the inauguration ceremony long after Christianity had taken hold in Ireland. When in 1099 the *craeb tulca*, or 'tree of the mound', was cut down in Antrim by the O'Neills, the offending family some years later uprooted the sacred *bile* of the O'Neills at Tullaghoge.

As there were as many as 100 local chiefs in Ireland at the beginning of the twelfth century, we may assume that there were many sacred inaugural trees throughout the land. According to the archaeologist Barry Raftery, 'the *bile* leaves no trace in the archaeological record, but we can assume that this custom [inauguration of kings] is of pagan Celtic origin, for there are clear indications that it existed in Gaul in the pre-Roman Iron Age'.

How to Use this Book

This book attempts to outline all the significant places in every county on the island of Ireland and includes places in Scotland where the early stories of the two countries conjoin. Altogether there are over a 1,000 locations referenced.

Each location is identified by a number in square brackets that refers to the Ordnance Survey *Discovery Series* for the Republic of Ireland and the Ordnance Survey of Northern Ireland *Discoverer Map Series*.

Names that appear frequently in the text are explained in a glossary and are marked with an asterisk * throughout.

Various time periods are mentioned throughout the book and these are as follows:

Mesolithic:	*c.*7000–4000 BC
Neolithic:	*c.*4000–2400 BC
Bronze Age:	*c.*2400–500 BC
Iron Age:	*c.*400–500 AD
Early Christian:	*c.*400–800 AD
Viking period:	*c.*400–1100 AD
Early Medieval:	*c.*400–1100 AD

CONNACHT

GALWAY

Gaillimh, 'stony (river)', also *Gaillem*, 'the river and town of Galway' *Cnoc Medbha* ('Medb's* Hill'), also known as *Cnoc Magh* ('the hill on the plain') and now known as Knockma, is five miles south-west of Tuam and south-east of Castlehacket [46]. Although only a little more than 500 feet high, the summit of Knockma commands some of the finest views in Ireland; the hill in the early part of the twentieth century was part of the folklore of Galway and Mayo. The fairies of Connacht were said to dwell in the depth of the hill under their leader Finvarra. The great cairn on the summit of the hill is marked Finvarra's Castle on the Ordnance Sheet. Knockma is the south-eastern limit of the great plain anciently called *Nemidh* or *Magh-Ith*.

Fairy-fighting in the sky over Knockma and on towards Galway was held responsible for the famine of 1846–7. Or one might hint that if something disastrous occurred then the remnants of the fairy faith were somehow responsible.

There are four cairns in this area within which are said to be excavated passages and a palace where the *aes síde* live. Inside the cairn of Knockma there is believed to be an entrance to the Otherworld. It was common belief in this area that after consumptives died, they became well again with the *aes síde*.

The cult of the head which I have encountered in a few counties is found in a novel called *Hero Breed* by Pat Mullen, from Inishmore on the Aran Islands, published 1936:

> What it was she saw or how far into the future it went nobody has ever known, but she said it as a *geasa* on his eldest son that he must dig up his father's skull at the coming of the first new moon after one year had elapsed, and never part with it until his death, when it was to be placed in the care of his eldest son in turn. In this way it would be passed down through the centuries until time ceased to be. 'For', said she, 'while the skull is kept carefully in the possession of the eldest son the spirit of the great warrior will always be near to watch over the family. The name shall never die out, the men shall be fearless, brave and strong, the women beautiful and kindly.

A further example can be seen at St MacDara's Island, a monastic site almost two miles south-west of Mace Head. It is best approached from the village of Carna [44]. Here on 16 July, the saint's patron day, local people came to the island and celebrated mass. After this some put their hands down into the earth in that part of the church where the saint's skull lay and touched it. This ritual continued until one year when it was stolen by what some locals say was a tourist; however, no proof has ever emerged as to the guilty party. The thief destroyed a custom that lasted, supposedly, for nearly 1,500 years.

There are other less intense traditions associated with this sixth-century saint; passing fishing boats are said to dip their sails three times for luck. The distinctive-looking oratory, according to Estyn Evans in *Prehistoric and Early Christian Ireland*, may have been timber-built. 'The whole arrangement suggests a translation into stone of a timber building with its roof supported by elbowed crucks. This is the only surviving example of its kind, though miniature copies of similar oratories occur on top of high crosses at Monasterboice and Durrow.' As the name *Dair* means 'oak', it is fitting that the original oratory was of timber.

The sighting of *péists* or Otherworld beasts (most notably the Loch Ness Monster in Scotland), was a common enough occurrence in Galway in the twentieth century. These sightings occurred firstly at Loch Fadda [44] close to Clifden, Connemara, and at Loch Ána ('Ána's lake') [36] and at Loch Shanakeever (*Loch Sheanadh Chíamhair*, 'the lake of ancient mist') [37]. The beast was known as the *Ech Uisce* or 'water horse' as its head was similar to that of a horse. According to local reports it was black, had a large white stripe along its back and was about seven to eight feet in length. Georgina Carberry, librarian at Clifden, said that she saw it in 1954. In 1960 the Loch Ness investigation bureau came to Loch Fadda and used dynamite, with government permission, in order, one presumes, to bring the beast out of its lair. Some academics have dismissed the possibility of a monster by saying that the sightings may be merely of a group of otters, which, black and in procession, may appear humped. This *ollphéist* or monster was mentioned by William Makepeace Thackeray in 1842.

Loch Fadda features a *crannóg* or ancient lake dwelling; these were usually wooden enclosures. This lake dwelling is known as Beaghcauneen (*Beitheach Cháinín*, 'the lake of the birch groves'). Coincidentally, the lake west of Loch Fadda is known as Loch Each, or 'the lake of the horse'. Two miles south-west of Loch Each by foot (or by horse!) is Loch Naweelaun (*Loch na bhFaoileann*, 'the lake of the seagulls') where sightings of the *Ollphéist* have also been observed. For the enthusiast there is a megalithic tomb about 300 yards south-west from the east side of the lake.

Inchagoill Island on the northern end of Lough Corrib [45] has an important pillar stone associated with Lug,* the Celtic sun god. Known as the Lugaedon stone, it has been cited by Professor Etienne Rynne as one of the more important pillar stones in Ireland. It can be seen a short distance south-west from the old church called *Teampull Phádraig* ('Patrick's temple') which, though believed traditionally to go back to the time of the saint, most likely dates from the thirteenth century. The pillar stone has an inscription, 'LIE LUGUAEDON MACCI MENUEH', which there have been many attempts at translating over the years. The first attempt was in 1810 by a member of the Tipperary militia who interpreted it as reading: 'Underneath this stone lie Goill, Ardan and Sionan.' The names were supposed to be those of three brothers, the eldest of whom was said to be the head of a religious order there and gave his name to the island. A further attempt was made in 1904 and came up with the reading: 'To speak yonder on the graves of those who are blessed.' In the early nineties a local boatman taking a group to the island informed Rynne that 'the stone is a fossilized rudder of St Patrick's boat'! Further misreadings abound, one of which is as follows: 'The stone of Lugnaedon, son of Limenueh', Limenueh being identified as Liemania, the sister of St Patrick, and Lugnaedon as Lugna, Liemania's son. The ancient collection of manuscripts known as *Leabhar Breac* states that Lugnat was the foster son of Patrick and son of his sister and that he was also his navigator–thus the seed for the boatman's story.

Eventually it was acknowledged that the original markings on the Lugnaedon stone were in ogam and later in Gaelic script, presumably from the ogam. So finally, we end up with our old harvest and sun god Lug,* a Celtic deity found throughout Europe and along the coast of North Africa. Thus, we are left with two pre-Christian or pagan deities: namely, Lug or the 'shining one' and Aed 'the fiery one', both solar deities. The noted antiquarian R.A.S. Macalister suggested that the original ogam inscriptions were cut from the sides of the stone and substituted with what one can see today. According to Rynne, it is generally accepted nowadays that the inscription dates from the sixth century and 'is probably the oldest extant example of an Irish inscription in Latin characters'. It has also been pointed out that the word *gall* is an old Irish word for a stone, and that Inchagoill should be translated as 'The Island of the Stone', or the 'Island of Lug's Stone'.

Lough Corrib was originally known as *Loch Orbsen*, Orbsen being the proper name of Mannanán mac Lir.* According to legend, when Orbsen's grave was being dug, the lake burst forth over the land. Keating says:

> *Mannanán mac Lir ó'n sír sreath, Oirbsean a ainm, iar gcéd gcloth ég adbath.*
> Manannán son of Lear, from the 'loch' he sought the 'sraith' ['sraith', a level space by a river]. Oirbsean his (own) name, after a hundred conflicts he died the death.

[Translated by David Comyn]

Legend relates that a great fight took place between Orbsen mac Alloid or Manannán mac Lir* and Uillinn, the grandson of Nuadu Argatlám ('Nuadu of the Silver Hand', who was a king of Ireland and whose replica, minus his arm, can be seen today in the Anglican cathedral in Armagh).This fight took place on the western shores of Lough Corrib near Moycullen [45], which in Irish is *Magh Uillinn* or 'the plain of Uillin'. A standing stone known as Uillin's stone was said to commemorate this battle but seems to have disappeared by the middle of the twentieth century.

A different origin for the Corrib's name is given by O'Rahilly who says that it is named after Oirbsiu Már, who was son of Lugaid Conmac, thus providing another connection, beside that on Inchagoill, with Lug.* The Conmaicne were a pre-Gaelic race who worshipped Lug as their sun god.

Kilbennan [39], about ten miles north-east of Lough Corrib, also has an association with Lug,* its pagan name having been *Dún Lugaid* ('the fort of Lug'). A monastery was

FIGURE 2. The pillar stone on Inchagoill Island, Lough Corrib, associated with the god Lug.

founded there by St Benin, a disciple and successor of St Patrick at Armagh; the land here was given by a local chieftain, Lugaid, who was baptised by Patrick. He followed the tradition of incorporating the local god, the sun god Lug, into his name. The early church of Benin was burnt down in 1114, but there are portions of a round tower still standing there. O'Donovan in the nineteenth century wrote that 'the present coarb [successor] of St Benin is making every exertion to put a stop to these courses, because he believed that the tower was a pagan fire-temple and that the well was of druidical sanctity, and that St Benin was obliged to transfer them to Christian purposes to please the superstitious natives'. St Benin's Well (*Tobar Chill Bheinín*) is about 150 yards north-west from the ruins of the medieval church.

On the last Sunday in July a great pattern was held at ancient Dún Lugaid to commemorate Lug,* a day that was also known as the Feast of Lughnasa and later as Garland Sunday. John O'Donovan visited here in 1838 and found that 'stations were performed at the well on Domnach Chrom Dubh [the Irish name for Garland Sunday]'. The parish priest at the time, a Father Joyce, wished to put a stop to the practice because of its pagan origins.

A few hundred yards to the east of the round tower is a townland named Ballygaddy (*Baile an Gadaighe*, 'the townland of the thief'), and according to O'Donovan there existed here two heaps of stones and a larger monument named *Altóir Phádruig*, or 'St Patrick's Altar', on which the saint is said to have said mass.

St Benin also has a small church on Inishmore, Aran Islands. The church known as Temple Benan is on the hillside a few hundred yards south-west from the village of Killeany. The internal measurements are about eleven by seven feet, while the gables, rising to about sixteen feet, are quite steep. Why the roof here cannot be restored is a mystery, for the walls are very solid and have remained so for almost a millennium and-a-half. It would be a place of great pilgrimage and memory to the monk who was the first disciple of St Patrick and who practised religion on the ancient site of Dún Lughaid.

Twelve miles east of Lough Corrib is the townland of Coolfowerbeg (*Cuil Fobhair*, 'the back of the spring well') [46] in the parish of Killererin. Here Tigernmas defeated the descendants of Éber, the Milesian or Gaelic chief, according to Keating, but Hogan says that Tigernmas fought and defeated the Érainn here. This vagueness as to who fought whom is indicative of our prehistory. Yet it stands as one of the many battles fought by Tigernmas, High King of Ireland, as recorded in the annals.

To the south-west of Kinvara (*Cinn Mhara*, 'head of the sea') [52] is the Doorus Demesne, the summer home of Comte Florimond de Basterot, and during a visit to the Count there in 1898 Lady Gregory recalled that 'The Count remembered when on Garland Sunday [last Sunday in July] men used to ride races naked on unsaddled horses out into the sea; but that wild custom has been done away with by decree of the priests.'

The wild custom would appear to have been part of a central ritual during the feast of Lughnasa and reveals the connection between Epona, a Gaulish horse goddess who was the daughter of a man called 'nature of the sea' and is also the mother of a horse who returns to the sea, and Lug,* the foster son of Manannán mac Lir,* the Irish and Welsh sea god. Epona's Irish equivalent is Macha, a horse goddess and a goddess of fertility. The central motif in the ritual horse bathing at harvest time is that the mare goddess is married to the sea and at certain times returns to her lover. In Greek mythology, Demeter, often depicted with a mare's head, had intercourse with Poseidon, the god of the sea. A central part of this Indo-European rite was expressed with the horse race into the sea at Kinvara.

About ten miles south of Kinvara is the town of Gort [52], and about two miles north-east of here is Ballyconnell, which derives its name from a famous battle known as *Cath Carn Conaill* or 'the battle of Carn Conaill'. According to the *Annals of Ulster* the battle took place in 649 AD, and although firmly placed in the historic period, contains many elements discernible in the older tales. The battle was fought between Duirmuid Ruanaid, a powerful chief of the southern Uí Néill, and Guaire of Aidne, King of Connacht. Aidne comprised the barony of Kiltartan and the dioceses of Kilmacduagh.

Guaire held his court at his castle originally known as *Durlas Guaire* ('the strong fort of Guaire') but now named Dungory just east of Kinvara. A more modern castle stands here now, but in 1914 it was said that the remains of the original castle could be seen. According to P.W. Joyce, 'half a mile east of Kinvara, on the seashore stands an ancient circular fort; and this is all that remains of the hospitable palace of Durlas'. The castle that now goes by the name Dungory Castle was built by the O'Heynes and stands in the middle of this original circular fort.

Like Suibhne Geilt ('Mad Sweeny'*) from Magh Rath in Co. Down, Guaire is from an age when the ancient order was changing and saw a flowering of the poetic order. It was perhaps because his *durlas* was a meeting place for poets that he was named Guaire the Hospitable. In a tale handed down from the seventh century it is said that after Seanchan Torpeist was elected to *Ollamh* (chief *file* or poet) of Ireland, he consulted with his fellow poets as to which king they should honour with their first or inaugural visit according to ancient custom, and they decided to visit Guaire. Thus, they visited *Gort Insi Guaire* ('the field island of Guaire'), which is an accurate description of Guaire's fortress at Kinvara, as the castle was on a small island just off the mainland in Kinvara Bay. Today there is a small causeway which leads to the island.

Seanchan took with him 150 poets, 150 pupils and a corresponding number of women – which follows the storytelling tradition of giving numbers in fifties. However, an *ollamh* was only entitled to a retinue of thirty, and this number was lowered to twenty-four at the Convention of Drom Ceat in 590 AD. Seanchan was well received by Guaire, of whom it is said that one of his arms was longer than the other, thus earning him the soubriquet 'hospitable'. Seanchan was entitled to stay at the royal residence for 'a year, a quarter and a month'. While he was at the king's residence, a dish sent to his bedroom by his wife Brigit contained nothing but gnawed bones, and the servant said that this was due to rats. Here Seanchan used his power in verse to rhyme the vermin to death. The following is a translation by O'Curry of his rhyme:

> Rats, though sharp their snouts,
> Are not powerful in battles;
> I will bring death on the party of them
> For having eaten Brigit's present.
>
> Small was the present she made us,
> Its loss to her was not great;
> Let her have payment from us in a poem,
> Let her not refuse the poet's gratitude!
> You rats which are in the roof of the house
> Arise, all of you, and fall down.

Ten rats then fell dead from the roof, and Seanchan said that it was not the rats that should have been satirised but the cats for failing in their duty. He then satirised the chief of the cats who was said to reside in the cave of Knowth near Slane. However, regardless of the rats and the delightful setting, the poets became troublesome to the extent that the king's brother, a hermit named Marbhan, put a *geis* or obligation on them to depart and to devote themselves to the discovery of the ancient tale of the *Táin Bó Cúailnge*.* Seanchan Torpeist was aggrieved at this and on his departure presented a short farewell poem to Guaire.

> We depart from thee, O stainless Guaire!
> We leave thee with our blessing;
> A year, a quarter and a month,
> Have we sojourned with thee, O high king!
> Three times fifty poets, – good and smooth, –
> Three times fifty students in the poetic art,
> Each with his servant and dog;
> They were all fed in one great house.
> Each man had his separate meal;
> Each man had his separate bed;
> We never arose at early morning,
> Without contentions without calming.
> I declare to thee O God!
> Who canst the promise verify,
> That should we return to our own land,
> We shall visit thee again, O Guaire, though now we depart.

[Translated by Eugene O'Curry]

Seanchan was later successful in retrieving the great epic of the Táin. He originally set out from Durlas Guaire in search of the epic to Scotland and then to the Isle of Man but had no success. He then returned to Ireland and went to St Caillin of Magh Rein in Leitrim, who was the poet's brother, after which he went back to Durlas Guaire. In order to help them in their endeavour, Guaire sent for his brother Marbhan from his hermitage at *Glenn-an Scail* ('the glen of the shadows'), now known as Gleananscaul [46], about two miles north of Oranmore. Marbhan arrived at Durlas Guaire and here they discussed the best way to recover the lost tale. Many saints went to the burial place of Fergus mac Roich, a prominent person in the tale, and through prayer persuaded God to raise him from the dead, and thus the tale was retrieved.

Guaire had a daughter named Créde who was in love with Dinertach of the Uí Fhidgente of east Limerick, who had come to support Guaire in his fight against Diarmait of the Uí Néill in the battle of Carn Conaill. A poem she composed, known as the 'Song of Crédne, Daughter of Guaire', was transcribed by Gilla Riabach mac Tuathail ui Chlérig who lived in the first half of the sixteenth century. Whether Dinertach was slain or survived this battle is not clear, but the poem tells us that he suffered seventeen wounds, which prompted Créde to keen the following:

It é saigdi goine súain
cech trát[h]a ind-oidc[h]I adhúair:
sercoi lie gnása íar ndé
fir a tóib tíri Roighne.

Rográd alathíre
romsíacht sech a comdíne:
rucc mo lí, ní lór do dath,
nímlécci do tindabrad.

Im-sa náidi rob-sa náir,
ní bind fri dula do dái:
óttalod I n-inderb n-aois,
romgab mo thédi toghaois.

Tathum cech maith la Guairi
lie rig nAidne n-adfúaire:
tocair mo menma óm thúathaib
isin iath I n Irlúachair.

Canair a n-íath Aidne áin
im thaobu Cilli Colmáin:
án breó des luimnech lechtach
dienad comainm Dínertach.

Cráidid mo chridhe cóinech,
a Chríst cáidh a forróidhedh:
it é soigde gona súain
cech trátha a n-oidchi adhúair.

These are the arrows that murder sleep at every hour in the bitter cold night: pangs of love throughout the day for the company of the man from the side of the land of Roigne.

Great love of a man of another land has come to me beyond all his mates: it has taken my bloom, no colour is left, it does not let me rest.

When I was a child, I was bashful, I was not used to go to a tryst; since I have come to an untried age, my wantonness has beguiled me.

I have every good with Guaire, the king of cold Aidne; but my mind has fallen away from my people to the meadow at Irluachair.

There is singing in the meadow of glorious Aidne around the sides of Cell Cholmain: glorious flame, lovely mantled, now sunk into the grave, the name of whom is Dinertach.

It wrings my pitiable heart, O chaste Christ, what has been sent to me: these are arrows that murder sleep at every hour in the bitter cold night.

[Translated by Kuno Meyer]

Gort, mentioned above, four miles from Lough Cutra [52], and between Lough Cutra and Derrybrien, is where the first resting place of Diarmuid* and Gráinne* was, namely *Doire dhá Bhóth* ('the oak wood of the two bothys'), which was also known as *Coill idir dhá mhaide* ('the hiding between the two woods'. The place-name makes clear that they did not stay in the same bothy – or small hut or cottage – because of Diarmuid's loyalty to Finn.* However, this arrangement did not last long, and they proceeded to have a family. In this area between Lough Cutra and Derrybrien there are ten townlands beginning with *doire*, which means oak wood, so this area must have been one large oak forest. Running through it is the Derrywee River, known in Irish as *Abhainn Dá Loilíoch*, or the 'river of the two milch cows'.

FIGURE 3. The Turoe Stone.

Four miles north-north-east of Loughrea is a decorated stone known as the Turoe Stone, which originally stood outside the rath of Feerwore in the townland of Turoe but now stands nearby on the lawn of Turoe House [46]. The nearby rath of Feerwore is an Early Iron Age habitation and was investigated by Joseph Raftery in 1938, the first Iron Age habitation to be excavated in modern times. According to Raftery the work on the site did not make any 'clearer the date or purpose of the Turoe stone'.

The community in which the stone stood was a settled agricultural one which concentrated on stock-raising and a small amount of tillage. The underlying limestone would have enriched the soil and the grass, which was the mainstay of the cattle. These conclusions were prompted by the number of animal bones recovered at the site. Raftery says that the animal most adapted to the locality was the ox of the Celtic shorthorn variety. Sheep and pigs were also present, but in smaller numbers. Recovery of the bones of red deer and wolf together with a flint arrowhead shows that hunting was a likely activity and possibly on occasion a necessity for survival. That grain was grown was surmised by the existence of one fragment of a rotary quern. Iron was smelted on the site, and the objects were likely wrought by a travelling smith. An iron fibula or brooch found on the site suggests the first century BC as the latest date, according to Raftery, for the 'beginning of the settlement at Turoe'.

The Turoe Stone would seem to demonstrate a spiritual aspect to the community. And it is here that the prevailing mythology should be investigated. The stone with its three smaller standing stones may have nothing to do with the fort and may have existed prior to its establishment. It may also have constituted a pre-Christian sacred centre, and the fort may have been set up in order to care for and manage any ceremonies that occurred there. It is usual for communities to develop close to sacred centres. As the stone was only ten yards outside the banks of the fort, the inhabitants would have been very close to the stones and very protective of them. It is also possible that the fort may have been inhabited only at certain times of the year during specific rites. Similar forts can be found at Magh Slecht in Co. Cavan, where Crom Dubh* was worshipped. Raftery mentions that the site may have been used as a sacred grave, which would make the presence of the stones more understandable. However, the desire to be buried within the precincts of a holy place generally comes after the site is no longer used as a ritual centre. For example, the burial of bodies within chuches throughout the length and breadth of the country almost always occurs when the church is in ruins.

Feerwore is most likely derived from *fear mór* ('great man'), a local term for those standing stones considered to represent the phallus. Cloghafarmore (*Cloch an Fear Mór*, 'the stone of the great man') is another example found at Knockbridge [36], west of Dundalk, Co. Louth; the great warrior Cú Chulainn died fighting while tied to this stone. The phallus symbolised the generative power of nature. In ancient Greece an image of the phallus was carried in procession during the Dionysian festivals. It was a central part in many religious systems and thus was widely venerated.

The stone has been described as a massive granite boulder 'hewn to its present shape from a glacial erratic'. It is nearly four feet high and worked into the shape of a domed pillar, cylindrical and with a domed cap. Raferty describes it as 'decorated with an asymmetrical series of double interlocking spirals, trumpet designs, circles and meandering curves, motives which continue downwards on the cylindrical portion of the stone. Near the base is a narrow band with a step-pattern, or "Wall of Troy" design.'

Professor Michael V. Duignan, from Galway University, in his analysis of the stone's designs compared it to British La Tène art, in particular to the British mirror style. Although there are five examples of this form of La Tène art in Ireland, the stone seems to be of Irish manufacture. A similar design can be found on the gold collar from Broighter in Co. Derry. It has been suggested that an old Atlantic route between France and Ireland in the second and first centuries BC may have been the conduit which introduced these highly decorative stones. A Breton craftsman may even have chiselled the great Turoe stone.

Three islands – Inishmore, Inishmaan, and Inisheer – collectively known as the Aran Islands [51] lie in a north-east to south-west direction about ten miles off the coast of Galway. The name Aran comes from the Irish word *ara* meaning kidney, which probably refers to their shape. Inishmore (*Inis Mór*, 'big island'), the largest of the islands, is about eight miles long by two-and-a-half miles wide, though its width is less than a mile at some points. The population of Inishmore is about 900, while that of Inishmaan (*Inis Meáin*, 'the middle island') is around 160 and Inisheer (*Inis Oírr* or *Inis Oirthir*, 'east island') about 260. Irish is the main language spoken on the islands.

FIGURE 4. Dún Aengus on Inishmore.

The most distinctive feature of the islands is the plate of limestone covering them, which is a continuation of the limestone lands of the Burren in north Clare and south Galway. This carboniferous limestone, in which many fossils can be seen, was the muddy base of the Atlantic Ocean about 300 million years ago.

The great fort of Dún Aengus on Inishmore is the most striking of all the monuments on the islands. It stands on the edge of a vertical cliff more than 300 feet above the Atlantic. It has an inner enclosure which contains a rectangular platform of limestone. This platform is central to how one 'sees' Dún Aengus. There are four enclosures or ramparts surrounding Dún Aengus and there is a *chevaux-de-frise* (upright protective stones) between the third and fourth ramparts. For many archaeologists, though not all, Dún Aengus is seen as a fortress. The 'outer wall' presumably fell into the sea. The contention that the monument was a fortress is backed up by the presence of the defensive *chevaux-de-frise*.

However, if the wall did not fall into the sea and the *chevaux-de-frise* was merely for reasons of prestige, then what you see is a magnificent amphitheatre, with terraces for sitting and a platform or raised structure for ceremonial celebration, where celebrants looked out to sea and the setting sun to the sound of Bronze Age horns and drums. A probable time for these ceremonies was mid-summer during the Late Bronze Age. This raised platform is a ceremonial site of the Late Bronze and Early Iron Age for the ritual of mating and harmony. When I was lecturing in Dublin, I brought foreign exchange students from Europe and America to this site and we were joined by Simon O'Dwyer, the Irish expert on Bronze and Iron Age horns, and his wife Maria who plays the *bodhrán*, a leather drum. After a brief talk on the site from the platform, Simon and Maria played Bronze Age music. When they finished, we were surprised by the arrival of a group of women who sang many old songs in Irish and continued singing while the sun went down, leaving in its train a long, golden pathway to the distant horizon.

Because of its outstanding presence, Dún Aengus has a continuous stream of tourists. If one wishes to see a lesser and quieter version of the great monument, one should begin one's Aran experience at the promontory fort on Inishmore known as *Dún Duchathair*. Being less known, it is peaceful and spectacular in its own way, surrounded as it is on both sides by the sea, with magnificent views.

Inishmore can be comfortably explored by foot. A half hour's walk in a westerly direction from Kilronan will bring you to Cowragh. Here, you take a boreen signposted for *Teampall an Ceathrar Alainn* ('the church of the four beautiful women'). Head south along this path and you will come to a megalithic tomb known as the Eochaill Wedge Tomb, which is about 4,000 years old. It is locally known as the Bed of Diarmuid* and Grainne.*

Return then to the main road and walk about one mile to the beach at Kilmurvey, and continue along the road for about half a mile until you come to a crossroads; here turn right and walk a short distance to *Clochán na Carraige*, a rectangular stone-built hut in good condition with a corbelled roof and two entrances. Whether it was a retreat house for the Seven Churches nearby remains a moot point.

FIGURE 5. Simon O'Dwyer playing a reconstruction of the Loughnashade trumpa at the Technological University Dublin, watched by Etienne Rynne and Helene Conway. In the background are sculptures by John Behan inspired by the Táin.

The Irish Church has many connections with Arainn; at the centre of this is the Community of Enda (*Teaghlach Einne*), a ninth-century church at the beach end of a large graveyard at Killeany, about a mile south-east of Kilronan. Traditionally the Aran Islands were known as *Ara na Naomh* (Aran of the Saints), and many of these saints are buried on Inishmore. A half-mile walk uphill from *Teaglach Einne* to *Teampall Bheanain* will bring you past the stump of a round tower, several wells, and a Mass rock, and at *Teampall Bheanain* (St Benin, a disciple of St Patrick) you can see the extent of the monastic settlement. St Enda's Church and later a Franciscan friary were demolished by Cromwellian forces in the middle of the seventeenth century, and the stones were used to build Arkin Fort, also known as Castle Arkin. These same stones eventually found a new lease of life when local houses were built. A disciple of St Enda, St Ciaran, had his monastery at *Mainistir Chiarain*. Within the church grounds is a standing stone which has a sundial.

Aran has a fine legacy of poets and writers. Máirtín Ó Direáin, wrote solely in Irish while Liam O'Flaherty wrote both in Irish and English, his notable work in Irish being *Duil* ('instinct') and in English, *The Informer* and *The Famine*. A lesser-known but interesting writer is Pat Mullen, whose most noted work is *Hero Breed* about the fishing community in Killeany in the 1930s. The American director Robert Flaherty made the famous drama documentary *Man of Aran* in the 1930s, using only local actors.

The writer most associated with Inishmaan is the playwright John Millington Synge. He went there at the behest of Yeats to learn Irish and to establish a literary tradition based on the speech he heard everyday on the island. Synge visited the island between 1898 and 1902 and integrated with the community, attending weddings and funerals, and was also witness to an eviction. Synge's plays avoided a patronising manner and described life as it was experienced by the islanders. He thus elevated the people from being stage characters to being vivid, recognisable people.

Dún Chonchuir is the largest stone fort on Inishmaan. Synge often came here to smoke and relax. It is a fine, oval stone enclosure possibly dating from early historical times and has several ruined stone huts on the inside. The fort has a dominant view of the island. It measures about 200 feet east–west and over 100 feet north–south, and has two terraces on the inside. It may be named after Conchuir, a brother of Aengus, who probably gave his name to the great fort on Inishmore; according to legend, they were the two sons of Umor, a chief of the Fir Bolg,* and had fled to the Aran Islands after the defeat of the Fir Bolg of Connacht. On the south-east coast of the island is a place named *Leaba Chonchuir* ('Conchuir's bed'), a natural rock bridge. Another fine fort is *Dún Fearbai*, perhaps similar in age to *Dún Chonchuir*. It gets its name from the local area, *An Fhearbach*, meaning abounding in cows.

FIGURE 6. Dún Dúncathair on Inishmore.

LEITRIM (SEE ALSO CAVAN)

Liathdroim, 'grey ridge'

The Black Pig's Dyke (*Claí na Muice Duibhe*), a 'linear earthwork', is sometimes seen as the defensive fortification of Ulster. It gets it name from a legend concerning the Black Pig, which is as follows: A druid had a school in Co. Louth, and he had a magic stick which he used for maintaining discipline. When pupils were unruly, he used it to turn them into animals and then chased them through the country. The father of one of these pupils went to the school and struck the master with the wand and changed him into a pig. This pig was chased westward and as he went he made a great trench with his snout, and a blacksmith is said to have shoved a red-hot iron into his mouth and the pig went up in smoke.

Two lakes in Leitrim are steeped in mythology, Lough Allen [26] and Lough Garadice [26, 27A]. To the east of Lough Allen lies Slieve Anierin or *Sliabh an Iarainn* ('iron mountain'). Here, Goibniu* the smith (*goba*) had one of his many forges, and it is close to here that he reputedly forged the weapons for the Second Battle of Magh Tuiredh which was fought between the Tuatha Dé Danann* and the Fomorians* near Lough Arrow (see under *Sligo*).

The smith played a hugely prominent role in ancient Irish life, underlined by Kuno Meyer in one of his books on 'Irish Triads' as follows: 'There are three renovators in the world – the womb of a woman, a cow's udder and a smith's *ness*.' This *ness* was the moulding clay of which the furnace was made from time to time. The word *ness* was applied to both the shaped furnace and to a bag of moulding clay for making it.

The ore for the Goibniu's* forge was taken from *Sliabh an Iarainn* and brought to the townland of *Doire na Tuan* ('the ancient oak wood'). Derrynatuan [26] is near the source of the Shannon, and it was here that the ore was smelted, and according to the noted antiquarian John O'Donovan, 'there has been a forge ever since'. In April 2014, I went in search for this forge and met someone who suggested that I speak to Ted McHugh, a local farmer, who then directed me to what is locally described as the remains of a mill. If this building was once a forge, where the entrance has collapsed and been replaced by concrete blocks. However, it is more likely the remains of an unclassified mill, possibly horizontal in form. The remains of the forge, I was informed, were in the area and close by but very much overgrown, and I could not find it. These remains bear testament to a possible site of the original smith's forge. The Shannon is within a stone's throw of the general area and, though here only a stream, would be enough for the Gabha* to take his metal workings.

Derrynatuan is in Cavan, and that is why it is important to consider the two counties together, for both share adjacent places connected to the Goibniu* or Gabha. Derrynatuan is to the north-west and broad end of Glangavlin or *Gleann Gaibhleann* or 'the glen of the grey (cow) of the Gabha'. The smith kept the mythic cow here in the glen, where she was famous for her milk yield; according to legend, if she slept in a field, the 'grass would become luxurious'. Legend also says that the tsumami of milk from her udder formed the mountain pass at Bellavally Gap or *Béal a'Bhealaigh* ('the Mouth of the Pass') [26], three miles east from Glangavlin.

Many verses have been written in praise of Gleann Gaibhleann, and the following is from a late medieval poem written by the fifteenth-century poet Tadhg Óg Ó hUiginn where he addresses the Shannon:

> *Dúthcha dhuit bheith againne*
> *dá bhféachtha dona fáthaibh:*
> *Gleann Gaibhle as é t'athairsi,*
> *an Bhréifne is í do mháthair.*

> By nature thou art ours, if sound reasons be regarded: Glen Gavlin is thy father and Brefney is thy mother.

[Translated by Osborn Bergin]

The Gabha* also had ale which preserved the Tuatha Dé Danann* from old age and disease; he was also invoked for a good yield of butter, which was possibly connected to his famous cow. The smith had several names signifying his different roles; as the Gobán Saor he enters folklore and legend as the man who built the round towers and as an all-around artificer, while as the Gabha he is the mighty smith and one who officiates at rites, such as the rite of coming of age and weddings. As the Goibniu,* he is the god of the smiths and holds the Otherworld feast in which no one ages and which presumably never ends.

The River Shannon takes its name from the goddess of the Tuatha Dé Danann,* namely *Sinann*. The legend of the Shannon's origin is preserved in a sixteen-stanza poem by the medieval poet Cuan O'Lothchain. The first verse is as follows:

> *Saer ainm Sinna saighuidh uaim*
> *nadad Loind a lom luaid*
> *ni h-inand a gním sa gléo*
> *dia mbai Sinand co saer beo.*

> The noble of *Sinainn* seek ye from me;
> Its bare recital would not be pleasant,
> Not alike now are its actions and noise,
> As when *Sinann* herself was free and alive.

[Translated by Edward Gwynn]

The source of the Shannon is at a place known as the Shannon Pot [26], the fame of which can be traced back to Finn mac Cumhail* who gained wisdom from the salmon that dwelt there. Legend says that the goddess Síonann, the daughter of Lodan, a son of Manannán mac Lir,* the sea god, came to the Shannon Pot in search of the great Salmon of Wisdom. The salmon was angered at the sight of Síonann and caused the pool to overflow and drown her. Thus, the Shannon Pot, *Log na Sionna*, was created and bears the name of the goddess to this day. The drowning of a goddess in a river and thus giving her name to it is a common motif in mythologies – for example, Boand, the white cow goddess, drowning in the Boyne.

If one wished to be pernickety, one could claim that the source of the Shannon lies in the western banks of the Cuilcagh Mountains astride Cavan and Fermanagh. But, regardless of argument, the Shannon Pot is one of our sacred pools together with Loughnashade (*Loch na séad*, or 'the lake of the jewels') and the artificial pool known as the 'King's Stables', both of which are at Emain Macha or Navan Fort in Co. Armagh.

MAYO

Magh Eo, 'plain of the yews'

Around Rathfran Bay, to the south-west of Killala Bay [24], there are a number of megalithic tombs dating from the Neolithic, about 4,000 years ago, which consist of large capstones resting on upright stones. They are generally referred to as 'cromlechs', a term that has the same meaning as the Breton word 'dolmen'.

One distinguished structure lies about four miles from Killala at Mullaghnacross crossroads. It has been termed *Baal Tien*, or 'The House of Baal', though one would think that *Baal Teine*, or 'the fire of Baal', would be more accurate. It was seen by nineteenth-century scholars as a sort of low temple. It has a simple *pronaos* – the space in front of the body of a temple enclosed by the portico and projecting side walls – formed by four upright stones on each side, which led to an altar. The altar was placed over a deep pit, at each end of which a great stone was fixed to support a large table stone. This table or altar stone has been displaced. It has been suggested that the pit may have been used to receive the blood of victims sacrificed on the altar. Similar pits were used by the Greeks and the Romans when sacrificing to *Sol*, the sun god. In Italy at the Temple of Serapis at Puzzuoli there is a deep square pit which was used for receiving the blood of those sacrificed. A powerful example of 'The House of Baal' is the Temple of Baal at Palmyra in Syria. I was fortunate to walk around this temple but unfortunate not to gain admittance in order to see the fire altars. Many of these precious sites at Palmyra have since been destroyed by militant Islamists.

Baal in Irish mythology is sometimes referred to as Bel, but usually as Balor or Balar. The month of May in Irish (*Bealtaine*) takes its name from Bel as in *Belteine* or the fire of Bel or Balor. Balor has never been fully acknowledged as being another name for Bel, but his epithet 'Balor of the Baleful Eye' seems to indicate an original sun god. *Samain*, which continues today as Hallowe'en, was one of the four great festivals of pre-Christian Ireland. In Indian mythology the great feast of fire is held in honour of Baal-Samin—Sahm or Sahman being one of the sacred names of the sun and corresponds to *samain* in Irish mythology. In India, cakes of flour are spotted with poppy and caraway seeds and stained with saffron. The Irish equivalent at this feast is the spotted cake or *Bairin-Breac*, the barnbrack or speckled cake. In India, all the devotees at this ceremony stain their bodies with saffron. In Ireland, the saffron-coloured kilt was a sign of royalty.

The fires of Baal were lit upon particular days in Ireland. They fires were said to purify the devotees and preserve them from harm. Cattle in Mayo were driven between blazing fires in order that the smoke might delouse them. This custom continued in Mayo up to the middle of the twentieth century. John Toland in 1747 wrote:

> The writer has more than once been a personal witness of the ceremony of driving the cattle of a certain village through the blazing fire; whilst the young people and children followed, and each seizing a lighted brand, formed a sort of irregular winding dance, waving the flaming torches over their heads, and shouting in a sort of rude chorus. Can there be a doubt as to the source of this custom?

Other places associated with sun worship are Carngrainey in Co. Antrim; Altoir na Greine, 'the altar of the sun' on Mount Callen, Co. Clare; and Knockainey in Co. Limerick, to name but a few. Although these practices had their origins in the Middle East, they never fully died out in the west and the south-west of Ireland.

Seven miles south-east of Castlebar is another place associated with and named Baal, now known as Balla [31]. St Mochno or Cronan founded a monastery here in 637, of which there remain a round tower and and the ruins of a small church. The tower is nearly fifty feet in height and the church is of similar stone and workmanship. In one of the walls of the church is a monumental inscription of 'great antiquity'.

According to the nineteenth-century antiquarian L.C. Beaufort, the place was noted for 'superstitious practices, particularly at one season of the year'. This time could have either been the *samain* to honour Baal-Samin or in early May for the feast of Belteine. However, both times would have merited ceremonial rites. Dr James McParlan in 1801 described a festival at Balla as follows:

> And this Baal is to this day a most extraordinary place of superstitious worship. Here are a couple of small chapels vaulted over a river which runs through the town; and once a year, I think in autumn, immense swarms of people crowd from all parts to perform certain circuits and evolutions on their knees, dropping as they proceed in describing those figures, a certain number of beads to various intentions, and in expiation of various sins; but the day closes most cheerfully in eating and drinking. Mr Lynch who lives just at the town, assured me that not less than three hundred sheep are consumed at this festival.

In the early nineteenth century some English antiquarians believed that round towers such as that at Balla were erected to display the sacred fires of Bel, and were thus not Christian but had been built at a time when sun worship was the prevailing religion. In this they had the support of Charles O'Conor, a noted Irish scholar. One might even say that the prevailing consensus in the nineteenth century was that the round towers had their origin in the Middle East and were brought to to Ireland by the Phoenicians. It was also said that they were astronomical centres for observing the stars, or more mundanely to observe sunrise at important festivals.

These opinions were severly criticised if not dashed by George Petrie in his *Inquiry into the Origin and Uses of the Round Towers in Ireland*. Petrie systematically refuted all of these scholars and proved their theories to be 'fallacious'. Petrie saw the event of 'quadrangular architecture' in Ireland as contemporaneous with the primitive Irish Church and the round towers as a distinctive expression of ecclesiastical architecture.

Folk customs connected to the sun can be found in Ballinrobe (*Bailean Róba*, 'town of the River Róba) [38] on the eve of the feast of St John on 24 June. This night is known as *Féile Eoin* in Wexford. On this night the summer solstice is celebrated by bonfires or, as they are sometimes called, 'bonefires' or *tine cnámh*, as originally the bones of dead animals were burnt at this time. It was also custom for people to come to the fires carrying bones. After the fires, the remaining coals were thrown into adjoining fields to bring luck to future crop-growing. Burning wood was thrown into the air; these 'fireballs' were a

FIGURE 7. Croagh Patrick.

way of acknowledging that the sun had achieved its height and that soon the days would be drawing in. These customs were common in Europe as far away Poland and Estonia. Jumping over the fires was another feature of the customs at this time in Ireland and in Spain.

Croagh Patrick (*Cruach Phádraig*, 'St Patrick's Reek or Peak', commonly referred to as 'the Reek') [30, 38] is one of the great assembly points, both in pre-Christian and Christian Ireland. Five miles west of Westport, it rises 2,530 feet above sea level to give a panoramic view across Clew Bay, and from it one can see Inishbofin, Inishturk, Clare Island and the Nephin Beg range of mountains. It was traditionally associated with the pagan god of the harvest, Crom Dubh;* today it still remains a place of pilgrimage, its quartzite summit pointing to the heavens, beckoning all those who fall within its gaze. Originally named *Cruachán Aigle*, it is refered to in the ninth-century *Book of Armagh* as *Mons Egli*, and it was here that Patrick, in imitation of Christ, and of Moses on Mount Sinai, fasted for forty days. According to the account of Muirchu Maccu Mactheni given in the *Book of Armagh*, as Patrick fasted the landscape was darkened by the wings of spirits in the form of birds, those with black wings representing demons and those with white representing the redeemed.

The most famous legend associated with Patrick was written in the twelfth century and tells how the saint brought all the snakes and demons of Ireland to the top of Cruachán Aigle and from there drove them into the sea. This highly popular tale of the snakes is a later addition to the observation by the third-century Roman writer Solinus that Ireland was free of all reptiles. To the south of the mountain is *Loch na Corra*, written as Lough Nacorra on the *Discovery* map; the name can be translated as 'the lake of the heron' but also as 'the lake of the Serpent' [37]. St Patrick is said to have driven a demon bird into a hollow which subsequently filled up with water to form the lake. This bird-demon is reminiscent of *in tEllén Trechend* ('triple-headed Ellén'), a bird associated with the Otherworld cave at Cruachain in Roscommon. After a while, the bird flew out of Lough Nacorra and flew north to land in Lough Derg [17], where she continues to observe the pilgrims.

Another lake associated with Croagh Patrick is Lough Carra (*Loch Ceara*, with an older name being *Finloch Ceara*, 'the white lake of Carra') [38]. An eleventh-century verse by an unknown author where, unlike at Lough Nacorra, the birds are 'angelic' is as follows:

when St. Patrick, glorious in grace, was suffering on goodly Cruach – an anxious toilsome time for him, the protector of lay men and women –

God sent to comfort him a flock of spotless angelic birds; over the clear lake without fail they would sing in chorus their gentle proclamation.

And thus they called, auspiciously: 'Patrick, arise and come! Shield of the Gael, in pure glory, illustrious golden spark of fire.'

The whole host struck the lake with their smooth and shadowy wings, so that its chilly waters became like a silver sheen.

Hence comes the bright name *The White Lake of Carra* of the contests; I tell you this triumphant meaning as I have heard in every church.

There is a hollow on the northern face of Croagh Patrick known as Lugnademon [30] or 'the hollow of the demons', *lug* meaning 'hollow'. This is where the demons retreated prior to their banishment. A more solid edifice of Christian presence on Croagh Patrick is a dry-stone oratory that was discovered in an archaeological excavation. It has been compared to St Gallarus's oratory in Co. Kerry and has a carbon dating from between 430 and 890 AD.

Cruachán Aigle is mentioned in a poem from the *Dindshenchas*, (a work of early Irish literature recounting the origins of place names)* the following being the first two verses:

Oighle mac Deirg, derg a dhrech,
romarb Cromderg mac Connrach:
don gnim-sin co ngairge ngus
as de atá Oighle ar Gharbrus.

Cruachán Garbrois gairmdís de
lucht eólais in tiri-si:
Cruachán Aighle ósin amach
a ainm co tí in bráth brethach.

Aigle son of Derg (red his face); him Cromderg son of Connra slew: from that deed of savage force the name Aigle is given to Garbros.

Cruachán Garbrois the learned of this land used to call it: thenceforth name Aigle is given to Garbros.

[Translated by Edward Gwynn]

The location of Garbros is problematic, but Edward Gwynn in his commentary to the *Dindshenchas** says that it probably was a district extending from Mayo across to north Sligo. Garbros can mean a 'rough tract of arable land', and this may well have described a large section of the land in Mayo and Sligo during Patrick's time and even up to the present day. As the *Dindshenchas* is often mentioned in these pages, perhaps it is time to define precisely what the word means. Essentially it means 'hill lore' or a topographical explanation of noted places both in verse and in prose. Most of these commentaries are in verse, and are to be seen in the *Book of Leinster* compiled in the late-eleventh century, although Cruachán Aigle is in other manuscripts.

Although the chapel on the summit of Croagh Patrick is the central attraction for most of the pilgrims, the landscape surrounding the mountain contains evidence of a Stone Age and Bronze Age ritual nature, as shown, for example, by the number of hillforts, which was revealed as the result of an archaeological dig in 1994. However, its pre-Christian role is seldom alluded to.

The pilgrim route to Croagh Patrick was known as *Tóchar Phrádraig*, and it is along this route that many of the monuments which testify to the importance of the ancient landscape can be seen. The Christian pilgrimage starts at Ballintubber Abbey (*Baile an Tobair*, 'homestead of the well') but the earlier or pagan pilgrimage started at Aghagower (*Achadh Ghobair*, 'field of the horse'), which previously was called *Achadh Fhobair* ('field of the spring well'). At both starting points the spring wells would have supplied the liquid essentials for a rocky journey.

At Aghagower [31] begins the ritual landscape connected to Croagh Patrick. One finds here the *Leacht Tomaltaigh* or the 'stone of feasting', but before one gets carried away with an image of gluttonous pilgrims, the meaning is far more likely to mean 'the stone in memory of Tomaltach'. Tomaltach was a fifth-century King of Connacht, and this stone may have signified his standing before or during the early Christian period. The stone is just beyond Aghagower to the left of the pilgrim path. Pilgrimage to the Reek was customary among kings, and Hugh O'Rourke, King of Breffni, was captured while returning from Croagh Patrick in 1351, according to the *Annals of Clonmacnoise*.

As we walk about two miles west beyond Aghagower, we find a landscape strewn with monuments from the Stone Age to the Iron Age. And one may presume that among these monuments is the original route. A starting point may be at Cloghan Bridge [38], underneath which the River Carrowbeg flows from south to north. Less than a mile beyond Cloghan Bridge is a crossroads, and shortly after this is the Lankill stone, and about a third of a mile south of this is the Lanmore standing stone. These two stones can be seen as the grand gateway to the ancient landscape. A mile further on along the pilgrim's walk is the Boheh standing stone, which is on a mild elevation on the right side of the road. From here, in order to immerse yourself in the landscape, walk due south for a little over a mile and climb to the top of Liscarney Hill, and from there you should see the Liscarney stone row and ring barrow. Walking from the barrow in a south-west direction, you cross the N59 and from here you can see, about 200 yards away, Lough Moher Lough (*Loch Mothar*, 'the lake of the thicket') [38]. The name presumably refers to the cluster of trees and bushes that were once around the lake; There is a *crannóg* on the lough, a word that comes from the Irish *crann*, 'a tree', and signifies a dwelling made of wood; *crannógs* were built on artificial islands on lakes as homesteads at roughly the same time as ring forts, from the fourth to the seventeenth century.

Back on the N59, Liscarney village [38] is merely one mile north along the road. One mile north from Liscarney you pass two lakes on your left, which are known as Boheh Loughs, and beyond them you are back on Tóchar Phádraig. At this point you should turn right to view the rock art on a rock outcrop, which consists of cup and ring motifs and is regarded as one of the most highly decorated forms of rock art in Britain and Ireland. Archaeologists such as Corlett, Bradley and Johnson researching in the 1990s have suggested that this form of art may have its origins from as early as the fourth millennium BC. In Offaly, another example of this art can be seen at Clonfinlough, close to Clonmacnoise [47].

Croagh Patrick can be seen from many locations both near and far, and observing it from ancient sites adds to its appeal. A cairn in the townland of Aillemore on a hill two miles south-east from Bunlough Strand [37] is an excellent viewing location. Slightly north of the megalithic court tomb at Formoyle, three miles east from Sruhir Strand [37], is another viewing point. Carrowkeel megalithic cemetery overlooking Lough Arrow [25], at a distance of forty-five miles, presents a memorable view. Once, while visiting Reilig na Rí at Rathcroghan [40], a student pointed out a cone-like peak in the distance, and fifty miles to the west Croagh Patrick could be seen from this trivallate ring fort.

The *Táin Bó Flidais* or 'The Cattle Spoil of Flidais' derives its name from Flidais Foltchain, or 'Flidais of the beautiful hair', who was the young wife of Ailill or Oilill Finn, a chief of Erris (*Irrus*) [23] in north-western Mayo just prior to the Christian era. Ailill lived on *Nemthann*, the present Nephin Mountain. The tale concerns a raid on Ailill during which Fergus mac Roich, an exiled King of Ulster and lover of Medb,* carries off Flidais along with 100 cows, 140 oxen, and 3,000 calves. Medb then decrees that Flidais live with Fergus and, feeling that the proceeds of the raid will feed her army while on the Táin Bó Cúaligne,* requests Flidais to provide food for them every seventh day during the expedition.

Ailill Finn was the son of Domnall Dual Buidhe 'of the yellow locks', who was deferentially named 'Emperor of Erris and Western Europe'. Flidais owned a wonderful hornless cow, the *Maol*, which could give milk for 300 men (not counting women and boys) in one day. In the Ulster version of the *Táin Bó Flidais*, 'the lady's cows every seventh day gave milk enough to support the men of Ireland'.

Few stories contain so many previously unrecorded place names as does this tale. The place names associated with the story in east Connacht, Roscommon and Sligo can, according to Dobbs, be placed by the references given in Hogan's *Onomasticon Goedelicum*. 'But those in north-west Mayo seem,' as Dobbs writes, 'to have been outside the works of the earliest writers.'

One part of the tale concerns a journey from Cruachain, the ancient capital of Connacht, to the fort of Ailill at Dún or Rath Morgain in north-west Mayo, and is described with so many place names that make it a worthy pilgrimage to take should one wish to go back to late-Iron Age Ireland.

The route from Cruachain [33] to Rath Morgan [22] is about fifty miles. Medb* thus began her cattle raid by travelling across Magh Ai, the plain running south from Cruachain, past the east of Sliab Treblainde, across the top of Cruad-luachrai and across Dub Abuind mBreasa where, according to Hogan, Dún Diarmada or Dundermot was built. This would appear to have been past Castleplunkett [40] and across Caran Hill, towards Dundermot north of the River Suck and crossing the Suck River below Ballymoe [39]. There are two Caran Hills, the first two miles south-east and the other three miles south of Castleplunkett. Both contain barrow graves.

In describing this part of the *Táin Bó Flidais*, Dobbs writes: 'In Dundermot townland, east of Ballymoe and down stream from it, on the east bank of the Suck, is a large rath, standing on the high bank above flood level and overlooking the river. The ancient name for the Suck may have been *Dublind Brea* or 'the bank above the dark water'.'

The interior of the rath, which is roughly circular, measures between 165 and 180 feet in diameter. The fort guards the fords at Ballymoe, and the approaches are over high, dry ground. Before crossing the causeway, Medb* may have stayed at Dundermot [39].

Medb* then goes east towards Slieve Dart on the Galway–Mayo border, which is above *Móin Connedha* or *Tóchar Móna Connedha* ('the causeway across the Bog of Connedha') between Ballymoe and Dunmore [39]. She presumably used this causeway as she travelled west towards Rath Morgan. Medb then travelled west of Cloonfad in Roscommon and came to the ford at the present Blackford Bridge at the head of low-lying ground on the borders of Roscommon and Mayo. This was an area noted for floods, and here Medb headed north to cross the River Dalgan on the borders between Galway, Roscommon and Mayo. She then headed north along the high ridge near the present road (N83) from Cloonfad to Ballyhaunis. North of present-day Ballyhaunis, she would have come to Loch Mannin [32] which, with Island Lake, was probably a turlough (a type of disappearing lake found mostly in limestone areas) joined by the Mannin River. In Medb's time this was known as *Loch n-Airnedh*. Her army, as Dobbs writes, would probably 'have camped at the southern end of this lake'. Dobbs further says that 'after leaving Loch n-Airneadh they went to the eastern border of Mothar, and past the west of Magh Sanais'. Hogan also says that Mothar is in Crích Guaire at Damh-inis, in Clew Bay [31]. This is probably the island called Inishdaff, about two miles south-west of Newport.

Medb* then moved north-eastwards to the valley of the River Newport, passed Loch Beltra and camped at the foot of *Nemthainn hua n-Amalgaidh* or Nephin Mountain. Her men then ran up the mountain, either to get some exercise or simply to see the cairn at its summit, presuming it was there nearly 2,000 years ago. At about a 1,000 feet above ground it was quite a run!

After leaving here, the army was met by the poet Torna who is buried at Dumha Torna, also known as Lios na gCorp, a few hundred yards south of Lahardaun [23/31]. The townland of Tonacrock is south-east from Lahardaun, and one may wonder whether this is Torna's Rock. This poet should not be confused with Torna Eigeas who fostered and educated Niall of the Nine Hostages, a Leinster king from the fourth century.

A probable route for the army then was to take the high ground to the north of Loch Beltra, leaving the wet marsh of Glen Nephin on their right flank. A stone fight during the night left some of Medb's* horses dead, and this place was known as *Ech Oilech* ('the pillar stone to the horses'). A suggestion for the location of Ech Oilech may be Ballynafulla [31] – *Baile na Folanna* ('the bloody townland'). There is a standing stone here, and on the north-west slopes of Nephin Mountain there would have been plenty of available stones. Two miles north of Lahardaun [23] was Dún Átha Fen, three miles south from the Deel River, and it was here that Medb rested after the encounter with the stone attack. Some have associated this fort with Knockfarnagh, a hill one mile south-east from Lahardaun and one mile west from Tonacrock.

Aldridge suggests that on the south-eastern slopes of Nephin lies the burial place of Medb's* warrior Nochta and that she is buried at *Cruach na h-Oinseacha* ('the burial hill of the foolish or giddy women'), though 'loose' women may also be implied. This area is close to Cloghbrack [23] (*An Cloch Bhreac*, 'the speckled stone'). As to the existence of this stone now, one is left in the land of conjecture. However, local people in the early twentieth century referred to this place as the 'rath', and there are two ring forts close to Cloghbrack in the present day, though again if one of them were a mound or a ring barrow then one may well be the burial place of Nochta.

The Glenmasan Manuscript, a fifteenth-century Scottish document, which has the fullest version of the tale, states that Dara Derg cast a spear at Medb* but she bent her head to avoid the weapon, which then pierced the heart of Cainner 'so that she fell dead'. Cainner was taken out of her chariot, *agus do gabastar Meadb lam ar a fert do claide, agus do rindi an laidh* – and Medb dug her grave with her hand and sang this lay:

> *Claidfid fert Cainnire,*
> *Fuil sund sa duma ar n-á dith;*
> *Oir Fermenn mac Dara Deirg*
> *Do telic an t-selg diá ro-d-bí.*
>
> *Cainner derg ingen Oilella*
> *Agus Medba, is I ro bith,*
> *Ac duma an sgáil,*
> *Ar bhaid ré h-ogaib Emna.*
>
> *Cele Lugdech mic Conraí*
> *Re secht laithib, lith n-gaili;*
> *Togthar a lia os a lecht,*
> *Dentar a fert do claide.*

> Dig ye the grave of Cainner
> Lying here on the mound slain;
> Fermenn son of Dara Derg,
> Threw the spear which caused her death.
>
> Red Cainner daughter of Oilill
> And Medb, she is the victim,
> At the mound of the shade,
> The darling of the warriors of Emain.

The spouse of Lugaid son of Curoi,
During seven (short) days, delight of valour;
Raise her pillar above her gravestone,
Dig ye her grave.

[Translated by Professor Donald Mackinnon]

After leaving Dún Átha Fen, Medb's* army split into two columns, one party camping at Rath Ruadh ('the red fort') in the present-day townland of Rathroe, where there is a ring fort south of the river named both the Belladooan and the Rathroe. After this, Medb's column stopped at Knockroe [24], which is north of the Cloonaghmore River just as it enters Killala Bay; there are five megaliths within a mile of Knockroe and an ogam stone. The area was anciently known as *Tulaig Liath* ('stone knoll') from the huge stones found here. This area has been described by O'Donovan as having 'several remains of druidical monuments, consisting of great round stones spread over the hill, among which are two of great size that evidently crowned a Druidical Altar'. A townland closeby is named as Carrowmore or *Ceathrú Mhór Leacan* ('the district of the great stones').

Leaving Rathroe and crossing the Belladooan/Rathroe River, Medb* travelled north-west and crossed the River Glenedagh and marched up the Keerglen [23] and into Erris. Prior to this they would have crossed the Ballingen River, which is a continuation of the Keerglen. The Keerglen River was also known as Glen Cainner; another possible burial place for Cainner was Dún Draighin or the 'Dragon's Grave'. This grave is noted on the six-inch survey maps. It was possibly a cromlech or burial place; it possessed huge flagstones, and there was, according to Aldridge, a passage from the riverbank running into the dún. Today there are megalithic tombs between the Ballinglen River west of Ballyglass Bridge, which is less than a mile west from Ballycastle [23] and the Bellananaminnaun River.

Up Keerglen or Cainner's Glen on the north side of the river is said to be a townland named Skahaghna-shee or *Sceach na Síd* ('the fairy bush'). According to Aldridge, it was known to the owner of the land as *Sceach na h-Oinseacha*, or 'the thorn tree of the female fool', which one may compare with the earlier-mentioned Cruach na h-Oinseacha. Both of these places were on Medb's* route, and one of these places may be the supposed site of Cainner's grave. Aldridge mentions that *Sceach na h-Oinseacha* is the burial place of Cainner. There is an enclosure here and an ancient track to this ring fort or barrow.

The route from Keerglen follows an ancient track to Erris, also known as Bangor Erris or simply Bangor (*Beannchar*, 'peaked hill'). This route may well be part of the present *Slí an Iarthair* or the Western Way. Medb* crossed the Maumakeogh and Benmore mountains into Glenamoy. According to Aldridge, this route was used for pony traffic across the mountains up to the nineteenth century. Apparently the road from Crossmolina and Ballina to Bangor were under forest and swamp and thus impossible for chariots.

South of Benmore, Medb* and her army went north-west to Glencalry, apparently named after Calraide, a warrior who fell there. From here they went west along the Glenmoy River valley. Aldridge writes that they kept to the high ground south of the river. They then crossed the Munhin River, termed the Munkin River in the *Discovery* map [22]. This river is at the southern end of Carrowmore Lake. From here they went to Rath Morgan, which is two miles north-west from Munhin Bridge. Significant parts of this saga occur at Rath Morgan, sometimes referred to as Dún Morgan. It was here that Flidais disclosed her love for Fergus to Bricriu, the great Ulster satirist, confiding to him that should Fergus come to visit her she would supply him with horses, weapons and armour in preparation for the cattle raid described in the *Táin Bó Cúailnge*.*

According to Aldridge,

> the present owner discovered what must be a souterrain at the north-east side of the rath, opening up flagstones at the base of the earth wall of the fort; but he covered these up again. Under the floor of a stable about thirty yards to the north-east of this there are more flags, either the continuation of a souterrain, or perhaps a grave; without digging it is not possible to prove the connection; but it is very similar to the souterrain at Rath Munhin (Castletown townland, east of Carrowmore Loch).

Rath Morgan is also where Ailill Finn summoned his household and counsellors when he found that he was surrounded by Medb.* Ailill also sent his chief messengers, Engán and Édar, to summon the clans to his aid. Engán came from his fort on the north side of a stream called Muingingaun which flows into the the north-east corner of Lough Carrowmore. The stream derives its name from Engán, though the fort is not included on the *Discovery* map. According to Aldridge, the rath existed in the early 1960s and was called the Liss by the villagers of Muingingaun. South of Muingingaun there is a gap in the long ridge running between the valleys of Muingingaun and Glenturk More [23], which is called *Bearna na Maoile* ('the gap of the hummel cow' or 'the gap of the hornless cow').

The second messenger sent, Édar, probably gave his name to Ederglen [22], a townland one mile north-east of Rath Morgan. Although, as Aldridge writes, 'Édar is forgotten', his fort still exists, and that fort presumably is the promontory fort which overlooks the stream flowing into Trawmore Bay. From here Édar could watch his cattle as they grazed down the valley.

As an emissary, Édar journeyed around Broadhaven [22], the Mullet and Lough Carrowmore. Engán's journey was longer, as he went along the ancient Bronze Age route to Cruachan Aigle, now known as Croagh Patrick, and he also travelled to Clew Bay, Achill and Blacksod Bay. The calling together of the chiefs shows that these clans opposing Medb* were located in north-west Mayo and beyond. At least fifteen clans are named in this area and their names are recorded. This shows a prevailing sense of place and a desire to locate each tribe or clan within a particular district. As an example: the two sons of Curnan Blackfoot lived in the area known as Ros Inbir da Egonn, now known as Es-Ruaidh or Assaroe, the modern Ballyshannon at the mouth of the River Erne [16] in Donegal.

The end of this saga is as follows:

Acus ro ergedar ceithre holl-cuigid Érend and sin, ocus in dubloingeas mar aen riu, ocus ro greis Oilill go mor, ocus Fergus, ocus Medb iat, ocus tucsat anaigthi a naenfecht ar in dunadh, ocus ro shendit a Stuic ocus a Sturgana leo i comfuagna catha, ocus ro thogbadar gairi aidbli uathmara.

And then arose the men of the four great provinces of Ireland, and the dark exiles of [Ulster] along with them; and they were excited greatly by Ailill and Fergus and Medb; and they altogether faced the fortress; and they sounded their *Stuic,** and their *Sturgana** in proclamation of battle, and they raised tremendous terrific shouts.

[**Stoc*, a horn or trumpet, *do stoic Catha*, 'battle trumpet', *Sturgan*, trumpet or horn.]

[*Translated by Eugene O'Curry*]

Close to Newport (*Baile Uí Fiacháin*, 'the townland of O'Feehan') [31] is Cillin Daire, a place that contains a number of fairy paths; the local man with knowledge of these ways is Mickey Joe Doherty. Fairy processions generally began as soon as night fell and the tracks they followed as well as fairy palaces were much respected.

According to an account in the *Daily Mail* on 23 April 1959, the construction of a new road at Toorghlas, Co. Mayo, would mean a fairy palace would have to be destroyed, which led to a strike by twenty-five Land Commission labourers who wanted the domain of the Good People preserved. After negotiations, workers had their way and the direction of the road was changed.

Mentioned above in relation to the *Táin Bó Flidais* is the birthplace of Flidais at Bangor Erris [23]. The original name is *Irrus Domnann* or 'the promontory (fort) of the Domnann'. The Dumnoni were, as O'Rahilly says, 'a pre-Gaelic tribe' with whom other places in Connacht are associated. Another of these sites is the promontory fort south of Glencastle Bridge in the valley of Glencastle [22] known as *Dún Domhnaill* or Dundonnell. It has been suggested that these sites are the remnants of early Atlantic settlements which were not included in Ptolemy's map of Ireland, which may suggest that they came later. However, if the Dumnoni did arrive from the Atlantic and came into Tramore Bay [22], they presumably sailed along the Glencastle River and built their defensive fort just two miles in from the bay on the north bank of the river south-east from Bunnahowen. Both these forts associated with the Domnann are in a continuous line from Tramore Bay and lead to *Magh Domnann* ('the plain of the Domnann') to the west of Killala Bay in the barony of Tirawley (*Tír Amalgada*) and thence to *Inbher Domnann* which, according to Hogan, is the present Killala Bay. They may well appear to have been a coastal people as they also appear in coastal regions on the east coast (see under *Dublin*).

The warrior most associated with the Fir Domnann is Fer Diad; the *Book of Leinster* reads: *Fer nDiad mac nDamáin meic Dáre, in míled mórchalma d' fheraib Domnand*, or 'Fer Diad son of Daman son of Daire, the soldier of great deeds of the Fir Domnann'.

The tribe most associated with the Fir Domnann are the Gamanrad or the 'calf tribe' (*gamhain*, 'calf'), who are credited with importing calves and milch cows. They are also connected to *Irrus Domnann* [22] and are said to have built the ramparts about Cruachain (see under *Roscommon*) around 100 BC. They are said to have come from Britain, where they are associated with Devon and south-west Scotland. In Ireland, they came to the coastal areas of Leinster and Connacht. The settlement of the Fir Domnann and the Gamanrad in north-west Mayo may be because of the Gaelic conquest of Connacht. Eochaid Fedlech, King of Tara, banished Tinne mac Conrach, King of Connacht, from Cruachain to the wilds of Mayo and bestowed the kingdom of Connacht at Cruachain to his daughter Medb. The Gamanrad are said to have been one of the three warrior races of Ireland, the other two being the Clann Dedad (the Érainn) and the Clann Rudraige (the Ulaid).

Whether the Fir Domnann or the Gamanrad ever heard of the tale of 'The Children of Lir'* is a moot point, but if they had, they would not have had far to go to see their final resting place by taking to the sea from *Irrus Domnann* (Bangor Erris) and sailing down to Inishglora (*Inis Gluaire*) [22]. 'The Children of Lir' is one of the great tales of Irish myth, and its original title is *Oidheadh Cloinne Lir* or 'The Fate of the Children of Lir', which is counted as one of the 'three sorrowful tales of Ireland'.

The Children of Lir* spent 900 years as swans because of a curse placed on them by their stepmother. They spent the first 300 on Lough Derravarragh in Westmeath, the second 300 on the Sea of Moyle, the North Channel between Ireland and Scotland, and the last 300 on *Irrus Domnann*. At *Irrus Domnann* they turned back into human shape and met a man named Ebric, who wrote down their tale. They then went to Inishglora where they died. The four Children of Lir are Fionula, Aodh, Fiachra and Conn; before they left the Moyle, Fionula chanted a lay, part of which is as follows:

> We leave forever the stream of Moyle:
> on the clear, cold wind we go;
> three hundred years around Glora's isle,
> where wintry tempests blow.

[Translated by P. W. Joyce]

Their grave can be seen today as four standing stones about a well; the central stone is said to be Fionula's headstone.

Moving to the early Christian era, also found on Inishglora are three round beehive huts or cells close together as part of the same block of masonry. They have the same corbelled dome as the Skellig huts off the coast of Co. Kerry [83].

Less well known than the Children of Lir* but a vital force in both pre-Christian and Christian mythology is Brigit. In addition to the numerous places in Ireland, Britain and throughout Europe, she also has a strong connection with *Ceann na Corra* ('headland of the bend') on Clare Island [30]. Kinnacora is on the most easterly point of the island, where there is a holy well known as *Tobar Féile Brighde* or 'the well of Brigit's Feast'. A pattern was observed here on Lady's Day, 15 August, with worshippers walking seven times around the nearby cashel or enclosure in a clockwise direction or *deas sol* – 'right to the sun'. Devotional exercises are also practised at it on 1 February, St Brigit's feast day.

At Murrisk (*Muraisc*, 'low-lying seashore') [30], towards the south-east end of Clew Bay and five miles west of Westport, a battle was fought between the invading Gaels under Édan and the pre-Gaelic Tuatha Dé Danann,* supposedly around 100 AD. Here the older tribes with their allegiance to the goddess Anu were slaughtered, and the Gaelic chief Édan established a fort named Rath Rígbairt. This fort is mentioned in the *Book of Leinster* as *Argain Ratha Rigbaird*, meaning the 'destruction of the fort of the supreme bard'. Did Édan destroy an existing fort or did he establish one? Another reference to a battle in the vicinity is the Battle of Glaise Fraochain where Fraochan Faidh fell. *Glaise Fraochan* or 'the stream of Fraochan' is said to be close to Rosreaghan.

Clare Island [30], three-and-a-half miles from Roonagh pier and fifteen miles west from Westport, is situated in the middle of the entrance to Clew Bay. Covering an area of almost 4,000 acres, it is five miles long and three miles wide. Knockmore in the Bunnamohaun mountain range rises to 1,500 feet above sea level. Here are also found the Bunnomohaun group of sod huts, said to have been huts or shelters for herders and milkers rather than part of a 'booley' settlement (a summer settlement in which pastoral communities lived close to their herds on high ground).

A comprehensive natural history survey was carried out in 1909 under the direction of the botanist Robert Lloyd Praeger. Between 1909 and 1911, over 100 field workers collected material which was published in a series of reports by the Royal Irish Academy. A member of this team, Jane Stephens, was part of the dredging expedition which collected sponges. A sponge she found in Ballytoohy More to the north of the island was five million years old, making it one of the oldest fossils found in Ireland. More recent discoveries by the archaeologist Paul Gosling have included court cairns, *fulacht fia* – cooking sites – and a court tomb.

The island was owned for a while by the O'Malley clan, although it had other owners. The most famous O'Malley is undoubtedly Grace, more frequently known as Granuaile. She was born in 1530 into the chief family of the O'Malleys. She was a formidable woman and controlled the waters of the western seaboard during the sixteenth century. The Lord Deputy Henry Sidney, writing to the English Council in 1576, stated: 'O'Malley is powerful in galleys and seamen.' This observation followed him being offered three galleys and 200 fighting men by Granuaile in 1576 at Galway. However, the government did not give enough money to allow Sidney to hire her ships.

The O'Malley castle close to the harbour is one of eleven castles associated with the O'Malleys and the one which Grace used as her base. Her father was Owen Dubhdara O'Malley, the chief of the clan. When not engaged in piracy, she spent much of her time defending her realm againt the invading Elizabethan forces. At one time she ended up in prison in Dublin and at another sailed up the Thames and met Queen Elizabeth. Their conversation was in Latin and is recorded in the Elizabethan State Papers. She was offered the title of countess but refused, saying that she herself was a queen. Her son Tiobóid became the first Viscount of Mayo after her death. She is said to be buried in Clare Abbey close to the harbour on Clare Island. T.H. Mason, the antiquarian and authority on St Brigit's crosses, was once shown a skull in the abbey which local people said was that of Granuaile. This, if it existed, has either been hidden or more likely stolen. The O'Malley arms are displayed in this abbey. The coat of arms is topped by a white seahorse, below which is a boat with six oars, and to its right a bow with an inlaid arrow. The inscription is *Terra Marique Potens O'Maille* (O'Malley powerful on land and on sea).

The Legend of the Seal Wife played a big part in the folklore of the island. Many versions of the tale can be found in the Hebrides and the west of Ireland, but the fullest version was recorded by Nathaniel Colgan in the early part of the last century on Clare Island:

> Three Clare men went out seal fishing in a canoe one day, when they got out to the island they were making for, one of them landed in a cave to see if any seals would be in it, and the other three pulled away to another cave to look for more seals. But by the time the canoe came back to pick up the first man, the wind had rose up and the sea was that coarse they didn't dare venture in with the canoe to take him off … So the end of it the man in the cave roared out: 'Go away with yous before the storm gets real bad and leave me here for the night.'
>
> So away they went and left him there all alone by himself, and he climbed into a skelp [cleft] of the rocks the way the high tide couldn't catch him. But it wasn't long he'd been there when a big herd of seals came swimming and splashing into the cave and got up and lay down on the round stones on the floor, and he could see them without they seeing him, for its well hid he was in the skelp of the rock above them. And he kept watching them; and when the night began to fall what does he see but all the seals taking off their cuculs [*cochall*, 'cowl or hood'] and hanging them on to the rocks. And the minute they took off the cuculs they all turned into men and women and began to talk to each other, the way you and me is talking at this present. And when they got tired talking they all lay down to sleep, the women seals lying up at the top of the cave by themselves where the stones were dry, and the men seals lower down near the water.
>
> And they slept there all night; and as the light of morning came creeping into the cave, the canoe man rose up softly in the skelp he was hiding in and put his hand down and pulled up one of the women's cuculs and hid it under him in the skelp. It wasn't long till all the men and women woke up and went putting on their cuculs and swimming off into the sea as good seals... as ever they were when they came in. But

one of the women couldn't find her cucul at all, and she went up and down the cave in a terrible state, crying and calling to the others not to leave her there. But they wouldn't wait, and so they went off with themselves and left her alone by herself.

By this time the sea had gone down, and the canoe came out again to take the man from the cave; so he got down out of the skelp with the cucul hid under his *bawneen* [white flannel vest], for well he knew the seal woman once she got hold of the cucul would slip it on and turn back into a seal and swim off with herself. A real handsome woman she was, and after speaking to her fair and kindly, he took her into the canoe and brought her home to the island, and they were married there by the priest. And they lived very happy there, and had two children, and the husband took care to keep the cucul hid in the thatch the way the wife wouldn't see it.

But one day he was out fishing, and the wife was drying flax by the fire – for at that time flax was grown on the island – when the flax caught fire and before she knew where she was the house was all in a blaze. So she ran out with the children, and the flax caught fire in a few minutes and she got a queer smell coming from the thatch and she looked up and what did she see but her cucul, and it singeing with the fire. With that she made a leap at the cucul and caught it, and ran down to the shore with it, and slipped it on and made a seal of herself, and away she swam off with herself, leaving the two children behind her.

So the husband was left forlorn there with the children till one day a neighbour came and told him how he'd seen his wife come out of the sea and throw off her cucul and walk up on the rocks and hug and kiss the children and cry as if her heart were breaking. 'And,' says he, 'if you go your way down now to the shore and hide till she comes up again you've nothing to do only dart out and snap up the cucul, and you'll have her back with you.' With that the husband goes down to the shore and hides behind a rock where the children were sitting, and sure enough a seal comes swimming up and throws off its cucul and he seen at once that 'twas his wife that was in it, and she takes to hugging and kissing the children as if she'd like to eat them. Then out he leaps and grabs at the cucul; but he wasn't smart enough, for she caught it up before he came near it and on she claps it, and away with her into the sea. And the poor man never seen sight or light of her after that. He was a man that lived over there at the other end of the island, but I disremember his name.

The word cucul, more correctly cuculle, means a 'hood', or 'cowl'. The islanders, according to Colgan, had various translations for the word: some thought it was a cap, others thought it meant a cape or the whole skin or vesture of the seal. Larminie, in his *West Irish Folk Tales*, translates it as a 'transforming cap', whereas the Scottish folklorists MacDougall from Argyleshire and Campbell of Islay render it as 'husk'. It is also connected to the infant's caul, which is the inner membrane enclosing the foetus before birth, a portion of which may sometimes envelop the head of the child at birth. It is regarded as lucky and is supposed to be a preservative against drowning, particarly by sailors.

According to Westropp in *A Folklore Survey of County Clare*,

> the belief that seals are disguised human beings prevailed, I am told, in Clare forty years ago, at least along the Kilkee coast. I never heard it myself from fisherfolk. A little further north, from Connemara up to Mayo the Kinealys are reputed to be descended from a beautiful seal-woman. The belief is nearly universal and is attached even to a few of the family in Clare.

In the *Book of Lismore*, St Brendan changes fifty seals into horses, which carry into the sea their riders who are then also changed into seals. In Galway, it is said that the O'Connollys or *Ó Conghaile* are of seal descent.

Caher or Cahir Island [37], south-west of Clew Bay and ten miles from Westport, is known in Irish as *Cathair na Naomh* ('the stone enclosure of the saints') as well as *Cathair Phadraig* ('the monastic settlement of St Patrick'). It is about one mile in length from its north-western extremity to its south-eastern one, covering about 130 acres. It rises to about 270 feet on its western side, and here are several daunting cliffs. Uninhabited for more than a century, it has no harbour, so landing is only possible on a calm day. The usual landing spot is at Portatemple, which is on the north shore.

The monastic settlement associated with St Patrick, close to the landing place at Portatemple, is in ruins. The smallness of the site would seem to make it an oratory. Around it are twelve crosses, and above it on a hilltop a stone cross has a human face in relief. Of the two entrances to the oratory, one is Romanesque in design and the other has a lintel stone above the door; this may have been an earlier entrance. On the *leacht* or altar there is a stone dish with coins placed by people in recognition of favours granted.

There is a horizontal slab in the graveyard known as 'St Patrick's Bed', which is said to cure ailments such as epilepsy and nervous disorders. There are marks on this bed which are said to be the marks of hands, feet and hips. All that is required of the person seeking a cure is that they stay on the bed overnight.

Stones on the island can be used to put a curse on wrongdoers – such 'cursing stones' also feaure on both Inishmurray and Tory. Also like Tory, Caher has sacred soil which can be used to keep rats at bay and, like the stone bed, has many curative powers. Perhaps we can expand from this and assume that, with its sacred stones and earth, the island itself is sacred and that simply being there induces a state of blessedness.

Close to the monastic ruins are traces of an old path known as *Bothar na Naomh* ('the way of the saints'), which is said to traverse the seabed and join the ancient pilgrim track from Croagh Patrick. This would make this pilgrim track about twenty miles in length. Interestingly, there is also a *Leaba Phadraig* or 'St Patrick's Bed' on the top of Croagh Patrick. In keeping with this lore and coincidence, Caher island formed a part of the pilgrimage on Reek or Garland Sunday on the last Sunday in July each year.

As in the case of Mac Dara's island off Galway, boatmen can occasionally be seen lowering their sails as they pass Caher. This is in recognition of its holy esteem and the rumour that St Patrick is said to lie beneath one of its carved stones.

Inishturk Island [37], measuring three by two miles, lies about four miles west of Louisburgh and has a population of about ninety, in contrast to its pre-Famine population of 577, recorded in the 1841 census. The name of the island may mean 'island of the hog', but *torc* also means a pile or a heap and may refer to the rugged landscape that the island presents.

The island is of special interest to the geologist; the sandstone here dates back to the Lower Palaeozoic era and is from the Ordovician period about 500 million years ago. The sandstone ridges are still visible today. From the Iron Age, about 2,000 years ago, one can find a standing stone, a *fulacht fia* and a promontory fort situated on the south coast of the island. North of this is a *cillín*, which can be accessed from the road. Less than a mile north-west from the standing stone and at a height of 500 feet is a signal tower.

From either the graveyard or the promontary fort, one can look south-east and, weather permitting, see Inishdalla, which may mean either a dark and gloomy island or 'the island of the blind' or possibly 'seers'. South of this isle is a place called Ooghnamuirish which may well mean 'a sea cave' but could also mean 'the cave of the mermaid'. And there is a legend that it is the home of a seal with horns like that of a cow. It is said to be seen once every two or three generations.

The island has a connection with a son of Grace O'Malley or Granuaile. His name was Owen O' Malley, and both he and his family were massacred by Bingham, the then Governor of Galway.

ROSCOMMON

Ros Comáin, 'Coman's grove'

The royal centre of Connacht was based in Roscommon at Cruachain [33], the high status of which is testified in many sources. The other royal and assembly centres in Ireland were Emain Macha in Ulster, Tara in the kingdom of Meath, Dind Ríg in Leinster and Cashel in Munster.

The following is an extract of a poem from the *Dindshenchas** that testifies to the importance of Cruachain:

> *Estid a churu im Chrúachain*
> *fri dumu cach dag-núachair:*
> *a shlúag ónad sír-blad smacht,*
> *a rígad fer n-Olnécmacht.*

> *A shlúag na nglond fata fír*
> *col-lín drong ndata is dag-ríg,*
> *a dremm is déniu dolud,*
> *diargell Ériu il-torud.*

Listen, ye warriors about Cruachu!
with its barrow for every noble couple:
O host whence springs lasting fame of laws!
O loyal line of the men of Connacht!

O host of the true, long remembered exploits,
with number of pleasant companies and of brave kings!
O people, quickest in havoc
to whom Erin has pledged various produce!

[Translated by Edward Gwynn]

Cruachain, overlooking an extensive plain that slopes north-east to the River Shannon, comprises over seventy earthworks, and it preserves the landscape for Ireland's prehistory like none other, excepting Tara. Here one can find the royal palace of the prehistoric Queen Medb known as Rathcroghan (*Rath Chrúachain*). According to E.E. Evans in his *Prehistoric Ireland*: 'Rathcroghan has at 500 feet the appearance of a natural glacial hillock some 70 yards across the top and about 25 feet high; near the centre is a low mound five yards across which looks like a denuded ring barrow, and there is a small standing stone near the edge

FIGURE 8. Dathi's Stone at Cruachain (Carole Cullen).

of the hillock.' Rathcroghan remained a royal residence until the seventh century, and the festivities of *Samain* or Hallowe'en were celebrated here.

The pillar stone at Cruachain is known as Dathi's Stone, named after Dathi, a King of Connacht who was said to have been killed in Switzerland and was brought home and buried here. Dathi's pillar is south-east of Relignaree (*reilig na rí*, 'the graveyard of the kings'). The following extract is from the poet Torna Eigeas who, addressing the stone, says:

> *Atá fút-sa fionn Fáil,*
> *Dáthí mac Fiachrach fear gráidh;*
> *A Chruacha ro cheilis sain*
> *Ar Ghallaibh ar Ghaedhealaibh.*

> A fair king of Fail lies beneath thee,
> Dathi son of Fiachraidh, a man of dignity;
> O Cruacha, thou hast concealed this
> From foreigners and from Gaels.

[Translated by Eugene O'Curry]

Although Relignaree is described as a royal cemetery, particularly as it contained a number of small mounds, excavations have not discovered any signs of burials. To the south of the main entrance is a mound named *Cnocán na gCorp* ('the hillock of the bodies'), a place where corpses were laid out to be wept over before burial.

Medb* is a major protagonist in the epic *Táin Bó Cúailnge** or 'The Cattle Raid of Cooley'. And Cruachain also contains the bullring (*rath 'a tairbh*) in which the Finnbennach, one of the two competing bulls in the *Táin Bó Cúailgne*, was kept. It was here that this bull fought the Donn bull of Cooley to the death. The writers of the Táin used a ploy by which the remains of the bulls were figuratively gathered together to form the story of the epic in much the same way as two millennia later James Joyce used the scatterings of a midden heap to form the basis of *Finnegans Wake*. However, more than the bulls died in the bullring at Rath Tarbh. Bricriu the great satirist of the Ulster Cycle ('Clearer to me a whisper than anyone else a shout') was the umpire at this contest and was mauled to death by the competing bulls, so perhaps the scattered skin and flesh of Bricriu forms the basis of the *Táin Bó Cúailnge*.

An important ring fort at Cruachain is the trivallate ring fort known as Rathmore; trivallate forts have traditionally been connected with royalty, and this one is also known as *Rath na Rí*, or 'the rath of the king'. On a clear day from Rathmore it is possible to see Croagh Patrick rising up in the west.

Roscommon also contains the inauguration site for the Kings of Connacht at Carnfree [40] or 'the cairn of Fraoch', a prominent hill about 400 feet high in the townland of Carns, about two miles south-south-west of Tulsk [33]. Evans has suggested that as well as being connected to Gaelic royal dynasties: 'Its sanctity may well go back to the Bronze Age.'

A poem from the fourteenth-century *Book of Uí Maine* titled 'Carn Fraoich Soitheach na Saorchlann' or 'The Carn of Fraoch, a Vessel for a Noble Clan', describes the life of Fraoch in 105 quatrains and the following are a few verses:

Carn Fraoich, soitheach na saorchlann,
ríogha Dean 'na dhonnmhaothbharr,
sluaigh ó nach baothchranna breath
na saorchlanna dán soitheach.

Ó Fhraoch mhac Fhiodhaigh na n-arm
comhartha fuair an fionncharn;
sám don tulaigh mar tarla
don churaidh an comhartha …

Grádhaighis-si Fraoch Fabair,
grádhaighis Fraoch Fionnabhair;
glór aobhdha fa sámh snadhma
grádh laomdha na lánamhna.

… 'nathaobh (thaoibh)
ó do marbhadh 'na mhacomh;
is mór laoch a-muigh do mharbh
nó gur luigh Fraoch fán bhfionncharn.

Carn Fraoich, goodly house of the noble kindreds, the kings of Dean in its brown soft top; the nobles whose goodly house it is are a host not foolish or decrepit in giving judgements.

From Fraoch son of Fiodhach of the weapons did the fair hill get a name; a pleasant matter it is for the hill that it got the hero's name …

She [Fionnabhair] loved Fraoch of Fabhar, Fraoch loved Fionnabhair; the flaming love of the pair was [like] a pleasant voice that smoothed out difficulties.

… about him since he died in his youth; many a warrior did Fraoch slay in the field before Fraoch lay beneath the fair cairn.

The inauguration stone previously at Carnfree is not in its original place but has been removed to Clonalis House, Castlerea [32], the home of the family of the O'Conor Don. It lies today to the left of the front door of the house, and the footprint in stone, which Evans says is of 'doubtful authenticity', is still visible. The O'Conor Don is the longest continuous lineage in Britain and Ireland, and can be traced back to Rory O'Conor, High King in the twelfth century.

The *Táin Bó Fraích* or 'The Raid on Fraoch's Cattle' is an eighth-century tale in which Findabair, daughter of Medb,* falls in love with Fraoch, the son of Idath, King of the Connachta, and Bé Find from the Otherworld. From this it would seem that he has one foot in early history and the other in mythology. Fraoch asks Findabair's father, Ailill, for her hand and Ailill accepts as long as he gets the bride-price.

Afterwards they go with Medb* to the *Dublind Fraoich* or 'Fraoch's black pool' on the River Suck [39] to swim. While Fraoch is in the water, Ailill steals a thumb ring (*ordnasc*) that Findabair gave Fraoch as a token of their love. Ailill throws the ring into the pool and it enters the mouth of a salmon. He then takes the ring from the salmon and hides it in the bank of the river. Ailill then asks Fraoch to break a branch of a rowan tree growing out of the bank and bring it to him. He breaks off a branch and brings it across the water, holding it over his back. There follows a description of Fraoch by Findabair:

> *Ba hed íarum athesc Findabair, nach álaind atchíd, ba háildiu lee Fraoch do acsin tar dublind, in corp do rogili agus in folt do roáilli, ind aiged do chumtachtai, int shúil do roglassi, is hé móethóclach cen locht cen ainm, co n-agaid fhocháel forlethain, is é díriuch dianim, in chráeb cosna cáeraib dergaib eter in mhbrágit agus in n-agid nhgil. Iss ed atbered Findabair, nocon fhacca ní rosáissed leth nó trían do chruth.*

This is what Findabair used to say afterwards when she saw any beautiful thing: that it was more beautiful for her to see Fraoch coming across the [river] Dublind, the body for shining whiteness and the hair for loveliness, the face for shapeliness, the eye so blue-grey, and he a gentle youth without fault or blemish, face broad above, narrow below, and he straight and perfect, the branch with the red berries between the throat and the white face. This is what Findabair used to say: that she had never seen anything half or a third as beautiful as he.

[Translated by James Carney]

I include the above in its original Gaelic as, apart from its content, its use of alliteration shows it as an example of a 'run' of words which was used to give vibrancy to the storyteller.

According to the story, Ailill wants more berries, so Fraoch returns to the pool and meets a monster (*béist*) in the water, which he eventually kills by cutting off its head, thanks to Findabair derobing and plunging into the water with Fraoch's sword. This gives the name the *Dublind Fráech i mBréib*, considered by the *Dindshenchas** and Hogan to be the River Suck.

The story continues with a number of motifs that show much European influence, and then the cattle spoil begins. Fraoch occasionally returns to the *síd* or fairy mound at Cruachain, so we see how deeply he is a lightning rod for the early stories along Magh Aí or the plain of Connacht. With elements from the European Romantic Age, Fraoch is the romantic hero from Connacht, as Naoise is from Ulster and Diarmuid* Uí Duibhne from Munster. But without Findabair, Deirdre and Gráinne,* they would be merely heroes.

The allusions to the River Suck above is consistent with O'Rahilly's mention of Fraoch mac Fidaig being of the Gamanrad tribe, and that these people were of the Domnann and associated with the Suck and present-day *Irrus domnann* or Bangor Erris [23] in Co. Mayo. In *Tochmarc Treblainne* or 'The Wooing of Treblan Fraoch', Fraoch is said to be of the Domannann, a dominant tribe in Connacht. He may also have been from the Ól nÉcmacht, an older name for Connacht or the Connachtaí, who were dominant in Connacht but lost power and were moved further west. In pre-Gaelic times their territory extended from Limerick to Assaroe in Sligo, and from Uisneach in Westmeath to Inis Bó in Mayo.

About ten miles north-west of Cruachain is the River Boyle [33] and it is near here at Knockadoobrusna *Cnoc-a' dumha brusna*, or 'the hill of the burial mound of the wood for firing', that Cesair, the first woman to enter Ireland, is said to be buried. Cambrensis in his *Topographica Hibernia* wrote that 'the mound of earth in which she was buried is called the tomb of Ceasara to this day', which shows that the name and tumulus existed down to the beginning of the thirteenth century. The tomb can be seen from the town of Boyle as you approach the railway station, where, looking south, a mound can be seen on a hilltop about a mile away.

The name Ól nÉcmacht has been translated in several ways. In the late Middle Irish treatise on personal names known as *Cóir Anmann* ('fitness of names'), a tale purports to explain its meaning as follows: a banquet was held for the Ól nEcmacht by the druid Domma, and the Ól nEcmacht failed to share the food and drink – 'whereupon the host Domma said: "Uncomradelike (*écumachta*) is this drinking (*ól*) ye do"', so from that time the term *Ól nÉcmacht* clung to the province of Connacht. However, another possible meaning could be 'great horsepeople', with *macht* meaning either from 'across the sea' or 'death' or 'wonderful'. The *Echach* were at the heart of the Dál nAraide,* and the Cruithin* and were the horse people who came from east Co. Down and gave their name to Lough Neagh – 'the lake of the horse'. Eochaid Echbel (horse-mouth) was a noted leader of the Echach. The word *Echtrai* or 'horse-travelling' is the Irish word used for tales which come under the title of 'adventures'.

The Battle of Airtech was fought between the Ulaid and the Fir Ól nEchmacht close to Cruachain. It would seem that this battle marked the end of the Ól nEcmacht as a power in Ulster and in Connacht. A manuscript translated by R.I. Best alludes to this battle as follows:

Nir leicsit dono fir Ól nEgmacht Ailill no Medb léo insin cath. Digniet ierom catha commorae comardae dib cechtor dilina occus ro indsaigh cach i cheile dibh i rrói cath occus imbualtae; ro comraicsit iarom ocus ro gab cách dib for truastrad i ceili ocus for trencuma. Ba hacgarb ba haithaihge ro ferad in gleo eter firu Ol nEgmacht ocus Ulta. Bai tnuth ocus miscais ocus midduthracht oc cach dia cheile dibh. Bui muirnn occus seselbi isin cath chechtordae .i. buirfedach na fer, iachtad na miled, cnetu ocus osnadhach na trenfer, beimnech occus blesbarnach na cloidem, síanu ocus scretu na sleg ocus na soicchet, occus becedach ocus golbemnech na carruc n-adbalmor n-anbforustai oc beim fri sciathaib ocus luirechaib occus cathbarraib na n-arcon occus na n-arsed:

The Fir Ól nEcmacht did not let Ailill or Medb go with them into battle. They form battalions then on each side, one as great and lofty as the other, and they make towards one another on the field of battles and of conflicts. Then they encountered, and every man took to smiting his fellow and to hard hacking. Rude and sharp was the fight between the Fir Ól nEcmacht and the Ulaid. Envy and hatred and ill-will there was on every side. There was uproar and tumult on both sides of the host, namely the bawling of the men, the outcry of the soldiers, the groans and lamentations of the strongmen, and clashing and clatter of the swords, the whiz and whirr of the spears and arrows, and the roaring and wailing of the huge tottering rocks as they crashed upon the shields and breastplates and helms of the wardogs and veterans.

As to the meaning of *airtech* and its location, one is left in the land of supposition. The word may be related to *airtherach*, meaning 'eastern'; the *ind Airthir* were the 'eastern districts', and the Airthir were a tribe whose territory included the present county of Armagh and the capital of Ulster, Emain Macha.

Síd ar Cruachain, also known as Oweynagat (*Uaimh na gcat*, 'the cave of the cat'), is perhaps the most interesting site in Cruachain, as it has an entrance to the Otherworld.

FIGURE 9. An entrance to the Otherworld – Oweynagat at Cruachain.

From here at Oíche Shamhna or Hallowe'en emerged the *Ellén Trechenn* or triple-headed deity who laid waste to Ireland. It is also said that from here emerged a flock of birds that 'withered up whatsoever their breaths impinged on'. For many years Simon O'Dwyer and his wife Maria, along with their Bronze Age horn and bodhrán, joined me and many others in acknowledging the start of *Samain* from within this underground cave.

There are many caves in this area, and according to local tradition they go back as far as Sligo. In Christian times, Síd ar Cruachain was known as the Hell's Gate of Ireland, and it was the destiny of one warrior named Nera and his wife to live there until the Day of Judgement. At the entrance are a number of lintel stones which act as a ceiling; two of these contain ogam writing. The archaeologist Robert Macalister translated one inscription, VRAICCI MAQI MEDVII, as 'Fráech son of Medb'.

According to a poem by the seventh-century poet Fintan, festivities were also held at Cruachain at the Feast of Lughnasa or Lammas on 1 August 'on the sporting green of the palace'. The poem is in memory of King Raghallach, who was murdered by poachers on his land after he demanded recompense when they had killed and eaten a buck. Muirenn was Raghallach's wife, and their three sons were Fergus, Cellach and Cathal. Nindé, a prince from Tír Chonaill, made a predatory invasion into Connacht when the nobles of the province were holding the ancient games of Lughnasa. The following is an extract from the poem:

Raghallach on Lammas-Day,
Cellach and Fergus the choleric,
And Muirenn, with her necklaces,
Were preparing for the games of Cruachan.
When came Nindé the vindictive …
And they burned all before them to Ceis Corann …
The land was filled with burnings from
Sliab Gamh to Sith Seaghsa ['the Curlews'] …
Though our losses were numerous,
We did not miss them in our pride;
On the steeds of the men of *Tir Eoghain*
We perfomed the games of *Cruachan*.

[Translated by Eugene O'Curry]

From Owneygat also came a flock of white birds that throughout Ireland 'withered up whatsoever their breaths impinged on'. Not only are birds and cats associated with the cave but also pigs emerged from the souterrain and went south to Athenry, giving the name *Magh Muccrama* ('the plain of the counting of pigs') to that part of Galway. It was from here also in the *Táin Bó Cúailgne** that the great warrior–goddess, the Mórrígan, came in a chariot 'pulled by a one-legged chestnut horse towards Cúailgne'.

At Ogulla (from *Óghda*, 'pure, virginal, or attached to a monastery'), half a mile west from Tulsk [33], there is a holy well known as Clébach (*Clíabach*, meaning a wild boar, deer, wolf or fox). The two druids associated with the well were Máel and Caplit. A small modern chapel here now is testament to the Christianisation of the place. Close by is a ring barrow grave in which the daughters of King Laoghaire, who were sent to be fostered by the two druids, are said to be buried. Here also was an assembly point for the gathering of the forces of Connacht under Medb* prior to advancing on Ulster in the Táin. This area is known as *Tuaim Móna* or 'peat ridge'.

Certain customs have been associated with corpses throughout Ireland, and many of these have been recorded by the Irish Folklore Commission. One example is from John Flanagan from Mount Talbot [40]: 'I heard of a cure in the corpse. I saw a man got something in his jaw, some kind of a lump. He was discussin' this lump he had on his jaw and he said he got a dead woman's hand and rubbed it off it and it cured the lump.' It was also believed that the hand of a corpse could also cure toothache: 'If you take the hand of a corpse and rub it on your face, if you had a toothache, it would cure the toothache,' according to a Mrs Hanley from Derraghmylan in Rooskey [33].

Magh Aíi or *Magh Aoi*, also known as Machaire Chonnacht and locally as 'the Maghery', is the plain from Strokestown [33] to Castlerea [32] and from the hills two miles north of Roscommon town to Lismacoil, two miles north-east of Elphin [40]. On this plain is *Énloch*, or 'the lake of the birds', where Fergus mac Roich is buried, although its exact location is open to speculation. Fergus left Ulster due to King Conchobar mac Nessa's treatment of Deirdre and the sons of Uisnech. Legend states that he was the last person to be able to relate the great epic of the *Táin Bó Cúailnge** from memory.

Énloch is the starting point for the tale of *Echtra Laegaire meic Crimthainn* ('The Adventures of Laegaire mac Crimthainn'). A possible location for the lake is Lough Fergus [40], four miles north-west on the N60 from Roscommon town, and another possibility, though less likely, is Finn Lough, two miles south-east from Strokestown. Yet another contender is Loughnaneane, just west of Roscommon town. Some locals say that as the lake is so close to the town the stone or stones may have been removed for building purposes. This brings one back to Lough Fergus where there are half a dozen barrows within a slingshot of the lake and a ring fort close by named Lisnalegan (from the Irish for 'the fort of the flagstone'), and beside it is a moated site. Further close to Lough Fergus is Lough Creevin or 'the lake of the little branch'. Fergus was a dominant member of the *Craeb Ruad* or 'the Red Branch knights'. A townland nearby is named Creeve.

SLIGO

Sligeach, 'abounding in shells'

Two miles south-west of Sligo [25] in the peninsula between Lough Gill and Ballysadare Bay are the ancient tombs at Carrowmore (*Ceathrú Mhór*, 'large quarter') which, according

FIGURE 10. The sacred centres of Sligo (map by Jack Roberts).

to the Swedish archaeologist Goran Burenhult, are the earliest known in Ireland or Britain. He contended that the ancient structures were built by fishermen whose ancestors had been there for generations, and not by Neolithic farmers as previously supposed. And he explains: 'The traditional stereotype, farming community equals megalithic monuments, can no longer be upheld, and a development within a pre-existing Mesolithic population is supported by offerings of unopened seashells in the excavated monuments.' He dated the tombs to be from between 4580 and 3710 BC, which would make them as old as the first cities at Mesopotamia.

This passage-grave cemetery at Carrowmore contains a large number of chambered cairns, with as many as sixty passage graves in various states of repair. These graves fanned around the central and largest grave at Listoghil. Many of the cairns have retained only the chamber, the other stones presumably used for house building and for enclosing fields. The sites where only the kerb stones remain, and where once there were cairns, have sometimes been misnamed as stone circles. According to Séan Ó Ríordáin who worked on the site, the passage graves do not 'indicate a settlement pattern as many of their hill-top positions would have been inhospitable at any period'.

The passage-graves lack ornament and are a simpler design than those found in the Boyne Valley complex. This has led some to speculate that the passage-graves moved from west to east rather than east to west. However, the Carrowmore graves, which consist of uprights covered with a large capstone and surrounded by a circular stone kerb, are very different from the more elaborate structures found in the Boyne Valley. A rare example of megalithic art in the Carrowmore district was found at Cloverhill Lake. On one stone there are inscribed three circles, and one is tempted to ask whether these relate to the sun, moon and earth, which, as in Newgrange, would have been central to their religion and used as a calendar to the farming seasons. It is also noteworthy that the name for the shell middens found here in this sacred place can be traced back to *Sligeach* or 'shelly place', from which the county gets its name.

Carrowmore represents a fine example of sun alignment at *Samain* (*sam fuin*, 'summer's end') or Hallowe'en, when the sun rises over the 'Saddle' at the Ballygawley Hills, the eastern extension of the Ox Mountains. At *samain*, the sun lights up the underside of the capstone and illuminates the chamber. This event occurs at Listoghil at 7.45 a.m. on 31 October and at 7.48 a.m. on 1 November annually. The Ballygawley Hills are also known as the 'sleeping woman', who is the *Cailleach Bhéara*; these hills contain her head, breasts, belly and legs and, up to her thighs, the Lake of the Two Geese, *loch dá ghed*, which is a high corrie lake. From this lake is derived the Irish for these hills, namely *Sliabh Dá Én* or the 'mountain of the two birds'. According to Pádraig Meehan, author of *Listoghil: A Seasonal Alignment?*, 'the Ballygawley Mountain range, with its distinctive rounded forms, may also have been part of the narrative that informed the positioning and layout of the Carrowmore complex'.

W.B. Yeats is buried 'up the road' from Carrowmore at Drumcliff. He refers to the Cailleach Bhéarra in his poem 'Red Hanrahan's Song about Ireland' as Clooth-na-Bare. He also refers to Medb* at Knocknarea:

The wind has bundled up the clouds high over Knocknarea,
And thrown the thunder on the stones for all that Maeve can say …

FIGURE 11. Capstone in chamber at Listoghil (Jack Roberts).

> The yellow pool has overflowed high up on Clooth-Na-Bare,
> For the wet winds are blowing out of the clinging air;

Listoghil is at the centre of the Carrowmore complex and is a passage grave tomb; it is locally known as the 'Giant's Grave'. Passage tombs consist of a round mound or cairn with a passage leading from the edge to a chamber within. They belong to the Neolithic or New Stone Age period (c. 4000–2000 BC). Passage tombs occur predominantly in the northern third of the country.

Michael J. O'Kelly in *Early Ireland: An Introduction to Irish Prehistory* writes:

> There is only one monument in the Carrowmore cemetery which comes within the classic passage tomb definition. This is no. 51, known as 'Listoghil'. It is centrally placed with regard to the other tombs and is at a somewhat higher elevation. It consists of a large srone cairn, between 35m and 41m [114ft and 135.5ft] in diameter at present, with remains of a kerb. At the centre is a rectangular chamber roofed with a singular limestone capstone, 3m by 2.75m and the cairn must originally have covered it.

This last point by O'Kelly, namely that a 'cairn must originally have covered it', was verified for me by Pádraig Meehan. He mentioned that the cairn was about to be stripped for use in building, but when the workers came to the tomb they halted their labour, as they did not wish to interfere with the tomb. Thanks to this respect for the dead by the local workforce, this unique tomb still exists and the seasonal alignment can still be observed.

Megalithic tombs are plentiful in Sligo, and one can even be seen in the town of Sligo [25]. This is now surrounded by a roundabout, the first to be built in Sligo. At one time it was proposed that the tomb be destroyed, and its fate was in the balance until an old woman coming up the river demanded that it be preserved, after which she went away.

Some say that she was the *Cailleach Bhéara* who came up the Garvoge River (*An Gharbh Óg*, 'Rough Ogress'), though others say it was a local woman with a passion equal to that of the *cailleach*. The megalithic tomb standing today is a testament to folklore and the power of women. This first roundabout, which is near the fire station, is known locally as Garbh Óg Villas and archaeologically as Abbey Quarter North. A testament to folklore in the area was a letter to the *Sunday Times* in late July 2017, in which Martin Ford from Sligo stated:

> One night when my sister was four years old, she went looking for my mother who was out visiting. She stopped at a fairy fort to tie her laces, and the 'little people' appeared and were playing around her. She asked did they know where her mammy was, and they said, 'we will take you to her.' They led her to a neighbour's house. When my Mum came out, my sister said, 'Meet my new friends.' But when she turned around, they had disappeared. That fairy fort is still there, at Garavogue Villas in Sligo town.

The Garvoge flows into Tobernalt Bay and close by is *Tobar an Ailt* ('the well by the cliff') which is both a Christian and a pre-Christian well and an example of the two traditions melding together. One problem with the continuing pre-Christian custom of placing votary offerings on trees, generally hawthorns, is that the old custom of not allowing pieces of cloth to be left for more than three days is not adhered to. I have seen this in Sligo, both at Creevykeel and at Tobar an Ailt, where the rotting offerings show an ignorance of the older custom and are aesthetically unappealing.

Four miles south-east of Ballymote [25] on the R295 is one of the most remarkable hills in Irish legend, namely Keshcorran (*Céis Chorainn*, 'the harp of Corann'). The plain from which the hill rises was known as *Magh Chorainn*, or 'the plain of Corann'. The *Dindshenchas** describes Magh Chorainn and Céis Chorainn as follows:

> Magh Corainn whence the name? Not hard to say. Corann, harper to Dian Cécht the Dagda's son, called with his harp Caelcheis, one of Drebriu's swine. And Caelcheis ran forward as fast as his legs would carry him; and the hounds of Connacht and their soldiery pursued him as far as Céis Chorainn; hence the names of Céis Chorainn and Magh Corainn.

Céis Chorainn may also mean 'the young sow of Corann'. Also known as *Céis Chorainn na bhfiann*, or 'Keshcorran of the Fianna', it is a humpbacked limestone hill 1,200 feet in height. There is a cairn on top of the hill and, to keep it company, a triangulation pillar. Halfway up the hill, about 200 feet from the base, is a vertical limestone cliff-face with panoramic views over south Sligo, east Mayo and Roscommon. The caves here comprise sixteen chambers all aligned east–west with the entrances facing the west. They are identified by the letters A to P from north to south. Some were named after archaeologists who investigated them, as, for example, cave J or the Coffey Cave, named after George Coffey who was involved in the first excavations of Kesh in 1903. This cave is about eighteen feet deep and nearly seven feet wide at the entrance, narrowing to just under a foot at the rear. Artefacts unearthed over the years include a medieval armour-piercing projectile head, an Early Medieval bone comb fragment and two bone pin fragments. A human tooth was radiocarbon dated to the Iron Age.

In the nineteenth century, it was thought that caves could be the long-sought repository of 'Early Man' in Ireland, but this was unfounded; the human remains were more often Neolithic rather than Mesolithic or Paleolithic. In earliest times, caves were used for burial rites and offerings, and from Early Medieval times for occupation and shelter; archaeological evidence shows that the caves at Keshcorann were used for short-term occupation during the Early Medieval period. Though archaeology states that certain activities occurred at the 'entrance to the caves' at Keshcorann, we need to go to mythology to get some idea as to what these activities were.

The earliest story relating to the caves was written about 800 AD and is found in the *Book of Leinster* under the heading of *Turim Tigi Temrach* or 'The Enumeration of the House of Tara', and as *Cath Maige Mucrima* or 'The Battle in the Plain of the Counting of Pigs'. The book also refers to Keshcorran as the cave where Cormac mac Airt, High King of Ireland, spent his early childhood: *Conamail … ruc. Cormac mac Airt a hÚaim Céise Coraind* ('houndlike Cormac mac Airt was brought up in the cave of Corann'); it also states: *Cormac mac Airt ina ucht altram* ('Cormac mac Airt was suckled by a she-wolf'). Both these statements give body to the legend that Cormac was taken by a she-wolf shortly after his birth and was reared by her in one of the caves at Keshcorran. On a six-inch Ordnance Survey map of 1838, Cave P is named *Owey Cormac mac Airt* ('the Cave of Cormac mac Airt'). A local legend recorded in 1836 told how the mother of Cormac mac Airt gave birth to him while collecting water at Tober Cormac to the north-west of the caves; this well is situated in the townland of Cross [25], a mile north of the village of Kesh. It is in the corner of a field on a north-facing slope. The area is overgrown and muddy, and some moss-covered stones mark the site of the well at a T-junction along an old road known as *Bóthar an Corann* or *Bóthar na Slieve*. This road was built by Richard de Burgh, the Red Earl of Ulster, and is situated between Keshcorann and the R295.

Similarities can be seen with the suckling of Romulus and Remus by a wolf, both going on to found Rome, as Cormac is credited with the founding of Tara. So often our early history is seen as mythology, and this is partly because our history is seen as *beginning* in 431 AD with the arrival of Christianity. In the case of Cormac mac Airt and his cave, his story fits into the motif of the European hero–king, but this is not to say that it is necessarily borrowed from the tale of Romulus and Remus and it may stand on its own.

Another later story relating to Keshcorran is included in the 'Lays of Finn' or the *Duanaire Finn* compiled in the seventeenth century. This is a story known as 'The Lay of the Smithy', in which Finn* and his Fianna* find themselves on Sliabh Luachra in Kerry, where they are approached by Lon mac Liomtha, the chief smith of Norway. He challenges the Fianna to race him, and he leads them all the way to the caves of Keshcorran. Lon makes swords and spears and presents them to Finn and his warriors. He names all the weaponry, *Mac an Luin* being the name given to Finn's sword. At sunrise the next day the Fianna wake up to find themselves once again on Sliabh Luachra. Here is an unusual tale where no one dies nor is injured. It possibly has a derivation in an ancient warrior route from Sliabh Luachra to Ard Patrick in Limerick, and from there to Clare and Galway and finally to Keshcorran.

A more famous tale relating to the caves, *Bruidhean Chéise Corainn*, or 'The Otherworld Hostel at Keshcorran', tells of Finn and the Fianna* being trapped here by three *cailleacha* or hags, the daughters of Conaran mac Imidel of the Tuatha Dé Danann,* and then being rescued by Goll mac Morna, the same Goll who in time rescued Finn in hell from the 'demons of the blue host'.

The caves were a meeting place for the goddesses or *cailleacha*, later demoted to hags but still retaining their power. In Mayo folklore, according to Máire Mac Neill, the caves were home to Áine, as were Knockainey in Co. Limerick and the Paps of Anu (the mother of the Irish gods) on the Cork–Kerry border. The Mórrígan ('great queen') had a tryst with the Dagda* on the River Unshin, three miles north of Corann Hill. In Old Irish, *Uinnius* means 'ash tree', one of the sacred and venerated trees both in these islands and in Norse mythology, as it was seen as the tree that connected the earth with the Otherworld. The Unshin was a living manifestation of the goddess, in this case the Mórrígan, with nine loosened tresses, who was washing herself, 'one foot on the south bank the other on the north'. She and the Dagda conversed and then mated over water, this being part of an ancient fertility ritual. The 'Bed of the Couple' is the name of this place. Here on this river she prophesied the second battle of Magh Tuiredh, telling the Dagda to summon the skilled men to meet her at the River Unshin. Here the Mórrígan killed Indech, a Fomorian giving handfuls of his blood to the waiting warriors. At a more local level, the *Cailín Cennruad* or 'red haired girl' was one of the *cailleachs* connected to Keshcorran.

Several ring forts connected to the Fenian saga of Diarmuid* and Gráinne* are just north of Keshcorann at Graniamore (*Gráinne Mór*) [25]. There are at least five in the townland of Graniamore and one in the townland of Graniaroe. A rath or ring fort at the base of the hill to the north is termed by Máire Mac Neill as *Ráth Gráinne*, and here she says the two lovers stayed during a lull in the trouble with Finn. This ring fort is at Carnaweeleen at the north base of the hill about a third of a mile north of the megalithic tomb from which Carnaweeleen gets its name. However, as the territory of Corann was part of Gráinne's dowry given to her by her father, Cormac mac Airt, she was not restricted to any one homestead but had her pick of a large number.

The identification in south Sligo of so many Early Medieval homesteads or ring forts connected with Gráinne gives this story, one of the great tales of early Irish literature, a strong resonance of place, and specific places at that. Many ancient places are named 'the love beds of Diarmuid* and Gráinne';* altogether there are said to be 366 of them throughout Ireland. They are mostly associated with dolmens or ring forts.

Perhaps the most significant site associated with this saga is Ben Bulben, or more accurately Ben Gulban [16], an imposing flat-topped plateau with its cliffs formed of limestones. It was on this plateau that Finn and the Fianna* finally caught up with the couple, and in a wild boar hunt Diarmuid* died from wounds received from the swine. Finn let him die unaided and Gráinne returned to Finn and the Fianna. Diarmuid was killed at a place known as *Leacht na Muice* or the 'grave of the pig', identified as *Áth Doimhghlais*, which may be in the townland of Ardnaglass between Ben Gulban and Grange on the N15. The legend relates that Diarmuid was taken by his guardian god Aengus of the Brú back to the burial place of the gods at *Brú na Bóinne* along the Boyne Valley in Co. Meath.

Ben Gulban is named after Conall Gulban, whose adventures in eastern lands are described in the sixteenth-century manuscript *Eachtra Chonaill Ghulban*, as it was here that he was fostered. Conall was a son of Niall of the Nine Hostages, who lived in the fifth century. *Tír Conaill Gulban* is the Irish version of Donegal, named after Gulban. Conall, together with his brothers Énnae and Eógan, were founders of the northern Úi Néill.

Three miles north-west of Drumcliff is Cooldrumman (*Cúl Dremne*, 'the back of the ridge hill'), the ridge hill referred to being Ben Gulban. Cooldrumman [16] is about two miles west of Ben Gulban. Here another O'Neill, namely Colm O'Neill, otherwise known as St Columcille or St Columba, was involved in the first recorded act of plagiarism, which led to the so-called Battle of the Books fought at Cooldrumman in 561 AD.

The origins of this battle go back to a visit by Columcille to St Finnian in Droma Find or Dromyn near Ardee, Co. Louth, to ask him for a loan of his book of the Psalms. Without Finnian's knowledge he began copying it, and when he was nearing the end Finnian sent someone to ask him for it back. The messenger observed Columcille transcribing the book, and when it was revealed to the saint that he had been observed, he spoke in saintly language to a pet crane he had, saying: 'It's all right with me if it's all right with God for you to pluck out the eye of that youth that came to spy on me without my knowledge.' The crane dutifully whipped out the eye so that it was left hanging externally on the cheek of the observer. St Finnian did not like this, and he blessed and healed the eye and put it back in its socket. He then approached Columcille and complained about his copying the book of Psalms without his consent. To this, Columcille said: 'I will need the ruling of the king of Ireland about this.' The king at the time was Diarmait mac Cerball.

Finnian replied: 'I will accept that.'

After that, they both went to King Diarmait at Tara for judgement. Finnian said: 'Columcille copied my book unknown to me and I say that the "son" [copy] of my book is mine.' To which Columcille replied:

> Finnian's book that I copied from is none the worse for it, and it is not right that the divine words in that book should perish or that I or any other should be hindered from copying or reading them or from spreading them among the people; and further I claim that I was entitled to copy it, for if there was any profit for me in copying it I

would want to give that profit to the people, without consequence to Finnian or his book.

Then Diarmait gave his famous judgement: 'To every cow its little cow, that is its calf, and to every book its little book, that is its copy: and because of that, Columcille, the book you copied is Finnian's.'

'That's a bad judgement,' said Columcille, 'and you will be punished for it.'

Around the same time a row broke out between the son of the King of Connacht and a steward during a hurling game, resulting in the prince killing the steward. The prince sought the protection of Columcille, but to no avail –he was taken away and executed. It seems that the execution of the prince while under the protection of the saint was more the cause for the ensuing battle, but the plagiarism has had a greater impact on our scribes and historians. In the battle of Cúil Dremne, the Úi Neill were victorious against Diarmait the King of Ireland. After this victory, Colum left Ireland due to his guilt at instigating this battle with all its loss of life, but he returned on occasion. His departure was not voluntary but in accordance with a ruling by St Molaise of Devenish, whose account of the battle is preserved in the *Cathach* or 'Battle Book', a most precious book in the possession of the Royal Irish Academy in Dublin. It is Ireland's oldest Latin manuscript. The book shrine in which the manuscript was originally contained may be seen in the National Museum of Ireland.

There were two Battles of Magh Tuiredh. The first, between the Tuatha Dé Danann* and the Fir Bolg,* was fought near Cong in Co. Galway, and the second, discussed below, near Lough Arrow. In the first battle, the last King of the Fir Bolgs, Eochaid mac Eirce, fell. He and his tribe were routed by the mythical Tuatha Dé Danann. Eochaid mac Eirce was buried at *Trá Eóchaille* at Beltra Strand in Ballysadare Bay west of Ballysadare [25]. A verse of a poem written by Tanaidhé O'Mulconry (who died in 1136) describing the death of Eochaid mac Eirce is as follows:

Tucsat Tuath de Danann dil
laigne leó ina lámaib,
dibsein ro marbad Eochaid
la sil Nemid nertbrethaigh.

The brave Tuatha Dé Danann brought
pointed spears in their hands with them.
Of these was killed king Eochaid,
by the victorious race of Nemid.

[Translated by Eugene O'Curry]

Eochaid was pursued by the sons of Nemed from Magh Tuiredh to *Trá Eochaille*, a distance of fifteen miles, and there a fierce battle ensued. Both Eochaid and the three sons of Nemed died here. The sons of Nemed were buried at the west end of the strand at a place known as *Leca Meic Nemedh* or 'the gravestones of the sons of Nemed'. King Eochaid was buried where he fell, and a large cairn was erected to him. This cairn was, according to O'Curry, 'one of the wonders of Ireland'. In the nineteenth century, it was known as the Cairn of Traigh Eothaile, Eothaile being a softer pronunciation of Traigh Eochaille. His cairn was raised over him by the Nemedians. The modern word for *Traigh Eochaille* is Beltra or in Irish Béal Trá, 'mouth of the beach'.

Trá Eochaille or Eochaid's Strand was three miles west of Ballysadare, and at low tide it was about a square mile in extent; today it is known as Trawohelly, an anglicised version of *Traigh Eothaile*. It is just east of Tanrego, a townland less than four miles west of Ballysadare. The historical importance of *Trá Eochaille* diminished when in 1858 a rampart was constructed which cut out the sea. Up until then, roads from the north, south-east and west crossed this strand, which is now marshland covered in sedge and rushes. As a result, the monuments to King Eochaid and the sons of Nemed were destroyed. The larger stones were used to build the rampart, and according to a writer in 1928, 'only a couple of little heaps of small stones at present mark these ancient sepulchres'. One wonders if these small stones are visible today.

Ballysadare (*Baile Easa Dara*, 'homestead of the waterfall of the oak') [25] mentioned above in relation to Moytura has an older meaning, namely, 'the home of Dara by the waterfall'. Dara was a Fomorian druid who was slain by the Tuatha Dé Danann* chief, Lug of the Long Hand. The Fomorians* are said to have landed in Ballysadare Bay. They were seen as pirates, and as the Vikings had a name for piracy, both groups often became confused in the popular mind.

The god of the Fomorians* was Balor, and Balor was the god of the Phoenicians who were a trading people; this leads one to speculate that the Phoenicians and the Fomorians were one people. Many statues of Balor stand today in the Lebanon at Tortosa in territory anciently connected with the Phoenicians.

The plain south of the River Duff and north of Ben Gulban and extending to the sea was known as *Magh Cétne na bFomorach* [16], possibly 'the first plain of the Fomorians'. When the Fomorians* were in power, the Nemedians had to bring their taxes of cattle, corn and children to *Magh Cétne*. A poem by Eochaidh O'Floinn who died in 1004 includes a reference to this:

> To hard Magh Ceitne of weapons,
> To Ess Ruadh of wonderful salmon,
> They deliver it to them every Samhain eve.

[Translated by R.A.S. Macalister]

Henry Morris the early twentieth-century antiquarian says that the Fomorians* settled on Dernish Island facing *Magh Cétne*. Dernish Island extends to 115 acres and at its centre rises to over 100 feet. So, it was to here that the taxes were paid from Magh Cétne, and the Nemedians also paid their taxes to the Fomorians at *Magh Itha*, which was an older name for the plain of *Magh Itha* or *Magh Ene* or *Magh Céthne*. This place is so old that it has been identified as the *Magnata* of Ptolemy. This would seem to suggest that *Tor Conaing* ('Conaign's tower') was located in Dernish and not on Tory Island. Ptolemy's names refer to the second century, and at that time this stone-built tower presumably would have still been standing.

The foundations of the Fomorian tower on Dernish Island were dug up in 1910 by the owner of the land, a Peter Mulligan. According to Henry Morris, it was still possible to see the trace of the circle in 1925. The tower was on the highest part of the island which in the early twentieth century was still called *Cnoc a' Dúin*, 'the Hill of the Dún or fortress'. Up until the middle of the nineteenth century there existed the remains of a stone fort which has been compared to the stone fort at *Dún Aengus* on *Inis Mór* on the Aran Islands off Co. Galway. The trace of the circle measured thirty-three yards in diameter, and Peter Mulligan found the remains of a *fulacht fiadh* or ancient cooking place which contained pieces of blackened stone. Mulligan was the first farmer to grow a crop on the spot, and presumably used the stout stones of the remaining tower to build field enclosures.

Around the site of the tower are immense stone fences, and Morris suggests that the Nemedians built a stone wall near the tower to 'attack the defenders on equal terms'. As the Nemedians had to give a quarter of their firstborn children and their corn and cattle as a tax to the Fomorians,* it is no wonder that they rose up and attacked their oppressors.

Dernish has associations with the Spanish Armada; a little rock to the west of the island is named *Carrig na Spainneach* ('the Spaniard's Rock'), commemorating the spot where one of the ships of the Spanish Armada went down. On the north-west of the island is a place named *Crochan na gCorp* ('the hillock of the corpses') where a number of the Spanish were buried. And going back in time 1,000 years we find a well dedicated to St Patrick in a little wood on the south-west side of the island.

About twenty miles south-east of Dernish is *Loch na Súil*, now named Lough Nasool [25] or 'lake of the eye'. This lake is associated with Balor, the god of the Fomorians,* and recalls another appellation for Balor – Balor of the Evil Eye. Balor was the name all subsequent chiefs took, and because of this a confusion can exist between the mythological and the early historical telling of tales. Balor is said to have lost an eye in the Battle of Moytura and tears flowed from it, flooding the valley and forming *Loch na Súil*. This small lake is all that remains of this watery cataract. In 1933, the waters of the lake disappeared overnight through an opening in its bed known as Balor's Eye; the phenomenon reoccurred in 1964 and again in 2006.

Overlooking Ballysadare Bay from the north side is the famous cairn of Medb* known as Knocknarea (*Cnoc na Riadh*, 'the hill of the races or journey') [25]. This is one of two passage tombs associated with the legendary queen; another is at Knockma, Co. Galway. It is a stunning setting for this Iron Age leader, a massive passage tomb built up over the years by the custom of bringing a stone and placing it on the top of the cairn. According to Dr

FIGURE 12. The cairn marking the burial spot of Queen Medb on Knocknarea.

Stefan Berg from the Knocknarea Archaeological Project, another six passage tombs have been found at Knocknarea. The term *Miosgán Medbha* has been used to describe this cairn, *mios* being the Irish for table or altar, and as the top of the cairn is flat, 'Medb's Altar' would seem quite a good description. It is possible that Neolithic rites involving sun worship took place here, where one has a splendid view of the setting sun and the night sky, which were so much part of early man's religious experience.

About ten miles west from Knocknarea is Aughris Head [25] or *Each Ros*, 'the headland of the horse'. The territory here was traditionally known as *Tír Fhiachrach* and was a probable inauguration site for the O'Dubhda or the O'Dowds, who were the ruling clan in this area. Elizabeth Fitzpatrick writes in *Notes on the Gathering Place of Tír Fhiachrach*: 'The place names of the district and its recorded folklore remain the only ancillary supports to our understanding the field monuments,' and presumably she also implies the customs, rites and early history as well. With the help of Joe Fenwick, she opens the salient aspects of early Irish society in relation to kingship and its customs.

The name *Each Ros* underlines how important the horse was in the culture of the society, and this is further supported by an area south from the headland known as the 'hoof-mark of Ó'Dubhda's Horse', which is a natural indentation in the rock; also, south of here a racecourse is marked, its name in Irish being *Ruball na Sionnach*, or the 'clearing area for the foxes'. The horse is remembered in the folklore of the area and was recorded in the Folklore Commission's collection for 1937. The myth of the king's mating with a white mare is part of the rite of kingship but is not to my knowledge part of the lore. As in Christianity, miracles are part of the lore, but the myth of resurrection is at the core of Christian mythology.

The story of the white horse from folklore and told by John Furey from Skreen is as follows:

> Long ago a family named O'Dowds reigned; they were chieftains of Tireagh and lived at Ardglass not far from here and at Ardnaree near Ballina. Of course, they had many horses to convey them from place to place as there was no other means of conveyance at the time. At any rate, they had a white horse that never left his stable. He was about seven or eight years old and was always well fed. One day when his master was away a man who lived nearby said to himself, that it would be great fun to go for a ride on the lovely horse. He went to the stable with a bridle and put it on the horse. Then he took him out and jumped up on him and off with them. He galloped until he came to Dunmoran river and it was no trouble for him to jump across it. Then he turned for Aughris pier along the shore all along the shore and all the way jumped the ditches as lively as another horse would run on level land. He kept on at this rate until he came to Córa Donn. When he saw the deep hole and the water going up under the land he turned on his heel and left a deep mark from his hoof on the solid rock, which is to be seen yet.

The cavern called *Comhra Donn*, which follows a deep cut in the cliff, is also mentioned by Máire Mac Neill in *The Festival of Lughnasa* – 'wherein there is a flagstone bearing hoof marks. Finally, there is a fort in Kilruiseighter where, people say, the kings used to be crowned and in this fort there are two tracks of feet which always remain an everchanging green'.

As mentioned above, the white mare was an integral part of some inaugural rites of kings, and a dramatic example of the white horse can be seen at the Vale of the White Horse at Uffington in Wiltshire. This figure, some 370 feet in length, was cut into the chalk of a hillside close to an Iron Age fort in the first century BC. Though legend purports that the acre site on which it stands was the idea of Alfred the Great as a commemoration of a victory against the Danes, the figure is not too far from the tomb of Wayland Smithy, a character similar to the *gabha* or smith in Irish mythology who could see into the future.

The horse goddess is a manifestation of the mother goddess, and thus the union of the king with the mother goddess is another variation of the sovereignty myth where the white horse as a symbol of life represents the *cailleach* as one who legitimately bestows sovereignty on the king-to-be.

Inaugural connections with other Celtic tribes can be found, and Herodotus mentions a Celtic tribe in Carinthia, north of the Adriatic, with similar inauguration rites to the Irish. He writes:

In Carinthia as often as a new prince of the republic enters upon the government, they observe a solemnity nowhere else heard of. In the open fields stands erect a marble stone, which when the leader is about to be created a certain countryman, to whom through his race the succession to that office hereditarily belongs, ascends, having on his right hand a black heifer in calf, while on his left is placed a working mare ... he in the common dress of the country, wearing a hair cap, carrying shoes and a pastoral shaft, acts the herdsman more than the prince ... the man in charge says that the mare and the heifer shall be his [the prince's] and that he shall be free of tribute ... then the king to be gently stikes the cheek of the official in charge and commands him to be a fair judge. Then the prince takes possession of the stone and turns himself around to every part and brandishing a naked sword addresses the clans and promises to be an equitable judge.

O'Donovan in *Tribes and Customs of Hy-Fiachrach* writes that in Ireland the king-to-be turns himself around thrice forwards and thrice backwards in order to view his people and territory in every direction.

The inauguration rite of kings is generally associated with the Iron Age, which straddled the late pre-Christian and early Christian era. At the inauguration site at Aughris Head, we may assume that a man became eligible to succeed as king, as Mac Neill writes in *Celtic Ireland*, if 'they belonged to the *derbfine* as a king who had already reigned'. The *derbfine* consisted of four generations in direct line – that is, father, sons, grandsons and great-grandsons. All those within the *derbfine* were eligible to succeed, subject to election. Those in line for kingship were classified as *rígdomna*, or 'crown prince', or 'royal heir'. Given the number of possible contenders to the throne, one can see how this led to the continuous series of battles that are at the basis of our early history.

Moytirra West and Moytirra East [25], three miles east of Lough Arrow, are the location of the Second Battle of Moytura (*Cath Muighe Tuireadh*, 'the battle of the plain of reckoning or keening or lamentation'). There are five megalithic tombs in the area as well as mounds, cairns, sweathouses and ring forts. There is also a *crannóg* on the northern end of Lough Arrow. The plain of Moytura is about ten miles from Ballysadare Bay, which would have been a good landing place for an invader.

The Second Battle of Moytura is possibly the most widely known of all the inter-racial battles in Ireland. It was fought between the 'native' Irish, the followers of the sun goddess Anu, whose people were known as the Tuatha Dé Danann,* and the invading force, the Fomorians* – *Fomoiri* (a race from 'across the sea') – more generally known as the Phoenicians, who were traders from Lebanon.

Like the Tuatha Dé Danann,* the Fomorians,* who had become the overlords of Ireland after their invasion, also worshipped a sun god namely Balor, so this story has often been regarded as a great tale of the Irish gods. Perhaps more than any other tale, this legend presents a roll call of the gods who combine to defeat the invading force led by their king, Elatha Mór mac Dealbhaoi, who reminds the Fomorians of their supremacy and charges them to defeat their vassals. The Tuatha Dé Danann forces are led by Lug,* who is a man, a sun god and a master of all the arts (*samildánach*).

The story is interwoven like many a biblical one with elements of the godly and the earthly. The great goddess the Mórrígan previously had predicted the battle when mating with the Dagda* on the River Unshin. The Dagda was the king and god of the Tuatha Dé Danann.* Prior to the battle the Mórrígan killed the Fomorian warrior Indech and gave handfuls of his blood to the Dagda's warriors. She then went with Badb and Macha to the Mound of the Hostages at Tara and from here they sent forth 'a cloud of mist and furious rain of fire, with a downpour of red blood from the air onto the warriors' heads'.

Then the battle begins and Nuadu mac Echtach of the Tuatha Dé Danann engages Elatha in combat and wounds him. Lug* then arrives and strikes off Elatha's head – *Is ann sin do riacht Lug an láthair agus sealluis a cheann de.*

Balor's eye, which no one could look at directly, is eventually pierced by a sling shot from the Goibniu,* the smith to the gods. Balor awakens from his injury and beheads Nuadu, then escapes from the field of battle followed by the remainder of the Fomorians;* they go to *Carn Eóluirg*, alternatively called *Carn Uí Néid* or Mizen Head [88], at the southernmost part of Ireland – *agus do Carn Eóluirg risa raitear Carn Í Néid I n-iarthur Éireann.* It is named after the father of Elatha.

Brian Ó Cuív who edited *Cath Muighe Tuireadh* came across a summary of the battle in a Trinity College manuscript written about 1630, or twenty years earlier than *Cath Muighe Tuireadh.* The following extract refers to the form that the tributes imposed by the Fomorians* took:

Tángatar Fomhóraigh go hÉrind, agus do chuirset dáorchíos uirre .i. dá ttrían etha, bleachta, cloinne, agus conáich do tharclamh ó fhearaibh Éirionn gacha Sámhna go Magh gCéidne na bFhomhórach .i. uinge dh'ór ón tsróin, nó an tsrón ón chionn amach.

The Fomorians came to Ireland, and they put a severe tribute on them, namely two thirds of arable land, of milch cows, of their progeny and their wealth to be collected from the men of Ireland each *samain* [Hallowe'en] at Magh Céidne of the Fomorians [a plain between the rivers Erne which extends eighty miles between Cavan to the west of Ballyshannon where it flows into the sea at Drowes], for example, the wealth tax being the nose tax for which an ounce of gold was to be paid or one's nose to be cut off.

[Translated by the author]

Donegal Bay, which is shared by Donegal, Leitrim and Sligo, may have been the entrance for the first recorded people to have arrived in Ireland, namely Cesair with fifty women and three men; they possibly arrived at *Dún na mBárc* or present day Mount Temple, and close by at *Trá Tuaidh* or *Traig Eba* [16] is where Eba or Eua or Eve, one of the fifty women who arrived with Cesair, is said to have drowned. *Machaire Eba*, or the Plain of Eba, is a name for a stretch of the Sligo coast which goes from Drumcliff Bay to Cliffony. The name is now reduced to Magherow, a townland north of Lissadell Strand west from Drumcliff.

At Streedagh [16] south-west of O'Conor's Island is a megalithic tomb mentioned in *Acallam na Senórach* or the Colloquy of the Ancients, a twelfth-century tale of discourses mostly between Caoilte of the Fianna* of Finn mac Cumhail* and St Patrick. According to Caoilte, this tomb, which still stands, was where the remains of Finn's deer-hound was buried, and in this tomb were later found 'the two lower jaws of a hound or wolf'. Whether or not this animal was Finn's, it certainly enriches the tale.

A mention of *Trá Eba* in the *Dindshenchas** gives credence to the suggestion that Sligo rather than Kerry may have been the location of *Dún na mBárc*, the port of call where Cesair and her followers entered Ireland:

'*Tráigh Eaba, cídh diatá? Ní ansa. Día tanic Cesair ingen Betha mic Naoí lucht curaigh co hÉrinn.Tainic Eaba in banlíaidh léi, cho rocodail isin trácht, co robáidh in tonn iarom. Conidh de raiter Rind Eaba agus Traigh Eaba dona hinadhaibh sin osin ille.*

Traig Eba, whence the name? Not hard to say. When Cesair daughter of Bith son of Noah came with a boat's crew to Erin, Eba the leech-woman came with her. She fell asleep on the strand, and the waves drowned her. Hence these places were called Rind Eba and Traig Eba from that time forth.

[Translated by Edward Gwynn]

Cesair has been connected to Noah in the *Book of Invasions* and in Keating's *Foras Feasa ar Éirinn* but she is also regarded as a Greek princess and as a French woman in other stories. Many early scholars connected or dovetailed Biblical events with early Irish history and mythology in order to set the events within a plausible timeframe.

Cesair possibly entered by Dernish Island, where her landing would have been sheltered by the peninsula known as Conor's Island. The *Book of Ballymote* and the *Book of Lecan* mention that Cesair and her womenfolk landed at Cairns which is now known as Mount Temple 'to flatter a local landlord'; according to Morris the territory of 'Cairns' extended from the present day Drumfad to the coast. Morris gives a number of reasons for his contention that Cesair landed in the estuary between Dernish Island and *Trá Tuaidh* [16]. Among the reasons Morris gives is that *Dún na mBárc* is a landlocked harbour with a fortress commanding it; the name 'cairns' was still in use when he was writing in the early twentieth century. One could also add the number of references to the area, many of which are mentioned above.

Cesair and her followers travelled south towards the Boyle River and, having crossed the Curlew Mountains, arrived on the wide fertile plain of *Magh Luirg* or 'the Plains of Boyle'. It is in a tumulus overlooking the Boyle River [33] that she is buried (as her burial place is in Roscommon, I have included this part of her story with that county). The area is regarded as a meeting place from ancient times.

Inishmurray (*Inis Muirdeach*, 'Muirdeach's island') [16] is a low-lying island one mile long and half-a-mile wide, with a maximum height rising to about seventy feet. Its name is derived from Muirdeach, who was bishop of Killala and was consecrated by St Patrick. The island is four miles from Streedagh Point in Co. Sligo, at the entrance to Donegal Bay, and is ten miles south-west from Mullaghmore Head. Muirdeach was also known as St Molaise and is credited with founding the monastery on Inishmurray about 520 AD. The remains of the monastery are fairly intact after 1,500 years – in stark contrast to the houses, which have gone to ruin after just 100 years. The remaining islanders left on 12 November 1948. It is a sign of their strength and persistence that in 1926, seventy-four people were able to make a living from the island and surrounding waters. The decision to abandon the island is said to have been due to isolation rather than poverty, but more likely was influenced by the letters and parcels coming from America and Britain telling of a better life.

A possible reason for the preservation of the monastic settlement is that it is enclosed behind a thick circular wall or *caiseal*, which was built during the Bronze Age. The wall is fifteen feet at its highest and is between six and nine feet wide. It encloses about a third of an acre of land. The presence of cursing stones and the name of a chapel as 'the temple of fire' would suggest that it may have been a druidic site before the arrival of the monks. There are three internal walls that result in the enclosure being divided into four areas. The largest enclosure contains *Teampall Molaise* or 'Molaise's church'. It was also known as *Teampall na bFhearr* or 'the men's church'. North-west of the church, there are two praying stones, and to the west is a font. To the south-west are *Na Clocha Breacha*, literally 'the speckled stones' but generally translated as 'cursing stones'. The stones were turned about while 'praying' by the person wishing to curse another. The ritual involved fasting for three days, and if the reasons for applying the curse were justified, it would have its effect; otherwise, the curse would rebound on the person who turned the stones.

In one of the smaller enclosures within the cashel is a building known as *Teac na Teine* or 'the house of fire'. This may have been the kitchen of the monastery, but some authorities say that its real name was *Teampall na Teine* or 'the church of fire'. This could place its origins in pre-Christian druidic times. The remains of the stone at the centre of the church are known as *Leic na Teine* or 'the stone of the fire'. Tradition has it that if all fires on the island were extinguished, then a sod placed on this hearth would spontaneously ignite. This 'miraculous hearth' was broken up by workers reconstructing the gable in the 1880s. When the antiquarian John O'Donovan visited the island in the 1830s, he recorded that there was a flagstone on the floor of this church which 'was always kept lighted for the use of the islanders'.

The enclosure contains three *clocháns* or beehive huts, each of which has a corbelled roof. There are also two standing stones and a holed or fertility stone where women prayed in order to have a healthy child. Outside the cashel there is a sweathouse, known as a *teach an allais,* from the Irish *allas,* meaning 'sweat'. This has been compared to the Turkish bath:

the house was filled with smoke, presumably from turf, and when it became very hot, the embers were swept away and water was thrown on the hot stones; then a person wrapped in a blanket entered to breathe the steam and 'sweat' for a while, after which they washed in the nearby well. Although we often refer to these baths as Turkish baths, in Germany and Bohemia they were known as Roman-Irish baths. The sweathouse was used as a cure for rheumatism as well as several other ailments, and there are hundreds throughout Ireland.

According to legend there is an invisible enchanted island between Inishmurray and the mainland, which is said to be seen every seven years. In the nineteenth century, a Sligo man named Patrick Waters claimed to have seen it. The island is said to be inhabited by the invisible 'gentry'. Hy Brazil, another enchanted place, is said to have been seen at the same time. Some say that Hy Brazil is associated with a place known as *Bruach Gráinne* or Grace's Bank, about one mile south of Inishmurray, which appears occasionally on the surface of the water. The last 'sighting' of Hy Brazil was during the summer of 1908; it too 'appears' every seventh year.

As on Tory Island, holy clay was used on Inishmurray to expel rats, and thus no rats are said to survive on the island. The clay was apparently given to St Molaise when he was on a pilgrimage to Rome. Swans on the island were never harmed, as it was felt that they might be the Children of Lir.* Other customs persisted on the island; for example, when pointing to a boat, you never pointed with your finger but rather with your thumb or with your whole hand. As on much of the mainland, it was always better to move clockwise in order to avoid bad luck; this particularly applied to boats, for when bringing a boat around it was always turned clockwise or *deas sol* ('right to the sun').

LEINSTER

CARLOW

Ceatharloch, 'four lakes'

The four lakes, according to tradition, were formed by the River Barrow (*An Bhearú*), but today of these lakes there is no trace. The tradition of the lakes existed up to the end of the eighteenth century, as the following verse from a 1798 song shows:

> That glorious plan, the rights of man,
> with sword in hand we'll guard it;
> the power to quell these infidels,
> *down by the lakes* of Carlow.

The plain surrounding the River Barrow is called *Magh Fea*, after one of the oxen of Brigit in her role as fertility goddess.

Dind Ríg ('the fortress of kings') [61], the palace of the Kings of Leinster and the ancient capital of the province, is on the River Barrow, a quarter of a mile south of Leighlinbridge in the townland of Ballyknockan. It has been equated with *Dunon* as listed among the city names given in Ptolemy's *Geography of Ireland* written about 150 AD, in which the Barrow is named *Birgos*. *Dind Ríg* today stands well off the tourist track, and the visitor may see it either as ancient and neglected or as a royal fortress and residence untouched by time and retaining its Iron Age atmosphere in a calm river setting. *Dind Ríg* is a high, steep-sided and flat-topped mound, similar to Bruree (*Brug Ríg*, Co. Limerick) and to Cú Chulainn's* mound at *Dún Delca*, Castletown, Co. Louth. The mound at *Dind Ríg* is situated at the S-end of a gravel ridge and junction of two rivers. It measures 237 yards in circumference at base, is sixty-nine feet above the river and forty-five yards in diameter at the top.

The site is also known as *Duma Sláinge* or 'the burial place of Sláinge', a king of the Fir Bolg* who died in the fourth century BC. The *Lebor Gabála Érenn* ('The Book of Invasions') states: 'No king, so called, took the kingship of Ireland, till the Fir Bolg came, and they gave the kingship to Slanga son of Dela, for he was the eldest of the sons of Dela. A year at first had Slanga, till he died in Dind Ríg.' It continues:

> *Bliadain do Shláine, is fír so,*
> *conerbailt 'na dég-dumo;*
> *cet-fher d'Fheraib Bolg na mbend*
> *atbath I n-inis Érend.*

A year had Slanga, this is true,
till he died in his fine mound;
the first man of the Fir Bolg of the peaks
who died in the island of Ireland.

[*Translated by R.A.S. Macalister*]

The Laginian invasion (from which Leinster, or *Laighean* in Irish, derives its name) was the last invasion before that of the Gaels, and their story is contained in the tale *Orgain Denda Ríg* or ('The Plunder of *Dind Ríg*'), the hero of which is Labraid Loingsech. Known as the first story of the Leinstermen, it was probably written in the ninth century. According to the *Lebor Gabála*, 'The Plunder of *Dind Ríg*' is dated to 307 BC. This date is not seriously contended by scholars, as the third century before Christ is generally agreed to be the time of the Laginian invasion. Although the invasion of the Lagin is not disputed, the idea of Labraid being exiled, a word implied in the epithet *Loingsech* or 'exile', is not given much credence. However, it allows for a good story while preserving the invasion and the plunder intact. In the original version, rather than being exiled Labraid is the leader of an Armorican (*Fir Morca*) invasion from north-west France. The later story also allows Labraid to lay waste to *Dind Ríg* as an act of legitimate revenge rather than a work of invasive destruction. Labraid was said to have come up from Munster and failed in his first attempt to capture the royal fortress and its king, Cobthach, who was within. Thus, the tale provides a solution, namely that the harper Craiphtine was to lull the enemy to sleep by playing sleep music (*suantraighe*) on his harp while the besiegers put their faces to the ground and their fingers in their ears. The result was that the defenders of *Dind Ríg* fell asleep and were slaughtered and *Dind Ríg* was destroyed. According to the original version, Cobthach was spared and lived in peace with Labraid who then became King of Leinster.

A later version tells how Labraid invited Cobthach to a feast in *Dind Ríg*, where he and his followers were roasted in an iron house that Labraid had spent a year building in total secrecy (thus giving rise to the proverb: 'every Leinsterman has his secret'). The *Book of Leinster* has the following verses:

Ro hort in rigrad moa ríg,
(ba gním olc, ba domna hír);
loisc Labraid méit gaile
Cobthach Cóel mac Ugaine.

Ba Túaim Tenbath cosin olc
in ríg-dind rán, in rochnocc,
coro n-oirg Labraid, lán ngaile,
diar chuir ár a maccraide.

The princes were slain round their king
(it was an ill deed, it was matter for wrath):
the Dumb Exile of martial might burnt
Cobthach Cael, son of Ugaine.

Till that crime, Tuaim Tenbath was the name
of the noble kingly hold, the noted hill,
till Labraid full of valour sacked it,
when he made a slaughter of its young men.

[Translated by Edward Gwynn]

Tuaim Tenbath was the old name for *Dind Ríg*. *Tuaim* has been translated as a moat mound or burial mound, and *Tenbath* has been glossed as a 'red flaming wall of fire'.

In 1934, *The Irish Times* reported that a 'most compact and regular cist' containing cremated bones had been found in the townland of Ballyknockan. The precise location of this site is unknown, but that a Bronze Age burial should be found close to this Late Bronze Age site is significant.

At Killinane, a mile south-south-east from *Dind Ríg* and on the same side of the River Barrow is an Early Bronze Age burial site, or cist. During the Early Bronze Age, from about 1800 to 1300 BC, funeral rites involving both cremation and inhumation were popular, many of the bodies being buried in a crouched position. Burials were sometimes accompanied by a range of distinctive pottery and grave goods (a sign of Christian burial being an absence of grave goods). The cist at Killinane contained the cremated remains of two individuals as well as rock crystal and quartz fragments and a food bowl. If *Dind Ríg* were plundered in 307 BC, as stated by the *Lebor Gabála*, then the cist at Killinane as well as that at Ballyknockan would presumably have been known to the inhabitants of *Dind Ríg*, and may well have been the graves of Slanga and of earlier kings from this famous royal site.

Perhaps the largest Bronze Age site in Carlow, and possibly in the country, was found at Ballon Hill [61], about six miles south-west of Tullow. Much of Ballon Hill was a Bronze Age cemetery and included pit and cist burials; cist burials were often under mounds and contained in a box-like structure of stone slabs. Ballon Hill contained two ring barrows, which are generally small mounds with an encircling ditch and bank. They are burial mounds, and excavations have shown cremations of a Bronze Age or Iron Age date. A good example of a ring barrow is *Rath Gráinne* on the Hill of Tara, Co. Meath [42]. Julius Caesar and other writers note that burning the dead was customary among the Celts. Generally, this was reserved for the upper stratum of society, but with such a large graveyard as that on Ballon Hill, the custom of cremation may have been more inclusive.

Another custom associated with burial was the burying of white stones or lumps of quartz crystal with the dead. Beneath one of the graves at Ballon Hill a funeral urn was found upside down and beneath it, placed in a triangular position, were three small pebbles, one white, one green and one black. This custom can be seen all over the country as well as in Scotland and within what is known as the Sacred Circle on the Isle of Man. A stone's throw from where I write in Co. Cork is a *cromlech* with a large quartz stone beside it, a material that seemingly had a religious meaning for our ancestors, though in what precise way we do not know. We do know that stones were regarded in many primal societies as the abode of supernatural beings. At Plouër, in the French part of the Côtes-du-Nord, since earliest times, girls have been sliding down a large block, and if a girl manages to do this without scraping her flesh, she is assured of soon finding a husband. The custom can also be seen in other parts of France and is no doubt connected to an earlier form of stone worship.

We do not have any poets or bards from the Bronze Age to weave a picture of the world they lived in, but we can possibly get a glimpse into their beliefs and world view from the way they buried their dead. An excavation at Ballon Hill in 1853 unearthed three skeletons 'huddled together in a small space not above two feet in length'. They were buried beneath an immense boulder, and urns were found close by. Beneath the boulder were granite slabs and beneath these a bed of charcoal was found. Some of the urns found here are the finest examples discovered in Ireland, and they along with the food vessels show that these peoples believed in an afterlife. Their 'sitting-up' positions also showed that they were ready to attend some ceremonial gathering in the afterlife, but the presence of a dagger blade of bronze seems to suggest that one needed to be on one's guard even in the Otherworld.

About five miles north-east of Leighlinbridge is Kelliston (*cell osnaid*, 'the graveyard of the groans') situated on *Magh Fea* or the Plain of Fea [61], the site of a noted battle in the fifth century AD. The King of Leinster at that time was Fraoch son of Fionnchaidh. This battle probably took place in the late fifth century AD. Aonghus who was King of Munster at that time and his wife Eithne Uathach both fell by Muiredach and by Oilill. This battle is remembered in the following verse from Keating's history:

Atbath craobhdhos bhile mhóir
Aonghus Molbhthach mac Natfraoich
Fágbhaidh lá hOilill a rath
I gcath Cell Osnadha claoin.

There died by the spreading branch of a great tree,
Aonghus Molbhthach, son of Natfraoch;
He lost his success by Oilill
In the battle of Cell Osnaid the vile.

[Translated by P.S. Dinneen]

A possible site for this battle is at Kelliston East where there is a graveyard in an area locally known as Kilomeel. It is a circular, raised area, and there is a local tradition of bones being buried at the site. About 400 yards north-west of the graveyard is St Patrick's Well. To get to the graveyard, go to Kelliston Crossroads, which are approximately four miles south-east from the town of Tullow. At the cross, turn right and continue for one mile, and here you will find a church on your right; looking north-east from the church is the likely battle site. A few hundred yards before the crossroads is a mound with steep sides and a small, rounded summit. This may well have been the site of the local king, and the battle may have been an attempt by a provincial king to extend his kingdom. Oilill, one of the invaders, eventually became King of Leinster. Legend has it that around this time St Patrick and Caoilte mac Ronáin, a warrior of the Fianna* who had miraculously survived into Christian times, came to Kilomeel, where they were entertained by a dulcimer player and where St Patrick performed a miracle.

St Mullin's (*Tigh Moling*, 'the houses of Moling') is situated on the east side of the Barrow River six miles south from Graiguenamanagh [68]. St Moling, who flourished in the seventh century, is cited by Aengus the Culdee (a bishop from the ninth century) as one of the early ecclesiastics who was distinguished as a literary figure. The story of the building of the oratory of St Moling involves the legendary builder of round towers, castles and oratories, namely the *Gobán Saor*,* the famous smith whose buildings and whose antics are a necessary part of the storyteller's bag. As payment for building the oratory, the *Gobán Saor* wanted the chapel filled with corn, rushes, apples and nuts. Whether he was successful or not leads to a long story, way beyond the remit of the present work. An oratory still stands at St Mullin's, although in ruins; whether this is the one that the *Gobán* built is anybody's guess.

The association of St Moling with that great personage of Irish myth, Suibhne Geilt* or Mad Sweeney* – the inspiration of the Ulster poets – is an example of a blending of Irish mythology with Christian saga. Some people say they are one and the same person due to the fact that Suibhne was said to have flown from place to place around Ireland, and the etymology of Moling's name is *mo ling* or 'my flight'. Be that as it may, St Mullin's is special insofar as it encloses these two notable people within its grounds. Suibhne* eventually settled down at *Tigh Moling*, where he was looked after by the saint. His wanderings have inspired the imagination of many poets to which the following verses give testament:

Duairc an bhetha-sa
bheith gan maeithleaptha,
adhbha úairsheacha,
garbha gáoithshnechta …

Gloomy this life,
to be without a soft bed,
abode of cold frost
roughness of wind driven snow.

Cold, icy wind,
faint shadow of a feeble sun,
shelter of a single tree,
on the summit of a table land.

Enduring the rain-storm,
stepping over deerpaths,
faring through greensward
on a morn of grey frost.

The bellowing of the stags
throughout the wood,
the climb to the deer-pass,
the voice of white seas.

[Translated by J.G. O'Keeffe]

St Moling told his cook, Muirgil, to give Suibhne* fresh milk to drink each day. She used to 'thrust her heel up to her ankle in the cow dung … and leave the full of it of new milk for Suibhne'. Suibhne* would come cautiously into the yard to drink the milk. Muirgil's husband was Moling's swineherd Mongán, whose sister provoked him to jealousy, leading him to throw a spear at Suibhne as he was drinking the milk. The spear passed through the nipple of Suibhne's left breast and broke his back in two. At this, Suibhne, Moling and Mongán utttered a lay between them, Suibhne speaking the following:

There was a time when I deemed more melodious
than the quiet converse of people,
the cooing of a turtle dove
flitting about a pool.

There was a time when I deemed more melodious
than the sound of a little bell beside me
the warbling of the blackbird to the mountain
and the belling of a stag in a storm.

There was a time when I deemed more melodious
than the voice of a beautiful woman beside me,
to hear at dawn,
the cry of the mountain grouse.

[Translated by J.G. O'Keeffe]

Suibhne died because of Mongán's assault and was buried at *tobar na ngealt*, 'the madman's well'. There is a possibility that the well in question is St Mullins' Well, about 100 yards north of the wheeled cross, which contains a rectangular stone with a circular basin. However, as this was a significant centre in the seventh century, it is possible that there were a number of other wells, any one of which could be his resting place. *Tigh Moling* is sited on a field known anciently as *achadh cainida* ('the field of keening or wailing'); whether there is any connection with this and Suibhne's* burial place is open to speculation. St Moling died in 697 AD.

Another impressive earthwork is at Mohullen or Mohullin (*magh-chuilinn*, 'plain of holly'), an earthwork locally known as 'the Rath'. This place is associated with numerous traditions and beliefs. Bones were found when the field was tilled. It does not have a record in the annals like *Dind Ríg* but is nonetheless full of local folklore. Mohullen is three miles south-east of Borris [68] on the R702; before you get to Ballymurphy, turn right onto the R703 and about a half-mile on your right is Mohullen.

Two miles west from Leighlinbridge is Oldleighlin [61] (*Seanleithghlinn*, 'the old half glen'), named from the configuration of the Madlin riverbed. This place was celebrated as an ecclesiastical establishment with a cathedral, and prior to that in pre-Christian times it was celebrated as possessing one of the sacred trees of Ireland, namely the *Eó Rossa*. The *Eó Rossa* was a yew, one of the five famous trees of Ireland as mentioned in the *Book of Leinster*. The *Eó Rossa* has been in the Rennes *Dindshenchas** as 'noblest of trees, glory of Leinster, dearest of bushes'. In the *Book of Leinster*, it receives a thirty-three-line stanza in its praise, ascribed to Druim Suithe ('ridge of science' – so this poet has presumably taken a pseudonym), and his or her praise in the form of epithets for this sacred tree is as follows:

> *Eó Rosa*
> *roth ruirech*
> *recht flatha*
> *fuaim tuinni*
> *dech dúilib*
> *diriuch dronchrand*
> *dia dronbalc*
> *dor nime*
> *nert n-aicde*
> *fó foirne*
> *fer ferbglan*
> *gart glanmár*
> *tren trinoit*
> *dam toimsi*
> *maith máthar*
> *mac Maire*
> *muir mothach*

miad maisse
mál menman
mind n-angel
nuall betha
blad Banba
brig búada
breth bunaid
brath brethach
brosna suad
saeriu crannaib
clu Gálion
caemiu dossaib
dín bethra
brig bethad
bricht n-eolais
Eó Rossa

Tree of Ross; a king's wheel; a prince's right; a wave's noise; best of creatures; a straight firm tree; *a firm strong god*; the door to the sky; a powerful bond; possessing great strength; a generous tree; full of hospitality; the strength of the trinity; a silent hero, fully measured; good mother; son of Mary; beautiful sea of honour and glory; worthy prince; treasure of nobles; proclaimer of life; renowned Banba; of prevailing strength; of ancient bearing; fame in judgement-giving; inspiration of bards; noblest of trees; the pride and glory of Leinster; beloved to them; shelter of water; force of life; an incantation of wisdom; Tree of Ross.

[Translated by the author]

Assemblies were held under these sacred trees and there was a *geis* or taboo placed on anyone who damaged them in any way. The name for a sacred tree was *bile*, meaning 'large tree'.

The *Eó Rossa*'s power and veneration may have led the local saint, Laserian of Leighlin, to covet its wood for church-building and to incorporate this strong pagan tree into the body of his church. It was not only Laserian who desired the tree but 'all the saints of Ireland' as well. The saints of Ireland assembled around the tree and prayed for its fall, and as they prayed the roots moved but when Laserian uttered his prayers the tree fell down. It is also possible that in the tree-chopping tradition of St Boniface, St German and St Ninian, the abbot of Cluain Conaire in Kildare, that it was chopped down as the idolatrous centre of an earlier spiritual tradition. However, according to O'Flaherty's *Ogygia*, all the sacred trees were blown down in 665 AD at the same time as a plague desolated Ireland, a plague known as the *Buide Conaill*, or the Yellow Plague.

It is said that St Moling asked Laserian for some of the sacred tree and was granted enough to build his oratory. The *Gobán Saor* then built the roof from the shingles, or parallel slats of wood, from the *Eó Rossa*. From a passage in St Bernard's life of Malachy we learn that the custom of building oratories of wood continued in Ireland as late as the twelfth century.

DUBLIN

Dubh Linn, 'black pool', the name preferred by the Vikings and later by the Anglo-Normans; later in Gaelic as Baile Átha Cliath, *'the homestead at the ford on the wattles'*

The earliest mention of Dublin is as *Eblana polis* on the map of Ptolemy from the second century AD. This is the oldest contemporary document for Irish history. Ptolemy lived in Alexandria in Egypt, and his map of Ireland (*Iouernia*) was derived from sailors and merchants who presumably had their information from other mariners. The map's blank interior of Ireland is testament to the fact that knowledge of the island was limited to its shores. Howth is named *Edros*, which corresponds to *Edar* in the Gaelic name for the place, *Beinn Edair*.

Three miles south from Tallaght on the R114 is Glenasmole (*gleann an smóil*, 'the glen of the thrush') [50], which is at the source of the River Dodder and possesses a large lake now used as a reservoir. Oisín,* a son of Finn mac Cumhail* and a hero of the Fenian Cycle of sagas, has a strong association with Glenasmole. It was at this place that tragedy struck for the warrior when he returned to Ireland after 300 years in *Tír na nÓg* ('the land of eternal youth'). A group of men asked him to help them raise a huge stone onto a wagon, and when he stooped to do so the reins on his horse snapped and he fell to the earth. As a result, he changed suddenly to be a very old man, and because of his fall he could no longer return to *Tír na nÓg*. Oisín had been taken to this world, also known as *Tír Tairngire* ('the land of promise') and *Magh Mell* ('the plain of honey'), by Niamh, an otherworldly princess. She told him that:

> It is the most delightful country to be found,
> of greatest repute under the sun
> trees drooping with fruit and blossom
> and foliage growing on the tops of boughs.

Finn mac Cumhail's* father was Cumall mac Trénmór, and he fought in a battle at Castleknock at the Battle of Cnucha located in present-day Castleknock at the north end of the Phoenix Park [50]. Cumall was King of the Leinster Fianna,* and he was defeated and killed in this battle by Goll mac Morna of the Connacht Fianna who were supported by the Lagin. The 'hills' referred to in the word *cnucha* are within the grounds of Castleknock College; a request to walk around the site should be made to the school authorities. The cause of this battle was Cumall's abduction of Muirenn, the daughter of the druid Tadg who complained to the king, Conn Cét Chathach, or 'Conn of the Hundred Battles' (177–212 AD). Cumall refused to either send Muirenn back or pay restitution, and he refused to attend a meeting at Tara with Conn to seek a resolution. As a result, Conn promised leadership of the Fianna to Goll mac Morna. After the battle, Muirenn who was now pregnant with Finn mac Cumhail, attempted to return home to her father, but he refused to admit her because she was pregnant. He told his people to burn her, but mercifully this was not carried out. On the eve of the battle, Cumall sent the following message to Muirenn: 'When my son is born, flee away with him, and let him be brought up in the most secret places you can find. Conmean the druid has foretold his fortune, and that under his rule the Fianna of Érinn shall much exceed what it enjoys under mine. Entreat the forgiveness of the golden haired Muirrean for me. Farewell.'

Another battle involving the Fianna* was fought at Garristown [43] in 285 AD (although it has on occasion been mentioned as having been fought in Meath, presumably because of changing boundaries). Known as the Battle of Gabhra, it ended the power of the Fianna in Ireland. The background is as follows: King Cairbre Lifechair wished to marry his daughter Sgéimh Solais ('beauty of light') to a prince, but the Fianna wanted her to marry one of them – or, failing that, they demanded to be paid a ransom of twenty ounces of gold. When Cairbre refused both requests, the Fianna marched on Tara and both sides met in a field known as the Black Acre in Garristown, where Oscar, the son of Oisín,* was carried from the field on a bier after being fatally wounded. The *Book of Leinster* tells a different story, stating that Cairbre was slain by Oscar, and *Acallam na Senórach* ('Discourse of the Elders') concurs with this. However, the local people to the present day believe that the Fianna lost the battle, and as an act of respect to the Fianna who fell at the battle they erected a large Celtic cross towards the end of the nineteenth century. This was blown down by a strong wind in the twentieth century, and the author met some local people who had removed the shaft of the cross to an adjoining ditch. A headstone has been erected in front of the library at Garristown, and the ogam writing on it commemorates the Battle of Gabhra; it translates as 'Oscar son of Oisín, grandson of Finn'.

The name Gabhra is interesting linguistically in so far as *gabhar* generally means a goat, but here may mean a white horse or brightness or even the sun; whether there is a connection to Sgéim Solais, the daughter of Cairbre, is open to debate. The *Annals of Ulster* refer to this battle as follows: 'Kalends of January third feria, twelfth of the moon [285 AD]. Cairpre Lifechair son of Cormac Ulfhota was killed by Oscar son of Oisín* son of Finn in the battle of Gabhra, and Oscar was killed by Cairpre at the same time.'

Two miles east from the north end of the Glenasmole Reservoir stands Montpelier Hill [50], to the north of which is a megalithic tomb and, to the east, a standing stone; up to the early eighteenth century there stood a large cairn here bounded by a circle of large stones. This site was desecrated in 1725 by William Conolly of Castletown, who used the stones of the cairn in the construction of a hunting lodge generally known as the Hell Fire Club. The roof was originally slated but a sharp wind stripped the roof of its slates so Conolly built a stone roof in its place, much of which stands today.

Local people said the lodge was haunted, due to the desecration of the site and that the devil was responsible for the original damage to the roof. Although Montpelier Hill is mainly associated with the club, most of its meetings were held at the Eagle Tavern on Cork Hill, which was part of a high ridge extending from Dame Street to beyond Christ Church. The drink of choice was known as *scaillín* or 'scaltheen' – a mixture of hot whiskey, butter, sugar and hot milk, which was apparently used as a remedy for a cold in the chest. The Hell Fire Club was founded by Richard Parsons, the first Earl of Rosse, and James Worsdale, the painter. Worsdale's painting of five members can be seen in the National Gallery of Ireland Dublin. A black cat supposed to represent the devil presided at the meetings, and on occasion at midnight a member of the club would emerge as the devil, wearing the horns and tail of a cow. On one occasion the cat, after being immersed in the punchbowl and set alight, ran out of the tavern on fire, reinforcing the belief among onlookers that the devil was truly present at these sessions.

Two miles north of the post office at Rush on the R128 you come to a crossroads, and here, if you turn right and then take the first turn to the right, you will arrive at Carnhill. To the east you should see Loughshinny, and walking south-east you will arrive at Drumanagh (*Druim Manach*, 'the ridge of the Manach') [43]. It is probably here that the great hero Cú Chulainn* came to woo Emer, the daughter of a local chieftain. The older name for Drumanagh was *Luglochta Logo*, 'the gardens of Lug'. Drumanagh is a forty-acre promontory fort overlooking the Irish Sea with Loughshinny to the north and Rush to the south. Emer's father was Fergal Manach, or 'Fergal Monks', and there are still Monks living in the area. The townland of Rathmooney is *Rathmanach*, 'the rath of the monks'. This fort of Fergal Manach is four miles due west from Drumanagh. To get there, take the north-west road from the post office at Lusk and turn right after a mile to bring you to Rathmooney. The fort at Drumanagh has three ramparts, and according to the 'Wooing of Emer', a story whose earliest extant version comes from the twelfth century, 'Cú Chulainn reached the fort of Fergal within a day, and performed the Salmon leap across the three ramparts, so that he landed in the centre of the fortress.'

Fergal did not see 'this wild man from the north' as a suitable suitor for his daughter and had Drumanagh guarded. Cú Chulainn* slaughtered all the defendants except the three brothers of Emer. Fergal tried to escape but failed and was left 'lifeless'; Cú Chulainn then took Emer with him and bolted across the three ramparts. Talking to local farmers in the 1970s, I was informed that I could better spend my time with other aspects of folklore rather than with this 'immoral man'; two millennia later, 'the wild man from Ulster' is still seen as one to be avoided.

Drumanagh entered the news in 1996 when an article in *The Sunday Times* led to a war of words with some academics. The article stated that: 'A nondescript patch of land fifteen miles north of Dublin has shattered one of Ireland's strongest myths [that the Romans never invaded Ireland]. It indicated that the country was, after all, invaded by the Romans.'

Drumanagh was here being described as a Roman promontory fort and a bridgehead for the invading Roman legions. This extrapolation was based on a find of Roman coins and small pieces of jewellery on or near Drumanagh, and further supported by Roman burial finds at nearby Lambay Island. Another point of view stated that the artefacts discovered were 'most likely due' to Irish trading with Roman Britain.

Farmers ploughing in the 1950s and 1970s found Roman and Gallo-Roman ware. However, as no scientific excavation took place, the way was open for pillagers with metal detectors. A preservation order was put on the site, but this was contested by the local landlord as far as the Supreme Court, where he lost the case. Although artefacts reappeared at Sotheby's in London, many have been recovered and are now in the National Museum in Dublin; for legal reasons, however, they are not open to public viewing. Loughshinny just north of Drumanagh was an established port from earliest times, and it appears that trading with Roman Britain did occur, as the artefacts testify. But whether this constitutes an outpost of the Roman Empire remains a moot point. One thing that is not open to debate is that Drumanagh should be the subject of a scientific survey, and the results should be on public display.

Rathmooney, mentioned above, was also known as *Bruiden Fergaill Manach*, the ancient *bruiden* ('hostels') being centres of feasting as well as lookout posts. There is a well here known as St Bride's well, which is most likely a Christian gloss on the ancient name. There were five *bruidne* (the plural form of the word) in Ireland, and these were places of perpetual feasting, the four others being *Bruiden Da Derga*, *Bruiden Da Choca*, *Bruiden Meic Da Réo* and *Bruiden Meic Da Thó*. According to legend, the god of the Otherworld presided at these banquets.

Six miles north-west of Rathmooney is the village of Naul [43], also known as 'The Naul' (*an Ail*, 'the cliff' or 'the rock'), apparently relating to the rock on which the original castle stood on the banks of the River Delvin (*Ailbine* or *Ollbine*). A cave close to the village fits into the story that Máire Mac Neill tells in her work *The Musician in the Cave*. Here she writes of tales of musicians in caves from Rathlin Island to Inish Maan to Ceis Corann; but here in the Naul lies a tale in the world of empirical reality in so far as the piper Seamus Ennis played his pipes in a cave down the side of a cliff just north of the village. I was taken to this cliff and wondered what those unaware of Seamus's sense of creativity thought of the music and its source.

Malahide Bay [50] is where a people known as the Domnann entered Ireland, as preserved in the Irish version of the name, *Inber Domnann* ('the rivermouth of the Domnann'). As they were a pre-Gaelic people, they are sometimes seen as either aboriginal or primitive. According to T.F. O'Rahilly, they were 'a branch of the Dumnonii of Devon and Cornwall'. They also had connections with Scotland, especially around Dumbarton and extending to Ayr. O'Rahilly states that their tribal name is derived from the name of a deity, namely *Dubnonos* or *Dubnona*. They were also known as the *Fir Domnann*. The academic Sharon Paice Macleod has suggested in *Mater Deorum Hibernensium* that they may also be related to the Tuatha Dé Danann,* insofar as the form Tuatha Dé Domnann is often used to name the same people. The Broadmeadow and Ward rivers flowing into *Inber Domnann* would have been the conduits along which they entered the island. At the estuary of Malahide Bay is a dangerous sandbank called Mol Downey Bank which perpetuates the name of the Domnann in *Mael Domhnann* ('the whirlpool of the Domnann').

Perhaps the most famous person to enter *Inber Domnann* was Tuathal Techtmar or Tuathal the Legitimate, who was a king of Ireland in the second century AD. Tuathal arrived at *Inber Domnainn* or Malahide Bay with a fleet of foreigners and defeated three tribes: the Fir Bolg,* the Domnann and the Gálioin. He is seen by some as an historical character who led the Gaels across the sea, gradually conquering Ireland. He became King of Ireland about 130 AD after subduing the *aithechthuatha* or vassal tribes of Ireland. Some say that Tuathal was a Roman legionary who was supported by the Gaels.

About fifteen miles north of Malahide Bay is Balbriggan; once there, take the R132, and two miles north you cross the River Delvin, which today forms the northern boundary of Co. Dublin and flows into the sea through the townland of Knocknagin. It marks a boundary of *Fine Gall* (a name for the Vikings), now Fingal. The river takes its name from *Ollbine*, 'great crime', the story of which concerns a king named Rúad mac Ríg Dúnd from Munster, who set out with a number of boats for a meeting with men from the south-west of Scotland. After their ships were becalmed, Rúad jumped into the sea to investigate the cause and he found nine women there, who confessed that they had stopped the boat. They brought nine ships of gold to him, and he in turn spent nine nights with them. One of the women conceived a child and said she would bear a son, and that she would return to them before his birth. The king took the other women to his men, and they all remained carousing for seven years. When they eventually landed in the estuary of the Delvin (*Inber Ollbine*), the women left the boy behind at the landing place, which was stony and rocky, where the men threw stones at him and killed him. The women then began to scream '*bine oll, bine oll*', or 'great crime, great crime'. That is how the Delvin got its name. The area is still stony and rocky. If you go one mile south from the estuary at Knocknagin Bridge and take the second turn left until the end of the road, you will find yourself in the vicinity of five mounds. And this, apart from its ancient associations, is the perfect viewing place from which to see the estuary and conjure up the story of Rúad and the fate of the newborn boy.

To the north and west of Donabate is the townland of Turvey, referred to as *Traigh Tuirbhi*, 'the strand of Turvey', in the annals [43]. The *Books of Lecan* and *Ballymote* say that Tuirbhi was the father of the *Gobán Saor*. His full name was *Tuirbhi Tragmár* or 'large-footed Turvey'. He apparently owned all the land attached to the strand. Like Canute,

King of England and Denmark, Turvey had a penchant for controlling the tides. Whereas Canute tried it by shouting orders, Turvey tried it by throwing a hatchet from *Tuladh an Bhiail* ('the hill of the hatchet'), into the face of the flowing tide. Needless to say, legend has Turvey stopping the tide. *Tuladh an Bhiail* may well have been situated at Portrane on the hill overlooking the Irish Sea. The present hospital at Portrane was built on this hill in 1898, and workmen digging the foundations 'found a subterranean sepulchral chamber lined with small stones; a long approach also lined with stones led to it, and in it was the skeleton of a man of large size; the whole was cleared away and the skeleton was thrown over the bank of rubbish' (Hogan, *Onomasticon*). Another example of the past being consigned to the rubbish tip!

The *Dindshenchas** encapsulates this story in verse as follows:

> *Tráig Thuirbe, turcbaid a hainm,*
> *do réir anctair ria imshaidm:*
> *Tuirbe trágmar ós cach thráig*
> *athair grammar gú Gobáin.*

> *A thúaig notelged iar scur*
> *in gilla mergech mór-dub*
> *ó Thulaig Béla buide*
> *fri cach ména mór-thuile.*

> *Cían nodcuired a thúaig the*
> *in muir ní thuiled tairse:*
> *cid Tuirbe thess na túag tré,*
> *ní fess can cúan nó chenél.*

> *Manip don tshíl dedgair dub*
> *luid a Temraig ria láech-Lug,*
> *ní fess a chan fri dáil de*
> *fir na cless ó Thráig Thuirbe.*

> The strand of Tuirbhi received its name,
> according to authors I relate,
> from Tuirbhi of the strands, lord over all strands,
> the affectionate acute father of *Gobán*.

> His hatchet he would fling after ceasing from work.
> The rusty faced, black, big fellow,
> from the pleasant Hill of the Hatchet,
> which is washed by the great flood.

The distance to which his hatchet he used to send,
the tide beyond or within flowed not;
though Tuirbhi in his land in the south was strong,
it is not known of what stock was his race.

Unless he was of the mystical black race,
who went out of Tara from the heroic Lug,
it is not known for what benefit he avoided to meet him,
the man of the feats from the strand of Tuirbhi.

[Translated by Edward Gwynn]

Tuirbhi was quite possibly a Pict, and his darker skin, as mentioned in the verses above, could possibly be explained by this. Like Cú Chulainn* he was swarthy, yet unlike the great Pictish warrior he was a 'big fellow', and the skeleton of 'large size' that was treated with such glaring disrespect could have been him or a relative of his. Turvey Castle is in the townland, and it was here that Edmond Campion wrote his *History of Ireland*.

Ten miles north-east from Turvey's Strand are two rocks in the sea beside each other, with a lighthouse on one. They are known as Rockabill, having been originally known as *Da-bille*, 'two little (rocks)'. An old *Dindshenchas** legend tells us that they got their name from Dabilla, a famous dog that was drowned there. Another legend associates these rocky outposts with the *Glas Gaibhleann*, the cow and calf of the *Gobán Saor*, turned to stone here by the Fomorian* god Balor.

On the south side of Dublin Bay lies Merrion Strand which comprises the strand from Sandymount to Blackrock, which in Irish is *Trácht Muirbthen* or *Muirbech* (a level strip of land along the coast). The name for the strand in the manuscripts is *Trácht Fuirbhi*, which seems very close to *Trácht Tuirbhi*. This leads to the possibility that Tuirbhi was chief (*tuire* meaning chief or lord) of the land from Donabate to Dún Laoghaire. This strand has strong associations with Conaire Mór, a third-century King of Ireland. The story of his death is told in the tale *Togail Bruidne Da Derga* ('the destruction of the hostel of the red god'), which was compiled in the eleventh century from two earlier versions. Conaire left *Bruidne Da Derga* close to Lough Bray Lower and walked to Tara along the *Slighe Cualann* and across Merrion Strand. At the same time, a group of marauders under Ingcél, a British or Welsh prince, was setting out to plunder Da Derga's hostel. They landed at Howth but, hearing that Conaire was on Merrion Strand, they sailed across Dublin Bay. Not finding him, they sailed further south and landed at Leamore strand in Wicklow. At that time an ancient rite was being carried out at Tara to determine who would be King of Ireland, and it was prophesied that the king to be was walking naked along *Trácht Muirbthen* on his way to Tara. When Conaire arrived at Tara he was proclaimed King by the druids. James Joyce's character in *Ulysses*, Stephen Dedalus, mirrors Conaire's appointment with destiny when he asks himself while strolling along the beach at Merrion: 'Am I walking into eternity along Sandymount strand?'

Around 5,500 years ago Howth Head [50] was an island, and as the waves fell back, they left an isthmus of sand and gravel about sixteen feet above sea level, which today links the promontory of Howth to the mainland. For 6,000 years there have been fishermen on Howth, and in ancient times they traded fish for polished stone axes from the incoming Neolithic farmers who would go on to build the great astronomical calendar in stone known as Newgrange. In more modern times, a popular folktale from Howth is known as 'Conall Gulban from Howth', more than sixty versions of which are recorded in manuscripts of the Irish Folklore Commission. They are all recorded in Irish, but English versions are published in *Hero-Tales of Ireland* by J. Curtin. This tale was also well known in Gaelic-speaking Scotland.

The present Baily Lighthouse [50] on the south-eastern extremity of Howth is built upon the fort of Crimthann Nianar, who was High King of Ireland around the time of Christ. He was buried here, having died in a battle with the *Aithech Tuatha*, an underclass of serfs.

According to the *Annals of Clonmacnoise*, Crimthann was brought by a fairy woman into her palace 'where after great entertainment and after they took their pleasure of one another by carnal knowledge she bestowed a gilted coat with a sum of gold on him as a token of her love, and soon after [he] died'. This would seem to be an example of the sovereignty myth wherein it was necessary for a king to sleep with a local goddess in order to be a proper king. The goddess herself was sovereignty and only through her could the king claim legitimacy. We see reflections of this in the Egyptian/Greek myth of Oedipus who, after sleeping with an older woman, his mother, becomes king. Crimthann himself shares with Oedipus an incestuous history in so far as his own father Lugaid Réoderg is said to have slept with his own mother Clothru, daughter of Eochaid Fedlech. Thus, Crimthann's mother Clothru was both his mother and his grandmother.

High Street in the centre of Dublin [50] is the starting point of a line of low hills stretching from Dublin to Clarinbridge in Co. Galway known as the *eiscir riada*. The Irish word *eiscir* has 'passed into international geological usage', the anglicised word being 'esker'. These eskers were formed after the Ice Age when sand or gravel that had built up inside tunnels in the ice remained after the ice melted away. In boggy country they provide natural causeways, the literal meaning of *eiscir riada* being the 'sand-ridge of chariot driving'. The *escir riada* was also a boundary between the north and south of Ireland, the southern half being known as *Leth Moga Nuadat* ('Mug Nuadu's half'). Mug Nuadu means 'the servant of Nuadu', a god venerated both in Britain and Ireland. Mug Nuada may have been a title which the King of the Eoganacht carried for life. The northern half was known as *Leth Cuinn* ('Conn's half'); this Conn was known as Conn Cét Chathach or 'Conn of the hundred battles'.

Ireland's Eye [50] lies about one mile from Howth, just north of Dublin Bay. Its area is about ten acres or half a square mile. The island has had a bevy of names, starting with *Inis*

Ereann or the island of Éire, the goddess from whom Ireland is named. With the Danish influence it became Erin's Ey, to the present Ireland's Eye. In a Papal Bull from Alexander III to St Laurence O'Toole, Archbishop of Dublin, in 1179, it is described as *Insula Filiorum Nessani*, 'the Island of the Sons of Nessan', which was originally gaelicised as *Inis mac Nessan*. The ruin of the church on the island is known locally as Mac Nessan's Church. A scriptorium presumably existed close to the church, as a copy of the four gospels was penned there in 690. It has two illuminated pages and is known as the *Garland of Howth*. The book was used to drive away evil spirits and as a swearing rite for making oaths. It can be seen today in Trinity College Dublin; perhaps the 'Book of Ireland's Eye' would be a more appropriate title! The church is essentially a small oratory and was part of the early Irish Church which spread throughout Europe in the Dark Ages. The church is mentioned by George Petrie as belonging to the seventh century.

The oldest rocks on the island are from the Cambrian Age and are therefore more than 500 million years old. Both ends of the island have quartzite, but the north side of the island contains the main mass of this stone, a hard, sandstone rock of quartz grains cemented together by silica.

One may take an open boat from Howth Harbour to Ireland's Eye, a journey of about fifteen minutes. The boat lands near the Martello Tower, which is on lower ground, and was built at the same time as the tower on Dalkey Island (see below). This tower was built by order of the Duke of York in 1803 as a lookout point and fortification against a Napoleonic invasion. On the east side there is a rock known as Puck's Rock, with a cleft in it which is said to have been formed by the devil, and its lore is like that of the Devil's Bit Mountain, a few miles north-west of Templemore, Co. Tipperary. Around here is a gannet colony, established in 1989. There are now a few hundred of these birds, and in time it may rival the vast colony on the Skelligs off the coast of Co. Kerry. As well as the gannets, breeding seabirds include kittiwakes, guillemots, fulmars, cormorants, shags and razorbills. There are also a few puffins; during winter, brent and greylag geese can be seen grazing the land. Indeed, with good eyesight or with a pair of binoculars one can see them from Howth Harbour. For a view of the nests it may be necessary to persuade the boatman to encircle the island, and if that happens, you may see seals as well.

Lambay Island [50] is situated about six miles north of Howth Head. The island is privately owned by the Revelstoke family and landing is not encouraged; when embarkation does take place, it is usually done from Rush Harbour, but if the weather is rough travelling takes place from the sheltered harbour of Lough Shinny. The island possesses the largest colony of cormorants in Ireland, and the second-largest colony of guillemots. In winter there are as many as 1,000 greylag geese on the island. Puffins can also be seen here. It is also home to a large colony of shag and herring gull. The Romans called the island *Limnios*, and Roman coins have been found on the nearby peninsula of Drumanagh on the mainland. The first Viking raid in Ireland occurred here in 795 AD. After the Battle of the Boyne in 1691, a fifteenth-century castle was used as a holding centre for the defeated Jacobite troops. This was converted into the present mansion about 1900. A shipping tragedy occurred on the east side of the island in 1854 when the *Tayleur*, a passenger ship of the White Star Line bound for Australia, floundered in shallow water and many passengers lost their lives. More than 100 are buried on the island.

Dalkey Island [50] is situated south of Dublin Bay, Co. Dublin. It covers an area of about twenty-five acres or a third of a mile by a third of a mile, and is less than half a mile from Coliemore Harbour, close to the village of Dalkey. The early name in Irish is *Delginis Cualann*. It is referred to in the twelfth-century *Book of Leinster* in the chapter concerning the sovereignty of Ireland:

> 7 *Cumtach Delginsi Cualand la Setga.*
> And [a fort] at Dalkey Island was built by Setga.

Dealg (*delg* in Old Irish) means 'a thorn' or 'a brooch'. It is to be found also in the village of Delgany, Co. Wicklow, and in Dundalk (*Dún Delca*), Co. Louth. It was an ancient custom for an important woman to encircle a piece of land prior to building on it, thus making it sacred. This custom goes all the way back to Medea and beyond. The pin or clasp on many brooches was often about a foot long. The present name of 'Dalkey' shows a Viking influence in that the suffix *ey* is Norse for island; this word appears again in Ireland's Eye north of Howth Harbour (see above).

Dalkey's 'history' begins in the Late Mesolithic Age about 7,000 years ago. Flint blades, which had long cutting edges and were possibly set in handles to be used for cutting and for whittling, were found at Dalkey Island, showing signs of habitation during Mesolithic times. Domesticated animal remains have been found on the island going back to these times, showing contact between hunter–gatherers and a farming community; Neolithic hollow scrapers and Bronze Age arrowheads have also been excavated.

Easily visible from the mainland is the church of St Begnet. Little is known of the saint, and the church has undergone many changes since her time. There are pilasters at each corner of the church and a lintel over the doorway. There is a fireplace at the east gable, apparently built for the workers who were constructing the nearby Martello tower between 1801 and 1803. The bell tower was possibly added during the fifteenth century. On a rock close to the west gable of the church is a rock with a circular or Greek cross incised upon it. This may be associated with the original settlement of St Begnet; another church associated with Begnet stands beside Dalkey Castle and Heritage Centre and is accessed through there.

KILDARE

Cill Dara, 'church of the oak tree'

Kildare town [55] still celebrates the feast of *imbolc* on the eve of 1 February. *Imbolc* is referred to in Cormac's Glossary as *óimelc*, or 'sheep's milk' (*Óimeilg .i. Is í aimser andsin tic as cárach melg. i.ass arinni mblegar*, 'at this time the sheep comes for the purpose of milking'); this ancient event became in time contemporaneous with the old pagan festival celebrating the first day of spring. As the festival is believed to have been at first connected with shepherding, it is understandable that a sheep was part of the ritual. It finds its origins in Greece and beyond, where it is associated with Pan, and in ancient Rome, where it is associated with the festival of the Lupercalia. This latter festival was held on 15 February: during it goats and dogs were sacrificed, and their skins were cut up and twisted into thongs with which women would run through the streets striking all in the hope that the gods of fertility would be propitious towards them. The place where the festival was held was called the Lupercal and was situated at the foot of the Palatine Hill. It contained an image of Lupercus covered with a goat's skin.

The early Christian Church responded to the Lupercalia with the Feast of Lights, also known as Candlemas. This festival took place on 2 February. Processing through towns with waxed candles which had been blessed in the church was the answer to the torches people carried through the streets of Rome even centuries after the arrival of Christianity.

An important part of the rites during the feast of *Imbolc* centred on fire, and the pit in which it was begun still exists within the grounds of Kildare Cathedral. This pit no longer contains fire at *Imbolc*, but the fires and festivities connected with Brigit now continue outside the church gates. The goddess associated with the rites at *Imbolc* is Brigit, whose name has been translated as *breo-shaighead* or 'arrow of fire'; as Brigit is the goddess of fertility, her symbol is fire represented by her sun symbol, Brigit's Cross. The sacred fire of Brigit was kept alight from pre-Christian times until it was extinguished by the Normans in the twelfth century. This fire, which may originally have been looked after by vestal virgins, was protected by nuns after the Christian Brigit became Abbess of Kildare in the sixth century. It is recorded in the *Historia Pontificalis* that these nuns took precedence over the bishops until the papal envoy directed otherwise in 1151. As Brigit was the goddess of *éicse* or divination, and was thus associated with supernatural knowledge, her centre, which stood at the heart of present-day Kildare town, was presumably enclosed within an oak wood.

Five miles north-east of Kildare town on the R415 is the Hill of Allen [49], standing 676 feet high. A large part of it has been quarried, and the erection of a monument in the late nineteenth century nearly destroyed the ancient mound at the summit of the hill. Its ancient name was *Almu*, who was the wife of Nuadu. Legend says that they were both buried on the hill. In the *Dindshenchas*,* there are twenty-two verses to Almu, three of which are given here to help with an early understanding of the place:

> *Almu rop alaind in ben*
> *ben Nuadat móir mic Aiched*
> *rachunig, ba fír in dál,*
> *a ainm ar in cnocc comlán ...*

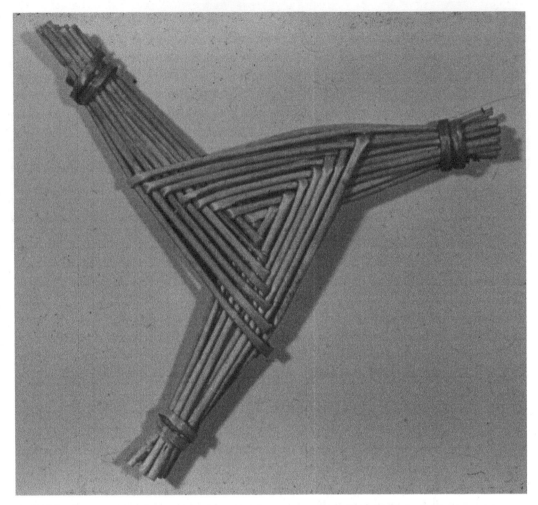

FIGURE 13. An earlier form of Brigit's Cross known as a triskel – a symbol of the sun.

Almu, beautiful was the woman!
the wife of Nuadu Mór, son of Achi;
she entreated—just was the reward—
that her name should be on the entire hill.

Nuadu the druid was a fierce man;
by him was built a fort strong and high:
by him alum was rubbed on the rock
over the whole fort after it was marked out.

All white is the fort (bitter strife),
as it had received the lime of all Erin,

from the alum he put on his house,
thence is Almu so named.

[Translated by Edward Gwynn]

The Hill of Allen was originally a *síd* where the Otherworld, ruled by Nuadu, was located. The naming of the hill is further contested by the piece of verse which states that 'Almu is the name of the man who got the place in the time of Nemed', while another extract from the poem alludes to a woman 'from whom Almu is so called'; a name ending in '*u*' signifies a goddess, and Almu is named as the wife of Nuadu, also a deity.

The hill also has a strong association with Finn mac Cumhail*; according to the *Dindshenchas,** Muirne, the granddaughter of Nuadu, married Cumall (although in truth she was carried off by Cumall in an act that led to the Battle of Castleknock – see the section on Dublin) and their eldest son was Finn. The hill was granted to Finn by his mother and became his chief seat and that of the Fianna.* Finn was watched over by an Otherworld woman known as a *bean faith* or *fée*; this blending of the mythological cycle with the Fenian cycle is a product of eleventh- and twelfth-century storytellers plying their craft to create a romantic set of tales.

This sacred hill became a centre of the Fianna* and not, as some suggest, a possible seat for the Kings of Leinster. O'Donovan wrote in 1837: 'I traversed the hill but could find upon it no monuments from which it could be inferred that it was ever a royal seat.' It is easier to see Almhain during the third century AD as the centre for the Fianna who represented the military wing of the Kings of Leinster, who were based at *Dún Aillinne* (Knockaulin) [55] less than ten miles south (discussed below).

A number of battles were fought here, but the most detailed is the battle of *Almhain* fought between Fergal mac Maelduin, King of Ulster at Grianán of Ailech, and Murchadh mac Brain, King of Leinster, over the *bóraime*, a tribute imposed on the Leinster men by the King of Tara. The payment was in cattle, and its imposition was for generations a cause of domestic warfare. Whether or not Fergal saw himself as a King of Tara is a moot point, but he left his fortress in present-day Donegal and travelled south-east to claim what he felt was a just tribute. According to ancient historians, the battle, in which Fergal was defeated, was the 'fiercest ever fought in Ireland'. According to the *Annals of the Four Masters*, 160 Ulstermen were killed at this battle:

At mid-day at Almhain,
in defence of the cows of *Breaghmhainé*
a red-mouthed beaked vulture raised
a shout of exultation over the head of Fergal.

Murchadh put off his former disability,
many a brave man did he cut to the ground;

he turned his arms against Fergal,
with his immense body of Fianna at Almhain.

[*Translated by John O'Donovan*]

In this battle there is reference made to musicians being in the train of the king while the king was pursuing warfare. The instruments played were harps and pipes [*cúisech*]. The Druid's Shout or *Géim Druadh* was a chant which was performed at the Battle of Almhain.

Murchadh's kingdom extended to *Breaghmainé*, which is in Meath; the Ua Brains kingdom extended to Meath at that time. The mac Brans are an east Ulster family and take their name from the raven, that is, '*Bran*', the Irish for the said bird.

Ten miles south-east of the Hill of Allen and two miles south-west of Kilcullen on the N78 is Knockaulin (*Dún Ailinne*), the royal seat of Leinster. It is a large hillfort with the bank outside the ditch or fosse, where the earthen rampart of the fort still surrounds its summit. Having the ditch on the inside gives credence to the probability that Knockaulin was a royal enclosure of assembly and ceremonial activities. The fort, which covers nearly forty acres, lasted from the Late Bronze Age through to the Iron Age and up to the Middle Ages. Excavation revealed that a large, circular, wooden structure probably existed within the enclosure. The defences are built on a steep hill slope to strengthen the fort against attack. Evidence of Neolithic occupation has been found here, and the discovery of glass beads, coarse pottery and a sword of the La Tène type is evidence that habitation existed here during the second century BC, the Early Iron Age. Although O'Rahilly has conjectured that *Dind Ríg* is a possible site for Ptolemy's *Dunon*, *Dún Ailinne* must also be considered as a serious candidate for this honour.

Ederscél, who was King of Ireland for five years, was slain at *Dún Ailinne* by Nuadu Necht, a king with strong associations with the Hill of Allen. Ederscél's father was Eógan, a grandson of Oilill Olum, who reigned for five years as King of Ireland. His son was Conaire Mór, and he also reigned as King of Ireland. Nuadu may have been connected to the Nodons from the River Severn, and thus the slaying of Ederscél may well have been the result of an invasionary force. They may have stemmed the flow of the Munster clans under Ederscél. These places present fragmentary historical evidence from a people living during the Iron Age. The name Nuadu figures prominently both here and at Almu, ten miles over, may well have been applied to sons, grandsons and so on, so that the progenitor's name was held through many generations. During the Late Iron Age, Finn mac Cumhail* kills Nuadu, who has by now become a god with his *síd* at Almhain.

The *óenach* or fair at Carman possibly tells us more about the early history of Kildare, and by extension, Leinster than any other place in Leinster apart from Tara, which was a kingdom unto itself. Generally it was seen as being located on the Plain of the Liffey (*Magh Life*). The River Liffey runs nine miles through Wicklow, nine miles through County Dublin and thirty-one miles through Kildare.

The following verse includes noted places connected to the fair at Carman:

The noble Aillinn he shall inhabit,
The famous Carman he shall obtain;
He shall rule over the venerable Almhain,
The impregnable Nas he shall strengthen.

The above verse is part of the will of Cathair Mór, King of Leinster, in the second century, and is addressed to his son Fiacha, the progenitor of most of the subsequent Kings of Leinster.

In the *Críth Gablach* (laws of settlement or agreement) it is stated that every king is expected to hold an *óenach* for the people of his *túath*. Other laws stress the duty of the king to have the site for the *óenach* cleared and prepared. The legal sources do not explicitly say so, but it is generally agreed that the *óenach* was held in early August, corresponding with the Feast of Lughnasa.

The *túath* may be described as a people, tribe or nation; in legal terms it may be a territory or a petty kingdom. At any time, the king could summon the *túath* in order to convene an *óenach*, which was a regular assembly for political, social and perhaps commercial purposes. Thus, the *Óenach Tailten*, 'Fair of Tailtiu', was held each year at the festival of Lughnasa under the auspices of the King of Tara. That these gatherings were lively events is attested by the *Corpus Iuris Hibernici* or *Body of Irish Laws*, edited by D.A. Binchy and quoted by Fergus Kelly in his *Guide to Early Irish Law* as follows: 'By attendance at a fair (*óenach*) a person is evidently felt to have willingly exposed himself to the risk of being killed or injured by horses or chariots, and there is consequently no recompense for such accidents.' The most famous of these fairs were the *Óenach Tailten* and the *Óenach Carmain*. These *óenaige* were presided over by the local king and were an important occasion for him to present himself to the *túatha* at this principal political gathering in early Irish society. The *Óenach Carmain* was the principal gathering of the many *túatha* connected to the Lagin. As with the *Óenach Tailten*, the *Óenach Carmain* occurred in early August.

The *óenach* or fair at Carman was possibly held every three years, and there are many opinions as to whether it was held in Kildare or Wexford. The fair of Carman may have been a moveable feast with the name 'Carman' remaining consistent but the location depending on the king's judgement, or it may simply have been held at different places at different times. One thing is that this harvest festival of celebration was a great social event, with horse-racing, music and storytelling. As well as storytelling, the recital of history may have included the genealogies of many notables present, and this gave public evidence to the general structure of the society, with the king representing the apex and the rest of the tribes in following order. E.J. Gwynn states that legal matters were discussed and that there was a market for food and a market for livestock; seemingly, we can look to these fairs for our original 'marts'. He also states that men and women stayed in separate assemblies similar to churches and dance halls of the not-too-distant past.

The siting of Carman, also named Carmun, is a matter of controversy; John O'Donovan identified it with Wexford, possibly influenced by the old name for Wexford Harbour being Loch Garman. According to G.H. Orpen, the fair at Carman was for the King of Leinster a festival of the same significance as was *Óenach Taillten* for the King of Tara, and as was *Óenach Cruachna* for the royalty of Connacht. As with the above suggestion of the 'moveable feast', Orpen suggests various sites where this festival was held, among them being Naas or *Nás na Ríg* – 'the assembly place of kings' [55], which is in Kildare. He also mentions Knockaulin (*Dún Aillinne*) ten miles south-west from Naas, which overlooks the Curragh. Five miles north from Newbridge is another place he associates with Carman, namely the Hill of Allen or *Cnoc Alúine* which is very similar to Knockaulin; this similarity in names can lead to confusion. Both sites are about eight miles apart. Orpen's work on the fair at Carman states that all references to the Fair of the Liffey, or at the Curragh, refer to *Óenach Carman*. In 954, Conghalach, King of Ireland made a hosting into Leinster and afterwards held the Fair of the Liffey; he was eventually ambushed and murdered by the Leinstermen and Danes, and presumably buried at the Curragh. The Plain of the Liffey, *Magh Life*, became the burial site of kings. Orpen records that 'an examination of the spot and excavations have proved the existence of pagan interments on the Curragh, such as we might expect on the site of Aenach Carman'. We may also add that from the Late Iron Age to the coming of the Normans, the political centre of Leinster was *Magh Life* or the Plain of the Liffey.

The following extract from a poem in the *Book of Leinster* is ascribed to Fulartach, whose date is unknown. It was translated by Eugene O'Curry.

Ni farlaic Cathair Carmain.
Acht dia maicni moradbail;
Na thosach co saidbri sain.
Síl Rosa Falge fegaid …

I kalaind auguist cen ail
Tiagait ind cech thres bliadain.
And luadit co dana ar daig.
Cert cech cana agus costaid.

Ith, blicht, síth, sáma sona,
Lína lána, lerthola,
Fir ríglaich, combáid cind
Dirmaig forráin for Hérind.

Acra tobuch frithir fiach.
écnach écraite anriad.

Ni lámar la graiffni in gáid.
Élud aithni athgabáil.

Cathair of Carman left nothing
save only to his mighty offspring:
at their head with special wealth,
behold the seed of Ros Failge!

On the calends of August free from reproach
they would go thither every third year:
they would hold seven races, for a glorious object,
seven days in the week.

Corn, milk, peace, happy ease,
full nets, ocean's plenty,
greybearded men, chieftains in amity
with troops overbearing Erin.

Suing, harsh levying of debts,
satirising, quarrelling, misconduct,
is not dared during the races …
evasion, injunction, nor distraint.

The Annals of Ulster mention Carman under the year 841, the year that a cleric named Feidlimid led an army near Cloncurry [49] and lost his crozier in 'the blackthorns'.

Finally, we come to Carman herself, who gave her name to the *aenach* or fair; Carman was a goddess in whose honour the festival was established. According to Anne Ross (*Pagan Celtic Britain*, p. 289):

[She] exhibits to a marked degree the concept of the *magical* powers of the female as opposed to the physical force employed by the male. Her divinity is emphasied by the fact that, appropriately, she had *three* sons, Dian 'violent', Dub 'Black', and Dothur 'Evil'. The mother is described as using charms and spells and incantations to bring about destruction. The sons brought it by violence, dishonesty and plundering. They blighted the corn of Ireland in order to destroy the Tuatha Dé Danann.* The Tuatha Dé Danann sang lampoons, witchcraft and spells on them until by their superior magic they drove them across the sea, retaining Carman as hostage. She died of grief and her *oenach* [fair] was held at her burial place. Here we have a local goddess, retained and overcome by an incoming race, and finally honoured by means of a seasonal feast at her grave.

Orpen concludes his work on Carman with the following: 'Finally it may be asserted without fear of contradiction, that nowhere in Leinster is there a place more suited than the Curragh for the holding of such assemblies, festivities, and races as are described in the account of the Fair of Carman which has come down to us, and that nowhere in Leinster is there a larger or more imposing *dún* than Knockaulin.'

About eight miles north-east from the Hill of Knockaulin is the great mound or hilltop fort of Naas (*Nás na Rí*, the 'commemorative assembly of the king') [55], another seat of the Kings of Leinster, which lasted as such until 804 AD, which sounds specific enough, though some say that it continued as a royal seat until the tenth century. Eochaidh, King of the Fir Bolg,* chiefly held his court at Naas. The last King of Leinster here was Cerball son of Muiregan – *Atá an Nás gan ríg anall ón ló ro torchair Cerball* ('Naas was without a king since the murder of Cerball'). Naas features in the story of Finn and the 'Salmon of Wisdom', the taste of which made him aware of everything that was happening, particularly in the courts of Tara, Emain Macha and Naas. Naas today is a thriving town, a testament to its ancient importance. In earlier times, *Crích Náis* meant the province of Leinster.

Three miles south from Naas is Mullacash Hill [55]. This area is on the Liffey Plain (*Mag Liphi*), the River Liffey flowing thirty-one miles through Kildare. The plain has a strong connection with Loegaire, a High King of Ireland from 428 to 458 AD. He broke his word over guarantees to the Lagin and was struck down between two hills known as Ériu and Alba. There are a number of small hills here, and the place where he was struck down 'by the sun and the wind' is known as *grellach da phil* ('the bog between the two ridges'). The exact location may well be lost.

Legend says that Mullaghmast (*mullach moisten* and *maistin na righ*, 'the hill of the kings') [55] in south Kildare and five miles north-east of Athy is named after Maistiu, the embroiderer to Aengus mac ind Óg, the harper to the gods. Maistiu's father, Aengus Umor, is attributed with building Dún Aengus on the Aran Islands off Galway Bay. The Mullaghmast pillar stone stood here until it was taken to the National Museum in Dublin. It possesses various La Tène motifs such as spirals, trumpets and a triskele. It is made of limestone and is four-sided. Stones such as this are seen as symbols of pre-Christian religious beliefs. The Mullaghmast Stone may be of the Late Iron Age or later. Perhaps the finest example of these stones is the Turoe Stone from Co. Galway.

Around the time of Christ, Mullaghmast was the final encampment of the Munstermen, who had overrun Ossory and Laois. They were then driven back to the River Barrow by Cú Chorb, the King of Leinster, and were routed by him at Ath Troisten, which today is called Athy on the Barrow. A millennium later, after the Battle of Clontarf in 1014 AD, the returning armies stopped at Mullaghmast, and the chief of the Dál gCais,* Donnchadh, son of Brian Boru, ordered that the wounded be tended in the ring fort there (*Ráth Maistean*), which involved the use of bog cotton and moss for the wounds.

At the base of Mullaghmast, according to Hogan, is a glen known as *Glenn Treicím* ('the glen of the flocks'). This is most likely the glen running east of Mullaghmast from the high cross at Moone, along the River Greese (*grís*, 'heat, fire, hot ashes'), which joins the River Barrow 3.5 miles above the town of Carlow at Ballitore (*Béal Átha an Tuair*, 'the field of the bleach green'). This, however, is more likely a contracted form of 'tuairgnín' which would translate as the 'ford of the smiting or hammering', underlining the fact that this glen has strong associations with the forge of Goibniu,* the smith god. Were this forge to be still extant in popular lore, then it would be at the ford where the Greese enters Ballitore. The Goibniu* is one of the *trí dee dana*, the three gods of artistic skill who, as pagan beliefs grew dimmer, became subsumed into the Tuatha Dé Danann,* a people from the mythic past with neither a hold on history nor place, and thus both vague and powerful at the same time.

At the south-east end of *Glenn Treicím* is the village of Moone (*Maoin*, 'a gift') [55], which is a possible location of one of the five famous trees, or *bile*, of Ireland around which tribal gatherings took place. This tree was known as the *Eó Mugna* ('the yew of Mugna') and got its name from Mugna, a district of which Ballaghmoon represents a remnant, and Ballaghmoon may also lay claim to the tree. Stories of praise about this tree abound; the *Dindshenchas** describes it as follows:

> *Eó Mugna, mór in crann cain;*
> *ard a barr ós na barraib;*
> *deich n-eda fichet, nir fhann,*
> *is ed tarla 'na thacmang.*
>
> *Tri cét, airde in chrainn cen chol,*
> *mile comged a fhoscad;*
> *fo díamair robói thuaid tair,*
> *co haimsir Chuinn chét-chathaig.*
>
> *Fiche cét láech, ní lúad lac,*
> *fri tóeb deich cét cethrachat*
> *noainced sin, ba garb gleó,*
> *co torchair lasna hécseo.*
>
> Eo Mugna, great was the fair tree,
> high its top above the rest;
> thirty cubits – it was no trifle –
> that was the measure of its girth.
>
> Three hundred cubits was the height of the blameless tree,
> its shadow sheltered a thousand:
> in secrecy it remained in the north and east
> till the time of Conn of the Hundred Fights.
>
> A hundred score of warriors – no empty tale –
> along with ten hundred and forty

would that tree shelter – it was a fierce struggle –
till it was overthrown by the poets.

[Translated by Edward Gwynn]

Lore about this tree says that it was said to bear apples, nuts and acorns; that it was a vast tree, 'the top whereof was as vast as the whole plain'; and that it lay hidden from the time of the Flood to the time of the birth of Conn Cét Chathach, a second-century High King of Ireland. It was also equated with being the 'son of the tree of the Garden of Eden'.

The story of how the *Eó Mugna* came to an end depicts how early Christianity brought an end to the earlier love of nature, and particularly the singular reverence for certain trees. John Francis Shearman, writing in the *Journal of the Royal Historical and Archaeological Association of Ireland* in January 1884, states:

> The abbot Ninian returned to Ireland from Candida (Casa) towards the end of the year 522, and dwelt in a monastery which he founded on a site given by the regulus of the locality, at Cluain Conaire (Cloncurry), four miles north west from Kilcock [49] just south of the Royal Canal on the Kildare/Meath border. He overcame some pagan superstitions in the neighbourhood, and like another St German, cut down a celebrated tree, because it was an object of superstitious worship – the Eó Mugna, the yew of Mugna – a place now called Monmehenoc or Dunmanoge, in the south of Kildare.

The yew is mentioned in a poem about Suibhne Geilt* ('Mad Sweeney'):

A iubhair, a iubhracháin,
i reilgibh bat reil.

O yew-tree, little yew-tree,
in churchyards thou art conspicuous.

The above translation was by J.G. O'Keeffe in 1912; a later translation by Seamus Heaney seems to me to more capture the essence of the poem:

The yew tree in each churchyard
wraps night in its dark hood.

A few miles north of *Glenn Treicím* is Narraghmore [55], and in this vicinity stood the *Bile mac Cruaich*, 'tree of the son of Cruaich'. According to Shearman, 'under its shade pagan rites were perhaps celebrated, and the chieftains of the territory were solemnly inaugurated'. The tree possibly stood at 'Nine-tree-hill', two miles south from Narraghmore. However,

Bull Hill to the north of Narraghmore may have been Buile Hill originally. Narraghmore and its sacred *bile* were sufficiently important to bring St Patrick here to found a church. In Irish the place was called: *An fhórac mór Patraich* ('Patrick's seat or meeting place'), but, with the 'a' becoming diminished over time and the 'f' silent, it was pronounced *Norrac Patrick*.

Less than two miles south of Old Kilcullen is the village of Calverstown [55], and here in 1788 labourers were digging in a garden when they came across a large stone which just appeared above the ground. Underneath this stone was a tomb consisting of large flat stones about five feet long and four feet wide and four feet deep. Here they found a skeleton, and near its head was an urn made of hard, baked earth and of a light-brown colour. The fact that the body was interred rather than cremated infers that the period of cremation was coming to an end. It was customary in early times, by which I mean pre-Christian times, to reduce the body to ashes and to place the ashes in an urn and raise the earth over the urn in a conical mound. Around the rims of these urns were mouldings which would appear to be artistic rather than symbolic.

King Eochaid Airem, who reigned towards the beginning of the Christian period, is said to have substituted burning for burying in Ireland. Christianity chose the latter, so we might surmise that burying in Ireland increased around the late fifth or early sixth centuries. One then has to ask, what of the urn? Was this grave found at a time when both methods of interment were practised? Between Kilcullen, Newbridge and Kildare town [55] lies a great expanse of gravely glacial deposits, six miles long and two miles wide, in an area known as the the Curragh (*An Currach*, 'low-lying plain or race track'). Cormac mac Cuillenan, the tenth-century Bishop–King of Cashel, whose celebrated glossary is known as *Sanas Cormaic*, writes that *Cuirrech* is associated with the Latin *curribus*, that is, *fich carpait*, which points to chariot races. The inference in Cormac's glossary is that chariot racing preceded horse racing in this country. This can be gleaned from the older stories about Cú Chulainn* in the Ulster Cycle, which involves chariots, and the later sagas with Finn mac Cumhail* and the Fianna,* which simply mention horses.

Cuirrech, or *cuirrectach*, was an epitaph of renown given to the Abbot Cobhthach, who died in the year 868 – *Cobhtach Cuirrigh Cuirrectach* ('the racing Cobhtach (or Coffey) of the Curragh') This would seem to confirm that the clergy in the Christian era rode with the chiefs.

The Curragh is part of a larger plain known as *Magh Ailbhe*, which extended from *Slieve Mairge*, now known as the Castlecomer Hills, to the River Barrow, including the ancient royal site of Dind Ríg and Ballaghmoon in south Kildare and from the Curragh eastwards to the foot of the Wicklow Mountains. A poet writing in the twelfth-century *Book of Rights* asks, 'where is there in any province in Ireland a plain like Magh Ailbhe?' To which John Hogan, an early-nineteenth-century antiquarian replies: 'It must occur to the reader that the extensive flat known as the Curragh of Kildare is identical with a portion of the ancient Magh Ailbhe; and of it too, may be said, "where is there in any province of Ireland a plain like the Curragh of Kildare?"'

Moving from horses to hounds, within a ninth-century fortified ring fort at Castlesize on the left bank of the Liffey and a mile north of Sallins [49], the ten-inch-long skull of an *ár chú*, or 'hound of slaughter', was discovered by Noel Dunne, a project archaeologist with the roads and rail agency. The skeleton of the hound is the largest yet found in Ireland and leads one to suggest that these hounds may have been guard dogs to tribal chiefs. Dunne says that these hounds 'were bred to guard and to attack and kill people if needed; this is the kind of animal referenced in the story of Setanta'. Setanta was named Cú Chulainn* after he slew Culann's hound with a hurling stick; he then became the 'hound of Culann'.

A story by Tómas Bairéad, 'Saidhbhreas na gCon', from his book *An Geall a Briseadh* ('the broken promise') published in 1938, begins with the following verse:

An chú ab' airde sa bhFéinn
Thigeadh gan chromadh fá bhléin;
Is a cheann ba gasta an roinn,
Ba chomhárd é le m'ghualainn.

Cheithre mhíol do leiginn uaim,
Míol ó dheas 's moil ó thuaidh,
Míol siar agus moil soir –
Do bhídís uilig I mbéal Bhrain.

The tallest hound of the Fianna
Comes with no sagging under his groin;
He is the fastest in the land
And equally balanced between the shoulders.

Four hounds I let go
Hounds from the south and from the north
From the west and from the east –
They all end up in Bran's mouth.

[Translated by the author]

Lifé was the old name for the plain of Kildare, and the river flowing through it, *Ruirthech* ('running swiftly'), was eventually named *Amhain Liffé* or 'River of the Liffey'. The poet and writer Oliver St John Gogarty, having escaped his captors during the civil war in Ireland by swimming across the Liffey to freedom, offered two swans to the goddess Lifé, and at his funeral near Islandbridge swans were said to be seen flying across the same river.

So it was to this plain of the Liffey that Conaire came, as Brehon Law prescribed, to preside over the assembly and partake in chariot contests. This he did before journeying to Dublin and then to Tara. Conaire, according to historical tradition, was king at Tara in the first century of the Christian period, and the Liffey valley was just north-west of the Curragh. This would make the Curragh the oldest racecourse in Ireland and a racecourse with an unbroken tradition up to the present day. When I drove by as a child with my parents, I was impressed that there were no fences along the road on the Curragh side of Kildare town. This was due to the fact that the Curragh was commonage, which is land held in common. It was used as a sheep or cattle way, and the Race of the Black Pig on the Curragh showed after excavation by Ó Ríordáin that the Race was not a road, but that it consisted of a trench with slight banks at the sides. These so-called 'hollow-ways' served as sheep ways, linking one pasture with another.

Fences have been erected for quite a while now, but that sense of open space made the Curragh a place of games, fun and sport, and above all a place to enjoy oneself and shed one's cares. In times past, it was a people's park, as the poem by the ninth-century poet Orthanach of the Curragh of Kildare states:

Marid Cuirrech cona li,
Ní mair nach Rí ro boi foir.

The Curragh with its beauty remains;
But there lives no king who was over it.

The Curragh was a commonage dedicated to St Brigit, and presumably before her was a commonage to the pre-Christian Brigit. Legend informs us that St Brigit received the plain of the Curragh as a commonage from the King of Leinster on account of having removed a deformity 'under which he laboured'. The king decreed that Brigit would be entitled to as much land as her mantle would cover, and to add to the tale it is further stated that were it not for a rent in her garment caused by the jealousy of one of her female companions, her mantle would have covered the island of Ireland. Tradition says that the Curragh was a commonage from 484, when Brigit founded her church beside the old oak of *Druim Criadh* ('Ridge of Clay'), but we may assume that on this commonage fires to pagan Brigit existed long before that on the plain of the Curragh. The old oak or sacred *bile* next to St Brigit's early chapel may have been the tree that gave its name to Kildare (*Cill Dara*, 'the little church by the oak')

An old custom demanded that any celebrated person visiting the Curragh had to do a circuit that was right to the sun, namely clockwise. This circuit was known as a *cor*, and this word has been suggested as the origins of the word *curragh*. Brigit's Cross is a sun symbol or swastika that shows movement, which the Christian use of the cross, which is always 'stuck' at 6 o'clock, does not. The little road leading from the priory or graveyard of Kildare was known in the nineteenth century as *Bóthairín na gcor* ('the little road of the circuits').

An important *aenach* ('fair or assembly') held here was known as *Currach Lífé*. The *aenach* could also be held on the accession of a king or for the purpose of holding the *aenach gubha* ('fair of sorrow' or funeral rites). Regardless of the circumstance, the fair was always followed by *graifne* or horse-racing. For about 200 years after the middle of the first century, chariot races were the most popular. The chariot was of Roman origin, and the Latin word *carpentum*, meaning a two-wheeled carriage or baggage wagon, is found in the Irish *carpa*. The chariot is said to have arrived in Ireland after the Roman invasion of Britain and throughout much of the Iron Age was the general mode of coach transport, and may well have lasted until the seventh century when the sons of King Aedh Slaine began to erect ditches, fences and stone walls to coincide with the erection of cashels and ring forts.

The change from chariot races to horse races is said to have occurred during the time of Finn mac Cumhail.* Finn's son, the legendary Oisín,* according to a poem in the twelfth-century *Book of Leinster*, laments his blindness and expresses his regret at not being able to enjoy the assembly or the *aenach* of the Liffey, that is of the Curragh, which he says was inaugurated by the King of Leinster. This poem begins as follows:

> *Oenach indium luíd in rí.*
> *Oenach Life cona lí*
> *aebind do cech oen téit and.*
> *ni hinund is Guaire Dall.*

> Then the king went to the assembly.
> The splendid *Oenach Life* [the Fair at the Curragh].
> The delightful [fair] to which everyone comes
> But being a noble prince who is blind, I don't share [its enjoyment].

An early account of the Curragh's history by John D'Alton (1830) says that there are about thirteen burial mounds or 'barrows' on the Curragh. These are generally assigned to the Iron Age, and their presence may attest to the desire of people to be buried close to sacred or ritual centres. Horse and army training over centuries did nothing for the preservation of these sites.

A significant early site north of Kildare town and known as the Little Curragh is a large enclosure known as Raheenanairy [55], which was excavated in the 1950s by Ó Ríordáin, who said that it was hard to distinguish between a large ring barrow and a ritual site. As a ceremonial site, the time for large gatherings here would have been at the autumnal equinox on 21 September. Tentative experiments have been carried out here in order to show that the sun comes between two gaps in the enclosure at sunset on the autumnal equinox. The enclosure is 150 feet in diameter and consists of a bank with an internal fosse or ditch and has an entrance on the west. No traces of habitation or burial were found here during excavation.

A further three ritual enclosures were found on the Curragh. The first was 45 feet in diameter and resembling a ring barrow. The second had an overall diameter of 110 feet, consisted of a bank with an internal fosse and had entrances to the east and west; at the centre was a burial site 'so disposed that the person seems to have been buried alive, presumably as a ritual sacrifice'. This conclusion by Estyn Evans from his book *Prehistoric and Early Christian Ireland* cries out for further information to support his interesting contention. The third enclosure was 110 feet in diameter with an entrance on the west. According to Ó Ríordáin, 'there is no clear dividing line between large ring-barrow and earth-circle ritual site'. He also states that the ditch and bank enclosures on the Curragh were almost certainly Iron Age in date.

To the south of Raheenanairy is the Rathbride Hare Park, and to the south-east of the park is a tumulus to an historical chief who for the moment remains anonymous. Across an ancient road from this tumulus is another rath, and these are divided by an ancient road called the Race of the Black Pig. Both to the east and to the north of this road is a rath known as Walsh's Rath. In some ways, the Curragh is a part of hidden Ireland, yet one would hope that imaginative teachers would use this area to reveal the roots of a culture that expresses an ancient and enriching past.

KILKENNY

Cill Chainnigh, 'Church of Cainneach' or St Cannice of Aghaboe

At Mullinabro (*Mullagh na brón*, 'summit of the millstone') [76], on the Kilkenny side of the River Suir close to Waterford city, there is a story relating to the banshee. This story is still causing ripples in the local area, as the latest 'hearing' occurred as recently as mid-June 2008. The story involves the Jones family, previous landlords in the area, and the death of one of them while out horseriding. The son of the landlord, while coming towards the gates of the estate, fell from his horse and was impaled on one of the gates. His sister put a *geis* or taboo on anyone opening the gate, and thus it remained closed for more than a hundred years. She said that she would return to haunt anyone who opened it. It was opened during construction work in the area and the wails of the banshee have been heard in the locality ever since. One construction worker claimed that, although he does not believe in such things, nonetheless the sound of the screeching made 'the hair on my neck stand on end'.

Within the environs of the spirit world, and at a later date, one encounters witches, though in Ireland they are fewer than found on mainland Europe. In Kilkenny city on Kieran Street is an old inn known as Kyteler's Inn, where Alice Kyteler was born in the late thirteenth century. She was said to have been a witch, perhaps due to the sudden demise of a number of husbands whom she was suspected of poisoning. Some of her customs were reportedly drinking blood from a human skull, and her inn was famed for its Rabelaisian 'goings on' mixed with a strong whiff of pagan ritual. A verse supports the above:

She drank blood from a chalice
made from a human skull.

About six miles due north from Mullinabro and two miles south-east of Mullinavat is the 1,000-foot-high Tory Hill [76]. The word 'tory' is derived from the Irish *tóraidhe*, meaning a highwayman or outlaw. The tory who gave his name to this hill was an outlaw named Edmund Denn who lived in the late seventeenth century. His family owned the hill, and after he was outlawed, he lived in a cave there. The antiquarian James Graves, writing in 1850, said that he spent a whole day unsuccessfully looking for this cave, called *Labby Emoinn* ('Edmond's Bed'). Denn was a popular hero locally, and his bed in the hill cave was pointed out by locals into the early twentieth century. Before Denn's time the hill was known as Slievegrian (*Slíabh gréine*, 'the hill of the sun'), which suggests pre-Christian sun worship.

The account of a local nineteenth-century folklorist quoted in Máire Mac Neill's *The Festival of Lughnasa* states that the hill was the place for pagan worship for the people of the surrounding country. There is a well-established circular track around the hill which people followed *deas sol* or 'right to the sun', and the hill's conical shape is reminiscent of Croagh Patrick in Co. Mayo, which was a centre of sun worship from Bronze Age times. On the summit of the hill is an altar which in Penal times was used for offering Mass, which was presumably also used in pre-Christian times. A megalithic tomb at the eastern base of the hill shows that it was held in high respect over a long span of time.

There is a difference of opinion about the original Irish name for the hill, that is, its name before Denn arrived. Hogan in his *Onomasticon Goedelicon* names it *Sliabh Gréine* ('the hill of the sun'), but O'Donovan names it *Sliabh gCruinn* or 'rounded hill'; on the hilltop there is a rounded space covered with stones. O'Donovan however disputes 'rounded hill', and both he and P.W. Joyce concur that its real name is as above, and that it 'no more denotes *mountain of the sun*, than it does Mount Ida!' Slieve Igrine, according to the above historians, was the mountain of the ancient territory of Igrine, called from the old tribe of *Ui* or *Hy Cruinn*, referred to as the lost sept of Co. Louth, who formerly held it. However, *Cruinn* meaning 'round', according to O'Rahilly 'suggests the sun deity'. That is, the tribe took their name from the sun, and if so then the hill was originally a pre-Christian centre for sun worship just as Croagh Patrick was. The *Discovery* map 76 concurs with O'Donovan who was a local man and a noted antiquarian. It would be nice to think that they are both right, but alas O'Donovan would appear to be correct in so far as he goes.

Some antiquarians in the more spirited times of the nineteenth century found what I have described as the altar stone, a cromlech on top of Tory hill. Reading an inscription on it, they leapt to conclusions based on fallacy rather than fact. Apparently, some local lads from Mullininavat used the cromlech for 'a running leap', having turned it on its side to give it some height. As a result, an inscription on the stone was turned upside-down to read 'IELI CIUO)3', which it was inferred was equivalent to BELI DIUOSE, and so 'Baal Dionusos' was interpreted from the reading. Howeever, when the stone was repositioned in its original position, the words ECONIC 1731 were the correct reading, and simply meant 'E. CONIC, 1731', referring to Ned Conic, a 'humble hewer-out of mill stones' at the time.

Over a mile south from Tory Hill is a townland named Fahy (*Faithche*, 'a field or exercise ground') [76], which is associated with great games of hurling with sixty players aside played during Fraughan Sunday on the second Sunday of July. South of the playing field is a lake named Lough Cullin or Holly Lake, which has a foundation myth associated with it as follows: one of the hurlers became thirsty in the course of the game and met an old woman (a *cailleach*, or hag) who said that if he lifted some rushes that water would come forth; this he did but he forgot to put them back, as he had been warned to do, and the water erupted and drowned everyone on the *faithche*. Finn mac Cumhail* and his dog Bran are also connected by legend to the lake. One could say that it is through these stories that control of the lake is still under the control of the ancient powers of the *cailleach*.

Unlike that on Tory Hill, what are genuinely ancient inscriptions written in ogam script can be found on a standing at Gowran (*Belat Gabhráin*, 'the Pass of Gabhrán') [68], fourteen miles south-east of Kilkenny city.

The stone was discovered in the foundation of the chancel of the old church of St Mary's when it was being rebuilt. It is now to be seen against the wall to the left of the altar of the rebuilt chancel. There are variations in the interpretations of the inscriptions on the stone. One is as follows: 'MAQI ERACIAS MAQI DIMAQA MUCOI', According to McManus in his authoritative *Guide to Ogam*, 'Maqi Eracias' or 'Maqi Ercias' translates as *Mac Erce*, 'son of Erc'. Erc was the son of Eochaid Muinreamhar, and his posterity are called the clan Eirc and the Cinéal Gabhráin in Scotland. He was the father of Fergus Mór mac Eirc, who led a single dynasty of both the Dál nAraide and the Dál Riata and controlled both sides of the North Channel in the fifth century. Gabhrán, who reigned in the sixth century, was great-grandson of Erc, and it was through him that the tribe became known as the Cineál Gabráin. Gabhrán's death is given as 558, around the time when the Picts defeated the Dál Riata in Scotland. Many tribes went to Scotland because of family ties, but also at times to take possession of land and use western Scotland as a source for collecting taxes. Erc's presence in Scotland was due to a military adventure.

A cross is inscribed at the base of the stone, the result of a fairly common practice of 'Christianising' pre-Christian stones; another good example of this can be found on the *Lia Fail* ('the grey understone', but more commonly referred to as 'the stone of destiny') on the Hill of Tara, Co. Meath. A small cross has been inscribed into the lower end of this stone in order to take away its pagan power. Rev. Canon A.V. Hogg read the ogam inscription in reverse as 'DALO MAQA MUCOI MAQUI ERACIAS MAQI LI' and translated it as 'Dalach, grandson of mac-Eirche, who was son of Lia'.

Gowran is mentioned in a tenth-century poem by Cormacan Eigeas, chief poet of Ulster, describing the king's tour of Ireland:

At night we passed at Bealach Mugna [Ballaghmoon].
We did not wet our fine hair.
The snow was on the ground before us,
In the stormy pass of Gowran.

103

Gowran is described as a boundary of Munster by Keating when he writes: 'The second division of Munster called *Urmhumha* or Ormond extends in length from *Gabhrán* to *Cnámchaill* in Tipperary.' Keating understood Gowran to be at the centre of Ossory, but the historian John O'Donovan confined it to the present town of Gowran. As for *Bealach Gabhrain* or 'the road or pass of Gabhran', it is difficult to pinpoint exactly where it was. According to Colgan, it extended from Gowran through where the present city of Kilkenny is and on to Cashel. Also, it is difficult to know where the *Bealach Gabhrain*, the supposed site of Donnchadh, King of Ossory, was, as it extended from Jonesbridge [68] to Gowran and to Cashel and consisted of a 'district of glens'. Of his daughter Sadb it is said, 'Sadb of Bealach Gabhran, district of glens'.

It has been suggested by John Hogan writing in 1865 that the 'district of glens' might more appropriately relate to the vales of the lower valley of the Nore River. The Nore River is about ten miles south from Gowran. Hogan also states that 'the present town of Gowran, except its name preserves no vestige of a pre-English existence'. Thus, Gowran possessed no architectural or historical interest prior to the settlement of Anglo-Norman nobles. If there was anything of note in the area was it treated in the same way as the ogam stone of Erc and literally buried beneath the earth?

A twelfth-century poem to Donnchadh Cairbreach O'Brien, the son of the last King of Munster by the poet Giolla-Brighde Mac Conmidhe, otherwise known as Giolla Brighde Albanach ('of Scotland') alludes to Gabhran as follows:

Cruit iBrian! binn a horgáin
re hucht bfleighe bfionngabráin;
ó bhéanadh stuaigh Gabrain gloin,
argáin truaigh as na téadaib.

O'Brien's harp! sweet its melody
At the head of the banquet of fair Gabhran;
Oh! how the pillar of bright Gabhran called forth
The melting tones of the thrilling chords.

A famous battle was fought at Gowran in which Conn Cét Chathach, 'Conn of the Hundred Battles', who was High King of Ireland towards the end of the second century AD, was defeated by Mog Nuadu or 'servant of the god Nuadu', who was regarded as being of Eóganacht descent. As a result of this and other victories against Conn, Mog Nuadu became sovereign of the southern part of Ireland. A pact must have been agreed between both kings, as south of the Esker Riada a line from Dublin to Galway is called *Leath Mogha* or Mog's Half, while north of the line is *Leath Cuinn* or Conn's Half.

When Cormac mac Airt ousted Lugaid mac Con from the high kingship in 227 AD, he introduced a seven-year period known as 'Cormac's Peace' during which no man should be slain. Finn mac Cumhail* responded that 'there are places where the slaying of a man is a vested right', namely *Slige Midluachra* or the great northern road from Tara, *Ath Firdiad* or Ardee, *Áth Cliath* or Dublin, *Belach Gabhráin* or Gowran and *Da Cich* or the Paps of Anu on the Cork–Kerry border. So even during times of peace Gowran was a potential battlefield.

Tales of the *púca* or Puck or the Pooka are found in Kilkenny. The word is sometimes translated as 'goblin' or 'sprite'. As Jack O'Lantern (*púca an duibh ré*), he is the 'sprite of darkness'. Shakespeare rejuvenated Puck in *A Midsummer's Night Dream*, where he is described as the 'merry wanderer of the night' and one who can 'put a girdle round about the earth in forty minutes'. A seventeenth-century Irish manuscript refers to *an pucadh da ngairir an spioraid phriobhaideach* ('the soulful solitary call of Puck').

In Kilkenny, Puck was seen as a large monster who frequented the glens of wild and mountainous districts. A particular Puck is said to dwell in a natural cave at the base of a hill on which stands the Dún of Clochanpooka [61]. He has variously been described as a bull with long horns, a horse or a goat, and is sometimes called the *Gruagach*, which means 'hairy one' or also an enchanter or magician. He is said to have uttered a 'mysterious buzzing sound which inspires terror in all who hear it'. W.G. Wood-Martin in his *Traces of the Elder Faiths* suggests that this 'strange superstition may be a lingering reminiscence of the former presence of the mammoth in these latitudes'. Cloghpook, as it is known today, is a townland at the base of a hill called Knockshanbally (*cnoc sean-bhaile*, 'the hill of the old homestead'). The *dún* mentioned above is likely to be the moated site within this townland. To get to Cloghpook, take the N78 south of Castlecomer and after three-and-a-half miles take a left turn for Gaulstown, travel two miles along this road and take the first right after Gaulstown. Then follow this road for about a mile and turn left along a boreen for about half a mile until you begin to rise from the base of the hill. The moated site is about a fifteen-minute walk due east from here.

There are many associations with monsters throughout Ireland, and these are often referred to as *péist*. At Freshford [60], ten miles north-west from Kilkenny city on the R693, there is a townland named Tobernapestia which means the 'well of the beast'. It was common to associate wells, pools and lakes with demons. The most famous place associated with demons in Ireland is *Poll na bPéist*, a rectangular water hole made by the ocean on Inishmore on the Aran Islands.

About ten miles north-north-east from Mullinabro is a townland named Listerlin (*Liss ar glinn*, 'the fort on the glen'). In this parish a thorn bush beside a holy well is believed to have grown from St Moling's walking stick (see under *Carlow*). Listerlin [76] is five miles west from New Ross on the R704; when you come to a crossroads, turn right and then take the next right after a 100 yards or so, pass the school on your right and stop. Along with the well there is a ring fort, from which presumably the area derives its name, as well as a moated site. It is usual to find a thorn tree beside a well, as both were regarded as sacred, and the thorn tree was often used as the site for inauguration of chiefs. Both the thorn, or *sceach*, and the well were a basic part of the fertility rite of young women.

Monabrogue [60] comes from *Móin na Burróige*, meaning 'the bog of the pits' – for making black dye. Black dye was made in the eighteenth century and earlier from the sumach tree and hot water, with the addition of copperas or sulphates of iron or copper. However, in early Ireland the black dye consisted of turf and water dug from the bottom of the bog. Woolens were soaked in this material and worn by men and women, and to this day black rather than white sweaters are worn by men on the Aran Islands. Another process of dyeing yarn or cloth was to boil the twigs of the alder tree or *ruaim* in Irish. The result of this was that the material acquired a reddish-brown colour. When the 'rimed' yarn or cloth (from the Irish *ruaim*) was then boiled in the peaty mud from certain bog holes and the peaty edges of lakes, the result was a dye of a fine black colour.

Six miles north-west from Monabrogue is the townland of Rathbreagh, adjoining the west bank of the River Nore. The plain here was anciently called *Mag Argatros* ('the plain of the silverwood'). Argetros [60] is said to have got its name from the silver shields that were made there by Enna Airgtheach (the second part of his name meaning 'a person rich in silver'), or it could simply be descriptive of a silver birch wood that extended from the confluence of the Nore and Dinin Rivers out to Rathbeagh and up to and beyond Coole on the Kilkenny–Laois border. The Milesian Gaels are said to have brought their metalworking skills from the mines of northern Spain. The addition of an engraved silver disc on a shield was an advance from the shields of yew that had been prevalent until the arrival of the Gaels from Spain. Argetros is recorded as being the seat of kings in an eighth-century poem giving an account of the Fair at Carman in Co. Wexford:

> The seat of the king of noble *Airget-Ros* [Ossory],
> on the right hand of the noble king of *Carmán*;
> on his left, for every happy enjoyment,
> the seat of the smooth-speared king of *Cruachan*.

The area has strong associations with Éremón, one of the sons of Míl and the progenitor of the Gaels. For a while Éremón was King of Ireland, but at the battle of Argatros he was slain. This battle probably occurred late in the third century BC. The *Book of Invasions* records Éremón's death as follows:

> The princedom of Éremón the perfect, the youthful,
> dug was his grave after the time of his death,
> in the the land of silvery Argetros,
> on the same chariot land.

At the centre of this plain, two miles south of Ballyragget, there is a large mound, and as he was a king perhaps it is there that Éremón is buried. But there is another mound, a further few miles north, at Coole. Although the battle that led to Éremón's demise is known as the Battle of Coole on the plain of Argatros (*Cath Cuile i nArgatros*), the *Annals of Clonmacnoise* state that he was buried at Rathbeagh (*Rath beothaigh*, 'the rath of the living'). This moat at Rathbeagh still exists and can be seen just right of the R694, two-and-a-half miles south of Ballyragget. Rathbeagh is also regarded as the place where Éremón had his royal fortress.

Unfortunately for Kilkenny, the mound at Coole [60], another mound associated with the burial place of Éremón, is a few hundred yards inside the Laois border! *The Annals of Clonmacnoise* state that Éremón reigned for fourteen years as King of Ireland and died at Argatros and was with great 'and solmne funerals buried at Rathebehie on the river of Feoire [the Nore]'. O'Curry concurs with this and says, 'the ancient fort of *Rath Betha*, in the present parish of Rath Beth, in the barony of Galmoy, near Ballyragget, in which Éremón died and was buried'. He was, according to the annals, the first Milesian chief to become King of Ireland and the nineteenth person to hold that title. He had two royal raths built, one at Rathdown, Co. Wicklow, and one at Rathbeagh. The rath at Rathbeagh is really a moat, and according to the *Annals of Clonmacnoise* the place where the first Gaelic King of Ireland is buried. As befitting the royal status of a chief, the mound at Coole between three rivers – namely the Nore, the Owenbeg and the Glashagal – may well be the entombment of Éremón or of another Gaelic chief, but this is open to conjecture. The word *Feoir* in Irish means both a stream and a border, and today between a stream and a border is where this burial mound is today. The Plain of Argetros is roughly between Freshford and Ballyragget. The plain has other historical associations, for it was here that Conall Gulban, ancestor of the O'Donnells, defeated the tribes of West Munster. At an earlier time, around 300 BC, Cionga, the son of the King of 'Western Europe and the Tyrennian Sea', namely Ugaine Mór, received Argetros as part of his kingdom.

The townland of Dunbell Big is five miles south-east of Kilkenny city and three miles north-east from Bennettsbridge [67]. Nineteenth-century accounts of the townland refer to it as Dunbel. Claire Foley, an archaeologist who worked on the site in 1972, says that it has been suggested that the 'bell' in the name may be derived from the Irish word '*bile*', which means a sacred or ancient and venerated tree. This is correct, as they are often also called *Bell* trees or *Bellow* trees. The name of the townland could thus be translated as 'the fort of the sacred tree'. The ring fort which Foley excavated was termed 'Dunbell 6' by her and was an important fort, possibly a chief's residence. It is not discernible on the *Discovery Series*, but for those who are truly interested it is marked on the 1842 edition of the six-inch Ordnance Survey map as a circular platform earthwork. It was situated, according to Foley, 'on the eastern tip of a ridge of dolomite, on the 210 ft. contour, with extensive views of the surrounding countryside and part of the Nore valley'. Given the elevated situation and the status of its inhabitant, the *bile* was probably sited here, and it would thus have been a place of gathering both during pre-Christian and early Christian times for the inauguration of local chiefs and possible seasonal rites.

A seasonal rite occurred every midsummer's day at Callan [67] less than ten miles south from Kilkenny city; this lasted into the nineteenth century and was recorded by Humphrey O'Sullivan of Callan, a schoolteacher who kept a diary, published many years after his death. For 23 June 1827 he wrote, 'The youths and young maidens are dancing around the bonfire', and three years later he wrote,

> There is no bonfire in Callan tonight as a man was killed this time last year at the fire. But from *Cnocán an Éithigh* at the end of the Green I can see many *Sop Seáin* [John's straws] alight. There are flames on every hill and mountain and loud voices to be heard in every glen around strong fires.

Walking three times around these fires, *deis sol* or 'right to the sun', was part of an ancient practice and was said to keep a person healthy for a year. Jumping across the fire was part of a virility rite aimed at impressing the local girls, and it was said that one who could achieve this was assured of a happy marriage.

LAOIS

Laeighis, 'the tribe of Leaighis'

Throughout this book, the Bronze Age (2400–500 BC) represents a period of enlightenment as manifested in the skills of mining, smelting and casting, and in applying those skills to the highest representations of the sun and the moon. Although we do not have a written record of these people, their bronze- and gold-plated objects tell us through their refined art that they had what might be termed a spiritual affinity with the sun and the moon, and that these observable bodies were an important part of their culture.

The Bronze Age hoard discovery at Knockshee, Ballytegan, one mile north of Portlaoise, in 1967 gives ample evidence to the richness of this culture.

The hoard was discovered by a Mr Joseph Smyth while sand was being quarried on his land at Ballytegan [54]; the place of discovery was near the top of a sand and gravel ridge called Knockshee (*Cnoc side*, 'the fairy hill'), and the objects, sixty in all, lay about a foot-and-a-half below the surface in a small pit. They were identified and catalogued by Dr Joseph Raftery, Keeper of the National Museum, who wrote: 'This group of objects from Ballytegan clearly constitutes a significant assemblage and the discovery raises several matters of interest. These include an assessment of the nature of the hoard and the reason for the burial of the objects. It must further be asked what the date of the hoard is and what is the cultural milieu into which it fits.'

Raferty wonders why so many similar Bronze Age hoards have been found throughout Europe and concludes that it is probable that some form of upheaval might have occurred in this period, or that communities in the Late Bronze Age were guarding their precious artefacts against the rise of the warrior culture of the Iron Age.

Five Late Bronze Age sunflower pins found in the hoard are the only ones to have been found in these islands; in Denmark, sixteen pins with decorated heads have been discovered. Thus, Raferty asks the question whether these Irish and Danish pins were made in Ireland under Danish influence or were direct influence from Denmark itself? So far, no mould for a sunflower pin has come to light in Ireland; however, it must be stated that the type with large head and prominent central conical boss surrounded by concentric zones of lightly incised rectilinear ornament appears to be absent in northern Europe and to be, therefore, most likely a native Irish adaptation of a foreign model.

The gold-plated sunflower pin was presumably used as a signal button in cloaks where it represented a sun disc and, apart from its aesthetic appeal, was a testament to a religious affiliation, just as in many cases is the wearing of a cross.

The ridge where the hoard was uncovered lies at a small distance from the Esker Riada (*Eiscir Riada*), a ridge of mounds which in earlier times formed a boundary between *Leth Cuinn* ('Conn's half') and *Leth Moga Nuadu* ('Nuadu's half'), namely, the north and the south of Ireland. The esker in this part of Ireland was known as 'The Ridge of Maryborough' – Maryborough, named after Mary Tudor, being the present day Portlaoise. *Riad* means travelling by chariot or horse, and *Esker Riada* is the 'sand-ridge of chariot driving'. For a long time there was a public road along its top, and today in parts it forms part of the old road between Dublin and Galway. The word 'esker' has its origins in the Gaelic word *escir*, which means a ridge or elevation separating two plains or depressed surfaces.

Along the Esker Riada in Laois is Timahoe (*Tigh Mochua*, 'the church of St Mochua') [55], who died in 657, and here along the same route is an example of the best of Christian architecture, namely the round tower, almost 100 feet high and with its decorated twelfth-century doorway and carvings of bearded men with interlaced hair. The Timahoe sixteenth-century tower house was said to contain two figures, one a *síle na gig* and the other a 'strange figure'; these, however, have fallen down and according to the archaeological inventory for Laois 'may be buried beneath debris'.

According to McMahon and Roberts in their book *The Sheela-na-Gigs of Ireland and Britain*, there are 101 recorded figures in Ireland, though seventeen of these are recorded as 'missing'. There are thirty-eight recorded in England, two in Wales and five in Scotland. We can thus say that they represent evidence of an early cultural history of Britain and Ireland. They are also found in France and possibly further afield. One possible meaning of the term is *Síle na gCíoch* ('Síle of the breasts'). *The Dictionary of the Irish Language* published by the Royal Irish Academy (RIA) fails to include this important woman in its pages, though it does include *cích* as 'pap' or 'female breast'. Dinneen's dictionary refers to the figure as follows: 'a stone fetish representing a woman, supposed to give fertility, generally thought to have been introduced by the Normans'. He also mentions *Síle Ní Ghadhra* ('Síle of the Hounds') as a personification of Ireland; there is a resonance here with the symbol of the Abbey Theatre of a young woman leading hounds. We should also mention that *síl* means seed or sperm, and thus we can begin to understand why Anne Ross in *Pagan Celtic Britain* stated that 'the origins of the Sheelas have eluded scholars' and that 'they are of "indeterminate date"'. The pillar stone at Tara known as St Adamnán's Cross is a *síle na gig* and precedes the Normans by over a millennium; the fact that these figures were secured or 'hidden' in the basement of the National Museum in Dublin bears witness to the prevailing puritanical ethos of Ireland in the nineteenth and early twentieth centuries.

The six *síle na gigs* found in Laois, apart from one found in a graveyard, are associated with tower houses. They are generally placed well above the ground so that, if you were not told where they were, it would be unlikely you would notice them. At Ballaghmore Lower [60] a *síle na gig* is situated on the south-west wall of Ballaghmore Castle at a height of over thirty feet above ground level. This female is carved in bold relief in soft white sandstone and is of local origin. As at Holy Cross Abbey in Tipperary, these figures were said to act as a protection against evil.

At Cullahill Castle in the townland of *Galesquarter* [60] there is a rude carving of a female figure at a height of about forty-three feet; however, if the ivy has not been cleared it remains well covered up and 'respectable'.

A *síle* in Rosenallis [60] among rows of inscribed tombstones found during a graveyard clean-up in 1991 is carved in relief on a sub-rectangular slab. This figure is now in the National Museum of Ireland. The power of the *síle* can be judged by the reaction to two of them at Tinnakill, two miles north-east of Mountmellick, which were built into a farmyard wall close to Tinnakill Castle [54], one reputedly having come from a window jamb in the castle and the other from Portnahinch, a few miles north. According to the owner of the castle and farm, they were broken up by a person or persons unknown and buried. Fortunately, Helen Roe of the RSAI took photographs of them and these photos can be seen in the Laois County Library.

Whereas the person or persons who smashed the *síle na gigs* in Tinnakill took a fundamentalist position, the *Dictionary of Irish Archaeology* takes a different kind of swipe with its tongue-in-cheek description of the figures:

> Sexually explicit female effigy in stone, from the medieval period depicting the Irish male's dream date as a woman who offers instant, no frills sex while bearing a passing resemblance to his mother.

The *síle na gig* is a later version of the *cailleach, who* confers sovereignty on presumptive kings. The sovereignty myth is at the heart of Irish mythology, for unless the king-to-be sleeps with her, he is not a righteous king. After he has slept with this old crone, she turns into a young woman and confers sovereignty; later, as an old man, the king meets a young woman in a wood, and after he sleeps with her, she turns into an old woman and kills him – thus the power of the goddess to confer life and death.

A poem by Patrick Pearse begins:

> *Mise Éire*
> *Sine mé an Chailleach Bhéarra.*
> *Mór mo ghlóir:*

Mé a rug Cú Chulainn cróga.
Mór mo náir
Mo chlann féin a dhíol a máthair …

I am Ireland
Older than the Cailleach Bearra
Great my glory:
I who bore Cú Chulainn the brave.
Great my shame
For my own clan to sell their mother …

Thus, we move in a triad from the *síle* to the *cailleach* and finally to the goddess Ériu, after whom this island is called and whose name means a 'regular traveller of the heavens'. The *síle* is not mentioned in O'Rahilly's *Early Irish History and Mythology*, nor for that matter is the *cailleach*, and the same is true of O'Curry's *Manners and Customs of the Ancient Irish*.

Two miles north-east of Clonaslee (*Cluain na Slí*, 'pasture of the path') [54] are the townlands of Reary Beg and Reary Mór, the site of an ancient battle about which information is vague. It was said (by Joyce in *Irish Names of Places*) to contain an ancient palace, but no remains would appear to exist; the only sign of antiquity is a rocky outcrop with bullaun-type holes. The *Dindshenchas** relates a poem which would seem to say that a battle occurred here between the Echaid, the horse people from Ulster, and the Fianna:*

Róiriu
Nímutánic ó thír thend
Róiriu mac Setnai in sith-chend,
a crích Néil, comul n-ena;
fuair forom féig fían-bera.

Ó condrancatar ind fhir,
síl nEchdach 's na láech-Lagin,
robeótar buidni bána
lasna ruibni rodána.

Dorochair Róiriu, réim rot,
lasna Féine I cét-chomruc,
co fil cen idus, nár mit,
a thirus nímmutánic.

Róiriu
Not luckily came from a strong land

Róiriu mac Setna, the long-headed,
from Niall's country, meeting place of waters;
he met the flight of a soldier's keen spear.

When the warriors met,
the sons of Echaid and the martial Lagin,
they pierced light-skinned troops
with intrepid lances.

Róiriu perished-fierce onset-
by the hands of the Feine, at the first encounter,
so that he was left without comeliness ...
on his enterprise not luckily he came.

[translated by Edward Gwynn]

The name Róiriu, the king of the Echach or horse people, is originally *Ro-Ech* or 'great horseman', and thus we can see Reary preserving in its name one of the many battles between the Echach of Ulster and the Fianna.*

The open land or bogland between Mountrath and Portlaoise was previously known as *Magh Riada* ('the plain of the kings'), as *Laoighis Riada* ('the royal [plain] of Laois') and as *Magh Rath* ('the Plain of the fort'). It was later known as the 'Great Heath of Maryborough'.

Eithrial, grandson of Éremón, the Milesian or Gaelic leader who entered Ireland in the early Christian or late pre-Christian period, was said to have built seven royal forts and to have cleared seven plains of trees, among them *Magh Rath*, which up to that time was controlled by the Uí Echach or horse people. Another battle occurred on the plain of *Magh Rath* at Coirtene where the Leinstermen under Laigsech Ceandmor were victorious against the Munstermen. It is plausible that Laois is named after Laigsech Cendmor, as *Laoighis Riada* was granted to him by Cucorb, a powerful Leinster king, in return for expelling the Munstermen from Leinster. Laigsech Cendmor was said to have been the son of Conall Cernach, one of the leading members of the Uí Echach tribe who came from Co. Down.

LONGFORD

Longphort, 'fortified house'

The name *longford* referred originally to the naval encampments or temporary beachheads of the Viking invaders; the more permanent meaning occurred around the fourteenth century, and in 1430 the *Annals of Ulster* refers to *Senlongphort* or 'old stronghold'. The early name for Longford was *Longphort Uí Fhearghail* ('stronghold of the man of valour', or 'O'Farrell's fortress'). The location of this fortress is a vexed question. However, a fortified house three miles north-west of Edgeworthstown [41] close to the townland of Moat Farrell may supply the answer. This fort, which is at the centre of the O'Farrell clan territory, is even today surrounded by a motte and a moated site, together with twenty ring forts.

Four miles south-west from Longford is *Sliabh calraighe Brí Leith* ('the mountain wood by the fair green') west of the village of Ardagh (*ard achadh*, 'high field'), which is now known as Ardagh Hill [41]. This is one of the most noted mounds or *síde* in our mythology. This mound, which is on half an acre, has connections with gods of the Tuatha Dé Danann,* namely Midir, Aengus and the Dagda.* It is said that Midir lives in the centre of the hill. This was the favourite abode of Midir, who is connected with Etáin in a great romantic tale from mythology. This tale is so complex that it makes *Finnegans Wake* by James Joyce seem straightforward. Apart from Etáin and Midir, we also have the more elusive tale of Brí and Leith, after whom the Irish form of Ardagh Hill is named. And to add to the confusion, we have the following from the *Dindshenchas*:*

Iarsin dochúaid 'na congaib
ingen Midir mór-glonnaig,
co n-érbailt co téith iar tain
túaid I mBrí Léith meic Celtchair.

'Cen co foam, clú cen geis,
mise ocus tú, a Brí co mbreis,
bíd hé do chomainm tréith tall
Brí Léith meic Celtchair Chulann.

The daughter of doughty Midir departed then in her battle-harness, and she died afterward an easy death at Brí Léith meic Celtchair northward.

'Though we mate not, thou and I, O Brí, cause of conflict, fame unforbidden! the place yonder shall bear thy gentle name, Brí of Liath mac Celtchair from Cualu.'

[Translated by Edward Gwynn]

Ardagh Hill is where Aengus, the harper to the gods, was given in fosterage to Midir. When Aengus became a man, he returned to the Boyne Valley where his father, the Dagda,* King of the gods, lived. His mother was the white cow goddess Boand for whom the River Boyne is named.

Midir lived at Brí Léith for a thousand years with his wife Étaín. It has been suggested that the association of gods with earth-mounds goes back to a time of nature worship when these along with rivers, trees and wells were worshipped – a time when the only route to the supernatural was through the natural.

The romance between Étaín and Midir was disrupted by a rival named Fuamnach who cast magic spells on Étaín who was then reborn as the daughter of Étar, King of the horse people. The story of Étaín is told in Old Irish in the romantic saga *Tochmarc Étaíne* or 'The Wooing of Étaín'. It belongs to the Mythological Cycle of Irish tales. Irish and Greek mythology feature the doctrine of rebirth, and since Étaín was reborn several times one can understand why 'The Wooing of Étaín' may appear difficult to comprehend without this prior knowledge. As to how many rebirths Étaín has, is almost impossible to judge, but here are several metamorphoses:

Fuamnach struck Étaín with a magic rod and turned her into a pool of water. The heat of the air and the earth turned the water into a worm, and the worm became a purple fly. Then Fuamnach became jealous of the fly and drove her away by causing a magic wind which carried her onto the rocks and waves of the sea. Then after seven years she alighted onto the breast of Aengus. He carried her about in a sunlit cage of crystal, but Fuamnach dispelled her again so that she arrived in Ulster and fell into the cup of the King's wife and the wife swallowed the fly and Étaín was reborn as the daughter of Étar, King of Ulster.

Swallowing a worm was a motif used in many royal births; in the case of Deichtine, daughter of Conchobar mac Nessa, 'a small creature slipped into her mouth with the liquid'. The motif here obscured the fact that the relationship between daughter and father was incestuous. Incest also comes into the story of Étaín; when Eochaid Airem, King of Ireland and another suitor of the irrepressible Étaín, set out to find Étaín he attacked Brí Léith. Fifty women identical to Étaín arrived, and the one he chose was another Étaín, namely his daughter. The resulting child, a daughter, was put out to die, but a herdsman found her and she survived. Later she married Etarscéle, King of Ireland, and became mother of Conaire, the protagonist in the saga known as the 'The Destruction of Da Derga's Hostel', a saga from the Ulster Cycle (see *Dublin* and *Wicklow*).

Myles Dillon writes of 'The Wooing of Étaín',

> as the finest of the stories from the mythological cycle, of which we have a ninth-century text. There is a strange beauty here which is perhaps unequalled in any other Irish story, the temper of love, the power of magic and a happy ending … Irish women were the vehicles by which the dead were reborn in generation after generation. The human husband has no spiritual role.

The following is a description of Étaín from one particular manuscript:

> *Bui ri amra airegda for Éiren, Eochaidh Fedleach a ainm, do luidfeacht; nann dar aenach mBreg Leith conaccai inmnai for ur in tobair, achas cirr, chuirrel argit conecor deor, achte oc folcud alluing argit, acas ceithri heoin oir for ri, acas gleoir-gemai beccai dicharrmogul chorcrai hiforfhlescuib na luingi. Brat cas corcra foloichain aichte; dualldai airgoidi ecoirside deor oibínnu ísibratt. Lene lebur culpatach isi chotut le mor deisitiu uainide foderginliud oirimpi. Tuagmila ingantai dior acas airget for a bruindi, acas a formnaib, acas a guallib isindlene dicachleith. Taitned fria ingrian cobbasdearg dona feraib tuidlech indoir frisin ngrein isin titiu uaindi. Da trilis norbuidi for a cind, fhige*

ceithrinduail ceachtarnde acas mell for rind cach duail ba cosmail leo. Dath ind foilt sin fri barr nailestair hiramrad, no fri deagor iar ndhenam a datha. Is and bui oc taithbiuch a fuilt dia fulcad, acas a dalaim tria derc asedlaig immach.

The following translation is by O'Curry from his *Manners and Customs of the Ancient Irish*:

There was an admirable, illustrious king over Ireland whose name was *Eochaidh Fedleach*. He on one occasion passed over the fair green at *Bri Leith*, where he saw a woman on the brink of a fountain, having a comb and a casket (*Cuirel*) of silver, ornamented with gold, washing her head in a silver basin with four birds of gold perched upon it, and little sparkling gems of crimson carbuncle (*Carrmogul*) upon the outer edges of the basin. A short, crimson cloak, with a beautiful gloss, lying near her; a *Dualldai* or brooch of silver, inlaid with sparkles of gold, in that cloak. A smock, long and warm, gathered and soft, of green silk, with a border of red gold, upon her; wonderful clasps of gold and of silver at her breast, and at her shoulder blades, and at her shoulders in that smock, on all sides. The sun shone upon it, while the men were all shaded in red, from the reflection of the gold against the sun, from the green silk. Two yellow golden tresses upon her head, each of them plaited with four locks or strands, and a ball of gold upon the point of each tress. The colour of that hair was like the flowers of the bog firs in the summer, or like red gold immediately after receiving its colouring. And there she was disentangling her hair, and her two arms out through the bosom of her smock.

We therefore see Étaín as sovereignty conferring kingship on three kings and giving birth to another high king, Conaire. She is always regarded as a beautiful young woman: 'All are lovely till compared with Étaín. All are fair till compared with Étaín.' This is a picture of the goddess untampered by neither Christian nor Gaelic influence; the goddess in this saga is not referred to as a 'hag' or a 'witch' or a 'crone'; she is fresh, sensual, beautiful and eternal. Her story is a tale of pre-Christian and pre-Gaelic Ireland and as such is possibly the greatest record we have from this part of our ancient past. This goddess has survived as the witness to a world still offering sustenance to poets and scholars and, perhaps more importantly, to all those who see in nature a link to our rich past.

Eight miles south-east from Ardagh is Clonbrin [41], noted for the Clonbrin Shield, a thick disc of leather less than two feet in width and in height. It was discovered in 1909 by Alexander Fry who came across it when cutting turf nine feet below the level of the bog at Clonbrin. It was brought to the owner of the bog, a Colonel King-Harman, who presented it to the Royal Irish Academy for their collection, which is preserved in the National Museum of Ireland in Dublin. The shield is made of a solid piece of leather about a quarter of an inch thick and was probably taken from the chest of a mature bull. It resembles a circular bronze shield found in Germany at Bingen on the south side of the Rhine between Mainz and Wiesbaden and two bronze shields of similar type found near Magdeburg, north Germany. A similar shield in bronze was found at Halland in southern Sweden.

It has been argued that all bronze shields of the round boss type had backings of leather. It was therefore thought that the Clonbrin Shield was the leather lining of a bronze one. However, according to E.C.R. Armstrong, its slightly oblong shape, the thickness of the leather, the lacing of the boss and the turning of the coarse side of the skin to the back all point to the shield as being complete in itself, but possibly copied from a metal shield. The indentations at the side of the German, Swedish and Clonbrin shields allowing access to the boss have been suggested as of 'magical import connected with the solar associations of these shields'. This gives us a vague but useful insight into the use of sympathetic magic in the affairs of war and life both here and in Germany and Sweden, and presumably throughout Europe.

A description from 'The Wooing of Étaín' describes one of Étaín's lovers as having 'a spear in one hand and a shield in the other with a white boss and ornament of gold'. The shield from Clonbrin had a central hemispherical shield boss laced to the shield with leather thongs. This served to protect the owner's hand. Surrounding the boss are three raised concentric oval ribs which follow the margin of the shield. It has been classified as an example of a prehistoric leather shield, in other words possibly an Iron Age possession of someone belonging to the warrior caste.

This shield may have been used in battle on *Dún Claidhe* ('earthen rampart'), which served as a frontier defence between the kingdoms of Brefny and Annaly, extending from Lough Gowna to Lough Kinale, a distance of six miles. The kingdom of *Angaile* (Annaly) was the tribal name of the Conmaicne sept of Uí Fearghail, the centre of their territory being in Longphort Uí Fearghail, as mentioned above, and so was *Caille Salaigh*, also known as *Brí Léith* west of Ardagh, mentioned above. The O'Farrells were thus the hereditary chiefs of Longford. A large part of this ancient entrenchment can still be seen one mile north-east of Granard [34].

On the north side of this entrenchment, known in Longford as the Black Pig's Race but in Cavan and Leitrim as the Black Pig's Dyke, was the kingdom of Brefny, which covered the present-day counties of Leitrim and Cavan. The O'Rourkes and the O'Rahillys controlled these lands, and the the Black Pig's Race is a living testament to the struggles between these clans.

The Black Pig's Dyke (*Claí na Muice Duibhe*) apparently was a continuous entrenchment from the Newry Valley along the southern borders of Armagh and Monaghan, as well as some fragmentary portions which are still extant in Cavan, Longford and Leitrim and went all the way to Bundoran and the Atlantic seaboard. It may be more technically termed a linear earthwork. It was also known as the Worm Ditch, the Dane's Cast and, in Longford, as the Duncla (*Dún Claí*, 'the fort of the earthen embankment'). This fortification once formed a continuous frontier which defined the southern boundary of Ulster possibly during the Iron Age (500 BC–400 AD). This great wall of Ulster was a line of defence for the Cruithin* or the Dál nAraide, now more generally known as the Ulaid. The Black Pig's

Dyke has been compared with the Wall of Antoninus running from the Clyde to the Forth, and to Hadrian's Wall running from Carisle to Wallsend-on-Tyne. Unlike Hadrian's Wall, the Black Pig's Dyke was never constructed out of stone and cement, though the structure was often strengthened with wooden piles.

The fragmentary portion of the dyke in Longford extends from Dring (*Drong*, 'a large gathering'), a village at the south-east of Lough Gowna [34], and six miles south-east to Lough Kinale. The direction of the dyke or 'race' is given on *Discovery* map 34. Although the fortification is delineated as a continuous line, it is unlikely that the remaining fragments are easy to discern or even that they exist at all. However, some evidence for their existence can be shown particularly on Longford's part of the jigsaw. The word 'dyke' refers to a ditch or fosse and bank. The Duncla in its travels from Lough Gowna to Lough Kinale may have started with a passage along the beach at Lough Gowna, but 'the dyke is visible as far as the shorebank' (Davies 1955); whether this is still so fifty years later would need to be verified. The dyke's western section travels through the townlands of Dring, Carrickduff and Clogh (O.S. Longford 6" Sheets 6 and 10), and follows the base of a shallow valley and consists of a wide ditch with two banks. After Clogh we approach Dalystown bog, and from here, according to Davies, the travelling earthwork 'may be traced fairly continuously to Lough Kinale'.

The purpose of the Irish dykes, according to Davies, was to 'concentrate traffic at defined crossings'. A possible reason for this was to safeguard territory against cattle raiding. If the only crossing was at fortified crossings which were defended, it would be difficult to engage in raids. To what extent the dyke curbed such raids is difficult to know.

At a more artistic level, Yeats included a poem on the dyke in his collection, *The Wind among the Reeds* (1899):

The Valley of the Black Pig

> The dews drop slowly and dreams gather: unknown spears
> Suddenly hurtle before my dream-awakened eyes,
> And then the clash of fallen horsemen and the cries
> Of unknown perishing armies beat about my ears.
> We who still labour by the cromlech on the shore,
> The grey cairn on the hill, when the day sinks drowned in dew,
> Being weary of the world's empires, bow down to you,
> Master of the still stars and of the flaming door.

Could 'The Wooing of Étaín' have connections with the great oak road built through the bog at Corlea [40], which was excavated in 1985? In order to win Étaín as his bride, Midir had, among other things, to clear twelve plains, to cut down forests and to build a causeway across the moors; one of these plains was by *Brí Léith*. And here Midir built a causeway, 'and into the bottom of this causeway all the men of the world were pouring a forest with its trunks and its roots'. Étaín in one of her earthly guises lived with Eochaid Airem, King of Ireland around 134 BC, and the road, according to archaeological records, was built around 148 BC, establishing both the tale and the road as almost contemporaneous during the Iron Age.

One could also, of course, propose a more 'reasoned' explanation for this Iron Age roadway, which would be that in prehistoric times the bogs were dangerous places with stagnant pools and waterlogged fen woods. Also, the growth of bogs from about 3000 BC was making travel hazardous. Barry Raftery in *Pagan Celtic Ireland* describes the Corlea Road as the 'Road to God knows where'. He writes:

> Before [excavation] timbers from the roadway had been exposed by the harvesting machines and sent off to Belfast for dendrochronological analysis. All the examples pointed consistently to a tree-felling date of 148BC. It thus seemed evident that the road had been constructed in a single phase. This was the first time that a trackway in Ireland had been dated to the Iron Age.

Corlea, six miles north-west from Ballymahon, has a marvellous heritage centre which has part of the conserved road on display and connects the great mythological tale to serious Iron Age construction and planning. The road was a little more than a mile in length, and

FIGURE 14. Iron Age roadway made of oak at Corlea.

200 to 300 large oak trees were needed to supply the wood for the surface and at least as many birches were used for the substructure, which was necessary to prevent subsidence of the upper oak timbers. Most of the thousands of pegs required to stabilise the timbers were of birch, though some were of oak.

According to Raftery, 'the road at Corlea was no ordinary road. It was quite different from the brushwood tracks of earlier times, which generally served as little more than footpaths across the bogs for the local farming communities ... Corlea is in fact among the largest of its kind in prehistoric Europe.' He adds that a roadway over peatland in Dümmer, south of Oldenberg in Germany, has trackways 'startlingly similar in all details of construction to that of Corlea'.

One would think that such a prestigious road would have the indentations of wheeled carts, but no such indentations are visible, as has been found in the German tracks. The Corlea Road was incomplete, and an attempt was made to destroy it as many of the timbers there were burnt. What was the function of this trackway? Seven miles away, at the modern village of Lanesborough [40], there was an ancient crossing across the Shannon, and about fifteen miles to the north-west is Cruachain, the royal centre of Connacht, and at the same distance south-east is Uisneach, known as the navel of Ireland and a centre dedicated to Balor, the sun god. Thus, one can conjecture that Corlea was part of a ritual path between ceremonial centres. Raftery has even postulated it as a toll road linking such centres of reverence. Between myth and reason lie religion and an open space for limitless conjecture.

Although similar sites have been identified in Co. Offaly, Co. Roscommon and Co. Tipperary, Corlea has remained the most important trackway site. Four miles north-west from Corlea is the trackway at Derraghan More, which was also part of a bog road and, like Corlea, was constructed of oak planks laid over large volumes of brushwood. The road at Derraghan was also radiocarbon-dated to the Iron Age and possibly built at the same time as Corlea. Other trackways in Longford date back to the Bronze Age and beyond, to the Neolithic period when farming began.

Barry Raftery writes that Corlea 'is the largest of its type in prehistoric Europe', and he adds that

> the road ... is a dramatic development in the means of crossing the marshy wastes and this might have been intended as a major highway in second century BC Ireland. It could well have been part of a wider communications network. Such roads imply the existence of wheeled vehicles. The widespread use of the horse during Iron Age times was also a significant development, for the horse, whether ridden or used in draught, increased appreciably the speed and comfort of human land transport. Horsepower is in fact as much as ten times faster than transport by oxen (which existed in Ireland from the early Neolithic). The horse must have acquired an increasingly high status in society, and the mounted warrior would have enjoyed an exalted position in the contemporary social hierarchy.

A stump of an ash tree has been described as a runner on the Corlea Road and regarded as zoomorphic, but it more likely represents a phallus, which was frequently found in standing stones from the Iron Age and specifically in the *Lia Fail* or 'stone of destiny' at Tara. This was possibly seen as a source of inspiration and power in the building of the road. The phallus represented reproduction, growth and fertility.

On the north arm of Lough Ree, on the River Shannon, is an island known as Inchcleraun (*Inis Clothrand*, 'the island of Clothru') [40]. Clothru reigned as queen of Connacht and administered the law from the island, which was also called 'the Seven Church Island'. One church, known as *Teampall Diarmaid*, with fragments of a Romanesque gateway, survives. It is situated within an impressively large ring fort.

Clothru was a sister of the famous Medb* of Connacht, and she was pregnant with a child by Conchobar mac Nessa, the King of Ulster at the beginning of the Christian era. Had this child been born, Conchobar would have had his line and kingdom extend to Connacht, but Medb was against such a possibility and had Clothru's child cut from his mother's womb. As a result of this, Clothru died but her child survived. His name was Furbaide Ferbenn mac Conchobair, and he is associated with the church mentioned above.

Furbaide means 'excised' or 'cut', and so it was that Furbaide got his name from his traumatic birth. The 'ferbenn' part of his name means 'man of horns', which were the two horns of silver and gold he had on his helmet.

Medb,* having disposed of Clothru, became Queen of Connacht. A site on Inchcleraun associated with Medb is a small cashel known as *Grianán Medbha*, 'the sunhouse of Medb'. This *grianán* is situated on the highest part of the island and thus favourably placed for the sun. Medb was under a *geis* or injunction to bathe every morning at the east side of this island, and while doing so was approached by Furbaide who placed a piece of hard cheese in his sling and hurled it at her. Another version is that he put a stone in his *crann-tabaill* or sling, and the cheese or stone went through her forehead and into her head, killing her. Thus Furbaide, son of Clothru, avenged his mother's death.

Although Furbaide never became King of Connacht, he was sufficiently recognised for legend to say that he was buried at the highest hill in north Longford, namely *Sliab Cairpri*, wedged in between Co. Cavan and Co. Leitrim. This hill was also known as *Sliab Uillind*. As to the exact location of this hill, a number of possibilities have been given; one, according to Hogan, is at the tallest hill in north Longford mentioned above at 686 feet high. But there are no cairns shown here, only a triangulation station, although it is possible that this, like so many others, was placed on top of a cairn [34]. Another possibility is Carn townland [41], two miles south of Ardagh or the ancient *Brí Léith*; however, Carn has simply a ring fort on a slight elevation. Another possibility is Corn Hill [34], which has two marked cairns; it is fifteen miles north-east from Inchcleraun and would appear to me to be the most likely burial place of Furbaide.

A poem, 'Carn Furbaide', in the Metrical *Dindshenchas* begins:

Atá sund Carn uí Chathbath
fors'rimred arm imathlam,
lechtán láechda laích col-lí,
fertán fráechda Furbaidi.

Here stands the carn of Cathbad's grandson against whom a nimble weapon was wielded; Furbaide's heath-clad grave, martial monument of a glorious soldier.

[Translated by Edward Gwynn]

Furbaide was fostered by Cú Chulainn,* who was either his half-brother or cousin. An alternative version is that Furbaide was the son of Ethne, Clothru's sister, and that she was slain by Lugaid trí-ríab-nderg. However, this version is incorrect, although mentioned in the poem above. Lugaid is said to have slain Furbaide at the crest of Corn Hill and to have made the cairn to Furbaide with a stone from every man who was in Lugaid's company.

LOUTH

Lugh, 'a hollow'

Although Louth is sometimes associated with the sun god and god of crafts, Lug,* I have kept with the custom of naming a place in accordance with its natural attributes and thus translated *Lugh* as 'a hollow'.

Mullameelan (*Mullach Maoláin*, 'flat-topped hillock') is less than a mile south of Ardee [36] on the N2, wherein from the left side of the road is a drystone-built souterrain forty-two feet in length and consisting of three passages aligned east–west. According to the late John Boyle of Kilmessan, Gerald Fitzgerald, a general in Hugh O'Neill's army, has often been seen coming from this souterrain. He is leading his horse and dressed in the old Irish costume with breastplate and carrying a spear. The local name for the hill above the souterrain is Mollyellen.

Doolargy (*Dúleargaidh*, 'black hillside') Mountain [36] in the Cooley Range has associations with the great Irish epic, the *Táin Bó Cúailgne*,* which will be discussed in the following pages, but first we shall look at the phenomenon of sweathouses, a number of which can be found in the townland of Ballymackellett in the lower reaches of Doolargy. Sweathouse is a literal translation of the Irish *Teach an Alluis*. The ancient use of medicines and poisons are closely connected to religion, so that in early times successful practitioners of medicine were raised to the level of a divinity after their death. Irish mythology has Dian Cécht as Greek has Aesculapius, who appears in Homer as an excellent physician and in the later legends becomes a god of healing. His temples, like the sweathouses, stood on hillsides and near running water. The Irish sweathouse is a simplified version of the healing temples of ancient Greece and Imperial Rome, and was in common use among the early Irish and lasted until the middle of the nineteenth century. A scholar of such sweathouses relates how 'what are called "Turkish" baths in Ireland and Great Britain are named as "Roman-Irish" baths in Germany and Bohemia'. He saw baths designated *Romische-Irische Bader* in 1879 at Prague as well as at Nuremburg. The Irish sweathouse was generally of beehive shape, covered with clay and with a low entrance. They were made of stone and were as far as possible airtight. The chamber was heated by filling it with turf and igniting the fuel; this fire was maintained until the 'stones were red'. The top opening of the house was closed, and the inside of the house was doused with water, putting the fire out and filling the chamber with steam. When a patient entered the house, the door was closed by means of a temporary screen. Inside the humid air was said to assist the sufferer. On leaving the sweathouse, the perspiring patient was plunged into a nearby pool or stream and as often as not was then returned to the warmth of the sweathouse. There is a marked similarity with the present sauna baths of Scandinavia, the main difference being that people from Scandinavia take the baths to refresh themselves whereas in Ireland they were used mainly as a cure for respiratory illnesses such as asthma, bronchitis, pneumonia and tuberculosis, as well as offering relief from rheumatism

S.F. Milligan, who pursued the study of the sweathouse in several counties, says, 'The hot air bath was known over many parts of this country as a cure for rheumatism. In the localities where the English and the Scottish settlers were in the majority it fell into disuse; but amongst the Irish speaking inhabitants its value was fully known and appreciated.'

The position of the houses on Doolargy Mountain made it easier to transport the large amount of turf required from the bogs on the upper reaches of the mountain, and the houses were generally placed near a mountain stream. There are seven sweathouses in the Doolargy area, in all. In more recent times, many of them have been used to house animals; indeed, they could be mistaken for farm buildings except for the blackened walls. The dimensions of one of the houses at Doolargy are as follows: door, thirty-six inches high by twenty-two inches wide; walls, fifteen inches thick; interior, seventy-nine inches high, sixty-six inches wide. The height of the building is above average; the width of the interior would mean that the patient was probably in a seated position.

Further up from Doolargy is Averna (*Áth na bhFearnaí*, 'the ford of the alders') Mountain, where there is a sweathouse that is smaller than usual and may have been used to treat children.

As with many of our saints, Brigit was originally a goddess. She is said to have been born near Faughart Upper [36]. The ruins of an ancient church can be found there as well as a holy well named after her. A hawthorne tree beside the well is covered with articles of clothing, a custom associated with magical practices. Brigit left Faughart and established a community at Kildare. She is associated with fire and her emblem, 'Brigit's Cross', is a sun symbol. Part of the ancient track that she walked along on her way south is still preserved west of Castletown in Dundalk.

According to the antiquarian Sir James Ware, 'She was born at Fochard, in the county of Louth, and was the fruit of an unlawful amour between her father Dubtach – a man of considerable rank in his country – and her mother, Brocessa or Brotseach, whom he had purchased for his servant.' Dubtach's wife, seeing or hearing that Brotseach was pregnant, ordered Dubtach to discharge Brotseach, and a poet bought her and brought her to Ulster where she 'was delivered of this saint'. This last sentence casts doubt on Faughart as the birthplace of Brigit but leaves no doubt to her being conceived there. Two dates are given for her birth: one is 439 and the other is 468.

The earliest name under which Faughart was known was *Ard Aignech in Cronech* or 'the 'height of the district of the swift [horses]'. According to the *Annals of Ulster*, 'the heathens defeated the community of Ard Macha in a battle at Aignig, and great numbers of them were taken captive'. This occurred in 831 AD, and in that same year, the annals say, that Conaille, which was close by, was 'invaded by the heathens and Máel Brigte, its king, and his brother Canannán were taken prisoner and taken away to the ships'. One is tempted to ask who these 'heathens' were. The Irish word used was *genntib*, which was employed to describe Norsemen, and the fact that ships were mentioned would seem to support the fact that these were the invaders.

This part of Louth as far south as the Boyne Estuary (*Inber Colptha*) up to the year 332 AD belonged to Ulster under the 'Horse tribes', later known as the Clanna Rudhraighe from Fergus Ro Ech or 'great horseman'. Their descendants today are known as the Mac Rorys.

It was on the plains of Faughart that Conchobar mac Nessa sent Cú Chulainn* to catch wild horses and to harness them prior to the Battle of Rossnaree (Co. Meath). In the time straddling the Christian Age there were large droves of wild horses, and these were caught and trained for battle; being able to break in horses was regarded as a 'hero feat'. It is no wonder therefore that the cattle raid described in the great Irish epic, the *Táin Bó Cúailnge** ('The cattle raid of Cuailnge'), took place in the territory of this stock-raising people. It was here that Cú Chulainn met Medb,* the Queen of Connacht, who was leading the cattle-spoil of Cúailnge. Before the meeting, Cú Chulainn had killed many of Medb's men, and Medb decided to arrange a meeting with the Ulster warrior and at the same time to lay an ambush for him. Fourteen men lay in wait for him, but he killed them all. Thus, the new name for the territory became Focherd from *fo* meaning 'good' and *cherd* meaning 'feat'.

Faughart was the headquarters for Medb's* army, where Cú Chulainn* came to attack them from his fort at *Dún Delca*, a little over a mile to the east. A few hundred years later, in 248 AD, Cormac mac Airt, grandson of Conn of the Hundred Battles, fought a battle here, presumably against the Ulaid or Ulstermen.

There are several ring forts in Faughart: three in Faughart Lower and four in Faughart Upper. Many of these can be seen from the Hill of Faughart. There are also souterrains, a *fulacht fiadh* and a motte to the west of the hill. There is a megalithic tomb half-a-mile south-west in the townland known as Connachtman's Corner.

As so many places in Louth are associated with Cú Chulainn,* we shall start by describing his fort at Castletown which, was known as *Dún Delca* and gave its name to the town of Dundalk to the east [36]. The fort is still referred to as 'Cú Chulainn's Castle' by local people. It may originally have been a tumulus, as suggested by Edmund Hogan in his *Onomasticon Goedelicum*. As in the case of Millmount (see below), the original fort at Castletown had a motte and bailey added to it by the Normans towards the end of the twelfth century. In the late eighteenth century, a pirate named Patrick Byrne built a castle on top of the mound, which is rightly regarded as a folly. Cú Chulainn, being a son or foster son of the King of Ulster, Conchobar mac Nessa, had a third of the territory of Ulster, his territory extending from the Hill of Uisneach to the centre of Baile Strand, Dundalk Bay. His fort at Castletown had a commanding view of his lands, and the view from *Dún Delca* remains truly impressive today.

A souterrain is set into the south side of the Norman motte. The souterrain consists of three drystone-built passages, all connected in a 'Z' shape and extending to about sixty feet. To the north-east of *Dún Delca* is a standing stone known as the *Lia Lingadon* or 'the stone of Lingadon', the herder of the cows of Deichtine, daughter of Conchobar mac Nessa and mother of Cú Chulainn.* The traditional account of this stone is that it is the brooch that was dropped there by Finn mac Cumhail's* mother on her way to Slieve Gullion, and that from this brooch, *Dún Dealgan* (*dealg Fhinn*) takes its name. This is a common trope in the storyteller's yarn, where all stones of note were dropped by the *cailleacha* on their various flightpaths. *Dún Delca* or *Dún Delga* may mean 'the fort of the pegs' upon which shields were hung or more likely 'the fort of the pin', meaning that the ground was originally encircled by a noted woman or goddess with a pin or fibula in a founding ritual.

After Cú Chulainn's* death, his body was brought back from Knockbridge on the plain of Muirthemne and his head was brought back from Tara where it had been used as a football. His wife Emer placed the body and head together on the green at Dún Delca and sang the lay:

> I know where my heart is
> O Cú Chulainn of the middle plain,
> No longer will your face be bloodstained,
> Once I have washed your head.
> Behold there a beloved mouth
> Ice-cold to the kiss, as is said of dead warriors.
> Alas for the smile that spread across your cheeks
> Let not the void diminish your deeds.

Cú Chulainn* died at Knockbridge, three miles south-west from Dundalk in the townland of Rathiddy. A standing stone here is about ten feet in height and a little over three feet in width. Locally this stone is pronounced as 'Cloghafarmore', that is *Cloch an Fhir Mhóir*, or 'the stone of the big man', presumably meaning big in the heroic sense, as Cú Chulainn was at most of average size.

One of Medb's* warriors, Lugaid mac Con Rí, threw a lance which struck Cú Chulainn* between his loin and his navel so that his entrails flowed out by his feet. Laeg, his charioteer, saw this and tended to him, and Cú Chulainn requested that Laeg bring him to the

> great pillar stone that is over there yonder, it is there that I shall die. Arrange my sword, the *Crúaidín Cadutchenn*, and put my shield and my spear close to each other. And if the men of Ireland see me in the distance, fear will not allow them to come and behead me; and tell Conall of all this.

When they came to the pillar stone Laeg tied his chest to the pillar and placed his hand towards his heart and adjusted him. When the men of Ireland saw that he was dead, Medb* commanded that he be beheaded, the act being carried out by Lugaid mac Con Rí, who took his head back to Tara.

Beheading the enemy was a custom among the warrior class, who kept the head as a trophy and in order to keep the soul of the dead warrior close by and to protect it. The Ulster warriors believed that the soul was contained in the brain rather than in the heart.

FIGURE 15. The Cloghfarmore stone at Knockbridge (Carole Cullen).

Macalister in *The Archaeology of Ireland* states that 'the skull was the seat of the soul'. Thus, heads hanging from the leather girdle around the waist of a warrior served as both a trophy and a sign that the hero was protecting the spirit of the slain enemy. In the first century BC, when Cú Chulainn* was born, the Greek stoic philosopher Posidonius remarked that this custom existed inland from Marseilles, 'where human heads hanging at the house-doors for trophies were an everyday sight'.

Local legend has it that in the same field as the *Cloch an Fhir Mhóir* there was a pool known as *Lochán in Tonaigh* ('the pool of the washing'); it was here that Cú Chulainn* washed himself before going to the pillar stone. The crossroads at Knockbridge is three miles south-west from Dundalk on the R171; the standing stone associated with Cú Chulainn at Rathiddy can be seen half-a-mile before the crossroads from the left side of the road on the summit of a slight rise in gently undulating countryside.

It is likely that Cú Chulainn* and Emer are buried less than half-a-mile south-west of *Dún Delca* in the townland of Lisnawilly (*liss na bhile*, 'the ringfort of the sacred tree or *bile*') [36], where there are two standing stones facing each other. The sacred tree in a notable ring fort close to Cú Chulainn's castle would have been a gathering place on special occasions for the Ulaid, and thus is the closest place of veneration most likely to have been chosen by Emer. As his body was still on the ground at *Dún Delca*, Emer composed a lay, which was answered by Conall Cernach, and Emer then asked that 'the body of the battle warrior be buried now'. She then requested that Conall make a broad and extensive grave for Cú Chulainn so that there would be room for herself, as was fitting for a lawful spouse.

Part of Emer's lament for Cú Chulainn is as follows:

O hand, O disfigured hand
whilst we were healthy
often was it placed under my head
O sweet to my neck his hand.

O head, O disfigured head
since you crossed the water
many times I have soothed
many the beatings this head has taken.

O eye, O blemished eye
always spirited and loving
identical will be our grave
dug equal for both of us.

Oh, for the summer days or a tree,
By a stream

Today I will not lift my head.
There will be no rejoicing only sorrow,
Och, O hand.

The 'Bull of Cooley', the target of the cattle raid launched by Medb,* was kept at Lissachiggel (*Lios-a'-tsiogail*, 'the fort of the rye') [36]. On the Ordnance Survey Map of Co. Louth (OS 4:12:6) and in the Archaeological Inventory of County Louth, it is found under the heading 'Ringforts' and is placed as one of Doolargy's nine ringforts; within the Inventory it is numbered 608. It is five miles north-east of Dundalk, and the easiest approach is by Cadger's Road from Ravensdale.

The fort appears to be composed of dry walling, but excavation in 1940 showed that it has a core of gravely clay. It was found to contain more than a dozen small huts, circular or sub-rectangular in plan. According to Evans in *Prehistoric and Early Christian Ireland*, these huts were 'probably roofed with timbers supported by sod walls; there were no post holes. Most of the huts had hearths and occupation debris containing potsherds, worked flints, glass beads, ox bones and fragments of iron and copper'.

Two miles south from Doolargy is *Ochaine* or Trumpet Hill [36] in the territory of *Conaille Muirthemne*. *Ochaine* was the name given to King Conchobar mac Nessa's shield. Here Cú Chulainn* threw rocks at the forces of Medb's* invading army on their way to Lissachiggel. *Ochaine* is 145 metres above the ground overlooking Dundalk Bay from the north. It was here, while Cú Chulainn was between *Ochaine* and the sea watching a flock of birds, that Lebarcham, a member of the court of Conchobar mac Nessa, came to plead with him to quell the noise of the oncoming army without engaging in single combat. However, Cú Chulainn did not heed the plea and fought Nath Crantail, one of Queen Medb's warriors. Nath Crantail arrived for battle 'with nine sharp and charred avenging holly arrows with him'. They fought by two large stones at *Ochaine*, and Cú Chulainn threw his spear so high into the air that it came down through Nath Crantail's head.

The stones around which they supposedly fought was, according to the owner of the land, blown up by an ancestor in the eighteenth century, but there the remnants still exist *in situ*. Where they lie is on private land, so you must get permission for entry from the owner.

Writing in 1906 Henry Morris equates *Áth Luain* ('the ford of Luan') with Luachainn, the ancient name for the river estuary about Dundalk. He further states that this was possibly the name for the open meadows and the unreclaimed land between the Blackrock Road and the sea. These open meadows were locally known as 'Low-kers' and pronounced as 'Lö-a-kers', which he equates with *luachrach* or an area covered in rushes. At the turn of the twentieth century Morris had not the same material that is available today; the great German tradition of translating our early sagas had not been fully assimilated by Irish scholars. *Áth Luain* is mentioned in the *Táin*,* but as a dividing area between Connacht and Meath, and is known today as Athlone in Westmeath. Hogan translates *Áth Luain* as 'the ford of Luan (son of Lugaid)'.

Two miles west from Carlingford and south of the Táin Way is a mountain associated with Queen Medb,* namely Barnavave (*Bearna meidhbhe*, 'Medb's Gap') [36]. Barnavave is 1,148 feet above sea level, and according to Paul Gosling writing in the *Journal of the County Louth Archaeological and History Society* (Vol. 27, No. 4, 2012): 'When viewed from the coastal plain to the south or south east, it presents a most remarkable appearance. From this aspect the summit is seen to be riven by a giant U-shaped cleft, for all the world as if an enormous bite has been taken out of the mountain top.' Barnavave Mountain is included in P.W. Joyce's *Irish Names of Places* as *Bearna-Mheidhbhe*, and he says Medb has been commemorated in this name since the first century; if so, it seems to have evaded folk consciousness for almost two millennia. However, it is fitting that she should have a mountain named after her, given the number of place names connected to the *Táin** in the vicinity and Medb's role in the saga as one of the main actors.

The tragic climax of *Táin Bó Cúailnge** is Cú Chulainn's* fight with his foster brother Fer Diad, who was among the many warriors from Ulster used by Medb* to increase her territorial ambitions. This single combat between these two great warriors on the River Dee, in which Fer Diad is finally slain by Cú Chulainn, is one of the great sagas from early European literature. There is a detailed description of the protracted battle and of the weapons used, and this bears comparison with Homer's description in the *Iliad* of the single combat between Achilles and Hector. Indeed, the *Táin* itself may well have had a historical core surrounded by legend and myth from an earlier era.

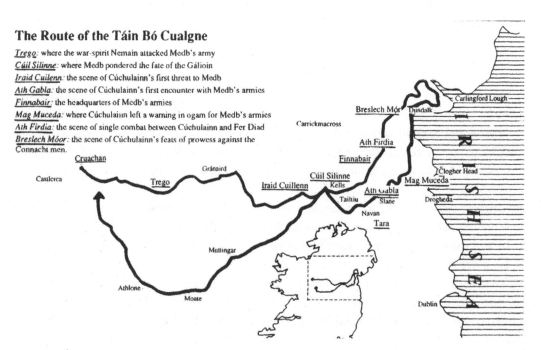

FIGURE 16. The *Táin* route – from *A Guide to Irish Mythology* by Daragh Smyth.

An aspect of the tragic nature of this single combat is that neither warrior wished to fight the other. Fer Diad resisted the goadings of Medb* until she called for satirists, druids and inciters to revile him and to raise blisters of misfortune, insult and disgrace upon his face. Thus, for the sake of his honour Fer Diad agreed to the contest but said: 'About the contest and fight with the hero tomorrow; I would prefer if it were with anyone else rather than with him' (*im chomlond im chomrac arnabárach. Ná im chomlond im chomrac ra Coin Culaind a oenur dambad assu leiss*).

When they meet, Cú Chulainn says:

> We were with Scáthach,
> where we learnt the craft of arms,
> where together we rode about
> and traversed through each camp.
>
> You my heart's companion,
> you my kith and kin,
> I had not realised before, beloved,
> how sorrowful your loss would be.

To which Fer Diad replies:

> Let you leave honour aside
> so that we may be battling.
> Before the cock crows
> your head will be on a stake.
>
> O Cú Chulainn from Cooley,
> frenzy and affliction have taken hold of you,
> since each tide of woe stretches before you.

Fer Diad was reputedly buried close to where he fell, and a rectangular mound was erected over his grave. This mound was recorded as being in existence in 1836; measuring forty-three feet long and just under ten feet wide, it was on the south side of the river, about 500 yards west of Ardee [36]. The site was known as 'Ferdia's grave' and is in a townland known as Townparks. Unfortunately, this site is now levelled without a visible surface trace. Ardee gets its name from Fer Diad, as the Irish form of the name is *Áth Fhir Diad* ('the ford of Fer Diad'). The epic battle between the two heroes is commemorated today by a fine sculpture facing the river from the road.

Millmount Fort [43] is a high mound on the south side of the River Boyne in the town of Drogheda. It has barely been mentioned by historians and remains open to a variety of interpretations. The archaeological Inventory for Louth does not mention Millmount in the index but does refer to Grange Irish as an earthwork. It describes Millmount as a 'high mound which may be glacial deposit. Traces of stone bank at perimeter on top (max. dimensions 11.5m [38 feet] by 10.5m [34.5 feet]) slight rise in centre'. The mound is locally known as 'Amergin's Fort'. Amergin,* son of Míl Espagne, is credited with being the Milesian Gael who founded Ireland around 200 BC. The antiquarian George Coffey, writing in 1912, writes that 'the Millmount of Drogheda, which a tradition makes the grave of Amergin, may have been a burial mound of the Boyne cemetery before being shaped for use as a fortress'. Amergin came from northern Iberia, and his descendants have been here ever since. It is also said to be in the plain of *Mag Breagh*; *Mag Breagh* is where the kingdom of Amergin's brothers, Eremon and Eber met. *Mag Breagh* is the plain of north Dublin which extends as far as the Boyne River.

The *Louth Archaeological Journal* for 1943 says that Millmount was the burial place of the *Bean Gabhann* or the wife of the *gabha*, a member of the *tri dee dana*, or the three craftsmen of the Tuatha Dé Danann.* Should this legend be true then the mound was there before the Gaels arrived, thus giving some support to the theory that it was Amergin's grave.

In his guide to the national monuments, Harbison refers to Millmount as 'possibly originally a Passage-Grave like Newgrange'. If so, Millmount goes back to Neolithic times and was possibly an entry tomb to the Boyne Valley complex of tombs established more than 5,000 years ago.

The mound holds a strategic position on the Boyne, just four miles in from where the river enters the Irish Sea. The Boyne Estuary is also known as *Inbhear Colptha*, or 'the estuary of Colptha', Colptha being the first to step ashore from the ships of the invading Milesians. The Boyne estuary is south of the village of Baltray and north of the village of Mornington. Both villages are about four miles east of the town of Drogheda. The estuary today looks similar to the way it must have seemed at the time of the Milesians. The land towards the sea is flat and therefore gives a clear view of the river from the summit of the mound. Whether or not its strategic position was recognised during the Neolithic phase, it was certainly appreciated 4,000 years later when Turgesius the Dane had his headquarters in Drogheda at Millmount, which he had strongly fortified. Later the Normans strengthened the existing fortifications. They converted the mound into a motte-and-bailey, and on the *Discovery* map today the mound is classed as a 'motte'. Hugh De Lacy built a castle on the mound in the twelfth century, a wooden structure erected for defensive purposes and known as the 'Castle of Drogheda'.

Despite the accumulations of all these layers over time, in Drogheda in 2015 a taxi driver told me that the mound is still locally known as 'the burial place of Amergin'.

What has been termed an 'epoch making battle' occurred at Crinna in 226 AD; its exact site is unknown so there are a number of suggestions as to its location. Somewhere between Dowth and Mellifont [43] has been suggested by Hogan, while others say it was fought closer to Stackallen Bridge, two miles south of Slane [43]. It could be seen as the first great battle of the Boyne, in which Fergus Dubdédach, 'of the black teeth', King of

Ulster, was defeated by Tade mac Cein, grandson of Oilioll Olum, in a struggle over the high kingship.

The Annals of the Four Masters describe the battle as follows:

The age of Christ, 226. Fergus Dubdédach, was king over Ireland for the space of a year, when he fell in the battle of Crinna, by Cormac, grandson of Conn [Cét Chathach] by the hand of Lugaid Laighe. There fell by him also (in the rout), across Brega, his two brothers Fergus the Long-haired and Fergus the Fiery, who was called Fergus Caisfhliaclach [of the Crooked Teeth]. Of them was said:

Upon the stone of Rathcro
Were slain the three Ferguses
Cormac said this is fine,
His hand did not fail Laighe.

After the death of Fergus, his army retreated and continued fighting in rearguard action until they reached *Druim-ineasclainn* ('the ridge of the strong stream or torrent'), which is known now as Dromiskin [36] and is about ten miles north-east from the probable site of the battle of Crinna. Near Dromiskin the followers of Fergus made their last stand. The final battle was at *Glais Neara* ('stream of iron') in the present townland of Newrath, two miles west of Dromiskin. The natural ridge here is favourable for a force taking up a defensive position against an army coming from the south-west.

A Major–General Stubbs writing in the *County Louth Archaeological Journal* of 1919–20 names some local places associated with this battle; they include *Mullaghghlinn*, which he translates as 'hill of the sword'; *Cros-na fuile*, 'bloody cross'; and *Cleggan-dinne*, 'hill of the skulls'. He states that near the latter place 'a large quantity of skulls and bones were discovered some ninety years ago, half a mile and corroborate the local tradition of a great battle having been fought here'. Unfortunately, I cannot find these places either on the *Discovery* map or in Hogan. Confirmation of their existence would enhance the credibility of the story told in the annals.

After this battle, Cormac mac Airt became High King of Ireland, and as a reward to Tadg mac Cein he granted him land from the Liffey to *Glais Neara*, but not including Tara. This territory took the name *Ciannachta* from Tadg's father Cian.

For those wishing to go back a bit further in time, the Paddock Wedge Grave a mile north-east from Monasterboice and west of the M1 motorway is known as the Cailleach Bhéara's House [36]. This Megalithic tomb is incorporated into a field wall. According to the Louth Archaeological Inventory, 'it consists of a gallery, 3.9m long and averaging about 1.2m wide, it is oriented east to west. The north side of the gallery is represented by five stones and the south side by six stones with the more westerly of these set in advance of the septal stone' (the stone which forms the partition).

As many ring forts were called 'love beds of Diarmuid* and Gráinne' from the Fenian love tale of the same name, so are many megaliths called after the *cailleach*, an early and persistent goddess originating in west Cork. The lore is that she travelled over the land with her apron full of stones, and those that fell became her dwelling house. About 350 yards north-north-east from here is the decorated rock in the townland of Tinure. Although mentioned by Eystyns, neither the *Discovery* map nor the archaeological inventory mention it. The concentration of rock art in Louth can be found east of Innishkeen and the River Fana; its distribution north of Derrygonnelly can be found in a four-mile radius, where five of the eight rock art examples can be found, and the other three are closeby.

The Tinure Stone represents a symbolic attempt at art or some deeper form of representation by a prehistoric people, presenting, like the Clonfinlough Stone in Co. Offaly, a physical and cultural connection to our ancient ancestors. Of it Evans writes:

> This little-known site is difficult to find, being overgrown with thorns and surrounded by marshy ground. The markings are on a slab of Silurian slate (7ft. high and 5ft. wide) which leans forward from a vertical rock-face from which it is partly detached; and apart from being damaged by the initials of visitors in 1869 and 1964, they are faint and difficult to detect. There are many clusters of tiny punched holes—miniature cup-arks—and fine incised lines with short cross-lines, single or double. Others have stars or crossbars at the ends. The Abbé Breuil interprets them as anthropomorphs. The closest parallel in Ireland is the Clonfinlough stone, *Offaly*, but there the markings are cut deeply.

The Tinure Stone is generally seen as an example of prehistoric art or rock art originating in south-west France and in Spain. The common assumption that these Stone Age peoples were simply involved in rock art is a possible underestimation of the culture of these peoples. Their art was more likely to express a form of sympathetic magic which may have involved a form of incantation and a pleading to spirits to bring success in hunting or in fertility. It is possible, given the apparent sense of motion in the art, that dancing was a part of these very early human rites.

Houghton Brodrick in *Prehistoric Painting* writes: 'Some of the later representations especially of human figures, became less and less life-like, gradually more and more stylised, until, like scribings on our Tinure Rock and elsewhere, no one without seeing the various stages depicted by the Abbé Brueil, could recognise the final pictograph as being a human figure.' H.G. Tempest, reviewing the book, writes: 'In Cantabria and Acquitaine, art went slowly on, modified in Mesolithic times to signs and patterns on pebbles until it became stylised into symbols reduced to their bare essentials. These are allied to the scribings on the rock face at Tinure in Co. Louth. These rock symbols represent the earliest evidence which we have of religion, myth and rite.'

The more abstract rock carvings of the later period of the Stone Age have left them free of interpretation, except possibly for N.L. Thomas, whose *Irish Symbols of 3500* BC attempts to unfold the riddle of many of these inscriptions. These inscriptions, he says, are mainly illustrative of the beginnings of agriculture during the Neolithic Age, and are interested in solar renewal and a 'stretch in the evenings' for the planting of crops.

MEATH

An Mhíde, 'the central area'

Meath, which gave its name to the historical fifth province of Ireland, is home to two highly important focal points of early Irish history and mythology: Newgrange, a religious centre from the Neolithic period, and Tara, once the royal capital.

One of the county's prominent geographical features is the River Boyne, which enters the Irish Sea four miles east of the town of Drogheda [43]. The river takes its name from *Bó Finne* or 'the white cow goddess' – formed by the junction of two rivers, namely the *Bó or Bó Guaire*, known today as the Blackwater, which flows from Lough Ramor [35], and the *Find*, the name for the upper Boyne before it is joined by the Blackwater in the centre of Navan [42]. A connection between Newgrange and the heavens can be found in *Bealach na Bó Finne, the Irish term for the Milky Way*. The area known as the Boyne valley (*Brú na Bóinne*, 'the dwelling place of the Boyne') contains one of the world's most important Neolithic landscapes and features the large passage graves of Knowth, Dowth and Newgrange [43].

Megalithic tombs have been a characteristic feature of farming communities over much of Western Europe as well as in Ireland from the Neolithic to the Bronze Age (c. 3500 to 1500 BC). The custom of collective burial in stone tombs persisted for more than 2,000 years, and the stone tombs became known as 'megalithic' or great stone tombs. The dead were placed in a chamber or chambers with walls built of upright stones and roofed by

FIGURE 17. *Brú na Bóinne* (Jack Roberts).

lintels or corbels of stone. But just as churches and temples are centres of Judeo-Christian myth rather than solely graveyards, so too are the megaliths of the Boyne Valley keepers of a Late Neolithic–Early Bronze Age culture.

Tom Condit in *Archaeology Ireland* (Autumn 1997) writes:

> That Brú na Bóinne was not just a place for the interment of the dead is amply demonstrated by the presence of monuments dating to the Late Neolithic/Early Bronze Age, such as the henge monuments, the timber circles and, in particular, the Newgrange cursus. Such monuments tell us, from their shape and design, that they were used for gatherings … The cursus is slightly different in that it marks the route of a ritual procession through the landscape revealing discrete sections of the landscape itself and highlighting monuments and other ritual sites.

The cursus at Newgrange is situated in the field east of the monument and was seemingly used as part of the procession ritual for significant events such as the winter solstice. A similar cursus north of Tara, mistakenly named the Banqueting Hall, may have been used as an assembly point for rituals such as the *tarb fes* and the inauguration of kings.

One of the most impressive prehistoric monuments in Europe, the Newgrange tumulus, is nearly a hundred yards across and forty-five feet high. As well as being a resting

FIGURE 18. The entrance to the Great Chamber at Newgrange.

place for the dead, it also had an astronomical function, allowing the winter solstice to be established when the first rays of the sun travelled directly down the mound's 62-foot-long passage and lit up the inner chamber. The shortest day of the year was thus established, providing a base for a yearly calendar that was closely associated with farming. The annual re-conception of the earth and its livestock was symbolised (I suggest) by the light of the sun entering along the uterine shaft of the mound and in its wondrous way acting as a harbinger of new life.

Around the edge of the mound are ninety-seven large stones called kerbstones. Twelve of these bear symbols and should be observed when visiting the site. The massive kerbstone known as K1 or the Entrance Stone is inscribed with several spiral designs and dual vertical lines. To the left of the vertical lines are three anti-clockwise double spirals. N.L. Thomas in his *Irish Symbols of 3500* BC writes that the 'double-spirals, relatively large in overall size are presumed to represent the longer summer days. On the right are two clockwise double spirals, slightly smaller and supposedly representing the weak winter sun'.

It is over this stone that the sun rises on the morning of the winter solstice. Thomas assumes that the designs on K1 and on K52 at the diametrically opposite position were made at the same time as the mounds were built, 'otherwise the passage would not have been made on the chosen alignments'. Thomas also states that the 'Irish calendar of about 3500 BC is apparently the earliest evidence of man's attempt to measure the passing of the year in an accurate fashion'.

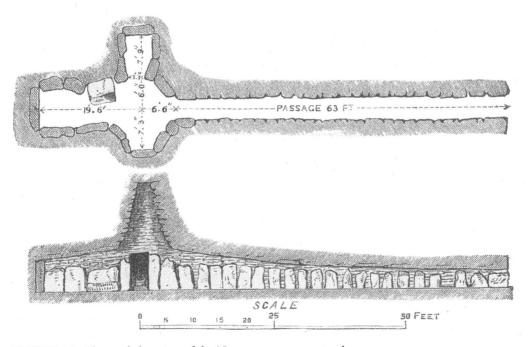

FIGURE 19. Plan and elevation of the Newgrange passage tomb.

The two other main sites in the Boyne Valley are at Dowth and Knowth. The early Irish for the first two of these passage entrances is *Dubadh*, or 'darkness or growing dark', and *Cnodba*, which cannot be found in some dictionaries as a single word, but in the *Dindshenchas** the following question is asked:

Cnogba, whence was it named? Not hard to tell. Englic, daughter of Elcmaire, Aengus mac ind Óc loved her, and could not win her. They held a gathering for sports between Cleitech and Síd in Broga, and the fairy people and the noble folk of all Erin used to attend these sports every *samain* eve, bringing with them provision of shell-fruit, that is, nuts. The three sons of Derg, son of Etaman, came from the North out of Síd Findabrach, and bore off the daughter of Elcmaire at a swoop, unknown to the young men. These, when they knew of it, pursued the reavers as far as the knoll that is called Cnogba. There they raised a loud lament, and this is the feast that sustained them there – the nut crop (*cnó-guba*).

There are nineteen megalithic tombs at Knowth, with Knowth cemetery Site 1 as the focal point of a large passage-tomb cemetery.

The *Archaeological Inventory of Co. Meath* describes Site 1 as follows:

This great kerbed mound has been the site of extensive excavations since 1962. Sixteen small passage-tombs are in close proximity to the main mound. The central mound is c. 90m [295.2 feet] by 80m [262.5 feet] by 11m [36.1 feet] in height. Incurving of kerb to E and W indicates entrances to two back-to-back passage tombs. The W tomb, 34.2m long, comprises a bent passage leading to a simple square chamber; a stone basin lies at bend in passage. The E tomb, 40m long, contains a cruciform chamber with corbelled roof; N recess contains an elaborately decorated stone basin. Many of the kerb stones and large numbers of the structural stones of both tombs are decorated with megalithic art.

Site 1, which lies a little more than half-a-mile to the north-west of Newgrange, produced evidence of Beaker activity, including areas where flint and pottery were present as well as cremation deposits. From this it has been concluded that the occupation of Knowth as well as Newgrange was of a domestic nature, and domestic debris was found both in the pits and hearths. Houses, both of a rectangular and oval design, were present through the Neolithic phase, although the archaeologist who did a great amount of work at Knowth, George Eogan, has suggested that the rectangular houses are earlier that the oval ones.

Like at Knowth, the megalith at Newgrange produced many sherds of vessels associated with a group known as the Beaker Folk, a name that comes from a kind of drinking bowl or cup, derived from the same root as the German *becher*, the Italian *bicchiere* and the Latin *baccarium*. The Scots call a hooped wooden dish a 'bicker'; in Irish the term is *bíocar*.

Macalister in his *Archaeology of Ireland* writes that the Beaker Folk came from east central Europe and that their 'type of pottery is especially associated with their remains'. He writes that they were more prominent in the east of Britain but less prominent in Ireland. He wrote that by 1932 only four beaker sites had been recorded in Ireland, but as has been shown above, many more Beaker sites have been discovered since the 1980s, which is a change from a 1918 archaeological map of Britain and Ireland, which shows no Beaker presence at all for Ireland.

Macalister goes on to describe the physical characteristics of these people as such:

> The Beaker Folk had short round skulls, with the normal concomitant of short round faces. In stature they varied considerably, but they were taller than the aborigines: the latter might average about 5 feet 5 inches, the newcomers about 5 feet 9 inches and might even rise to 6 feet. The limb bones are more slender than those of the earlier people. Their teeth show much more intensive wear than those of their predecessors, indicating the use of gritty food-bread, made of flour unavoidably mixed with fine dust from the quern stones.

One suggestion was that Ireland with its gold in the Wicklow Mountains may have lured Beaker communities to the east coast of Ireland. It was also suggested that these people, as well as the legendary Tuatha Dé Danann,* reached Ireland from northern Scotland during the Bronze Age.

The mound at Dowth corresponds closely to Newgrange in dimensions; it is about 47 feet high and measures 280 feet in diameter. As at Newgrange, the base is surrounded by large stones except that Dowth has no retaining wall. The Archaeological Inventory of County Meath describes Dowth as follows:

> This great mound, comparable in original size with those of Newgrange and Knowth, is not as well preserved. Much of the material to the west was removed at various times in the past and in 1847, when in the course of excavation, a large crater was dug into the top of the mound. This monument comprises a kerbed mound, 85m in diameter and 15m in height, covering two passage-tombs opening onto its west side. The north tomb 12.5m long is of cruciform shape; an annex of two chambers opens off the south recess. A reconstructed stone basin lies in the centre of chamber. The south tomb is 8.25m long and comprises a short passage leading to a sub-circular chamber with a single recess opening off its south-east side. A number of kerb stones and structural stones in both tombs bear megalithic art. There is a souterrain built into the mound.

Neolithic Newgrange enters our mythology from the Late Bronze Age to the Iron Age, and from then on it is recorded in the post-Patrician period by monks. Like the universe, which was without light for millions of years after the Big Bang, the Boyne Valley was without a memory until memory was 'inked' in manuscript form, and it is from these manuscripts that legends, early history and myths derive.

It is here in the Boyne Valley that *Brug mic ind Óc* ('the Hostel of Aengus mac ind Óg) has been tentatively identified by archaeologist Geraldine Stout. Site P is named as *Caiseal Aengus* and is an embanked enclosure or large henge. The site is described in the *Dindshenchas** where it is referred to as *Tech mic ind Óc* ('the house of Mac ind Óc') and *Síd I mBruig mic ind Óc* ('the fairy mound of Aengus'). The house of Aengus [43] is half-a-mile from Newgrange. Aengus was the harper to the gods, who tricked his father the Dagda,* the Irish Zeus and sun god, into possession of the sacred territory.

A poem attributed to Cináed úa hArtacáin (d. 981) is Late Medieval, but it relates the persistence of memory to this Neolithic tomb, which was originally an astronomical and ceremonial centre:

> *Focheil cúane calma cáin*
> *a mag mic in Dagda déin:*
> *ná dersat adrad Dé móir*
> *andso dóib hitát hi péin.*

> *Iatsom dimbúan, tussu búan,*
> *immotréide cech slúag slán:*
> *iatsom dosrogáeth a ngaés'*
> *tussu fogéb aq aés n-án.*

> *Bóand bale roglas réil*
> *mana sechut la séil slain*
> *cenn indais ui úabrig úaib*
> *Senbic a túaim immais áin.*

> *Congalach col-lí cond fían,*
> *dían a buille, dond a dál:*
> *is búale rán-tor co rian,*
> *is cúane n-ard-chon, is án.*

> Thou hidest a brood bold and kind,
> O plain of the son of the swift Dagda!
> let men not punish the worship of the great God;
> it is worse for them that are in torment.

> They are transient, thou abidest:
> every believing band rides around thee:
> as for them, their wisdom has befooled them;
> thou shalt attain a noble age.

Boyne, a spot right green and bright,
an omen with sound … beside thee
… from you of the proud grandson
of Senbec from the stead of noble poesy.

Warlike and splendid is the centre of champions!
swift their stroke, noble their assembly!
it is a fold of glorious chieftains, with a track,
it is a kennel of high-bred whelps, it is glorious.

[Translation by Edward Gwynn]

Finally, the mythic aspect of the Boyne Valley and Newgrange especially can be expressed as the sun, represented by the Dagda,* the 'good god', entering the uterine shaft of Newgrange on the winter solstice and mating with Boand, the white cow goddess who represents the moon, and this union then leading to a rebirth of the soil and the land. Legend then translates this union into human terms, with the Dagda mating with various women, principally Boand, wife of Nechtain, who bore him a son, Aengus, who in time became the principal lord of the Boyne monuments.

The Norsemen from north Leinster invaded the Boyne Valley in 862, and the *Annals of Ulster* states that for that year:

The caves of Achad Aldai (Newgrange), and of Cnogba (Knowth) and Boadán's Mound above Dubad (Dowth), and of Óengoba's wife, were searched by the foreigners— something which had never been done before. This was the occasion when the three kings of the foreigners, i.e. Amlaíb and Ímar and Auisle, plundered the land of Flann son of Conaing; and Lorcán son of Cathal, king of Meath, was with them in this.

South of Newgrange and on the south side of the Boyne is Rossnaree [43], a site associated with *Cath Ruis na Ríg for Bóinn* or 'the Battle of Ross na Ríg on the Boyne', a post-Táin encounter between Ulster and the rest of the island, including Connacht, Leinster, royal Meath and Munster. In this battle the Ulaid were victorious. Professor MacNeill took the battle to be one of the 'old constituent stories of the Táin', but the German scholar Thurneysen stated that it was a 'romantic invention and that the tale has no historical value'. The fact that Keating does not mention it may reinforce Thurneysen.

The area today leaves little evidence of its importance in earlier times; the Ross or headland was the place of residence of King Dathí's mother and the burial place of King Cormac mac Airt. The tumulus where he was reputed to be buried was destroyed in the 1940s when the body of a woman was found there. It is also the spot where Conn 'of the Hundred Battles' (*Conn Cét Chathach*) was slain. It was associated with being a Christian site as opposed to the more pagan tombs on the north side of the river and has connections with Saints Fintan, Finnian and Columcille, the latter of whom is said to have found Cormac mac Airt's skull, which he 'reverently put again into the grave'.

It is said that Cormac died in the ring fort of Spelán in *Cletech Brega* [43] south of the Boyne near Stackallon Bridge, on a height called *Ucht Cleitig* when a salmon bone lodged in his throat. He did not want to be buried in *Brú na Bóinne*, as he 'did not adore the god adored by those buried there'. Thus, later writers ascribed to Cormac a premonition about the arrival of Christianity. According to the annals, Cormac's death occurred during the first half of the second century AD.

Tuathal Techtmar, a second-century High King of Tara, formed the territory of Meath by a union of portions from the four provinces as mensal lands or lands for the benefit of the monarchy. Or as the *Book of Invasions* says, 'it was by Tuathal that every province in Ireland was decapitated (*dithcheannadh*) to form Meath'.

Tara [42, 43] was the royal centre of Ireland, as it is here that the high kings were inaugurated. In the *Dindshenchas*,* Tara is described as follows:

> *Tech Temrach imatá inráith,*
> *asa tardad dliged cáich,*
> *maraid fós míad dia samlaib*
> *ac rígaib ac ríg-domnaib.*

FIGURE 20. An aerial view of the royal enclosure at Tara.

Rí ocus ollam filed,
súi, brugaid, bertís dliged,
lepta ná loiscti lochit,
láraig ocus lón-chrochit.

The house of Tara, round which is the rath,
from it was given to each his due;
honour still continues to such as them
at the courts of kings and princes.

King and chief of the poets,
sage, farmer, they received their due,
couches that torches burn not,
the thighs and the chine steaks.

[Translated by Edward Gwynn]

Regardless of its pre-Gaelic influence, Tara has been credited by the annals with a solely Gaelic tradition, and this is evidenced by the *Dindshenchas** and by the *Annals of the Four Masters*. The former asks: '*Temuir, unde nominatur*? (Whence is Tara so named?)' and answers: 'Temhuir [i.e *Teamhur*, i.e. *Mur Tea*, 'the wall of Tea'], daughter of Lugaid, son of Ith, son of Breogan, the wife of Eremon, son of Milesius and [within this defence] she is buried'. The annals reinforce the *Dindshenchas* and state:

Tea daughter of Lugaid, son of Ith whom Eremon married in Spain, was the Tea who requested of Eremon a choice hill as her dowry and requesting that whichever place she might select she might be interred therein, and that her mound and her gravestone might be raised there and where every prince ever to be born of her race should dwell. The hill she selected was Druim Caein or the hill of Caen which is Tara. It is from her it was called, and in it she was interred.

However, the word Tara has been given fresh etymological meaning in recent times and is seen as being connected to the Indo-European verbal root *tem*, 'to cut', which is found in the Greek *temenos* ('sanctuary') and the Latin *templum* ('temple'). It has been suggested by Breathnach and Newman in an article in *Archaeology Ireland* that the 'physical act of cutting a ditch around the crown of the hill' [at Tara] cuts the bond between the human world and the world of the gods. Presumably this means that this connection is lost in such a sacred place and that here one enters a purely spiritual zone. Cormac mac Cuilennáin the tenth-century king–bishop of Cashel suggested that the word Tara was simply another word for a *grianán*, 'an open balcony exposed to the sun'. As *grianán* derives from the word *grian* meaning the sun goddess, we may assume that sun worship was part of the ceremonial order. Also, the fact that some high kings were named Lugaid from the sun god Lug* reinforces this idea.

Another possible meaning of Temair is 'a gate to the Otherworld'. This would apply to a rath named *Deisiol Temrach*, meaning 'right to the sun', which was regarded as a 'lucky spot' from which to enter the Otherworld. This site is shown on Petrie's map of 1838 as lying between two cairns, that of the Leinstermen and that of the O'Neill, one mile north of Rath Gráinne in the townland of Jordanstown. This site was not included in the Ordnance Survey Map of 1837, a possible reason being that nothing was included north of the ancient way known as *Fán na gCarbad* or the 'slope of the chariots'. An aerial photograph may be required to pinpoint it.

This *Deisiol Temrach* is recorded in the *Dindshenchas** as follows:

Etir dá Charn na nGillaí
Deisel Temrach tes Crinnaí:
fót co rath ria ndul ar cel,
a sóitís dáine deisel.

Between the two cairns of the lads
is the Deisel of Tara south of Crinna,
a sward that brings luck before going to death,
where men used to make a turn right-hand-wise.

[Translated by Edward Gwynn]

This rath is of importance for an understanding of the pre-Christian importance of Tara, as it was probably connected with an ancient rite. Here the sun god was acknowledged by walking sun-wise in a clockwise direction (*deas sol*); participating in this rite was regarded as a necessary function prior to death.

A fable quoted by Samuel Ferguson in 1876 in a reading to the Royal Irish Academy under the heading 'On the Ceremonial Turn Called "Desiul"' is as follows:

Arge a huntress, pursuing a stag, said, 'although thou followest the course of the Sun, yet will I follow thee;' at which the Sun, being displeased turned her into a doe.

The power of the sun god is seen here insofar as Arge's stag was acting in a ceremonial way by turning to the sun and Arge's crime was acting profanely towards an act of solar adoration. One may see this as somewhat obscure, yet it shows the power of the sun deity as told through Latin mythology.

It is important to see that the custom of *deisiol* was not just applicable to Ireland but throughout the extent of Europe as well, and its significance has been recorded by the writers of classical antiquity. Thus, these writers give evidence of some kind of rotation forming part of the ceremonial of religious worship.

Plutarch states that the Pythagoreans placed the element of fire at the centre of the universe and that the Earth made its revolution about this sphere of fire. He writes that:

> The turning around in adoration is said to represent the circular motion of the world. But I rather think that, as the temples opened towards the East, such as entered them, necessarily turning their backs upon the rising sun, made a half turn to that quarter in honour of the god of day and then completed the circle as well as their devotions with their faces towards the god of the temple.

Lucretius describes the worshipper making his gyration before the pillar stone:

> Call it not Piety that oft you're found
> veiled, at the standing stone, to make your round.

The custom was prevalent in the Scottish Hebrides in the nineteenth century when it was also common for Irish people to walk three times around the graveyard *deisiol* with the coffin. In Wales, the central council for the Eisteddfod is the *gorsedd*, which was held within a circle of stones – 'face to face with the sun and the eye of light, as there is no power to hold a *gorsedd* under cover or at night but only where and as long as the sun is visible in the heavens'.

St Findchua of Brigown, Co. Cork, found himself while at Tara under attack by British pirates and organised a defence party, directing them to march *deisol* to meet the invaders and thus came down on the enemy's flank and made short work of them. The *Cathach* (the 'battle book') of the O'Donnells was always borne three times *deisiol* around the army before battle in order to assure victory.

Tara was essentially the inauguration site for the High Kings of Ireland and the early-eleventh-century poet Flann Mainistrech wrote a poem, *Ríg Themra tóebaige dia tesband tnú*, on the pre-Christian kings of Ireland from Eochu Feidlech to Nath Í. There were about twenty high kings at Tara before St Patrick's time and many of these were of pre-Gaelic stock, such as Conaire Mór, Tuathal Techmar, Lugaid Mac Con, Eochaid Mugmedon and his son Niall Noígiallach or Niall of the Nine Hostages, to name but five.

The inauguration of the king involved a procession from the Rath of the Synods past a *síle na gig*, Christianised as 'St Adamnan's Cross', then past two small portal stones and towards the Neolithic passage tomb known as the Mound of the Hostages. On top of this mound stood a standing stone known as the *Lia Fáil* or the 'Stone of Destiny'. The king stood on top of this and turned three times to the right, acknowledging the sun god. If the stone roared, the man on top was a rightful king and was free to practice the *fir flathemon* ('the king's justice'). The goddess with whom the king must mate prior to taking the kingship was named Medb,* and she was the goddess of fertility and sovereignty. Another goddess performing a similar role was Eithne. As the role of the goddess was on a par with that of the gods during the Iron Age, so too was the role of women with men; had the Romans invaded Ireland they would most likely have have met an Irish Boadicea.

FIGURE 21. The *Lia Fáil* or the 'Stone of Destiny' at Tara with the Mound of the Hostages in the background (Carole Cullen).

A final rite associated with Tara was the *tarb fes* ('bull feast'), carried out at the Rath of the Synods and harking back to a time when dreams played an important part in the rituals of the tribe. The twelfth-century *Lebor na hUidre* describes the rite as follows:

> Firstly a white bull was killed and one took his fill of the meat and of the broth, and satisfied with that slept and four druids chanted an incantation for finding truth over him, and it would be seen from the dreams he had the kind of man who would be king, and from the spectre in the dream a description was made; thus the work was done. The man awoke from the dream and told the vision to the king: A strong noble youthful warrior with two red circles over him, standing above the pillow of a man in decline in Emain Macha.

The 'man in decline' was Cú Chulainn* while the man chosen as king was Lugaid Reóderg (Lugaid 'of the red stripes'), despite the consensus of the provinces to exclude the Ulaid or men of Ulster.

At Ringlestown Hillfort [42], two miles south-west of Tara and one mile north-east of Kilmessan, fairy music is said to have been heard here by a local man named John Graham according to Evans Wentz. A tribe of little red men are said to be living in Glen Odder between Ringlestown and Tara. The fairies here are supposed to be of Fir Bolg,* Tuatha Dé Danann* and Milesian stock. Hugh O'Neill on his march south in 1599 camped here with his army. The hillfort is just under 400 feet in diameter, so quite a few soldiers could have been accommodated. Legend has it that his army was assisted by the spirits of the dead who dwelt within the rath.

According to John Boylin from Kilmessan, speaking to Evans Wentz around the beginning of the twentieth century, the fairies were often seen 'serenading' around the western slopes of Tara. They were warrior fairies and would defend Tara against attack

FIGURE 22. Adamnan's Cross with a Sheela na Gig at the base.

from Cruachain in Connacht. To quote John Boylin: 'We were told as children that as soon as night fell, the fairies from Rath Ringlestown would form in a procession across Tara road, pass around certain bushes which have not been disturbed for ages, and join the *gangkena*'. The *gangkena* or *geanncanach* were 'one of the lower and more aggressive kinds of fairies'. The fairy procession was sacrosanct and was not to be interfered with. Thus, no houses or roads were to be built on its way. Some mystics regard these paths or passes as magnetic arteries, through which the Earth's magnetism circulates.

On a more historical note, there is Tlachtga, also known as the Hill of Ward close to Athboy (*Ath Buidhe Tlachtga*, possibly meaning 'the ford at sunny Tlachtga' – 'sunny' because an annual festival was held here on May Day). Tlachtga is six miles north-west of Trim on the R154 and on the road to Athboy. Today, it consists of a multivallate ring fort with a diameter of nearly 500 feet. It was reputedly founded by Tuathal Techtmar who led one of the Gaelic invasions of Ireland about 80 AD. Tuathal can be defined as *Teuto-valos* or 'ruler of the people', and *techtmar* means 'great traveller'. Specifically, he led the Gaels across the Irish Sea and in time conquered the indigenous people, namely the Dál nAraide or Cruithin.* He was the first person to impose taxes, the form of which was a tax on cows and was known as the *Boireamh Laighen* or 'Cow Tribute of Leinster'.

Tlachtga was one of four fortresses that Tuathal built, and it was here that the Fire of Tlachtga was commenced, and thus Tlachtga became a centre for a druidic assembly. These fires were lit on the eve of *samain*, when sacrifices were offered to the gods. According to Keating, *is ann san teinidh sin do loischtí a n-iodhbartha leo*, which has been translated by Dinneen as: 'it was at that fire they used to burn their victims'. I would suggest that the translation should be 'it was at that fire that their offerings were burnt'! If this is correct, then human sacrifice at Tlachtga may not have existed; if the former is correct, it did exist. According to Caesar, the druids in Gaul frequently sacrificed humans to their gods, and in the third century BC the poet Sopater stated that the Galatians sacrificed their victims by burning after a victory.

Any fire after the *samain* ceremony at Tlachtga had to be started from the ceremonial fire and a tax was imposed on one so doing, the money being paid to the King of Munster. This tax or tribute was known as a *screpall*; twenty-four grains of wheat made a scruple of silver, so presumably the price for taking a light from the fire of Tlachtga was minimal.

Tlachtga is named after the goddess Tlachtga who had a feast dedicated to her. She gave birth to three sons, each conceived of a different father, and died having given birth to them.

Tuathal Techtmar is also credited with building Taillte or the fort at Teltown, four miles from Kells on the Slane road heading eastwards. It is about a quarter of a mile in from the road on the south side. The fort is locally known as *Rath Dhu* or 'the black fort'. The original name for Teltown derives from the goddess Tailtiu, who lived there. She is said to have cleared the forest of *Coill Cuan* that stood there originally, and according to her wishes was buried on the resulting plain. Before she died, she also requested that funeral games be held every year to lament her, and so her foster son Lug* commemorated her with games a week before and after Lughnasa, the first day of August.

The games included a horse race from *Cnoc Aidi* just north of Kells to Teltown. The ancient assembly at Teltown was known as *Oenach Tailten* or the 'fair at Tailten'. It was held on the north bank of the Blackwater River in Teltown and was attended by people from all over Ireland as well as Scotland. Marriages were a special part of the fair and were held in a place called the 'marriage hollow'. The ordinary *oenach* or *aenach* was a periodical assembly, and the great provincial fairs of Cruachan, Carman and Tailtiu may be looked on as *mór dála* or national assemblies. Tailtiu was held every year at the kalends of August and Carman was held at August every three years.

On 2 August 1924, the Tailteann games were reinstituted, not in their original location but at Croke Park in Dublin. The revival was a great success, with athletes from all over the world participating, although one sport that was a big part of the ancient games was absent – that of pig-sticking! The games were opened by the poet W.B. Yeats who in an address to a banquet held that evening said: 'It is natural that we should call you together now that we are an independent nation, victor at last in the struggle of centuries'. A notable competition was a hurling versus shinty match between Ireland and Scotland in which Scotland won by two goals. An ancient aspect of the evening was the fact that the banquet was held by candlelight, but this was not in memory of the older games but rather that the municipal workers were on strike!

Tuathal's victory was at Achall, east of Tara, where he routed Éllim mac Conrach who led the *aithechthuatha*, the non-Gaelic tribes who were called the *aithechthuatha* or 'vassal tribes'. This battle was possibly one of many where the indigenous peoples were defeated by the incoming Gaels. Achall is about one mile due east of Tara. Today it is known as Skreen, or *Scrín Columcille*.

Five miles northwest of Tara is the town of Navan and three miles west of Navan is the townland of Ardbraccan (*Ard Breacáin*, 'speckled height'). It is here that one of the five ancient trees of Ireland stood – the *Bile Tortan* or the sacred tree in the land of the Uí Tortan. In the *Book of Leinster*, it is described as *Unnius I Tortain tuirmid* or 'an ash in arable Tortan'. The *bile*, which is an older Irish word for 'tree', was venerated as the tribal centre under which kings were crowned and around which tribal gatherings were held. The modern custom of holding hands and dancing around a tree may find its origins in communing with this ancient tribal centre.

The *Dindshenchas** commemorates this tree in a poem. The poem is recited by a number of saints, including St Ultán the patron saint of Ardbreachan who died in 656 AD, so presumably the tree was down by then. The following includes three of the verses from the *Dindshenchas*:

Bile Tortán dorochair'
doruart mór sin dia eochair:

cian comdatar minnian fris,
ba amne noscarfaitis.

Fir Thortan dia fertais dál
'mon crann ndeligthe ndermár,
nícostaidled siled sín
cosin lathe bad erchrin.

Bile Tortan, trom a fhúaim
fri hainciss sine rorúaid:
rolá sunn mór saithe de
osnad gáeithe gem-aidche.

Fallen is the tree of Tortu, whose skirts conquered many a storm … even so would they disperse.

When the men of Tortu used to meet around the huge conspicuous tree, the pelting of the storms did not reach them, until the day when it was decayed.

Deep was the sound of the tree of Tortu in the storm's fierce torment: the moaning of the wind on winter nights has torn from it here many a swarm of leaves.

[Tranlated by Edward Gwynn]

As well as Ultán, the poem was recited by St Ultán of *Tech Túa*, or Taghadoe, near Maynooth; St Mochua of *Cluain Dolcan*, or Clondalkin; St Mochuma of Terryglass; and St Sinche of *Cell Roiss*, who is the only female saint mentioned. The inclusion of these saints is interesting as to how emerging Christianity commented on the pagan past. The wind is mentioned, as is the gathering around 'the huge conspicuous tree', its past being traced back to Míl and the beginning of the Gaelicisation of Ireland. Nothing is mentioned of its ritual purpose, though nothing disparaging is said of it.

'The Banquet of *Dún na nGedh*' ('the fort of the geese') is a tale translated from a fifteenth-century manuscript by the scholar John O'Donovan in 1842. The story also features in the twelfth-century *Yellow Book of Lecan* and deals with real historical events from the seventh century – a battle between Congal Claen or Cáech, Cruithin* King of Ulster and the rising power of the Uí Néill, a prominent Leinster family whose king at the time was Domhnall, son of Aed mac Ainmire.

The fort of *Dún na nGedh* is difficult to place with any certainty, though a number of sources place it on the south side of the Boyne facing Dowth. Hogan says it 'was probably the large fort on the south side of the River Boyne near Dowth'. It is said that Domhnall modelled his fort on Tara; thus, he built seven great ramparts around the fort and included a banqueting hall. Unfortunately, however, the Banqueting Hall at Tara seems to have been a cursus or place for racing during the games at Tara, but at least we know where Tara is, while the location of *Dún na nGed* is speculative. South of the Boyne is bereft of large forts with the possible exception of Platin, an inland promontory fort less than three miles south-east from Dowth.

Platin [43] is situated on top of a rock outcrop and covers an area of two acres. Here within an oval area there is a raised, subcircular area with a diameter of just over eighty feet. This site is unmarked and is still unclear if it is *Dún na nGed*, but of all the existing sites south of Dowth it has the possibility of being the fort of the saga. As it is a raised promontory fort, this would add to it as a defensive location and as a meeting place for the Cruithin* or Picts. As promontory forts are generally assigned to the Iron Age, 300 BC–500 AD, this would put the building of the fort here by Domhnall out by about 100 years. However, this area has a long history of Neolithic and Bronze Age habitation, and a Neolithic house was identified here; also, the discovery of a *fulacht fiadh* would suggest a way of cooking that lasted from the Bronze Age down to the historic period when 'The Banquet of *Dún na nGed*' took place.

Dún na nGed was not the residence of King Domhnall for long, and thus its location may have been forgotten among the storytellers and early historians; after a while Domhnall moved his court to Ard Fothad close to the town of Donegal, and it is here that he died in the year 639 according to the *Annals of the Four Masters*.

'The Banquet of *Dún na nGed*' is a good example of an historical tale which is both accurate in terms of the people involved and bardic in its licence to tell history as a form of storytelling. Even its opening line has the approach of the bedtime story as told by adults:

> *Bui rig amra fror Éirinn, feachtus and …*
> Once upon a time there was a renowned king over Ireland …

'The Banquet of *Dún na nGed*' is in some way a preface to the Battle of Moira or *Cáth Maighe Rath* in County Down in 637. Historically these tales tell the end of the power of the Dál nAraide or Cruithin,* the aboriginal Irish and British or Picts. However, the bardic tradition of storytelling focuses on detail rather than give a broader picture of the historical realities. This has on occasion confused scholars and led them to believe that the whole process of early Irish history is one long rant, colourful, engaging and poetic but with a cultural rather than an historical core.

The background to this story is the legend that Congal Cáech, the King of Ulster and of the Dál nAraide, was slighted by Domhnall mac Áed, King of Tara. Domhnall was of the northern branch of the Uí Néill, a Leinster tribe which together with the Cenél Conaill and the Cenél nEógain had established themselves in the north-west. This slight, according to Mac Niocaill in *Ireland before the Vikings*, 'may have some basis in fact'; either way, it forms the basis of 'The Banquet at *Dún na nGed*'. The 'slight' concerned goose eggs, which were placed on silver dishes and given to all participants at the feast except Congal, who was given a hen's egg placed on a wooden dish. One wonders whether there was a connection between the name of the fort and the core of the story. To add insult to injury, Congal's seat beside the king was given to Maelodhar Macha, King of Oirghiall.

A relevant verse from the tale reads thus:

In Chuid sin Chaithise a nocht,
cen uabar, cen imarnocht,
ug circe o'n rig narsat car,
is ug géoid do Maelódar.

That meal thou hast taken tonight
Is without pride, without honour;
A hen's egg from the king who loves thee not,
And a goose egg to Maelodhar.

[Translated by John O'Donovan]

The wider historical context from the seventh century is the rise of the Uí Néill, and their rise to power and the decline of the Dál nAraide, or the rise of the Laigin or dominant Leinster tribe against the ancient peoples of the north-east of Ireland.

OFFALY

Ua bhFáilí, *a noted Leinster tribe and descendants of 'Foilgi Ross'*

Belief in the fairies (*aes síde*) existed until recently throughout Ireland, though customs relating to them may still exist in outlying pockets of the Slieve Bloom Mountains. There is, for example, the 'fairy tree' or St Kieran's Bush at Clonmore [54], south of the Seir Kieran ecclesiastical site, which is seven miles north of Roscrea on the R421. Seir Kieran means 'the heel of Ciaran'. This 'fairy tree' or *sceach gheal* (whitethorn) can be seen today covered in rags or old pieces of clothing, a remnant of a rite carried out by a young virgin or *pisóc*. The young woman walked clockwise or *deas sol*, 'right to the sun', three times around the 'fairy tree' and hung her piece of cloth fresh with her first menstrual blood on the tree. She then went to the well and perhaps washed. She had now manifested her coming of age and her readiness to procreate. After three days relatives took down the garment, and the rite was thus complete. Although the finer points of this rite have long gone out of our national consciousness, the word has retained its strength. The word now is spelt either as *piseog* or *pishreog* together with variations of the above. Examples of its modern definition include 'a charm or spell' or 'magic'. Dinneen defines it as 'witchcraft, sorcery' as well as a charm or spell, and goes on to say:

piseoga were chiefly directed to obtaining cures of man and beast and to conserving and increasing farm products such as butter, milk young stock, etc.; they were mainly of four kinds—(a) protective from witchcraft; (b) seeking increase through certain practices savouring of witchcraft. Of (a) an example is not allowing fire to leave the house while butter was being churned; of (b) the putting of a cows *broghais* or 'afterbirth' under the milk keelers set to throw up cream; a third class (c) included love charms which are obscure; a fourth class (d) concerned itself with the human person, how to ward off and cure diseases, etc., also how to inflict injury on others.

A more sinister side to (d) is inferred by the infliction of injuries on others. Dinneen gives the following example of this: *im an deataigh úd ar mo chuid bainne-se*, 'may the butter of that house be added to my milk' (an imprecation used by a woman twisting a spancel on May Day in the early morning as the smoke arose from the neighbouring chimneys).

The original *piseog* may be seen in aspects of (c) and (d); the very rite of the young woman may be seen as the performance of a love charm and (d) may be seen as expressing an act of self-purification.

The following was told to me by Paddy Heany of Cadamstown in Co. Offaly:

John Heany, a local farmer from *Bar na scairt*, would sharpen his scythe after scything and leave it in the whitethorn tree for the fairies. There was a ringfort in front of his door and one day John and myself came down from the bog and John said 'go out and bring me in a *breasna of cipíns* [a bundle of sticks]'. I did, and he told me to take them back as they were taken from the ringfort and the fairies would burn the house if I did not.

Another story relating to fairies was told to me by Oliver Devery. A friend of his, 'a very straight forward man and one not easily fooled', was apparently 'tricked' by the fairies one day as he was going from one field to another in the townland of Kilcamin about two miles south of the village of Cloghan in north-west Offaly. He was convinced that the fairies were constantly moving a gap in the hedge so that he found it increasingly difficult to move from one field to another.

The Slieve Bloom mountain range straddles a large part of Offaly. According to local legend, the Fir Bolg* had a palace on a hill in the Slieve Blooms. When they left to fight at Moytura they sealed up this palace with stones and earth, and as they were all killed at this battle it presumably remains sealed Paddy Heaney told me that Montgomery Hitchcock believes that this 'palace' 'is there to be found yet'.

There is a great richness to many of the place names found in the mountains. On the west side of the Slieve Blooms lies Kinnitty (*cionn eitigh*, 'the head of the horse') [47]. Local historian Paddy Heaney says that the name means 'the head of Ita', reputedly a local princess, though more credence is given to the first meaning. Heaney quotes Montgomery

Hitchcock as saying that the Slieve Blooms were 'the ancient place of the Tuatha Dé Danann* and it was here that Eochaid and his people once held dominion'. He mentioned that the horse was of local significance in the Kinnitty area, as he knew and heard and saw the stone horseman found in Knocknaman (*Cnoc Manannáin*, 'the hill of Manannán'). Manannán* was both a sun god and a sea god and was often depicted as riding through the waves on horseback. The hill is also known as the hill of the sun god and was a druidic centre. A few miles south-east from Knocknaman is Crochaun, an area in Glendine [54]; a festival was held here at Lughnasa, which is on the eve of 1 August.

The stone horseman mentioned by Paddy was found by workmen working on the Bernard estate around 1847. While digging a trench, they found about two feet down a circle of stone in the centre of which was the figure of a horse and a rider carved from local sandstone, measuring fifteen by fifteen inches. The Bernards brought over an archaeologist from London who said that the figure dated back to the time of Tuatha Dé Danann.* It was kept in Kinnitty Castle until 1947, when the family donated it to the National Museum after selling the castle. This figure is minus the head and part of the legs and is known as the Knocknaman Horseman. A replica of it can be seen on the entrance piers of the National Stud at Tully, Co. Kildare.

Other places in Kinnitty are also associated with horses. One of these is a massive limestone boulder on the side of the hill in Glenregan known as the *capall bán* ('the white horse'). It is what geologists call 'an erratic', possibly having been deposited there during the Ice Age. Due to afforestation it cannot be seen now. To the north-west of Kinnitty, near the hill of Knockbarron, there is a druidic circle and close by is a well known as *tobar na gcapall* ('the well of the horse'). Adjoining Kinnitty there is a field known as *baile eitigh* ('the place of the horse').

To the south of the village of Cadamstown [54] is the hill of Coolcreen (*Coil Crinn*, 'the corner of the old [wood]') on top of which was what was known as O'Flanagan's Fort, perhaps around twenty-seven acres in dimension. Although part of the ramparts can still be seen, it has fallen victim to land reclamation. Inside this hill were two Bronze Age burial mounds. The O'Flanagans were the chiefs of Kinnelarga, a territory comprising the west Slieve Blooms and from Birr down as far as Roscrea. They held this land until the O'Carrolls arrived in the twelfth century. The O'Carrolls, having established themselves, built Ballymacadam Castle close to Cadamstown, now destroyed.

A stone found in the fort, and locally described as either a turtle or an eagle, can today be seen in Kinnitty village, although it is known as the Ballykelly stone, after a nearby townland. According to local historians, Ballykelly derives from *baile ceile*, 'the meeting place', which is supported by the fact that there was a forge here. If this is correct, the association with the Kellys is meaningless.

Two stone walls, twenty yards apart, ran parallel up the hill of Coolcreen, between which cattle were run, possibly at *samain* or during the feast of St John. Fires were lit beneath the walls, so the ensuing smoke would delouse the cattle. An inauguration stone was also found here but was buried by a local farmer during land reclamation in the 1950s and 1960s. Close by in Ballykelly, two walls for running cattle were destroyed by a local farmer.

Paddy Heaney's ancestors lived at one stage inside the ring fort at Coolcreen and, according to his father, never had any luck there, which he attributed to the killing of two men there during the struggle of 1798. The remnants of the fort have not been included in the archaeological inventory for Offaly published in 1997, and neither was it mentioned in the archaeological survey for 1847–8. However, a ring barrow, a tumulus and an enclosure are noted as existing in this area from the most recent survey.

The large standing stone found here but then buried by the landowner was regarded by Montgomery Hitchcock as the inauguration stone of the O'Flanagans. There was a footprint in the stone in which the king-to-be would place his foot during the inauguration ceremony, similar to the inauguration stone of the O'Conors, which is now sited at Clonaslee house, Castlereagh, Co. Roscommon.

On the eve of 1 November, the great festival of *samain* was held on Glendossaun Mountain (*Glenn do samain*, 'the glen of *samain*') [54], the festival we now celebrate as Hallowe'en. There are some high flagstones on the top of Glendossaun, and these are said to have been part of an altar used by the druids and then destroyed by St Patrick. Nearby is Hugh O'Neill's well, formerly known as St Patrick's well; it is just on the other side of the border with Co. Laois.

About a mile from Glendossaun is a mysterious lake named Clear Lake. About 1,000 feet above sea level and surrounded by bog, it never goes dry and never overflows. The water is very clear, thus the name. As with many lakes throughout Ireland, legend has it that it is bottomless. One theory about its origin is that it is the result of a meteorite, which would explain its circular shape and the fact that it has a sheer drop on each side. However, had this happened, the bog would have burst out and would not be intact after such an impact. Like nearby Knocknaman and Glendossaun mountains, it was possibly a druidic site. A local archaeologist has suggested that this lake was made by the druids and that there is evidence of other lakes of a similar type throughout Ireland.

North-west of Coolcreen, 1,087 feet above sea level, is Spink Hill (*Spinc*, 'pinnacle') [54], on the south side of which is a Bronze Age burial mound. The stones are still there. Close by is a conglomerate stone known as 'the bracken stone', from the Irish word *breac* meaning speckled. In druidic times, as the sun rose to its height at midday this stone was said to flash throughout the glen. It was, and is still, also known as the 'cursing stone' of the druids.

To the south-east of Spink Hill is a hill known as Bandra (*bean draoi*, 'female druid') and within its surrounds is a place named Cruithin.* The Cruithin were among the earliest tribes to enter Ireland, settling first in the Ards Peninsula in Co. Down. They are also known as the Dál nAraide, and it may be contested that they were also the race known as the Picts. Their south-west migratory path brought them to the Slieve Blooms. While they were living here and in the surrounding area of Glen Letter (*Gleann Leitir*, 'glen by the watery hillside') and all the way to Kinnitty, another tribe arrived, and this led to a battle at Cruithin. Before the battle, the Cruithin buried their treasure under a whitethorn tree and left a wolfhound to protect it. After the Cruithin were defeated the victors killed the wolfhound, cut out his heart and put it on the tree. The location of that tree was known as *Cú na Croi* ('the heart of the hound'). Local lore has it that the Cruithin were horse worshippers; this makes the find of the Knocknaman Horseman all the more interesting.

Another place steeped in ancient lore is Croghan Hill [48], three-and-a-half miles north of Daingean. In Irish it is called *Cnoc Cruacháin*, and its earlier name was *Cruacháin Brí Éli* ('the mound of the hill of the Éli'). The Éli were a people who inhabited parts of Offaly, Tipperary and Laois. Their name is incorporated in the term Ely O'Carroll country. Other places in Offaly connected with the Éli are *Móin Éli*, part of the Bog of Allen and *Magh Éli la Lagnib* ('the plain of the Éli of Leinster'), identified as Moyally [48], two miles south-east from Moate, Co. Westmeath, and just inside the Offaly border. A turn to the right a mile-and-a-half east from Moate on the N6 leads one down a boreen and into the plain of *Magh Éli*. On the plain today one can see the ruins of the sixteenth-century Melaghlin Castle, and less than a 100 yards across the border into Westmeath at Ardnaponra, a ring fort.

The Éli were driven out of Offaly by the Gaels on their way north from the south-west. The Uí Fhailge tribe have been identified by O'Rahilly as a branch of the Éli. The Éli then became members of a subservient class or a tributary group and were known as the *aithechthuatha*, or 'subject-people'. The territory around the Hill of Croghan was known in days of antiquity as *Fotharta Airbrech* ('the wooded hollow of the great hosts'). The inhabitants here may well have been the Picts or Cruithin* or a pre-Gaelic people entering Ireland through Leinster. Croghan Hill is strongly associated with the Éli people. Éli in Irish means 'a charm or a chant or an incantation', and the goddess associated with the Éli may be the *ellen trechend* or the triple-headed goddess who sometimes assumes the form of a destructive bird. She emerges from the underworld site near Rathcroghan in Co. Roscommon every *samain*. She may be the eponymous deity of the Éli. Éli in Irish also means a flock of birds. Later this area was associated with the mythological figure of Brigit and later again with St Brigit.

Eight miles south-south-west of Croghan Hill as the crow flies is Geashill (*Géisill*, 'place of great clamour or shouting' – presumably a place of large gatherings). It was here that the Milesian or Gaelic conquerors of the Cruithin* eventually fought an internecine battle for sovereignty of all Ireland or for control of both sides of the *eiscir riada*. The two Milesian brothers seeking sole sovereignty were Éber and Éremon, and they fought on a plain by Geashill known as *Magh Smerthan*. This name has several possible translations; it may refer to the false beard worn by Cú Chulainn,* or it may refer to a marrow tub, *smirchomairt*, used for the healing of wounds after combat. According to Keating [FFÉ, vol. 2, 105], the battle was fought at *Bru Bhriodain*, at a pass between two plains in the district of Geishill':

> *Torchar Éibhear, anba an fear,*
> *Le hÉireamhón mac Míleadh;*

Fuair I dtuath Ghéislle a ghoin,
San maidin ag Maigh Smearthoin.

Éber fell, great the man,
By Éremon son of Míl;
He got his death-wound in the land of Geishill
in the morning on Magh Smearthoin.

[Translated by P. S. Dinneen]

Evidence for communities living in Ireland during the Mesolithic or Middle Stone Age time (7000–4000 BC) can be found at Ferriter's Cove, Co. Kerry; at Mount Sandel on the Bann Estuary, Co. Derry; and along the River Blackwater in Co. Cork. The settlement at Lough Boora [54] is the only Mesolithic habitation in Co. Offaly. These people survived by hunting, fishing and gathering, making blades of flint for cutting and scraping and flint axes for chopping. This site was only discovered in 1977 and excavated by the National Museum of Ireland. It has been described as a summer shoreline camp, a site where Stone Age communities spent the summer season. The flint they used was locally available chert – a flint-like quartz also known as hornstone. More than 400 objects were recovered, including three polished stone axe heads. The find here was because the midland bog was drained, and when the turf was harvested the fossil shore of the original Lough Boora emerged. To get to Lough Boora, go to Kilcormac and turn north at the post office for a mile-and-a-half; this road is known as the Offaly Way. After a twenty-minute walk, turn left and you are then in Stone Age territory and heading towards Lough Boora; a mild repast of salmon or ham would find you eating the same meal as our earliest ancestors.

The Bronze Age is well represented in Offaly by the Clonfinlough Stone [47]; it is sometimes seen as an example of rock art, though it may also depict an early example of a battle fought during the Late Bronze Age or Early Iron Age.

This stone is a large limestone slab from the Carboniferous Period and is also described as a large glacial erratic boulder. Elizabeth Shee Twohig in her description of this stone says nothing quite like the Clonfinlough carvings appears to have been recorded in Ireland or Britain. It is decorated with a series of figures and is unique among the stone monuments of Ireland. These engravings contain figures described as crosses and as '*phi* figures', of which there are eleven instances. Similar stones have been found in Cork, Kerry and Louth as well as in England, Scotland and north-west Spain.

These stones have been regarded as examples of Galician rock art of the Bronze Age. The Clonfinlough Stone may well describe pictorially an early tussle between the Milesian Gaels and indigenous people such as the Éli. This contention has been previously documented by two archaeologists, R.A.S. Macalister and Joseph Raftery. Macalister saw it as a battle between the 'loop men' and the 'cross men'. Raftery described the stone as being 'without parallel in Ireland'. He described it as having close parallels in the Iberian Peninsula and possessing the 'stylised representations of human beings'. Raftery states that this stone 'has usually been interpreted as being the first record in Irish history of a battle between two groups of people'. Before there is a collective wince from archaeologists, let me say that Raftery resumes reserve and states that 'it is not possible to say what the meaning of the Clonfinlough stone is'.

The possibility that it does represent some ancient struggle is strengthened by the number of battles fought on the south side of the eskers that make up the *eiscir riada*. Two battles spring to mind, firstly the Battle of Moylena (*Cath Maighe Léna*) at Moleen, the large plain south of the eskers, and then the Battle of Comhraire at Moyally (*Magh Éile*, 'the plain of the Ely'), also south of the *eiscir riada*. One may wonder why these battles between the Milesian Gaels and the aboriginal tribes were fought here; suffice to say that the south side of these hills were warmer because of their alignment and thus more productive for crops; also, the soil would be finer, as the north-facing land tends to be rockier even to this day. Also, Ireland was divided by these east–west hills, which constituted a borderland and a theatre for encounters between those arriving from the north-east and east coasts and those entering from the south-west. The word *escir* is an Irish word meaning 'a ridge or elevation separating two plains'. The *eiscir riada* or 'esker of the kings' marks the course of an Ice Age river, which was formed under the ice. When the ice eventually disappeared, the 'tunnel fill would emerge as an esker' (Mitchell 1976). At Tullabeg, in the area of the Clonfinlough Stone, and at Clonmacnoise fossilised shellfish were deposited hundreds of thousands of years before people arrived. In boggy counties like Offaly, the eskers provided natural causeways. The *eiscir riada* or 'gravel hills of the kings' is the legendary boundary between the southern half of Ireland, or *Leath Mhogha*, and the northern half, or *Leath Cuinn*. These hills stretch from Dublin to Clarinbridge, Co. Galway.

The Battle of Moylena was fought in the second century AD between the native tribes and the invaders from north-west Spain. O'Curry gives two dates for this battle, namely 180 and 137 AD. The oldest source for the battle comes from the eighth century and is titled *Do Bunad Imthechta Eóganachta* ('the original [story] of the adventures of the Eóganacht'). As so often happens in these tales, the narrative is a construct of a number of legends concerning the rivalry between the indigenous peoples and the invading army from Spain. It tells how Eógan, the leader or the eponymous deity of the Eóganacht, came to Ireland from Spain with 150 men, landed with his forces at Kenmare in south-west Munster and settled in the land. Apparently, there was a famine at the time, and Eógan was able to supply food to the famished. The condition for nourishment was that Eógan's son be made king.

After fifteen years, Eógan attempted to overthrow Conn, the King of Tara, but he was defeated and slain by Conn at *Magh Léna* alongside a fellow warrior named Fergus; two hillocks on the plain are said to be their tombs. The plain is about a mile north-east of Tullamore, in the townland of Ballynasrah. The heath named Moleen [48] is where this battle was fought and where the Cruithin* or indigenous tribes temporarily checked the

Spanish Gaels or Goidels. The best way to get to Moleen is to take the third-class road east of the hospital in Tullamore and head north-east for two miles, then take a turn left to a smaller road which runs for about 100 yards before entering a track over the gate – here ask permission from the local farmer to proceed. This track leads to the eskers and Moleen. South of here you are looking at the plain and the site of our earliest recorded battle. Local lore says that at a later time (1601) Hugh O Neill encamped here on his way to Kinsale, and the hollows within the eskers are locally known as 'the garrisons'.

The battle of Comraire at Moyally [48], south of the eskers, was fought at a later stage between two brothers of the Gaels, namely Un or An and Éremón, presumably for the kingdom of the southern part of Ireland. Again, this battle was fought south of the *eiscir riada*, about ten miles north-west of Moleen. Above this plain, at Comraire, is the burial mound of Un.

A few miles east of the Clonfinlough Stone is the village of Boher where the church houses the remarkable Shrine of St Manchan, the largest surviving medieval Irish reliquary. In technique and style, it is similar to the Cross of Cong. The reliquary, which is made of yew, was originally covered with fifty figures, but today only eleven exist on one of its sides. It contains bones of St Manchan. Adding to the beauty of this shrine is a number of stained-glass windows by Harry Clarke. Manchan was a sixth-century saint; his feast day is 24 January.

A few hundred yards west of the Clonfinlough Stone is Fin Lough, and south of the lake the site of a Late Bronze Age settlement was excavated in 1993. It consisted of three circular timber platforms of varying size, the platforms representing the remains of two substantial hut sites and one smaller hut site. Two boat paddles were recovered from one platform. At the centre of Fin Lough is a *crannóg*, a name derived from the Irish *crann*, meaning a tree. The word translates as a 'wooden lake dwelling'. This dwelling can be defined as a small, circular man-made island dwelling enclosed by wooden palisades. Access to the shore was either by a causeway or by dugout canoes. Although these structures date back to Neolithic times, their development was most numerous between the fourth and seventh centuries AD. This also was the time for the upsurge in the building of ring forts. *Crannóg* communities lasted for nearly 6,000 years until the seventeenth century; perhaps their defensive structures enabled their survival. The Late Bronze Age dwelling at Clonfinlough has been described as 'unique in the Irish archaeological record'.

One of the most remarkable finds from the Bronze Age is the Dowris Hoard, which was uncovered in the early part of the nineteenth century by two men trenching potatoes in the townland of Whigsborough [53], at a place called Derrens or Dowris. This place is so significant that the Bronze Age period in Ireland from 700 to 300 BC is known as the 'Dowris Period'. The Bronze Age community here not only farmed but produced many artefacts that led to the Late Bronze Age becoming the first 'golden age' in our history – a period during which it seems that the successful cultivation of crops gave people the time to develop other skills and crafts. The Dowris Hoard consists of 200 items, of which 190 can be seen today: 111 are in the National Museum of Ireland in Dublin and seventy-nine in the British Museum. The items include forty-four spearheads, forty-three axes, twenty-four trumpets and forty-four crotals. The trumpets were used to summon gatherings and presumably were used as an integral part of ceremonies. The Irish word *crothal* means a 'rattle'. The crotal is peculiar to Ireland and, though generally employed as a handbell or above doors to alert one to guests or strangers, could also be used around the necks of cattle. Ireland at that time was a supplier of copper to Europe, and this led to both wealth and innovation.

It has been suggested that the general expansion of farming at that time was due to the introduction of some sort of plough. Ard ploughs (the word *ard* is found in the root *ar*, 'to plough', and gives the Old Irish *arathar*, 'a plough') were being used at that time in Scandinavia, and finds of amber beads in Ireland show that there must have been trading connections with northern Europe. This plough was also found in Danish bogs with radiocarbon dating ranging from 900 to 350 BC. As it was used in Scotland, it was most likely also used in Ireland and is the only possible reason for the leap in farm yields. The ard plough was very basic, with a *share* or oak cutting-rod that ploughed just below the surface. Because of its limitations, cross-ploughing was necessary, and this resulted in square-shaped fields, which are sometimes described by archaeologists as 'Celtic fields'.

FIGURE 23. Hand ploughing lasted in Ireland for 2,000 years until the 1970s.

WESTMEATH

Iarmhí, 'western Meath'

The 600-foot-high Hill of Uisneach [48] was regarded as the omphalos or centre of Ireland, the omphalos, from the Greek word for 'navel', being a sacred stone in the temple of Apollo at Delphi, which was said to mark the centre of the known world. The omphalos at Uisneach is represented by the Cat Stone, a boulder also known as *Ail na Uírenn*, 'the Stone of the Divisions'. This stone is to the west of the Hill of Uisneach and was the common point touched by all the five provinces – that is, the four provinces of Ulster, Leinster, Munster and Connacht, with Mide constituting the fifth province.

A verse in the *Lebor Gabála* or the *Book of Invasions* states:

> About the stone in cold Uisneach
> In the plains of Mide of the horseman-bands,
> On its top—it is a fair co-division—
> Is the co-division of every province.

As well as the Cat Stone there was at Uisneach one of the five famous trees of Ireland, namely the *Craeb Uisnigh* or the *Bile Uisnigh* ('the ash of Uisneach'), which stood close to the Cat Stone.

> An ash in Uisneach, where the troops dwell,
> The branches fell; the truth is plain,
> In the time of the sons of Aed Slane.

[Translated by R.A.S. Macalister]

Apart from the fact that the tree fell in the time of Aed Slane, nothing more is known of what happened to this tree or how it was brought down. Of all the *biles* or sacred trees in Ireland, the *Bile Uisnig* is possibly the most important, situated as it was at a site generally believed to be the cosmological centre of Ireland. The ash was seen as connecting the physical and spiritual aspects of the world, and thus provided a link to the Otherworld. Trees were the oldest deities and were venerated worldwide. In northern Europe, the Norse tree Yggdrasil was said to have been situated at the centre of the world. One of its roots reached down to the depths of the subterranean kingdom, while its boughs reached the sky. Yggdrasil is associated with the god Odin, and Norse mythology is full of stories about this sacred tree.

The Germans also believed that the universe was supported by a famous tree, and it was a custom to have the framework of their houses supported by a huge tree trunk. Some tribes set up pillars made of a single tree trunk on hilltops. These were said to represent the tree of the universe. These were known as *Irmensul* or 'giant column'. While in Westphalia in 722, Charlemagne had, in the tradition of St Boniface, one of these venerated pillars destroyed.

The sacred tree at Uisneach is bereft of such a wealth of lore, but the hill on which it stood is associated with the god Balor or Bel, its original name in fact being *Cnoc Balair* or 'Balor's Hill'. With its great views across the central lowlands, Balor's Hill was the pagan sanctuary of one of the great assemblies of pre-Christian Ireland. St Patrick is said to have won over this ancient hill, but there are no Christian antiquities here, although the names St Patrick's Well and St Patrick's Bed are ascribed to a platform of stones on the summit of the hill.

At Uisneach, fires were lit every May eve in honour of Bel, the sun god. Beltaine, meaning 'Bel's fire', is the Irish word for this festival and also for the month of May. Fires were lit, and cattle were driven between them to protect against disease. The incantations of the druids could be heard, and cattle were sacrificed to Bel, who was locally known as Balor. The chief druid, who was named Mide and whose name is eponymous with the central province, lit the first fire at Uisneach. The great assemblies held here every May Day were known as the *Mórdáil Uisnig* ('the assembly of Uisneach'). Comparisons have been made between the druidic ceremonies at Uisneach and those in Brittany also led by the druids. Interestingly, that other sun god, Lug* of the Tuatha Dé Danann,* was killed or superseded at Uisneach by a later triad of gods – Mac Cuill, Mac Cécht and Mac Gréine.

Although Binchy states in relation to the *Mórdáil Uisnig* that there 'is not a shred of evidence that any such assembly was ever held during the entire historical period', a passage in the old list of royal auspices and taboos states that it was customary to hold a meeting at Uisneach about every seven years under the presidency of the King of Tara. The price of attendance at this meeting was a gold armlet, to be handed over to the King of Meath. Keating wrote that the *Mórdáil Uisnig* was held every year on May Day, and it was the 'custom to exchange with one another their goods, wares and valuables'. But, more importantly, they 'used to offer sacrifice to the chief god they adored, who was called Bel; and it was their wont to offer two fires in honour of Bel in every district in Ireland and to drive a weakling of each species of cattle between the two fires as a preservative to shield from all diseases during that year'. As Dinneen writes in his dictionary, '*idir dhá theine lae Bealtaine*' – referring to the practice of driving cattle between two fires with a view to their preservation. An older name for Uisneach was *Cnoc Balair* or Balor's Hill, and other names were *Cnoc Úachtair Erca*, 'the hill of the high heavens' and *Cnoc Úachtair Fhorcha*, 'the hill of the foremost fires'.

Numerous raths, cashels and cairns are scattered over the townlands of Uisneach Hill: Kellybrook, Togherstown, Mweelra, Rathnew and Fearaghafin. In the townland of Rathnew, south-east of the hill, an excavation by the Royal Irish Academy between 1925 and 1930 on a bivallate rath with a diameter of 200 feet discovered a series of pits and post holes. The many animal bones suggest habitation; a nearby souterrain was closed up.

The fact that no pottery was found has led some to believe that the art of pottery was lost and had to be reimported from Europe. The date given for the rath is between 150 and 200 AD. Contemporary with this rath is the Uisneach House, which is associated with Tuathal Techtmar or Tuathal the Legitimate, who is recorded as King of Ireland in the second century AD and who transferred his seat of power to Uisneach. Macalister writes that the house within the ring fort contains seven rooms together with a complicated series of ramparts fortifying the site. He further writes: 'We may consider ourselves as near to certainty as the conditions permit, that we have the actual dwelling in which the monarch was housed.' He wonders if a recess in the thickness of the walls was a sleeping chamber. He states that 'of this royal house we cannot in honesty say anything better than that a darker more uncomfortable and less sanitary dwelling it would be difficult to imagine'. He adds that it is the 'most elaborate dwelling of the Iron Age yet found in Ireland'. Due to pillaging by wall builders over the centuries, all that is left today are a few mounds.

Despite Macalister's pronouncements, later excavations concluded that 'little was found to support the identification of the site as a royal residence'. What was found included a bone comb; according to Raftery, 'only one find of silver has been ascribed to this period (the Iron Age) which takes the form of an inlay in the head of a ring headed bronze pin'. Also found in the dig was a sickle, a knife, a horse bit and a gilt-bronze saucer-brooch in one of the souterrains and dated to the sixth century.

Uisneach is ten miles south-west of Mullingar on the R390. It is three-and-a-half miles east of the village of Ballymore, so should you end up in Ballymore you have gone too far.

Another famous *bile* or sacred tree in Westmeath stood north of Kinnegad [42] and just south of the village of Killucan. This ash tree was known as the *Craeb Daithi* and was situated in the ancient territory of the O'Hannafys. This tree was in Farbill or *Fer-bile* ('the men or tribe of the *bile* or ancient tree'), and it is likely that under this tree the chiefs of the O'Hannafys were inaugurated. The name *Craeb Daithi* or *Bile Daithi* takes its name from *Daithi Éices*, or 'Daithi the seer or poet'. That he was buried in Cruachain, one of the five centres of Ireland in Roscommon, is an acknowledgement of the regard shown to him.

An ancient *bruidne* or hostel known as *Bruiden Da Choca* is situated at Breenmore Hill, which was anciently called Sliabh Malonn and lies seven miles north-east of Athlone [48]. This was one of the great ancient 'hostels' of Ireland, places of hospitality, each of which had a mythical caludron that provided enough food for any number of guests, and in this instance served the route from Connacht eastwards. It is at the centre of the saga *Togail Bruidne Da Choca* ('the destruction of Da Choca's hostel'). O'Donovan claimed that there was a circle of large standing stones around the fort. These presumably have been transmogrified into stone walls. The saga says that there were three separate buildings on the site: a house for soldiers, a house for women on the summit of the hill and a house for nobles on the slope below. The townland of Cloghbreen (*cloch bruidne*, 'the hostel of stone') has gone, but its name lives on in the present townland. At present there are five ring forts on Breenmore Hill, and their excavation might yield interesting results.

The townland of Breenmore (*bruiden mór*, 'large hostel') or Bryanmore appears on the *Discovery* map; the Breensford River [47] to the west of *Bruiden Da Choca* may have some connection to the site. Breenmore Hill is in the upper parish of Drumraney and in the barony of Kilkenny West. On Sliabh Malonn between Bryanmore Lower and Bryanbeg Upper there are five ring forts. Sliabh Malonn, which is not on the *Discovery* map, is an elevated site between Bryanmore Lower, Bryanmore Upper and Bryanbeg Upper.

The *bruidne* (plural of *bruiden*) were seen as Otherworld feasting places where the inexhaustible cauldron of the Dagda,* the King of the gods, was always on the boil. They were thus the centre of the Otherworld feast where the Goibniu* or the *gabha*, the smith god, presided over a perpetual feast. An existing remnant of the *bruidne* is the *tech n-oíged* or 'guest house', and many an Irish hostelry can still be found where four roads meet.

In the more mundane sense, they were places where the owner of the *bruiden* was obliged to hold seasonal feasts for the local king, and as such they were known as *ríg-briugu* ('the king's hostel'). One such *briugu* was the *briugu Buchet* ('Buchet's hostel') wherein was the 'cauldron of generosity among the Leinstermen', and this 'was reduced to near-penury by the frequent visits of the king's thirty-two sons'. *Bruiden Da Choca* was such a hostel, and the arrival of kings here has been documented. One such person to stay the night was Cormac Connloinges, son of Conchobar mac Nessa, King of Ulster. Prior to his night at the hostel, Cormac, having crossed the Shannon, came to *Magh Deirg*, a flat plain known as the Derries today and south of Athlone, where they encountered a band of Connachtmen returning from a raid on Ulster and slaughtered them. The battles took place around *Magh Deirg* and are named as *Druim Airthir*, *Dubthir-Átha-Luain* close to Athlone, *Tír Coibden* east of Athlone and *Muine Caindlige* or the 'Bog of Caindlech', which was a stretch of bog running towards *Bruiden Da Choca*. The name *Muine Caindlige* exists today as Bunnahinly [47]. The killing of the Connachtmen incensed Medb* and she sent a band of warriors to the hostel to avenge them; in the resulting battle, Cormac Connloinges was killed along with most of his warriors. A site named in the course of the fighting with Medb's army was at *Ard mBoccain*, now Ardbuckan [48], one mile east from *Bruidean Da Choca*, and another is *Ard na Crech*, now Ardnagragh, two miles east.

Cormac Connloinges' grave and mound were made at *Cluain Duma*. Is this the motte at Mount Temple [48]? It has been suggested that it was close to *Bruiden Da Choca*. The *Book of Druim Snechta* says that the head of Cormac was brought to Athlone.

> *Ó ro-mbéotar in dá ón,*
> *isin bruidin lasin cluain,*
> *ba cend Cormaic Condluingis,*
> *fácbais Anlúan oc Áth Luain.*

> When the two maniacs slew him
> in the hostel along with the pack,

it was the head of Cormac Connloinges
that Anlúan left at Athlone.

The above verse is from a doctoral thesis by Gregory Toner, which is an edited version of a fifteenth-century manuscript, *Bruiden Da Choca*. The original manuscript was written in the twelfth century, which makes it contemporaneous with the *Book of Leinster*.

Sliabh Malonn, or Breemore Hill, is nearly 500 feet high and has views over the Shannon Valley and the midland plain. The site of the *bruiden* on top is an oval fort standing ten feet above the surrounding ground.

As to the meaning of *da choca*, one almost screams out for a simple translation of the two words. Of the word *da* it has been suggested that it is a contraction of *dia* or 'god'; thus, we have the 'hostel of the god Choca', and this leaves us with the meaning of Choca. Dinneen's dictionary defines *coca* as 'cock', so *bruiden da choca* would translate as 'the hostel of the cock god'; however, with the verb *cóch*, meaning to attack, we could surmise a translation as 'the hostel of the god of war'.

Bruidean Da Choca was in the ancient territory of *Tethba*, more commonly known as Teffia, which was a district in central Ireland east of the Shannon from Lough Boderg [33], which on its west side straddles Roscommon and Leitrim down as far as Clonmacnoise [47] in Offaly. On its west side Teffia extended from Lough Gamhna in Longford [34] to the River Brosna at Ferbane [48]. It ran as far north as Cloncoose in Longford and as far east as Coole in Westmeath. Clonmacnoise may have been the property of the kings of *Tethba* at one time.

The great mythic tale of Midir and Étaín is centred in *Tethba*. King Eochaid Airem had a fort in *Tethba* known as *Dún Frémainn* and another, also known as *Dún Frémainn*, in Westmeath; this has been identified as Frewin Hill, west of Lough Owel [41]. The *Lebor Gabála* says that he was burnt to death 'in Frémainn of Tethba'. This fort may not be so easy to find, but a suggestion in the *Chronicon Scotorum* suggests that it is close to *Sliabh gCalraidh*, or Sliabh Golry [41], to the west of Ardagh. According to Hogan, it was known as *Sliabh gCalraidh Brí Léith*. The hill gets its name from the *Calraige*, a tribe associated with Westmeath, Longford, Roscommon, Mayo and Sligo. This tribe was termed as being *aithechthuatha* or a 'tributary' or 'vassal' class, which was generally the term applied to the pre-Gaelic or pre-Milesian races who were overtaken by the Gaels and forced to pay tribute to their new masters.

Eochaid Airem, mentioned above, had a daughter named Tethba, and from her the territory of *Tethba* is named in the *Dindshenchas**:

> *Dorat Tethba don tír thúaid,*
> *ná bad sechna dia sár-búaid,*
> *a comainm clethach, rochar*
> *ingean Echach Aireman …*

The final verse refers both to Tethba and her nurse Eitech:

Marait a n-anmann dia n-éis,
conas-fagbam fria n-aisnéis,
na mban co mbríg is co mblat:
rotag cách tír dia tarat.

Tethba, daughter of Eochu Airem, gave to the northern land that she loved her secret name – let there be no slighting of her excellence! ...

Their names endure after them, the names of the women mighty and strong, and we find them to tell their story: each chose the land to which she gave her name.

[Translated by Edward Gwynn]

Margaret Dobbs, writing in the mid-twentieth century, says that *Tethba* is barely mentioned in the annals. However, it seems that there was a Milesian or Gaelic involvement in *Tethba* as Irial Faidh, son of Eremon the Milesian chief, won a battle here at *Ard Finmaoith*. Tigernmas, King of Ireland in the second century BC, also won a battle in north Tethba at Cluain Cuas [34] on the Leitrim side of the Longford–Leitrim border. Clooncose village today is seven miles south of Carrigallen in Leitrim.

Ten miles south-east of *Bruiden Da Choca* and east of *Tethba* is *Áth an Urchair* ('the ford of the cast'), today anglicised as Horseleap [48]. 'Horseleap' for *Áth an Luchaire*, or the 'ford of the foal', may well be an error; thus, one can see how ancient history is lost through mistranslation.

Just as *Bruiden Da Choca* involved the death of an Ulster king, Cormac Connloinges, by forces from Connacht, so *Áth an Urchair* ('the ford of the cast') is the scene of the eventual death of Conchobar mac Nessa, King of Ulster. I first heard this story in the early 1950s from my national schoolteacher, a Mrs Golden, or Bean Ní Golden as we then called her. She told of how Cet mac Magach threw a 'brain-ball' into the head of Conchobar mac Nessa, where it remained for seven years until Conchobar heard of the crucifixion of Christ and the ball fell from his head and the king died. The story told thus wedded an event with prehistory and joined it to a significant event in the Christian story.

About fifteen miles north-east of the Hill of Uisneach is Lough Derravaragh [41], from *dairbhreach*, meaning 'abounding in oaks'. There is evidence of a Mesolithic culture here about 9,000 years ago. The earliest settlers here were hunter–gatherers and Frank Mitchell in his book *The Irish Landscape* says: 'On the [north-west] shore of Lough Derravaragh, just where the River Inny [flowing from Lough Sheelin] enters the lake, there were extensive fens which were visited by people living in Larnian fashion.' The name 'Larnian' comes from the people who used the implements, mostly flint and stone, from the raised beach levels at Larne, Co. Antrim. The Larnians lived by hunting, foraging and fishing, as they did not clear the forests and, unlike their Neolithic successors, were limited to the lake shores from where most of their food derived.

There is evidence of a Mesolithic chert quarry nearby on the slopes of Knockeyon Hill, at 700 feet the highest hill in the county; this find was a result of research carried out by archaeologists from UCD and geologists from the National Museum of Ireland in Dublin. The hill gets its name from *Cnoc naomh Eoghain*, or more commonly Saint Eyon. The partial drainage of the lake in the 1960s allowed 'a very small window of archaeological surveying potential'. Chert is a flint-like stone, sometimes known as horn stone. On the south of Knockeyon there are exposed limestone cliffs, and from these cliffs bands of chert were quarried. Many of these cherts were found on the southern slopes of the cliff extending into the oak woods from which Derravaragh gets its name. The lakeshore of Derravaragh has produced picks, butt-trimmed blades and one piece of flint.

Nemed mac Agnomain, one of the earliest colonists of Ireland, from whom the Nemedians are named, was said to have arrived from the Black Sea and during his time four lakes were said to have erupted: Lough Loughall, Co. Armagh; Lough Ramor, Co. Cavan; and Loughs Derravaragh and Ennell in Co. Westmeath.

From the summit of this hill you have a magnificent view of Lough Derravaragh. Of all the colour slides I took throughout Ireland, the transparency of this lake is the most stunning of all. For those seeking to get to the summit, it is advisable to beware of bulls at the upper reaches, and a good rule of thumb is to ask the landlord's permission to walk on his or her land.

The area around Lough Derravaragh was well inhabited in the Early Medieval period; today there are about thirty-four ring forts surrounding the lake. There are also seven *crannógs* around the lake. Aidan O'Sullivan, an archaeologist who worked on the site at Coolure Demesne (north-east of the lake) has written that 'the presence of the smaller lakeshore crannogs may suggest that both high-status and low-status sites clustered together there, representing the dwellings of a community who resided around their lord or gathered for public assemblies, hosting, feastings or other activities associated with kingship'.

The lake is connected to a classical tale from Irish mythology, namely the Children of Lir,* which seems to be a tale with many European motifs, namely shape-changing and a dream-like timelessness, as well as the vindictive stepmother who occurs in so many stories.

The children, who spents 300 years on Lough Derravaragh after being turned into swans, are addressed by their stepmother in the following words:

> Out to your home, ye Swans, on Darva's wave;
> With clamorous birds begin your life of gloom;
> Your friends shall weep your fate, but none can save;
> For I've pronounced the dreadful words of doom.

> *[From P. W. Joyce's Old Celtic Romances]*

The swans ended up on *Inis Glora* [22] off the coast of Mayo, resuming their human shapes and becoming converts to Christianity, thus neatly bringing together pre-Christian and Christian mythologies.

In Christian times an oratory halfway up the hill at Knockeyon [41] became a place of pilgrimage on the first Sunday in August. At certain places on the path, pilgrims walked barefooted and in other places they moved along on their bare knees. A record of this harvest pilgrimage was recorded by Sir Henry Piers in 1682 and is included in *The Festival of Lughnasa* by Máire Mac Neill. The following is an extract from Piers's description:

> Their devotions performed, they return merry and shod, no longer concerned for those sins that were the cause of so severe a penance; but as if now having paid off the old score, they longed to go on in the new again, they return in all haste to a green spot of ground on the east side of the hill towards the land, and here men and women fall a dancing and carousing the rest of the day; for alesellers in great numbers have their booths here as in a fair, and to be sure the merry bagpipers fail not to pay their attendance. Thus, in lewd and obscene dancing and in excess of drinking, the remainder of the day is spent, as if they celebrated the Baccchanalia.

So, one might say that underlying the pilgrimage, the festival of Balor had changed little from pagan times.

Lough Ree (*Loch Rí* and originally *Loch Ríb*) [47, 40] borders three counties, Westmeath, Roscommon and Longford, and takes its name from Ríb, the stepbrother of Eochaid, son of Mairid, King of Munster. Eochaid drowned in Lough Neagh after eloping with his stepmother Ebliu. A similar fate awaited Ríb who was in a fight with the semi-divine Midir, who killed all Ríb's horses but gave him one to continue his journey. As in the folktale connected with Lough Neagh (*Loch Echach*, 'the lake of the horse'), Ríb's horse urinates, creating a spring that grows and forms Lough Ree in which Ríb and his men are drowned.

A poem in the notes of the *Dindshenchas** contains the following:

> *Loch Rí, cred ba fail in tainm a eolca Fail re fir gairm?*
> *Raidhid ce in Rí o fuil a eolcha dana in domain …*

> Loch Rí, whence comes its name, truly given, O ye learned of Inis Fail?
> Say it was Rí from whom it is called ye learned poets in all the world!

> Rí, famous son of Muirid, of the bright joyous plain of Meath, got a home there for a while in Magh Airbhten of the angels.

> A gelding – the braver was he! When loosed of his burden staled and made a spring – it was theme of talk – of the abundant flow in mid-plain.

> The copious spring spread over Magh Airbthen famed in story; it drowned Rí – the braver was he – with his horse and all his cattle.

From that Rí – it was a masterful effort – the lake is named throughout Erin: from him – a title early won – bravely arose the noble lake.

[Translated by Edward Gwynn]

WICKLOW

The name Wicklow is of Norwegian origin and in Norse is *Vikingr-lo*, which translates as the 'meadow of the Vikings' and later took the form Wykinglo, changing to Wicklow in the late twelfth century. In Irish, the name used is *Cill Mhantáin* ('the church of the toothless one').

The earliest dated settlement in Wicklow occurred in the Neolithic period (4000–2500 BC) and is indicated by a number of burial monuments known as megalithic tombs found to the north and west of the county. A fine example is at Scurlocksleap [56], locally known as 'Seefin', or the 'fairy mound of Finn mac Cumhail'.* This passage tomb is situated at the summit of Seefin Mountain. It is a circular cairn with a kerb of large boulders. The passage is orientated north-east to south-west like the *grikes* (fissures between blocks of limestone), which can be found as a continuing fault on the Aran Islands. It has a corbelled roof, a style of roofing seen at Newgrange and later at the Tower House at Termonfeckin.

The word *Manntán* in the Irish name for the county means one who has lost some teeth. It may be a description of the saint or the saint's personal name. The former probability is the stronger, as Manntán was, according to the *Annals of Clonmacnoise*, with St Patrick when he tried to land in Leinster on the coast of Wicklow. This landing was strongly resisted by the King of Leinster, and as Patrick attempted to come ashore one of the king's men threw a stone, which struck the saint's companion and left him toothless. Thus, Patrick failed to land and left, but not before placing a curse on the shore so that little or no fish would be caught there.

On the coast also is Leamore Strand [56], which is the reputed landing place for Ingcél Caech mac hui Conmaicni, the son of the King of the Britons or the Welsh, who was expelled from the kingdom for lawless behaviour and became a pirate or a 'reaver', as he is described in translation. In the tale *Togáil Bruidne Da Derga* ('The Destruction of the Hostel of the Red God'), Ingcél is the principal leader of invading bands coming across the Irish Sea to attack Conaire Mór, a local chief who has a fortress at *Bruiden Da Derga*. This saga, compiled in the eleventh century from two earlier versions, is regarded as having the greatest literary interest of all the older Irish sagas.

The story tells of a young king foredoomed to a tragic death, to which end the fates play a pivotal part. It centres around Conaire Mór, who was King of Ireland and who had his kingdom at Tara. The nucleus of the story tells how a King of the Érainn, in what is now the province of Leinster, was attacked and beheaded by a force of invaders from overseas. The 'historical fact' underlying this part of early Irish history is, according to O'Rahilly, the invasion of Leinster by a people known as the Laginian tribes, who subsequently gave their name to the province. Some of these invaders were also from Ireland, namely the four sons of Donn Désa who were from Leinster and who had been banished from Ireland by Conaire.

When Ingcél along with the sons of Donn Désa arrived in Ireland, they climbed to the top of Howth Hill or *Benn Étair* in order to reconnoitre the landscape. They saw Conaire going south with an army of men and, not knowing exactly where he was directed, they returned to their boats and sailed south along the coast. Where they landed has been contested among academics, but the one who did his homework best seems to me to have been Henry Morris, who in a paper titled 'Where was Bruiden Da Derga?' read to the Royal Society of Antiquaries in 1935 delves deepest into the topography of the story. According to Morris, the invading party landed at Leamore Strand, 'having seen the bright light of the hostel at Da Derga'. It was the night of the eve of *samain* or Hallowe'en, when fires would have been lit.

Morris never got the opportunity to check the specific location of Da Derga's Hostel, which is a pity considering the amount of time he spent pursuing it. More recent research would seem to place the hostel closer to Calary [56]. If this is correct, then *Bruiden Da Derga* was a hillfort with a commanding presence and a possible tribal centre for Conaire Mór and his people. Generally, hillforts are dated to the Late Bronze Age, and Conaire Mór's reign in the first century BC would mean that this hillfort had been standing some time before then. As a place of gathering and defence, the hillfort would be an obvious target for attack by outside forces seeking to overcome the local tribes. It was during the Iron Age that hillforts, of which there are about seventy in Ireland, enter the sagas, and *Bruiden Da Derga* is no exception.

There is a hillfort south of Calary Lower known as the Downshill Hillfort; this is a semicircular univallate hillfort about 394 yards in diameter east to west and 240 yards in diameter north to south. The site encloses the summit of Downshill, which stands at 407 yards, and from here there are commanding views, including the wedge of the Glen of the Downs. According to the Archaeological Inventory of County Wicklow, the summit is now covered in forestry and the only accessible surviving part of the rampart is along the south-west side where it forms part of a field boundary skirting the plantation. The earth-and-stone bank has an upright stone, though according to the Inventory this may not be original. This hillfort is about a mile north-west of the medieval village of Downs. This would put Downshill closer to the site than Lough Bray. A trade route from the Hill of Tara to Wicklow may have passed by Downshill, and the old roads and walls on Downshill are said to be part of this route. A cremation pit is said to exist at Downshill, but this requires further research.

The marshy coastline between Wicklow town and Greystones, almost a mile in depth and six-and-a-half miles in length, was known as *Sescenn Fuairbeoil* or *Sescenn Uairbeoil* ('the cold river-mouth at the swampland'), and here apparently there was a hostel, for it is recorded that at the 'hostel at Sescann' *ar bru Seiscinn Fuairbeoil*, the daughter of Conan Cualann gave Finn mac Cumhail* a drink. *Sescann* means an 'unproductive ground' or a marsh a swamp or a bog. *Beoil* is likely the genitive of *beol* or *béal*, namely 'of the mouth'. So Ingcél and his 'reavers' entered along the east coast at an opening along the marsh at Leamore Strand, though the word 'strand' may be something of a misnomer as the coastline here is stony. Leamore Strand, simply translated as the 'great grey land', has also been translated as 'the house of Lug'.

Morris states a number of reasons for his conviction that the 'reavers' landed here and not on Merrion Beach or *Trácht Fuirbthen* or *Muirbthen*, but says that *Muirbthen* may well be the 'Murrow' or 'Murrough' of Wicklow from south of Greystones to Wicklow Harbour. The word 'Murrough' does not appear in the Shorter Oxford Dictionary, and the closest word is 'morion', which means an abundance of 'cloudy quartz stones'. The Irish *múr* meaning 'a wall' can by extension mean 'an embankment of earth and stones built over burial chambers' (RIA), or a 'sandbank shoal' from the same source. Although the exact meaning seems to have been lost, it would seem to mean a 'raised stony beach' and definitely not Merrion Strand. The 'embankment of earth and stones built over burial chambers' fits in with the narrative of the story where it says that 'every man of the raiders picked up a stone to make a cairn'. According to the tale, the raiders erected a pillar stone for a rout, but a cairn for when they decided upon destruction. Also, the story says the noise of the invading force could be heard at the Bruiden and was so powerful that it shook the hostel. According to Morris, local people said to him that the noise made on this long stony beach by a strong tide could be heard far up the hills and may well have been the source for the shaking of the hostel.

Finally, a description of the area given by a Mrs M. O' Faherty from Newcastle to Morris in the 1930s is as follows:

> A marsh one-quarter to five-sixths of a mile in depth and six-and-a-half-miles in length lies between Newcastle and the sea. It begins at Ballygannon about one-and-a-half-miles south of Greystones and extends over three miles south of Newcastle station. These marshes are locally called 'bogs' and are covered with water during winter, especially when east winds blow. No one remembers a Gaelic name for them, but the local farmers are not here for more than two generations, and the majority of them for even less.

Another mention of *Seiscenn Uairbeoil* concerns Muircheartach mac Erca, King of Ireland for twenty-four years prior to his being burnt to death at his palace at *Cleithec* on the Boyne, Co. Meath, in 527 AD. He had his palace roofed by sedge grass cut by Leinster women from *Seiscenn Uairbeoil*. For Morris, the site of the hostel was positioned between Upper Lough Bray and what then was the Glencree Reformatory; to be more precise, Morris located the site of Bruiden Da Derga at the borders of Wicklow and Dublin, at Mareen's Brook, the main tributary of the Dodder, coming from Kippure. But the post holes have, to my knowledge, yet to be discovered. Perhaps they are covered by bog, awaiting discovery.

Downshill [56], a hill west of the Glen of the Downs, is approached from Downs, which was a small medieval village.

Morris also states that on their way from Leamore Strand the raiders went along the Glen of the Downs and climbed the Big Sugar Loaf (which my mother said was called 'Cú Chulainn's Spear' in her time). This mountain is in the heart of the ancient territory of Cualu, and the reavers could get an excellent view of the surrounding territory from here. The original line from the story states: *I n-Óe Cualann fo chomrier* ('in the sheep (?) country of Cualu the [view] was unimpeded'). There are various opinions about the extent of Cualu; some state that the territory covered the present county. However, Hogan says that it extends from Arklow to the Liffey and was coextensive with the Diocese of Glendalough.

There are about 200 ring forts or sites of ring forts in Co. Wicklow. They were homesteads enclosing farmsteads, generally between 80 and 165 feet in diameter, erected between the fifth and the twelfth centuries AD. They are the commonest monuments on our landscape and the ones most under threat. As their name suggests, they are usually circular in shape. Although they have been assiduously recorded by the Archaeological Survey of Ireland, their local names, if any, are seldom mentioned, and any 'story' connected to them is virtually nonexistent. This is due to a number of factors, among which is the fact that few field archaeologists were familiar with the local areas and seldom used local historians, perhaps feeling that any non-archaeological information was outside their remit. However, as in everything, there are exceptions, and one example of this is the site of a bivallate fort at Killamoat [62], which is a mile south of Rathdangan. A survey of this ring fort in 1942 mentions that two horses dropped dead as a result of ploughing on the site. There are many such instances recorded throughout Ireland where interference was seen as being a source of ill luck, even to the point of fatality. Though some may see the *mí ádh* ('bad luck') as superstitious nonsense, it has resulted in certain families respecting these early habitats, and thus retaining the historical continuum of our culture.

If there is superstition attached to ring forts, there is even more attached to lakes and wells. Two examples in Wicklow are at Glendalough, *Glenn dá Locha* ('the valley of the two lakes') and at Pollaphuca, *Poll an Phúca* ('the hole of the sprite or goblin'). The *púca* originates in Old Norse lore as the *puki* or imp. Glendalough is a popular tourist spot close to Laragh and is renowned for its setting and for its monastical sites and round tower. Its only possible pre-Christian lore is attached to its upper lake, which is said to have no bottom and to provide a home for a serpent. A woman who legend states loved the local St Kevin is said to have drowned in this lake in an act of unrequited love. Pollaphuca, which is now a reservoir and extends from Blessington to Ballymore Eustace along the N81, is similarly associated with pagan 'goings on' as one of the best-known haunts of Puck. It was described as a 'wild chasm where the Liffey falls over a ledge of rocks into a deep pool, to which the name properly belongs, signifying the pool or hole of the Pooka'.

In Wicklow, the well as a venerated place exists to the present day. It was to the well and the hawthorne or *corr sceach*, 'a fairy thorn', that pilgrims came in early times. The well's reputation as a fertility symbol and as a source for cures has its origins in the Iron Age and possibly before that. Both tree and well are mentioned in this extract from a twelfth-century poem:

> Blackthorn, little thorny one, black little sloe-bush;
> Watercress, little green-topped one,
> on the brink of the blackbirds' well.

As well as fertility rites and healing powers, the well is also associated with wisdom. The custom of hanging articles of clothing on the branches of the *sceach geal*, or whitethorn, finds its origins in the ancient rite of the *piseóc* or literally 'young vulva' or 'young virgin'.

A hillfort on top of Tinoranhill [55] is associated with the sun god Lug.* The hill is connected to the nearby Brusseltown Ring, a hillfort of 320 acres surrounded by three miles of defensive ramparts. There are two stone circles, Boleycarrigeen and Castleruddery, in the area. Tinoranhill is two miles north of Baltinglass and one mile west of the River Slaney. It is one of a series of hillforts in the Baltinglass area, the others being at Hughstown at Rathcoran and Rathnagree [all 61], north-east of the Slaney River, and further north-east at Spinans Hill [62]. These forts have led to the area being known as 'the hillfort capital of Ireland'.

Twelve miles north-east from Baltinglass on the N81 and two miles south from the Hollywood crossroads is Dunboyke [56], lying in the south-west foothills of Slievecorragh Mountain. The cemetery of Dunboyke marks the spot where the fort or house of *Dún Buichet* stood. It is situated on a slope near the northern entrance to Hollywood Glen on the rising ground, opposite which stands the Athgraney Stone Circle.

Esnada Tige Buchet ('the Songs of Buchet's House') tells the story of the hospitaller Buchet and his foster daughter Eithne Thoebfhota, daughter of Cathaer Már, King of Ireland, who died in 122 AD. Buchet was from a group known as hospitallers, who were in charge of feeding the king's retinue at certain times of the year and thus were generally large farmers. He was the owner of large herds and is spoken of as *Buchet na mbó* ('Buchet of the cows') and *in briugaid bóchétach* ('a farmer with hundreds of cows'). The tale says that Buchet had seven herds with 140 cows in each herd; even by today's standards he would be seen as a large farmer. Buchet's foster daughter wedded Cormac mac Airt. To wander a bit, one may say that Ethne was the mother of Lug,* the sun god, and if Cormac mac Airt could be suckled by a wolf-bitch in the caves of Keshcorran, he might as well be the son of the Indo-European earth goddess. The hospitallers' feasts were often compared to perpetual feasts, around which mythic tales abound.

The Book of Leinster mentions Buchet in a verse as follows:

> *Bligrióir Buchet búasaig báin*
> *boaire Cormaic caemnáir.*

> The milker Buchet, wealthy cattlelord
> and hospitaller to Cormac.

Buchet's house, according to legend, always had a fire burning beneath its cauldron to provide food for all his guests. This house of hospitality is similar to the *bruiden* or hostel, of which there were said to be six throughout Ireland. The *bruidne* (the plural form) in folklore became centres for the perpetual Otherworld feast.

Some of Buchet's guests – 'nobles of Leinster, with companies of their followers' – were not satisfied with his generousity and abused his kindness by stealing his cattle, brood mares and horses to the extent that he was left with only seven cows and a bull. They may also have threatened him as he fled by night with his wife and his foster daughter. They went from Dunboyke to an oak grove near Kells in Co. Meath where Cormac mac Airt

FIGURE 24. Standing stone with ogam writing in the Glen of Imaal, Co. Wicklow (Carole Cullen).

resided. Cormac met Eithne and asked Buchet for her hand, and Buchet consented. After a while, Eithne bore Cormac a son named Cairbre Life. Buchet was granted the district of Odhran beside Tara with its stock of cattle for the remainder of his life.

A later reference to Dunboyke is given in the *Annals of Ulster* as follows:

> the killing of Cumascach son of Áed by Brandub son of Eochu, in Dún Buchat in January 596AD.

WEXFORD

Viksfjord, in Norse meaning 'sea washed' or in Gaelic *Loch Carman* or *Loch gCarman* or more generally Lough Garman.

> *Rí na Loch in loch-sa thess,*
> *Loch garman na nglan-écess,*
> *cúan cróebach lethan nal-long,*
> *óenach na n-ethar n-éromm …*
>
> *Fri ré Cathair na cath crúaid*
> *Maidm locha Garman glan-úair*
> *Fri ré Fer mBolg cen bane*
> *Maidm sunna na sen-Sláne.*

[Poem ascribed to Eochaid Eolach O'Ceirin,
eleventh-century poet]

> King of the lakes, this lake to the South
> Loch Garman of the bright poets:
> Branching broad haven of the ships,
> Assembly plain of the light boats.
>
> In the time of Cathair of the bitter battles
> came the outburst of pure cold Loch Garman:
> in the time of the unblenching Fir Bolg
> came the outburst here of ancient Slane.

[Translated and edited by J. O'Beirne Crowe]

Loch Carman is the present harbour or estuary of Wexford. An older name still is *inber saline*, or the mouth of the Slaney, which corresponds to Wexford Harbour. *Muicinis* was one of the names given by the sons of Míl to Ireland when they arrived at the mouth of *inber sláine*. It is translated as 'the island of mist or fog, gloom or darkness' (*múich inis*); it was given this name because the Tuatha Dé Danann* surrounded the sons of Míl with a druidic mist when they attempted to land.

The famous fair at Carman was revived in 718 AD by Dunchadh, King of Leinster, and was last celebrated by Donnachad mac Gillapatrick in 1023 AD. An ancient poem on the fair is found in the twelfth-century *Book of Leinster*, and part in the *Book of Ballymote*, written at a later date. According to the latter poem, Carman was a Greek woman left behind in Ireland as a pledge that the Greeks would never land on the island of Ireland again, 'as long as the sea flowed around Ireland'.

The fairs such as those at Tailtiu, Cruachu and Carman were named *oenaige*, and the *oenach* at Carman was held at the feast of Lughnasa in honour of the god Lug.* Edward Gwynn suggests that the *oenaige* may have had a ritual character. In its primary sense, an *oenach* was a 'reunion' and then was translated as a 'popular assembly' or gathering. Petrie remarked that the site of an *oenach* was usually a famous burying ground, but it is more likely that the place of burial was determined by the existence of the gathering. The gathering was also the place where various enactments were adopted with regard to the dues of the various tribal chiefs. Generally, people including freemen stayed within their own *túath* or territory, and the *oenach* gave people a chance to attend horse and chariot racing and sport and athletics along with the numerous enterprises of the fair. The annual ploughing championship held during autumn may be seen as a continuation of the Irish tendency to assemble in large crowds. The fact that the championship is the largest agricultural show in Europe is a testament to this.

The *Oenach Carmain* was also held to celebrate success in war or to demonstrate the ascendancy of a king. Thus, the *Oenach Carmain* was held in 1023 by Donnachad mac Gillapatrick to mark his conquest of the Kingship of Leinster.

A legend of Carman from the *Book of Ballymote* includes a version of the story of Carman, which says that she followed the seven cows of Echech in the company of Lena the son of Mesroída mac Da Thó, a Leinster landowner living at the time of Conchobar mac Nessa. These cows were stolen by Lena and represent a cattle raid on the followers of Echech, who were Cruithin* or Picts, by the Leinstermen or the Lagin, who were Gaels. Echech takes his name from the Uí Echech, which was a tribe of horse people. The Cruithin are said by Keating and Hogan to have landed in Wexford Harbour. They presumably crossed from Wales which was relatively close. If this is so, then the Picts were not confined to Ulster but had a second settlement along the east coast.

A poem by the poet Fulartach, found in the *Book of Leinster*, tells the story of the Fair of Carman. It begins thus:

Estid a Laigniu na leacht.
A slúag o Raigni ratchert
Co fagbaid uaim as cech aird
Cáemsenchas Carmuin chlothaird

Carmun cete oenaig Fhéil.
Co faicthi roenaig roreid.
In tshluaig tictis dia thaichmi
Arfigtís a glangraifni.

Listen O Leinstermen of the monuments.
You the host who never rises against justice,
Until you get from me from all directions
The fine old tales of far famed Carman.
The festival fair of Carman

Chanted on the smooth clear plain.
Over the heads of the host who come to compete
And do battle in the glorious horse races ...
At the calends of August without fail
They assembled every third year.
Performing before the fire
Each poet was rightly listened to.

[Translated by Eugene O'Curry]

The problem arises as to where Carman is located. O'Curry and O'Donovan say that the fair was held near present-day Wexford town, while Hennessy and Hogan assume that the fair was held on a large plain at the banks of the Burren and the Barrow, which unite at the town of Carlow. This plain would be close to Dind Ríg, an ancient home of the kings of Leinster, on the west bank of the Barrow river and a quarter mile to the south of Leighlin Bridge. Then there may be a case for saying that with its Cruithin* or Pictish origins it may well have begun its life at Loch Carman in Wexford and moved to the environs of Dind Ríg as the centre of power graduated north. According to the poem of Fulartach, the site for the fair consisted of twenty-one raths and seven mounds 'without touching each other'. The fair was held within the surrounds of seven fields, and three markets were held within its borders: a market for food; a market for live cattle; and a market of the Greeks in which gold and fine clothes were sold.

Ladhra, one of the three men who according to legend arrived in Ireland 'forty days before the Deluge' with Cesair, the daughter of Noah, is said to be buried at Ardamine Hill (*Ard Ladrann*, 'the hill of the rebels') [69] one mile south from Courtown, and south of the townland of Middletow where there is a mound. Fr Edmund Hogan in his *Onomasticon Goedelicum* states:

I have seen this remarkable Ardamine Hill, and the upright stone on it, near the sea, 1m south of Courtown harbour and near it on the road from Gorey to River-

Chapel is one of the most perfect raths in Ireland: it consists of a cupola of clay surrounding the platform, about half-an acre in area of an artificial mound, and on the north side of the platform is a rude erect stone cross, and adjoining the moat is the ancient cemetery of Ardamine; local tradition says that the mound contains a stone chamber.

The hill may have been the location of a residence of some of the early kings of the Uí Ceinnsealaigh, or the modern Kinsellas, a clan that covered much of north Wexford and were a sept of the Mac Murroughs. Some of them were Kings of Leinster in pre-Christian times. The hill is recorded in the Archeological Inventory of Co. Wexford as a 'tumulus'.

In the south-west of Wexford, in the barony of Shelburne, lies the Hook Peninsula, where the earliest settlements are possibly from the Bronze Age, 2300–500 BC. In the townland of Loftus Hall three miles south-west from Fethard [76] is a circular mound about sixty-six feet in diameter. A linear earthwork of two parallel earthen banks was once nearby, and this may have been a cursus, i.e. a running ground or final part of a gallop. Another cursus is at Tara (Co. Meath), and this was the conclusion of the final part of a journey to the ritual centre known as the Rath of the Synods. Whether this mound at the Hook is a burial mound of the bowl barrow type is difficult to say; as there are no 'stories' from the Bronze Age, conjecture about the original intent of these structures remains vague. However, on a good day this mound on the Hook peninsula is a pleasant introduction to Bronze Age Wexford.

Staying within the townland of Loftus Hall, I heard a story from two women whom I met while walking on the borders of the Wicklow and Wexford mountains. Their names were Kathleen Graham and Breda Breen. They told me a tale of the devil at Loftus Hall.

The Hall was originally known as Redmond Hall, as it was erected by the Redmonds from Kilcloggan, a townland about two miles north from Loftus Hall, and in 1666 was granted to Sir Nicholas Loftus. The house was demolished in 1870, for whatever reason, and the present house known as Loftus Hall was built on the site.

Loftus was regarded as something of a rake by the locals, and he was noted for the occasional spree or parties that involved much drunken carousing, aided by girls brought down from the slums of Dublin. The spree was always preceded by a hunt. The party would go to Johnstown, four miles south-west of Wexford, to hunt deer presumably on the grounds of Rathlannon House, which had been in the hands of the Esmond family for generations. When the party returned to Loftus Hall, the fun began; supper was followed by dancing or cards, and a general jollity prevailed. On one such occasion, when the party was just about to sit down to supper, a gentleman on a black horse and wearing a red coat rode up to the hall door. He was asked in by the owner and joined the party for supper. Later, he joined the revellers for a game of cards and played all night and some of the following day. At this point, it was decided to have the horses taken out and yoked, and a long line of carriages was assembled outside the front door. All the coachmen told the horses to 'go on', but the horses couldn't move.

They returned to their partying for a few more days but became suspicious. After a while, one of the servants suggested that they send for a priest. The priest was from Templetown and his name was Father Broaders. (Templetown is three miles north of Loftus Hall.) The priest tried to get the stranger to depart, but the stranger said that he would stay until 'everyone was taken'; the priest said that he would be confined to the house in a room for seven years and would 'take no one'. After seven years, the stranger left by shooting out through the roof. According to legend, the scorch marks could be seen on the rafters after the sudden exit.

Another version of this tale is that the daughter of the original owners, a Miss Anne Tottenham, befriended a stranger who came to the house asking for shelter, having survived a storm at sea. He was brought into the house and played cards with the family; during the game, Anne bent down to retrieve a fallen card and spotted his cloven hoof. On being recognised, the devil disappeared through the roof 'in a puff of smoke'. Within a short while of this event, a local parish priest performed an exorcism in the house. A room was blocked off, and this was the tapestry room in which the stranger had stayed prior to his dramatic exit. Thereafter, this room was said to have been haunted. After the house was demolished, it was dumped alongside the cliff edge to forestall coastal erosion.

The new and present building was erected in 1870, and in 1913 the Hall along with its reduced holding of sixty-seven acres was purchased as a convent for Benedictine nuns. The Hall was sold by the nuns in the 1980s and became a private residence.

An island of interest in Wexford is the Great Saltee Island [77], which lies about five miles south of Kilmore Quay. It is possible to embark from here and arrive on the shores of the Great Saltee within an hour. In spring, the island is a sea of bluebells and as it is fairly flat the swathe of blue is both visually pleasing and fragrant. The island has many palm trees, which further add to a sense of exoticism. It is a favourite bird-watching sanctuary, and many of the outlying rocks are teeming with all manner of gulls.

The island was inhabited by a few dozen people until the nineteenth century. It had been farmed, but when the farm labourers left, farming came to an end. After the Rebellion of 1798, Bagenal Harvey fled there but was later captured on the island.

Michael Neale bought the island in 1943 and crowned himself Prince Michael in 1972; he died in 1998. There are still monuments to him on the island. Folklore has it that while living at Kilmore Quay as a young boy, he looked out at the island and told his mother that one day he would be the King of the Saltees. A monument on the island is dedicated to children and to the hope that they may achieve their ambitions. When the family is in residence on the island the Prince of Saltee flag is flown. During these times visitors are not encouraged; should they arrive, they must leave by 4:30 pm. A promontory fort is situated on the north-east side of the island. An ogam stone once stood near the centre of the island but is now in the County Museum, Enniscorthy.

I was first introduced to the holy wells of Wexford by the late Dr Stephen O'Sullivan, a friend and a native of Wexford town. While on our way to the North Marsh to see the departing geese, we stopped at St David's Well at Oylegate [77], which is close to an ancient graveyard; it is walled, with several steps leading down to it. Patterns were held there on St David's feast day, 1 March, up to 1840, and the custom was revived in 1910. Many holy wells are noted for their cures, and St David's Well is associated with cures for goitre and warts.

At St Martin's Well of Kinnagh [76], for example, a lot of people leave badges and pictures there as a thanksgiving. One family keeps a small lamp burning by the side of the well. Old people say that blindness was cured by going nine times in succession to the well and putting the water on the afflicted place.

MUNSTER

CLARE

Clár, 'a plain'

Clare was originally part of Munster and was later incorporated into Connacht but finally reverted to Munster.

At Craglea (*An Chraig Liath*, 'the grey steep rock') [58] two miles north of Killaloe *Cill Dalua* ('Church of Dalua') is the holy hill of Aibhell or Aoibhell, the great goddess of north Munster. Craglea is situated at the south-west end of Lough Derg. The origin of Aoibhell is to be found in the word *aeb*, which means 'sheen, brightness, beauty and attractivness'; it is also applied to the radiance of the sun, which would make Aoibhell a sun goddess. In this latter context, Aoibhell can mean a 'live coal' or 'fire, spark'.

Aoibhell is said to dwell in the *síd* or fairy dwelling place of *Craig Liath*. There is a ring fort or fairy fort at Craglea and this may be her dwelling place, but the actual crag above Craglea is more likely to be her centre. It is told how Brian Boru cried out Aoibhell's name (*Aibhell Craicce Léithe*) before the Battle of Clontarf in 1014; it is a testament to the persistence of the earlier belief system after 500 years of Christianisation.

This influence of Aoibhell extended south to the Slieve Felim mountain range of north Limerick [65, 66], the Irish for which is *Sliab Éibhlinne*, after the goddess *Éblenn* or *Ébliu*. Aoibhell and Eibhlenn, however, are but slightly differentiated names for the one goddess. The mountainous district near Killaloe on the west of the Shannon was known as *an tír fa Eibhlinn uile*, 'the country under the other Eibhlinn'. It was precisely here – Craglea – that Aoibhell had her seat.

Aoibhell was clearly a tutelary spirit of the Dalcassians, the powerful tribe of which Brian Boru was the the most famous member. This is underlined in a tale about Dunlang O'Hartigan, a friend of Brian Boru's eldest son Murchadh, who was on his way to fight the Danes at Clontarf when Aoibhell met him and tried to dissuade him from fighting that day. She offered him immortality in *Magh Mell* (the 'Plain of Honey') if he would stay away, but he said that he could not abandon his friend Murchadh. She then placed a magical cloak (*féth fiada*) over him which made him invisible, warning that if he took it off he would be slain. Towards the end of the battle he threw it off and was killed. When this news got back to Brian he cried out, 'I shall not leave this place alive for Aoibhell of Craglea came to me last night and told me I would be killed this day.' Aoibhell would thus have performed the role of a *ban sí* ('woman of the fairy mound'), more commonly known as a banshee, whose function was to act as a messenger of death.

It was not only on the Irish side that strange appearances took place before that battle. A Danish leader while waiting at Caithness in Scotland before sailing to Ireland saw twelve women riding on horses towards a tumulus; he followed them in and noticed them weaving with 'human heads for woof and warp, a sword for a reed, an arrow for a shuttle'. While thus employed they sang these words:

> Glittering lances are the loom,
> Where the dusky warp we strain,
> Weaving many a soldier's doom,
> Orkney's woe and Radner's bane,
> See the gristly texture grow,
> ('Tis of human entrails made);
> And the shafts that play below,
> Each a grasping warrior's hand.

Local lore says that Aoibhell left her crag at Craglea when the woods were cut down. A well on the mountainside is known as *Tobar Aoibhell* ('Aoibhell's well'). In 1839 the antiquarian John O'Donovan was in the area and he heard from the locals that the precipice and well were still connected with Aoibhell. At Loch Rátha below Ráth Bláthmaic in Inchiquin [57] she was apparently seen as late as the early twentieth century in the company of twenty-five other banshees washing clothes. Loch Rátha is three miles south-west from Corofin and was originally known as *Loch Broigseach* or 'Badger's Lake', and high up on the precipitous side of a hill close to the lake there is a hole or cavern known as *Poll na Brocuidhe* or the 'Badger's Hole'. At Ráth Bláthmaic there are two ring forts side by side, about half-a-mile south-east from Loch Rátha.

Aoibhell's counterpart is Bronach, a banshee from Loch Rask, a lake within a mile north-east of Ballyvaughan, in north Clare [51]. Bronach ('the sorrowful or dismal one') was known as the 'Hag of Black Head'. The wail of the banshee was said to signify an imminent death:

> Hush be the banshee's cry,
> unearthly sound,
> wailing for one soon to lie,
> cold in the ground.

Bronach is referred to in the fourteenth-century manuscript *Cathreim Thoirdhealbhaigh* ('Triumphs of Turlough'), where she is recorded as having been seen prior to the battle of Corcomroe in 1317 at Loch Rask by the supporters of Prince Murchad O'Brien. What the invading army saw was 'a lone, ancient hag, stooped over the bright lough shore'. The detailed description is a good example of medieval bard waxing lyrical in his choice of adjectives and in his use of endless detail to build up as grotesque a figure as possible.

Thus, she was 'thatched with elf locks, foxy grey and rough like heather, matted and like long sea wrack, a bossy, wrinkled, ulcerated brow, the hairs of her eyebrows like fish hooks; bleared watery eyes peered with malignant fire between red inflamed lids'. Bronach was washing human limbs and heads until the lake was awash with blood, brains and floating hair. When asked her name she replied 'I am Bronach of the Burren, of the Tuatha Dé Danann.* This slaughter heap is of your army's heads; your own is in the middle.'

Two miles south from Corofin on the R476 is Ballycullinan Lough [57], and beside this lough there was fought a battle in 1318 known as the battle of Dysert O'Dea in which the Anglo-Norman lord Richard de Clare was defeated by the Gaelic King of Thomond. When Richard and his men came to the River Fergus, two miles north of Dysert O'Dea, they observed a woman at the ford washing 'armour and rich robes till the red gore churned and splashed through her hands'. De Clare asked an Irish ally to question her and was told that the armour and clothes were those of the enemy, namely the Anglo-Normans, and that few would escape from the ensuing battle. She then came towards them saying: 'I am the Water Doleful One, I live in the *sídhe* on the land but am of the Tribes of Hell. Thither I invite you; soon we shall be dwellers in one country.' The next day, de Clare lay dead with his son and his soldiers on the fields near the Ford of Dysert. For a while this battle prevented the establishment of an English lordship in what was later to be known as Co. Clare.

In the *Memoirs of Lady Fanshawe*, published in 1665, reference is made to the banshee. Lady Fanshawe was staying with the O'Briens at either Mountcashel overlooking Castle Lake or at Bunratty Castle [58] overlooking the Ratty River. She was awakened by screaming and saw a girl with red hair outside the window who then disappeared. The next day she was told that the girl was the spirit of a peasant wife who had been drowned in the moat by her husband, a former owner of the castle.

Brian Boru's fort once stood at Kincora (*Ceann Choradh*, 'weir head'). According to Keating, it was the largest household of any king of Ireland except those of Cormac mac Airt and Conaire Mór; now it is merely a grassy bank. The only artefacts found in the area were three axeheads found near the fort by a young boy in 1936; two of these axeheads went missing and the third is in the National Museum of Ireland in Dublin. There are to my knowledge no legends to unearth here but a poem about Kincora still exists, which was written by Brian's secretary and Chief Poet of Ireland, Muircheartach mac Con Ceartaich Mac Liag:

A Chinn Choradh caidhi Brian;
nó caidhi in sciamh do bhí ort,
caidhi maithe no meic righ,
Ga n-ibhmís fín ad port?

The concluding verse is as follows:

Is mairg atá beó gan Brian,
is mise Mac Liag o'n linn;

dom thoghairm go tigh na séd,
do tighedh fó chéd, a chin.

O *Ceann Coradh!* where is Brian?
Or where is the splendour that was upon thee?
Where are the nobles and the sons of kings,
With whom we drank wine in thy halls?

Woe that I live after *Brian!*
I am Mac Liag from the lake:
To invite me into his treasury,
He would come a hundred times, O *Ceann Coradh!*

[Translated by Eugene O'Curry]

The following are two verses of the poem as adapted by James Clarence Mangan:

Oh, where Kincora! are thy valorous lords?
Oh, whither, thou Hospitable! are they gone?
Oh, where are the Dalcassians of the golden swords?
And where are the warriors that Brian led on?
Where oh, Kincora?

And where is Murchadh, the descendant of kings –
The defeater of a hundred – the daringly brave –
Who set but slight store by jewels and rings –
Who swam down the torrent and laughed at its wave?
Where oh, Kincora?

Eighteen miles west of Kincora and three miles south-west of Tulla [58] is *Magh Adhair*, the mound marking the inauguration place from the fourth to the sixteenth century of the O'Briens, who were of the *Dál gCais* (Dalcassian) tribe and were the Kings of Thomond, or north Munster. Adar, after whom the plain is named, was the son of Umór either of the race of the Fir Bolg* or the Cruithin.* Estyn Evans in his work *Prehistoric and Early Christian Ireland* writes that *Magh Adhair* is 'placed in an amphitheatre of low hills ... and displays the usual features: a large mound and other earthworks. The mound over 20 ft. high has a flat top measuring 100 by 80 ft. and is surrounded by a fosse and external bank'. According to T.J. Westropp, the mound was built in the first century AD and contains the remains of the chief of a people who were predecessors of the Dalcassians. 'Adar of Magh Adair' is mentioned in the 'Lay of Carn Chonoill'. However, few kings are mentioned from the fifth to the ninth century, one of whom was Conall, son of Eochaid Balderg (Eochaid 'of the red wen or protuberance'). Eochaid Balderg was in a direct line of twelve generations an ancestor of Brian Boru, and was inaugurated here in the sixth century. In the ninth century, Lorcan, grandfather of Brian Boru, was crowned at *Magh Adhair*.

Geoffrey Keating writes: 'At Magh Adhar O Briain was inaugurated; it was Mac na Mara who inaugurated him (*do ghaireadh é*). O'Duibhidhir (O'Dwyer) was his marshal; the Flannchuidhe (O'Flanahy) were his brehons of native customary law; the clann Chraith his ollamhs or scholars in poetry; the clann Cruithin* (the Picts) his ollamhs in ancient history and tradition.' Gatherings at *Magh Adhair* were last recalled by old people as late as 1890.

Evans does not mention the *bile* or sacred tree, which was an essential part of any inauguration site. This tree stood on the plain of *Magh Adhair* until it 'was cut after being cut from the earth with its roots' – so recorded the *Annals of the Four Masters* for the year 982. The destroyer of this sacred tree was Maelshechlainn, also known as Malachy, King of Tara. The spiritual life of the Dalcassians was bound up with this tree, and cutting it down was an act of desecration and a challenge to war. Maelshechlainn probably did thus out of fear of the rise of Brian Boru; by destroying the *bile,* he stalled the crowning of Brian.

However, a substitute tree must have been planted shortly after Maelshechlainn's departure, as seventy years later in 1049 or 1051, depending on which annals come to hand, another tree was ready for further inaugurations; alas, it was also uprooted, this time by Aodh Ó Conchobhair of Connacht.

Besides the *bile*, which was the nexus or bond of the tribe, there are other places which would have been part of the assemblies. On the east side of a small stream is a small mound, and across the stream to the west is a standing stone over six feet tall in line with the two mounds. North of the larger mound is a boulder with an oval basin cut in its upper surface. Half-a-mile to the south-west is a large enclosure with a triple ring of stone surrounding, which may have been the site of the *bile* and the home of the local chief.

As there were as many as one hundred local chiefs at the beginning of the eleventh century, we may assume that there were many such sacred trees. Unfortunately, as the archaeologist Barry Raftery writes, 'the *bile* leaves no trace in the archaeological record, but we can assume that this custom is of pagan Celtic origin for there are clear indications that it existed in Gaul in the pre-Roman Iron Age'.

Lough Graney (*Loch Gréine* 'sun lake') [52] is named after the goddess Grian, which is the Irish word for 'sun'. *The Annals of the Four Masters* simply state that the lake is named after a woman, but like the River Graney and the Well of Grian, *Tobar Gréine,* it is in fact named after the sun goddess. Interestingly an older name for the lake was *Loch na bó girre* or 'Bó Guaire's lake', the Bó Guaire being a moon goddess. Around here and in Lough Bó Girre near Cahir in Tipperary, the Bó Guaire was a large, long-horned cow which used to issue from these lakes when the moon was up, the long horns representing the crescent moon. The *Bó Guaire* is a sister river to the Boyne and is known as the Blackwater in east Cavan.

Brian Merriman's famous poem, *Cúirt an Mheán Oíche* ('The Midnight Court'), written in the eighteenth century, captures the landscape of this spot nestled south of the Aughty Mountains:

Do ghealladh mo chroí nuair chin Loch Gréine,
An talamh,'s an tír is íor na spéire;
Taithneamhnach aoibhinn suíom na sléibhte
Ag bagairt a gcinn thar dhroim a chéile

My heart lit up when I saw Lough Graney, the earth, the land and the raging sky; a glowing delight at the lie of the mountains with their heads beckoning across the ridge.

Aoibhell also features in the poem, where she is depicted as presiding over an assembly of the *aes síde* at Craglea for the purpose of boosting and strenghtening the Dalcassian line.

Less than two miles south of Carran [51] is Cahercommaun, a triple cliff fort of the ninth century, which is somewhat difficult to access due to the cliffs, but a car park nearby leads to a track which will bring you to the monument. This is a superb example of a cliff fort, and it is one of the strongest of its kind in the country. There are walls here which are twenty-eight feet thick and rise to a height of fourteen feet. Although the fort is from the ninth century, stone axes were still in use and wooden containers employed rather than pottery.

For two miles between this fort and Knockans and in the general area of the Burren National Park was the grazing area of the *Glas Gaibhleann,* the famous lactiferous cow which reputedly belonged to Goibniu,* the smith god, but was also seen as the possession of Lon Liomtha, the smith living on the ridge of Glasgeivnagh in the townland of Teeskagh (*Taosca*, 'flowing', surging', 'gushing') [51]. Lon was credited as a teacher of the smiths of Bergen in Norway and has been described in folklore as possessing one leg, three arms, and an eye in the middle of his forehead. He represents a remnant of the pre-Milesian tribes who had escaped to this 'desert place', which was sufficiently fertile to support themselves and Lon's cow. As a working smith he was ideally suited here, as there were *seacht srutha na Teascaighe* ('the seven streams of Teeskagh'), for a blacksmith needs to be near running water.

In the cow legend of Corofin, as described by Westropp, a woman made a bet that she would find a vessel that the cow could not fill; she milked her into a sieve, and the milk ran down the hillside forming a waterfall and the seven streams, which run across a deep gorge to sink into clefts of rock. This tale would merge the seven streams into popular folklore. As the *Glas Gaibhleann* could not fill the sieve, she ran away and possibly went to Glangevlin [27] in Cavan, where she filled all her pails.

The following are some of the places associated with the *Glas Gaibhleann*: firstly, going east, one comes across Glasgeivnagh Hill [51] or 'the hill of the *glas gaibhneach*' and to the north-west of here is the grazing area of this cow which is known as *Mothair na Glaise* ('the thicket of the grey cow') [51]. Less than a mile north-east is Slievenaglasha [51], or 'the mountain of the grey cow'. A few hundred yards north from there are some bare patches of earth and these are known as the beds of the glas. North from here is the Thicket of Lon the smith or *Mothair na Ceártan* and further north is *Tobar na Glaise* or the well of the glas.

Turlough Hill [51] is noted for its large cairn, which may be Neolithic, and a large number of hut sites, which may have been used by shepherds bringing their cattle up in winter and down in summer in what is called 'reverse transhumance'. The large enclosure west of the cairn and on lower ground has, according to Westropp, associations with the Fianna.* He says that this enclosure, which he describes as 'a stone fort', probably belonged to the 'Irish Militia', or to the warriors of Finn mac Cumhail.* However, this fort is more than likely an enclosure from the Bronze Age, and as such was a meeting place for certain rituals associated with the sun. In this it is similar to the enclosure at Lough Gur in Co. Limerick and the great ritual site at *Dún Aengus* on the Aran Islands. It is likely that the Turlough Hill enclosure was one among many centres for the celebration of the festival of Lughnasa, which was celebrated not only in Ireland but in London (*Lugdunum*), possibly in the druidic temple now lying under the airport at Heathrow, in Lyon (also *Lugdunum*) and further away at *Lam Luada*, west of Benghazi in Libya.

Ten miles south-west from Kinvara in the Burren is Glencolumbkille [52], where there is a church and graveyard within which once stood a large oval enclosure which was bulldozed in the 1980s. Whether this was similar to the Turlough Hill enclosure is open to speculation, but if it were a ritual enclosure then it is easy to understand why it would contain an ecclesiastical site with a church and graveyard. The church is dedicated to St Columcille who is said to have founded this church after leaving the Aran Islands. His thumb and fingerprint can still be seen on a limestone boulder. This has echoes of the stone on Tory Island where St Columcille overcame the hound which attacked him. The imprint of the hound can still be seen just a few hundred yards to the east of the jetty.

The destruction of the enclosure led to the finding of a carved stone head by a University of California research team in 1989. A similar stone head can be seen on the exterior south-west corner at the medieval church (c. 1500) at Rathborney (*Rath Boirne*, 'the rath of the Burren') in the townland of Croagh North [51] less than three miles south-west from Ballyvaughan. The church, graveyard, souterrain and stone head are just south of the Burren Way, and there is a path leading from the road to the church.

This rath, or, more correctly, a large oval enclosure within which the church is located, has several similarities with Glencolumbkille, mentioned above. Both churches are sited within large enclosures and both possess stone heads which preceded the building of the churches. Sinéad Ní Ghabláin, writing in the *JRSAI*, Vol. 118 (1988), says that the

> closest parallel for the Glencolumbkille stone head in the area comes from the medieval church at Rathborney ... it may be coincidental that these stone heads come

from early historic sites. In one case there is a clear medieval context for the use of the carving. In the other such a use may be postulated although the possibility remains that the carving was produced at some earlier period.

I would suggest that both were produced at an earlier period and that the Glencolumbkille head may well be female. As to where the Glencolumbkille stone head is now remains a mystery; hopefully, the Rathborney stone head will remain intact and continue to allow us to fill in parts of the jigsaw of our pre-Christian past.

In the south-west of Clare, almost thirty miles from Turlough Hill, is Mount Callan or Slieve Callan (*Sliabh Collán*, 'the mountain of the hazels') [57]. Here, at 1,283 feet, is another hilltop assembly point for the festival of Lug.* Seven miles inland from the Atlantic, it has a commanding view of the ocean and can witness the setting sun across the broad Atlantic. As Lug was a sun god, it is easy to understand why this place had a relevance for Bronze Age sun worshippers, a relevance that probably lasted into the Iron Age and the early Christian period. Sun worship was a strong part of pre-Christian Irish culture, as it was through most, if not all, early societies; it had religious and ritual overtones, but it was not a religiosity insofar as it did not depend on belief or the *reliqua* (that which binds us to the narrative myth), as the sun could be observed and understood to be a benefit to nature and the growth of life sustaining plants.

A fear connected with the sun god was that he would not return unless propitiated to, and thus sun rites were born. Presumably Newgrange in Co. Meath had a Neolithic rite on the eve of the winter solstice, and these rituals existed throughout the country. The pilgrimage to Croagh Patrick in Co. Mayo possibly began as a Bronze Age rite to the sun until it was taken over in the Late Iron Age by the harvest festival associated with Crom Cruach* (the harvest god).

Mount Callan has a long antiquarian history. It begins with a presentation to the Royal Irish Academy in 1787 by a Theophilus O'Flanagan concerning an ogam inscription on the sepulchral mountain. This presentation is recorded in the first volume of the RIA and is possibly one that they would rather forget, as it is generally regarded as a forgery. However, O'Flanagan, in the tradition of James Macpherson in Scotland, did stir up debate and stimulate interest in the subject of *antient* places of note.

Westropp states that the *Dindshenchas** contains a legend about how

> Alestar, a contemporary of Queen Tailti, for a supposed slight on that lady, was compelled by her father, Eochu Garb son of Dua, King of Ireland, to make her a fort in Sengann's heritage. The third of Erin's rath builders chose as its site a slope on Mount Callan called Sliabh Leitrech, but though the place was long called after him 'Cluain Alestair', the name and site are now lost.

According to Westropp, 'the remote mythology of the region begins with the tribes of Sengann, and this is borne out by Ptolemy's Atlas, giving the Ganganoi (or the tribes of

Sengann) as dwelling at the mouth of the Senos or Shannon, before the second century (AD)'.

In her complete and splendid book *The Festival of Lughnasa*, Máire MacNeill describes Mount Callan in prose bordering on the poetic:

> West Clare is bleak and stalwart. Unlike the other Atlantic coast-lands it does not break the impact of the ocean on prongs of mountain and inlet but faces it squarely with a phalanx of cliff and low rocky shores. The waves come thundering against it in full force and the western gales blow across its craggy fields and bogs, wetting them with the salt spray and bending the sparse thorn bushes so that all their gnarled branches stretch to the east. Its landscape gets its character from wind, light and stone.

A local historian named Brian O'Looney, who was used as a source by MacNeill, was able to give his experiences of the hill and surrounding areas, and this has helped clarify certain stories. South of the mountain is a small lake named Lough Booleynagreany [57] (*Loch Buaile na Gréine*, 'the lake of the sunny pasture'). Here was a megalithic structure named *Altóir na Gréine* ('the altar of the sun'). There is today a megalithic tomb less than a mile south-south-west from the lake, and whether this is the tomb referred to by O'Looney is a moot point. However, many portal and wedge tombs in later times were subsumed into the general folklore as either altars of the sun or sacrificial altars, or more usually love beds of Diarmuid* and Gráinne.* O'Looney felt that the sun element both in the lake and the stone were simply describing a sun element in the names of these places, and that *Altóir na Gréine* was no older than a 1748 romance written by a Clare writer named Michael Comyn called *Eachtra Thoirdhealbhaigh mhic Stairn* or 'The Adventure of Turlough mac Starn'. Comyn was a Jacobite Protestant and Gaelic scholar.

According to Comyn, every third year a festival took place at *Buaile na Gréine* which involved worship and sacrifice to the sun. The animals sacrificed were bulls, rams and goats. An embellishment on this story was that three heroes came to Mount Callan and killed a monster at *Loch Buaile na Gréine*; they were also present at the above sacrifices, and they killed and roasted a pig and distributed its flesh to the assembly. The slaughter and roasting of a pig was a common feature of Iron Age culture, particularly at certain times of the year such as the *samain* or Hallowe'en and during the harvest feast of Lughnasa. As the harvest sacrifices to Crom* were attested throughout the land, it is likely that the sacrifices at Lough Buaile were in a similar vein.

One of the above heroes may have included a warrior from the Fenian sagas of the third century AD – namely, Conán Maol, a satirist of the Fianna* and the equivalent of Bricriu from the Ulster sagas. Conán was noted for his jibes and taunts or, to be more precise, his foul tongue:

Conán mac Morna
Fear mallachtach miolábhra.

> Conán son of Morna,
> a man of oaths and abusive speech.

O'Looney, a native of the area, discovered the tomb where Conán was buried in 1844; known as *Leaba Chonáin* or 'Conán's Bed'. it was situated on the south side of Mount Callan overlooking *Loch Buaile na Gréine*. This area was known as *Tulach na Féinne* or 'the Mound of the Fianna'..* According to Máire MacNeill, 'It consisted of a pillar stone or flagstone, called *Leac Chonáin* by O'Looney, resting on a half-reclining position on a pile of rough stones, perhaps remains of a *leacht* (sepulchral cairn).' As mentioned above, this stone was the subject of an apparent forgery in ogam.

Regardless of the veracity of this stone and its ogam inscriptions, and in the area of early history and mythology, who is to say what is what, except that the Mac Brodin family who lived closeby and were local historians, claimed that Conán Maol was buried in the cairn which contained the ogam inscription.

That MacNeill says that the sun-worshipping side of Mount Callan can be set aside as 'artificial' seems to run counter to the feast of Lughnasa. Particularly as Lug* the sun god was worshipped on this mountain.

O'Looney writes that when he went back to *Leaba Chonáin* in 1859 there was no trace to be found beyond a 'muddy hole and a few loose stones'. In Inagh village [57], there is a story of depressing regularity insofar as a woman and her sons, presuming that there was treasure there, split the stone or *leacht* in two; they found no treasure, for the tomb had previously been pillaged by an O'Flanagan, and bones and iron weapons and a helmet had been taken away. The objects were taken to a Mr Burton who had taken them out of the country. O'Looney with the help of some locals restored the inscribed stone to the best of their ability.

The grave of Conán Maol has connections with a so-called magic island known as Kilsafeen in Liscannor Bay [57], about eight miles north-west from Mount Callan. In 1839, an earthquake swallowed up what was said to be an ecclesiastical city on the island; other stories say that the island sank when its chieftain lost its golden key in battle and that the island would not reappear until it was restored from its hiding place under the ogam stone of Conán Maol. The tale relates that the island may at times be seen 'with its golden roofed palaces and towers, shining beneath the waves, but once in every seven years it rises above them, and those who see it are said to die before its next appearance'. A poem under the heading of the monks of Kilcrea is as follows:

> Point how high the billows roll above lost Kilsafeen,
> Its palaces and towers of pride
> All buried in the rushing tide
> And deep sea-waters green.

To continue the tradition of the Fianna,* in the 'Adventures of the Three Sons of Thorailbh' the island is connected with a raid in the time of Finn mac Cumhail.*

One version of this story says that a submerged reef off Moher at the mouth of Liscannor Bay marks the site of the lost city and church of Kilsafeen, the key of which lies buried with the hero Conán on the side of Mount Callan. Another says the city lies at the mouth of the Shannon, and whoever saw its domes and pinnacles was doomed to die within a week. The city under the sea is a global motif and perhaps finds its strongest example in the saga of Atlantis, which is a persistent myth and lends its story to Hy Brasil, Lough Neagh and many other tales.

Kilkee (*Cill Chaoide*, 'church of Caoi') [63] was noted for a belief in water divinities up to the late nineteenth century, though there may have been a connection with the white mermaid which was occasionally seen here, reinforced by a belief in 'mer-folk'. A stronger and more relevant connection to the sea, however, was the ritual horse-bathing which occurred at harvest time at Kilkee. The impact of this rite led to a resolution passed, at a meeting of the magistrates, visitors and lodge owners of Kilkee held on 7 August 1833, in which it was stated:

> We have witnessed the disgraceful practice of bathing on the Strand at Kilkee, at all hours of the day, to the great annoyance of females who are by such indecent exposures prevented from exercising on the beach. That it is expedient that some measures be adopted to prevent a recurrence of the practice; and with this in view, it is resolved that the strand shall be divided into three parts; that two sides thereof to the right and left, shall be appropriated to the use of the female visitors for bathing, and the portion of the strand defined by a post in the centre, shall be for the use of the male part of the visitors, up to the hour of ten o'clock in the morning of each day, but after that hour no *male person* shall be permitted to bathe on the strand.
>
> We are determined, by every means in our power to put an end to the shameful custom which prevails, of naked men riding horses through the water; and that the police shall receive instruction to seize all persons so offending, in order that they may be prosecuted according to law.

Thus, public order acts were used to limit this ancient rite which survived even if its origins were unclear; the fact that it was permitted to continue at all shows the fairness of the law coupled with the persistence of the custom. Unfortunately, the custom was stopped by the Church at Kinvara, Co. Galway, with no similar concessions.

Returning to the goddesses, banshees and *cailleacha*, we come to two headlands, namely Hag's Head (*Ceann Cailighe*) at the south end of the Cliffs of Moher [57] and Loop Head at the southern extremity of Clare [63]. The translation of *cailleach* as 'hag', 'witch' or 'crone' may be seen as placing the *cailleach* in a pejorative light, especially when later she is translated as 'nun' and 'senior nun' with *cenn cailleach* translated as 'abbess'. Loop Head was originally known as *Léim Chon gCulainn*, which translates as 'Cú Chulainn's leap'. Loop originates from the name given to it by the Danes of the lower Shannon – *hlaup*, a leap. Both headlands are associated with a story concerning the *cailleach* and Cú Chulainn,* in which the Ulster hero was pursued by an old woman named Mal of the eponymous Hag's Head as far as Loop Head. He was obviously afraid of her, as he leapt onto a nearby rock in the ocean in order to escape; the name of this rock, which rises about 25 feet from the ocean, is called *Oileán na Léime* or 'the island of the leap'. Cú Chulainn landed on the rock, and Mal alighted behind him; however, the hero bounded back to the mainland while Mal, attempting to do the same, fell short and into the sea.

The hag's body was swept northward by the tide and was found at the southern point of the Cliffs of Moher, which has been known since as *Ceann Caillighe* or 'Hag's Head'. The sea all along was dyed with her blood and was called *Tonn Mal* or 'Mal's Wave', which is reminiscent of 'Cliodhna's Wave' (*Tonn Cliodhna*) in Glandore in west Cork. Today *Tonn Mal* is known as Malbay, west of Miltown Malbay [57].

Twenty miles up along the mouth of the Shannon from Loop Head towards Kilrush is Scattery Island (*Inis Cathaig*) [63], the home of the *cata,* a *péist* or monster related to the cat-eared deity as exemplified by Cairbre Cinn Cait ('Cairbre Cat-Ear'), the chief of the vassal tribes known as the *aitechthuath*. The *cata* was a strong figure from Barleycove in west Cork to the Shannon Estuary and possibly beyond.

Around 500 AD, St Senan discovered that the *cata* dwelt on Scattery, and between *geasa* and saintly miracles, a battle for the minds of the inhabitants arose. The *cata* devoured the saint's smith, Narach, but Senan brought him to life again. The *cata* then resumed the fight with its cat's eyes and fiery jaws, but against this venom all Senan had to do was make the sign of the cross; the beast collapsed and was chained and thrown into Doolough (the 'black lake') five miles south-west from Mount Callan [57]. According to Westropp in his *Folklore of Clare*, 'in the fifteenth century details, of the "cathedral" of Scattery of a large-eyed dragon with crocodile jaws is conspicuous; there was another carving at Kilrush; and a third – the pattern-stone removed from Scattery and at one time at Kilkee – showed the cata as "the amphibious beast of this blessed isle"'.

St Senan was reputedly born on this island and is said to have founded both the churches and the round tower. The 'cathedral' or stone-built principal church is referred to by archaeologists as the *damliag*. The round tower at Scattery has, according to Macalister,

> its doorway on the ground level: its masonry, if we accept the classification formulated by Lord Dunraven and Margaret Stokes, is of the first and presumably oldest type, and therefore it is reasonable to infer that this tower was built before the advantage of the raised door was realised, and that it may actually be the oldest of the extant specimens, which set the model for all the rest. Its imposing dimensions—for it is the tallest perfect example – would carry its fame over the whole country.

If the story of Senan and the *cata* has any historical credence, then animistic religion existed and thrived here until Christianity took hold. St Senan apparently did not permit any women on the island, perhaps in fear of the return of the 'cat'.

The monastery on the island consisted of eleven churches at its height, the most conspicuous part being the round tower which still stands at 120 feet high and is Ireland's tallest round tower. It is unusual in that its entrance is at ground level; it has survived the ravages of time and bears excellent testament to Irish architecture and the early Irish Church.

The island remained a beacon of the Irish Church until the Vikings landed in the early ninth century. They used the island as a base and buried their booty there. Two ninth-century silver brooches found on the island are Viking in origin. Today they can be seen in the British Museum. Some say that Scattery was a thriving Norse community prior to the establishment of Limerick city.

Thomas Mac Greevy, a poet from Tarbert, Co. Kerry, and a friend of James Joyce, wrote his last poem, 'St Senan's Well', after undertaking a pilgrimage to Scattery:

> I made a response to lips I would kiss once
> And wonder where tangents finish
> The sunlit discs are small
> The end of a tangent is very far away.
> I began my rounds with the sorrowful mysteries
> Instead of the joyful
> Ready therefore, all ready, already
> For the without of glory.

CORK

Corcaigh, 'a moor or marsh or low-lying swamp'

Humans have been living in Cork for the past 9,000 years, with the earliest settlers perhaps living in limestone caves unaffected by the last Ice Age. This is supported by the finds of Mesolithic flint tools from ploughed fields along the east Cork coastline and in the valley of the Blackwater River which flows into Youghal [81].

The evidence for the Neolithic Age is scarce in Cork, although a Neolithic occupation was discovered in 1986, a mile-and-a-half west of Buttevant at Pepperhill [73]. The date of the site is similar to that at Tankardstown, Co. Limerick, which has been carbon-dated to about 4000 BC. Neolithic sites often included wedge tombs, and the greatest of these in Cork is at Labbacallee [73] (*Leaba na Cailleigh*, 'the bed of the goddess'). This tomb has a porthole, a ritual feature that allowed an exit for the passage of the soul after death.

North of Labbacallee is the Funshion River (*An Fhuinnsinn*, 'the river by the ash trees'). The Funshion Valley [73], which is inundated with Neolithic and Bronze Age artefacts, is a good place to explore for those wishing to understand the many layers of our past. In the Iron Age we enter the dawn of our sagas and early history. During this time the *cailleach* and the *aes síde* (fairy folk) make an appearance. Killawillin Mountain

[81], for instance, is known in Irish as *Sídeán na Mná Finge*, 'the fairy palace of the women of Finn'. The folklore associated with the *aes síde* first found book form in London in 1825, in a volume titled *Fairy Legends and Traditions of the South of Ireland*. The first collection of oral tales assembled in Britain and Ireland, it was compiled by Thomas Crofton Croker who was born in Cork in 1798. Sir Walter Scott and the Brothers Grimm were impressed by Croker's work, and within a year the Grimms had translated his work into German as *Irische Elfenmärchen*.

The *Cailleach* mentioned above in *Leaba na Cailligh* has strong associations with Cork, particularly with Bere Island [84, 88]. the *Cailleach Bhéara*, also known as the *Cailleach Béri*, is associated with the Beara Peninsula in south-west Cork, where she is recorded as being a mother goddess to the Corca Duibhne. A local story on Bere Island tells about a row between two *cailleachs*, one on the mainland the other on the island. They threw hurling sticks or rods at each other, and the large standing stone in the middle of Bere Island is where one landed; the other is close to Castletownbeare.

A powerful rite showing the power of the *cailleach* is the rite of sovereignty whereby a rightful claim to the kingship of Tara requires that the king-to-be sleeps with the *Cailleach Bhéara*. Lugaid Laigde, the father of the future King of Ireland Lugaid Mac Con, is forced to do this when the *Cailleach Bhéara* says to Lugaid and his companions, 'One of you must sleep with me tonight, or I will devour you all, unaided, hound and strongman alike.' Once Lugaid agreed, the Cailleach changed into a young woman of 'radiant form'. When Lugaid asked where she came from and who she was, she replied:

> *Atbér-sa frit, a meic min:*
> *limm-sa fóit na haird- ríg:*
> *is mé ind ingen seta seng,*
> *flathius Alban is hÉrend.*

> I will tell you gentle boy,
> with me the high-kings sleep,
> I am the graceful, slender girl,
> the Sovereignty of Scotland and Ireland.

> *[Translated by Edward Gwynn]*

'The Lament of the Old Woman of Beare' can be found in the *Book of Lecan*. It begins as follows:

> *Sentane Bérre, Digdi a ainm, di Chorco Dubne dí .i. di uaib maic Íair*
> *Conchinn. Is díb dano Brigit ingen Iustáin. Is diib dono Líadain ben Chuirithir.*
> *Is díb dono Ūallach ingen Muineghāin.Fo-rácaib Finán Cam doib ní biad cin*
> *Caillig n-amra n-áin díb.*

Is de ro- boí Cailleach Bérre forre: coíca dalta día mBérri. Secht n-aís n-aíted a
ndechaid co déged cech fer éc críne úade, comtar túatha agus chenéla a hui
agus a íarmy, agus cét mblíadna dí fo cailliu íarna shénad do Chuimíniu for
a cend. Do sn-ánic-si áes agus lobrae íarom. Is ant is-rubard-sii.

This was translated by Gerard Murphy as:

The Old woman of Beare, whose name was Digde, was of the Corcu Duibne, that is to
say of the Uí Maic Íair Chonchinn. Brigit daughter of Iustán belonged to them also,
and Líadain wife of Cuirithir, and Ūallach daughter of Muimnechán. Finán Cam has
bequeathed to them that they should never be without some wonderful old woman
among them.

This is why she was called the Old Woman of Beare: she had fifty foster-children
in Beare. She passed into seven periods of youth, so that every husband used to pass
from her to death of old age, so that her grandchildren and great-grand-children were
peoples and races.

We can clearly see from the above that the *Cailleach Bhéara* was a 'mother goddess', who
is remembered both in Ireland and Scotland. She was an ancestress of races, had husbands
in succeeding generations and had the power to confer kingship. Folklore tells us that she
dropped cairns from her apron, thus forming Rathlin Island off Co. Antrim and the 'witch's
hills' or *Sliab na Cailleacha* in Meath, and was the queen of the Limerick fairies.

If the *cailleach* is on an equal footing with the goddess Ériu from whom this island is
named, then the *púca* or Puck is on a less elevated plain. In *Bold Blades of Donegal*, Seumas
Mac Manus writes: 'The Púca is the only evil spirit to be met with in Ireland. He is of a
shadowy, dark indefinite form, set low as if he went on all fours ... always it is on his back
that he tries to carry off his victim. And woe to him that takes the Púca's ride.' Caheraphuca
(*Cathair an Phúca*, 'Puck's stone fort') [84] is in the townland of Knockroe East and is
six miles from Castletownbeare. Three miles west of Macroom [79], there is a townland
named Carrigaphooka (*Carraig a'Phuca*, 'Puck's rock'), from a steep-sided rock outcrop
north of the N22 and overlooking the River Sullane. Carrigaphooka stone circle is to the
east of the outcrop and 326 yards north-west of the confluence of the Foherish and Sullane
rivers. It was originally a multiple stone circle, but today only three stones survive. On top
of 'Puck's rock' stands a castle or tower house built by Donal Mac Carthy in 1436, which
was recently repaired by the Office of Public Works.

About fifteen miles south-west from Macroom is the burial site at Currane Hill [89]
of Lugaid Mac Con, one of two High Kings of Ireland from Munster. In the twentieth
century the hill was locally known as Carn Mac Con. Currane Hill, 757 feet high, is two
miles south-west from Ballineen and the River Bandon; a cairn was raised over the burial
place of Mac Con here, but in 1950 many if not all of the stones were used to build a cross
in commemoration of the Marian Year and a large Vodaphone aerial further works against

the special nature of this site. In pursuit of Lugaid Mac Con, the Ballineen and Enniskeane Heritage group journeyed to the Ulster Museum in Belfast in order to see an urn which they had hoped was the one that had once contained his ashes, but the expert in this area, Greer Ramsay, pronounced it to be of Bronze Age origin, around 1600 BC; consequently, as Mac Con was High King from 195 to 225 AD, this was not his urn.

Lugaid Mac Con is the ancestor of the Érainn, the ancient Celtic rulers of Ireland who chiefly reigned in the east, south-east and south-west of Ireland. The Érainn were one of three ethnic groups in Ireland which have historical credence, the other two being the Cruithin* or Picts and the Gaels (*Clann Miled*). As the Gaels were dominant in the early historical period, the Érainn and the Cruithin who preceded them have been consigned to pseudo-history or to legend. O'Rahilly says that the Érainn came to Ireland from Britain, 'where they had already acquired power'. Keating gives Mac Con a Gaelic pedigree, but this may simply be to make him 'respectable'. I highlight the word 'respectable', as Mac Con and his people were members of the *Aithechtuatha* or vassal tribe; this is generally the status taken on by a race overcome by an invader: they become subservient to the victor, though in Mac Con's case a desire to return to the status quo led to armed resistance, culminating in a number of battles.

In Munster, those who could not claim descent from Ailill Olum, the progenitor of the Eóganacht, such as Mac Con and the Érainn whom the Eóganacht had displaced, were ranked as *fortuatha* – 'people not descended from the ruling stock in an area which they inhabit'. Mac Con was fostered out to Ailill Olum so that this chief warrior of the Érainn could be kept under control. Ailill's son Eóghan defeated Mac Con at the battle of Cenn Abrat on the Cork–Limerick border, after which Mac Con fled to Scotland. After a time there, he sailed with his retinue around the north of Ireland and landed in Clew Bay [30]. Mac Con then challenged Eóghan to battle again, saying, 'I would rather be eaten by dogs than stay in exile any longer.' This led to the battle of Magh Muccrime, which was fought west of Athenry [46] in 195 AD, and here the *Aithechtuatha* under Mac Con were victorious. The fact that Mac Con became High King of Ireland meant that the vassal class was now in the ascendant again, if only for a while.

Mac Con's name is informative, as it points to a distinction between the Gaels and the pre-Gaelic peoples in Ireland; the pre-Gaelic tribes' surnames usually referred to a time when animals were venerated or perceived as ancestor spirits. The surname Mac Con ('son of a hound') is still found in Co. Down; other names acknowledging the hound include Mac Cullagh (*Mac Cú Uladh* or *Mac Con Ulad*, 'hound of Ulster'), and in Munster it is found in the name O'Doheny (*Ó Dubhchonna*, 'black hound'). Interestingly, Mac Con's mother was Sadb, and she was the daughter of Conn Cétchatach, another king of the hound or wolf tribe.

While Mac Con was king at Tara, it came about that Cormac mac Airt was in fosterage there. One day Mac Con passed judgement on a woman whose sheep had grazed the queen's woad garden. Garden woad (*satis tinctoria*) was extensively cultivated for the blue dye prepared from its leaves; it was thought to possess magical properties, and if one painted the guardian of one's tribe, such as a hound or a cat, on one's body, this would act as a protective shield in battle. The woman on whom Mac Con had passed judgement came to Cormac mac Airt, who said to her that the judgement was in error. He said that the judgement should have been 'one shearing for another' (*in lommrad tar héisi a chéli*), meaning that the sheep's wool should have been sufficient for the grazed woad. When Mac Con saw that he had made an error in 'the king's justice' (*fír flathemon*), he resigned.

He returned to his Munster kingdom but was murdered at a place called the 'Red Fort' in the townland known as Derrigra which is from the Irish *Dearg Rath*, which also means 'red fort'. Derrigra is close to the village of Ballineen [86]. A local historian, Michael O'Connell, thinks that Mac Con was killed in the vicinity of Ballineen; however, another suggestion was that he was killed by Feircheas mac Comáigh on the orders of Cormac mac Airt at *Gort an Óir* ('field of gold') close to Derrygrath ('red fort') east of Cahir [74], Co. Tipperary. The same name for the two townlands may have led to this confusion.

Keating writes: *Is é Feircheas mac Comáin Éigeas ar Fhoráileamh Chormaic mic Airt do mharbh Mac Con leis an nga da ngairthí rincne* ('Feircheas son of Comán Éigeas, at the command of Cormac mac Airt, slew Mac Con with the spear called *rincne*'). Mac Con's death was avenged by Finn mac Cumhail,* who slew Feircheas.

Mac Con was cremated, and his ashes were buried on Currane Hill [86]. In the mid-nineteenth century his tomb was robbed, and his urn was discarded; the local historical group believed that the urn was in the Ulster Museum but, as mentioned above, it preceded Mac Con by 1,700 years and was thus unlikely to have ever contained his ashes. A local story concerning the urn is that a 'long time back' a member of a local family put his hand into the urn in the belief that there was gold in it (possibly the memory of *Gort an Óir* was still in the popular mind), which indeed there was, but when he looked later it was only clay; this change in substance was attributed to the fairies. The Ballineen and Enniskeane Heritage Group has re-identified where Mac Con's cairn stood, and this has been supported by local famers who remember it prior to 1950.

As Currane Hill is of such significance to Munster, it is important to examine what is currently known regarding the site. In 1937, Adolf Mahr, curator of the National Museum of Ireland in Dublin, recorded an urn 'found in the centre of three concentric stone circles, rising in height from the inner to the other', each being covered with 'long flags extending round the uprights of each respective circle'. This unusual Bronze Age structure is one of the most unusual prehistoric monuments in Ireland; all that remains today is the site of a cairn a few feet south-east from the high cross erected in 1950. The cairn was destroyed in 1840. The destruction of the cairn unearthed an urn containing 'a ball of clay about the size of a large apple which by tradition contained the ashes of an Irish chieftain'. The chieftain in this case was Mac Con. The ball is reminiscent of the black balls of ashes found in some old churches and, like the *Síle na Gigs*, is incorporated into the wall of some churches as a venerated curiosity from an earlier age.

According to the *Book of Leinster*, Mac Con was King of Ireland for thirty years, from 195 to 225 AD.

> *Gabais Mac Con tír mBanba*
> *cach leth co glasmuir ngledend:*
> *tríca bliadan án naland*
> *ro boí Ir Rígu hÉrend.*

> Mac Con took control of Ireland
> each half to the blue sea he controlled
> for thirty years of splendid rule
> he was king of Ireland.

[Translated by Whitley Stokes]

Another important burial place lies three miles north-east of Currane Hill in the townland of Murragh (*Mór Átha*, 'big ford') [86] through which the River Bandon flows. In the graveyard of Murragh are the remains of an eleventh-century church. Bruno O'Donoghue in *Parish Histories and Place Names of West Cork* mentions that there was a tumulus here. This was also pointed out by the antiquarian John Windele in the nineteenth century, who gave its position as being west of the graveyard. Windele states that this tumulus is where Diarmuid Ó Duibhne* is buried. The following is an account given by Windele:

> At Moragh Glebe, we quitted the car to visit Diarmat's grave, a tumulus to the memory of Diarmot O'Duivne, one of the principal heroes of the Fenian romance, the successful lover of Grainne, daughter of King Cormac and wife of Finn. I had heard formerly of this tumulus, the situation of which had been pointed out by a countryman. 'Between Enniskeane and Bandon near a graveyard at Moragh is a Leabba Dermit's Grainne.' [*Leaba Diarmuid agus Gráinne*, 'love bed of Diarmuid* and Gráinne*'] We passed the burial ground which lies close to the high bank overhanging the River Bandon. The river we are told, has frequently encroached on this bank carrying away portions of the cemetery, coffins, headstones etc … We strolled along the bank a short distance to the west, until we came to the tumulus. This like its Christian neighbour just mentioned lies immediately over the river which has encroached so much on all this bank that one whole half length of the tumulus has been undermined and fallen down a considerable way on the slope of declivity, disclosing its materials, part of the surrounding alluvial deposit, but not showing sufficient of the interior to inform us whether it consisted of Kistaven or Cromleac. A little time and expense would soon inform us on this lead and I suggested the attempt to Mr. Hawkes. But will he do it? The form of the tumulus is a long ridge like mound. It measures 81 feet in length and 12 feet high. At the river side it has greatly fallen away.

Michael O'Connell and I can concur with the measurements given by Windele over 150 years ago; apart from slippage, the mound to Diarmuid* stands today in a beautiful setting on the banks of the Bandon at Murragh, a mile-and-a-half east of Enniskeane [86]. (The research that Michael O'Connell and I did on the tumulus or mound of Diarmuid can be seen in the book *Murragh: A place of Graves*, published by the Ballineen and Enniskeane Heritage Group.)

The River Bandon (which, like the Bann in Ulster and the Boyne in Leinster, refers to a goddess – Bandae) has a further connection to Diarmuid,* as the place where it rises, a hill known as *Cnoc na nAbhann* ('hill of the rivers') or more commonly Nowen Hill [85], has a cave which, according to George Bennett in *A History of Bandon* (1869), is called *Leaba Dhiarmada* or 'Diarmuid's Bed'.

After many attempts and serious 'rites of passage' through bogland, Michael O'Connell and I, on our third attempt and with the help of a kind guide, Robert Deane, were able to identify this cave, which is not on the *Discovery Series* map. There are many ancient walks around this hill, and apparently they led to Diarmuid's* cave. As Bennett says: 'Dermot's bed appears at one time to have been much frequented by visitors, as its sides are literally covered with the names and initials of many of those who came to see where Diarmuid and Finn mac Cumhail's* faithless wife concealed themselves from the fury of the great Fenian.' I can confirm this, as there are inscribed dates here from 1686, 1701 and 1881. The area is best approached from the farm of Mary Kingston O'Donovan, though permission should be sought in advance.

A stone circle south-west of the cave and locally known as a ring fort would presumably have been familiar to the lovers. When they left their love bed they went to Cullenagh Lake (from *Cuileanach*, 'place of holly'), and from there to Shiplough or Ship's Pool (*Cluain na Luinge*, 'pasture land of the ships'), west of Dunmanway [85]. From there they went to *Garrán Bán*, meaning the 'white grove' of maythorn or of silver birch (but other accounts say it means 'a white horse'), which is a massive stone with the handprint of Diarmuid.* It is just yards north of Dunmanway Hospital.

Close to Murragh and Enniskeane is Kilnacranagh West [86], and here another discovery awaits, possibly a Chalcolithic or Copper Age settlement area, including a lake, now reduced to a marsh but known to locals as the 'Loughy'. A mound to the east of this area known locally as the 'settlement' appears to contain a wedge tomb; another mound to the west may also contain a wedge tomb, but this remains to be explored. Wedge tombs were built between the end of the Neolithic period and the beginning of the Bronze Age. Outside the wedge tomb (about 400 of which have been so far discovered in Ireland) were two jamb-like stones or more simply two side stones of a doorway. The covered mound at Kilnacranagh would seem to suggest that the community placed a special religious significance to the tomb. The name *Cill na Cranagh* may well refer to the remains of a wooden church found nearby, but *cranagh* may also refer to the wooden structures found in the 'Loughy' or lake, as it may have been the local pronunciation for *crannóc* or *crannóg*, 'a wooden lake dwelling'.

The elevation of the tomb reflects the veneration that these communities had for the sun and the sky. The hundreds of wedge tombs found in Ireland are on a line west from north-east Antrim to Cork Harbour. None have been discovered in Britain, but they exist in Brittany, where they are known as *allés couvertes* or 'covered passages'. The large wedge tomb [73] at Labbacallee (*Leaba Callaigh*, 'the bed of the goddess') in Co. Cork is placed in the third millennium BC, as indicated by the radiocarbon date obtained from a human bone found in the tomb. An inscribed stone was found in the area, and this may come from the Late Neolithic period. The site is mentioned in a sketch sent to the noted English antiquary John Aubrey in 1675, and further sketches appear in Charles Smith's *History of Cork* published in 1750. The excavation of Labbacallee was begun by H.G. Leask and Liam Price in 1934 as part of the Relief of Unemployment programme of archaeological excavations inaugurated in 1934 and administered by the Office of Public Works in collaboration with the National Museum of Ireland. The chambers within Labbacallee may have contained cremated bones, but according to Leask these were removed and placed in a single chamber when Iron Age tribes used the chambers for accommodation.

A wedge tomb is also found on Sherkin Island [88], one of the many islands in Roaring Water Bay in west Cork. The name possibly derives from *sericin*, a 'heel', but according to Bruno O'Donoghue in *Parish Histories of West Cork* it is *Inis Oircin*, 'Island of the little pig' or possibly 'of the whale'. The tomb is found in the west of the island at Slievemore. On the south side is Kilmoon (*Cill Mugain*, 'St Mughain's church'), St Mughain being a virgin saint of the O'Driscolls and a relative of St Ciarán of Cape Clear. At the south side of the church is a holy well called Tobernagow (*Tober a Ghabha*, 'the smith's well'), at which 'rounds' were performed.

Cape Clear Island or *Oileán Cléire* [88] is, apart from the Fastnet Rock, the most southerly point of Ireland. As at Newgrange, Co. Meath, farming began on Cape Clear during the Neolithic Age, about 6,000 years ago. The Cape Clear Stone, now in the Cork Public Museum, is from Neolithic times, and one may see its symbols as either Neolithic art or symbols of an astronomical calendar signifying the seasons. To reinforce this, a passage tomb at Killickaforavane (*Cill Leice Forabhain*, 'church of the slatey strip of land') situated on a hill on the north side of the island has a stone decorated with symbols. At the summer solstice the sun has been observed entering along this passage. A facsimile of the Cape Clear Stone is to be seen at the Cléire Museum and Heritage Centre on the island. Other links to the Neolithic Age are to be found in two standing stones; a hole in one of these points to the spot on the horizon where the sun rises at the summer solstice. A custom has developed whereby lovers link hands through this hole and pledge loyalty to each other. Above the south-west cliffs of Cape Clear stands a line of standing stones; in the closing years of the eighteenth century, these stones were dressed up as redcoats to frighten off a feared invasion by the French. They are still known as *Na Fir Bréagacha*, 'the False Men'.

Of the islands in the south-west, Dursey [84] is a good one for earthing the myths; its Irish name is *Oileán Bhaoi-Bheirre*, 'the island of Baoi of Beare'. Dursey is from the Irish *doirse*, 'doors'. Westropp suggests that it may relate to the Cliffs of Illanbeg where a fort once stood. The name is as old as 1339, when it appeared in the form 'Dorrosey'. Edmund Hogan was told by local O'Sullivans that Baoi Bherre was Dursey. Philip O'Sullivan Beare calls it '*Bea Insula, in qua, sum ipse natus*' ('The Island of Baoi in which I myself am a native'). Regarding two townlands on either side of the Dursey Sound, Ballynacallagh ('the townland of the cailleach', though this has also been termed as *baile na caladh* or 'the townland of the harbour') and Ballaghboy ('the townland of Baoi'), we can see the possibility that both these islands were intimately connected to the mother goddess, the *Cailleach*. In other words, Baoi gives her name to both islands and both may be named *Oileán Baoi*. Between the Beara Peninsula and Bere Island is Dunboy or *Dún Baoi*, 'the fortress of Baoi', so we can see that the *Cailleach Beara* is interwoven with the folklore of the area.

Dursey is mentioned in a ninth-century poem, the second verse of which reads as follows:

> *Is me Cailleach Berre Bui,*
> *Do-meillinn lene mbithnui;*
> *Indiu tathum dom shemi*
> *Na melanin cid athleni.*

> I am the old woman of Beare, from Dursey,
> I used to wear a cloak of orange-yellow wort
> Today I am but skin and bone,
> And there is nothing to wear but cast-offs.

Dursey is also known as *Teach Duinn* or 'the House of Donn', as well as *An Tarbh*, or 'the bull'. This double name is, according to Westropp, a relic of the old myth belonging to the bull episode in the *Táin Bó Cúailgne*,* with a connection to the Donnotaurus ('brown' or 'kingly bull') of ancient Gaul. The Donn of folklore is frequently connected with cattle. The cult of the ancient bull god can be traced all along the Atlantic and Mediterranean countries to the Far East. Bull Rock on Dursey, a rocky island out to sea, is said to be the House of Donn. In a medieval manuscript, the souls about to go to hell visit *Teach Duinn*, which is the realm of the dead and gateway to the Otherworld. And this gateway gives its name to the island, for here are the *doirse* or 'doors' (Dursey) which lead from the land of the living to that of the dead. A lighthouse tower nearly 330 feet above sea level now stands on Bull Rock, exhibiting a light equivalent to that of millions of candles for a distance of thirty nautical miles, which means that over time the house of the dark has metamorphosed into a house of light.

The Book of Leinster gives the story behind the location of Donn's House. The invasion by the sons of Mil included Donn as part of the invading force, and he was asked to climb the ship's mast and cast incantations against the Tuatha Dé Danann,* the pre-Gaelic Irish. The Tuatha Dé Danann in turn cast incantations against the Milesians, after which Donn got an acute fever and entered his death throes. Amergin, a son of Mil, decided that it was best to place Donn's body away from the land, and the dying Donn requested that his body be carried to one of the islands off Dursey. 'Let his body be carried to yonder high rock,' says Amergin. 'His folk shall come to this spot.' Thus came about the name *Teach Duinn* or House of Donn.

The folklorist Kate Müller-Lisowski mentions part of a lost poem from the ninth century as follows:

> *Tech Duinn dámaig dún Congaile,*
> *Carrack rúad fáebrach rathaighte,*
> *Raith ríg fri lán lir féthaigthe,*
> *Fail nir, net gríphe grádaighte.*

> The house of Donn of the mighty host,
> The house of Congal's feast, red edged rock.
> King's fortress at the silent flowing of the sea,
> Lair of a wild boar,
> Nest of a griffin of high degree.

Many old customs are connected with Dursey; one is associated with *Imbolc* or *Oímelc*: sheep's milk; this is the ancient fertility festival associated with Brigit (mentioned below), whose feast falls on 1 February. Gobnat (from Ballyvourney), later St Gobnat, has also connections with Dursey; a *geis* or taboo is placed on anyone who plants or ploughs before St Gobnat's Day on 18 February. On St Patrick's Day, 17 March, farmers would use charcoal from burnt wood to place the sign of the cross on their right hand, on the forehead of a cow and on the base of a milk churn.

Diarmuid* Ó Duibhne of Diarmuid and Grainne* fame is also connected to Dursey, as he says, 'I am Diarmuid of the yew tree of Connacht and of Dursey and of Bearehaven.' Whether Coosdermit ('the foot mark of Diarmuid'), a few miles east from Dursey and Darriheendermot ('the oak wood of Diarmuid') and now marked as Derreeny on the south-east slope of Hungry Hill [84], are references to Diarmuid is open to conjecture.

The *cailleach* as noted above has strong connections with Bere Island [84]. Although in Gaelic it is generally named *An tOileán Mór* or 'the great island', it is also called *Inis Greagraidhe*, or 'the island of screeching', which is more in keeping with the *cailleach* as a hag or banshee.

The goddess Clíodna together with Aoibhell and Áine constitutes a triad of Munster goddesses. Clíodna's *síd* or fairy palace is close to *Carraig Clíodna* or Clíodna's Rock, which is in the harbour of Glandore between Skibbereen and Clonakilty [89]. Another rock associated with Clíodna is in the barony of Duhallow [72] north of Kanturk, where she was closely connected with the O'Keeffe family as its fairy guardian. Lore from Duhallow describes Clíodna as both a seductress of young men and a benefactor to farmers. To quote from *Traces of the Elder Faiths of Ireland* by W.G. Wood-Martin: 'In her neighbourhood no cattle die from the influences of the evil eye nor the malignant power of the unfriendly spirits of the air. Her goodness preserves the harvest from the blights which dissipate the farmer's hopes.' The nineteenth-century scholar J. O'Beirne Crowe stated that the Irish possessed foreign deities, and he identified Clíodna with the Gaulish Clutonda.

Clíodna is also regarded as the banshee that rules as queen over the fairies of south Munster and as such is possessed of powerful spells. As an Otherworld goddess, she possessed three magical birds which ate apples from the Otherworld tree. Clíodna's birds had a healing power which lulled the sick to sleep and healed them. The *Dindshenchas** contains a poem of verses named *Tond Chlidna* or Clíodna's Wave. The following is a sample of three of these verses:

> *Clidna chend-find, búan a bét,*
> *'con tuind-se tánic a héc;*
> *damna d'a máthair beith marb*
> *inní dia tarla in sen-ainm.*

> *Rígan ind óenaig thall tra,*
> *ingen dar' chomainm Clidna*
> *tar in ler lethan longach*
> *tuc leis Cíabán cass-mongach.*

> *Tond dúine Téite na tríath,*
> *'sí a hainm roime in bar n-íath;*
> *nocorbáided 'mon tuind tra*
> *ben diarbo chomainm Clidna.*

Clidna Cendfind, lasting her calamity,
at this wave came her death;
cause for her mother to die
was the matter whence arose the ancient name.

The queen of the gathering yonder in sooth,
the maiden whose name was Clidna,
Ciaban the curly-haired bore with him,
over the wide ship-ridden sea.

The wave of Dun Teite of the chiefs,
that was its name before in your land,
till there was drowned in the wave in sooth
a woman whose name was Clidna.

The deep roar of the sea as it enters the caverns in the cliffs at Glandore was said to foretell the death of the King of Munster. This surge has been 'from time immemorial called Tonn Clíodna or Clíodna's wave'. According to W.G. Wood-Martin, Clíodna was said to have been a beautiful but malignant fairy who attracted young men to follow her to the seashore, whereupon they were drowned in the ocean. One young man was able to counteract her spells and laid a plot for her destruction, from which she escaped by taking the form of a wren. She was to resume this form each Christmas Day, and hence comes the practice of hunting the wren at this time. In revenge for the way she was treated, Clíodna threatened to cause a very large wave which would completely cover Munster.

Clíodna is also associated with the Ahaglaslin [89] portal tomb one mile west from Rosscarberry and eight miles west from Clíodna's Rock at Glandore; this picturesque monument is visible from the road, though not easy to access. The local name for the tomb is Callaheencladdig, or 'the little witch by the seashore'.

Not far from Rosscarbery is the much-visited Drombeg ('small hill' or 'little ridge') stone circle [89], one of the finest examples of such in Cork. Outside the circle are traces of a cooking pit or *fulacht fia* with a supposed date of about 150 BC, though stone circles are likely to be of Bronze Age in date. A burial pit was found near the centre of the circle containing shards of a broken pot and some cremated bone. A stone circle is a monument primarily dedicated to ritual. They are very common in the West Cork area. They consist

FIGURE 25. Drombeg stone circle.

of free-standing upright stones and vary in number from between five and fifteen stones, while the diameter ranges from between ten and thirty feet. A feature of these circles is the 'recumbent stone' which looks like an altar stone, and the Drombeg circle was locally known as 'the Druid's Altar'. Opposite the recumbent are two large stones known as portal stones, presumably the site for a ritual entrance. The interior was originally paved with flat pebbles, and although submerged now the site remains tidy. The use of stone circles as observatories and places of sun worship is now generally accepted. Like many other circles, the orientation of Drombeg is aligned towards sunrise and sunset on the winter solstice. The circle is briefly lit up when the sun appears in the cleft between two hills to the south. A deeply etched mark on the north portal stone is said to be a marker for such observation.

Another impressive stone circle can be found at Templebryan [89]. There are only four of the original nine uprights in place. At the centre is a large block of quartz known as the *cloch gréine* or 'sunstone'. This is said by some to be the stone from which Clonakilty – *cloch na coillte*, 'the stone in the woods' – gets its name. However, it is also said that this stone is close to *Tadg an Asna* or the Pike Man, which is on the main road through Clonakilty. Other stone circles in the neighbourhood include those at Reenascreena and at Bohonoagh.

FIGURE 26. Reenascreena stone circle.

There are 234 stone circles in Ireland, and of these eighty-six are found in Cork. Of the 145 stone circles that exist in the Republic, about 100 exist in west Cork and south Kerry; they consist of the largest group to be found in the Britain and Ireland. These circles all possess an astronomical orientation which consists of a line extending from the middle of the gap between the entrance stones across to the centre of the axial or recumbent stone, so that the main axis of the circle is aligned north–east/south–west, i.e. those parts of the horizon in which the sun rises or sets at significant times of the year. These astronomical timings were used to ascertain the proper time for performing a spiritual ceremony rather than determining the right time for sowing crops.

Whereas stone circles had an astronomical function, the promontory fort was essentially a defensive structure. These are generally coastal promontory forts and occur on headlands, especially where the headland is connected to the mainland by a narrow neck. Almost 200 of these sites are known in Ireland and are mostly located on the western and southern seaboards. They may be seen as the Iron Age version of the Martello Tower. The fort which finds its way into the early sagas is the promontory fort on the foot of the Old Head of Kinsale [87]. This coastal promontory fort has two names: Dunmacpatrick and *Dún Cermna*. The former is a Late-Medieval stone-built fortification with part of the bawn wall still standing; the latter is an Iron Age promontory fort, which was a significant pre-Christian settlement. Only the site of this fort exists, although prior to the 1970s features such as hut sites were evident. However, there is a rich early history connected with the site.

In Keatings' *History of Ireland*, *Dún Cermna* was a part of the fifth division of Ireland. In this division, Ireland was divided into two parts, with the southern part extended south from a line between *Inber Colptha* (the estuary of the Boyne) at Drogheda and Limerick on the Shannon. The northern half was ruled by Cermna's brother Sobhairce, and his fortress was at Dunseverick, Co. Antrim.The southern half was ruled by Cermna, and his fort was the aforementioned *Dún Cermna* on the Old Head of Kinsale. Cermna was King of the Érainn, a pre-Gaelic race who came from Britain. This fort was not too distant from the burial site of their first king, Nemed, at Great Island in Cork Harbour. This may also have been the spot where the Érainn landed. The Érainn arrived in the fourth century BC and for a while were overlords of Ireland. *Dún Cermna* is named as one of the three *dúine* of Ireland in the *Irish Triads*. The other two are *Dún Sobhairce*, Co. Antrim, and Caherconree on Slieve Mish, Co. Kerry. The reign of Cermna came to an end when Cermna was slain by Eochaid Fabarghlas at the battle of *Dún Cermna*.

The southernmost point of Cork is Mizen Head or *Carn Uí Néid* [88], meaning 'the cairn of the tribe of Néid'. Where this cairn is today is a uncertain, but a suggestion has been made that it is at Mizen Peak, also known as Cairn Hill. Could it be part of the loose stones of Cloganes? It is hardly under the visitor centre or, worse still (like King Richard III), under a car park! Néid is a god of the Tuatha Dé Danann* and was son of Indai; he is associated with Mizen Head and with *Grianan Ailech*, the old name for which was *Ailech Néid*, in Donegal, a few miles west of Derry city.

FIGURE 27. The statue of King Puck in Killorglin, Co. Kerry.

On the Mizen Head peninsula and two miles north-west of Goleen is Knockaphuca or Puck's Hill. As a deity, Puck represents the goat. He is annually commemorated at Puck Fair every August at Kilorglin in Co. Kerry. Three miles south-west from Knockapuca is Knocknamaddree or 'the hill of the dogs', and to add to the animal motif, there is a place called Carraigacat (*Carraig chait*, 'the rock of the cat') about a mile south-west from Knocknamaddree. At first glance, one may say that these places are merely named after wild goats (Puck), or wild cats or dogs. But the association with dogs, cats and goats goes deeper than that, particularly in south-west Ireland. Cats, for example, are regarded as ancestor deities of the Érainn, and Cairbre Cinn Cait or 'Cairbre Cat-Head' is an example of the deification of the animal. Folklore maintains that he got his name because he had ears like those of a cat:

Amhail do bhí Cairbre cruaidh
Do ghabh Éire theas is thuaidh:
Dá chluas chait um a cheann cain
Fionnfadh cait tré n-a chluasaibh.

Thus was Cairbre the hardy,
Who ruled Ireland south and north:
Two cat's ears on his fair head,
Cat's fur upon his ears.

[Translated by P.S. Dinneen]

A description by the poet Egan O'Rahilly states, *srub chait dona lasin Carpre* ('the nose or snout of a cat was worn by Cairbre'). Cairbre's son Moran had a collar round his neck which referred to Cairbre as the cat-headed King of Ireland. This collar was known as *Tresin Moraind* or the 'triple Collar of Moran'. In later times Cairbre Cinn Cait led the *Aithechtuatha* or 'subject people', who were generally the Cruithin* or the aboriginal peoples of Britain and Ireland. Cairbre led a successful rebellion in 90 AD. However, Cairbre Cinn Cait was an ancestor deity, and the Cairbre mentioned above was more likely a chief of the same tribe or race which had been reduced in status as a result of invasion by a superior force, namely the Milesians or Gaels.

The cat deity originated among the Silures of Wales who, according to Ptolemy, inhabited the south-east of Wales. Their tribal centre was at Caerwent (*ventra silurium*), and their chief Caratacus was defeated by the Romans in 51 AD. The Silures had a fortress at Caerleon, and here many cat heads have been found in stone. These, it has been suggested, represent the feline deity of the Silures, which appears in Welsh literature as *Cath Paluc* or 'Paluc's Cat'. Carbery in west Cork is the largest barony in Ireland and gets its name from Cairbre. Its name is derived from Cairbre Riada who was King of Munster in the second century or possibly from Cairbre, King of the Cinéal Laoghaire or the O'Leary clan in the seventh century AD.

In ancient times, a battle was fought on the site of *Carraigacat* or 'cat rock', presumably between the 'cat people' of Cairbre or the Érainn and an invading tribe, possibly a force attacking the centre of worship. There are eleven stones here in a circle with a diameter of twenty feet, some upright, others recumbent. A burial ground is south and west of the stones. *Cloghan Cinn Cait* in Brandon, Co. Kerry, is also known as 'the stepping-stones of Cairbre'. The place is also associated with the Érainn, for whom Cairbre was an ancestor god.

P.W. Joyce in *Irish Names of Places* writes that *Carraig-a' chait* means 'rock of the wild cat, a haunt'. It is also seen as simply 'a wild cat haunt', in W.Y. Evans Wentz's *The Fairy Faith in Celtic Countries*. In the record of monuments and places by Dúchas, Carraigacat receives four mentions: as a mining complex, as a fish palace, as a burial ground and as a circular enclosure. We thus evolve from a haunt of wild cats to a circular enclosure and then to a ceremonial or ritual centre, like *Dún Aengus* on the Aran Islands, or like Crom's Circle at Lough Gur. To the north of this circular centre is a semi-circular wall of stone marking the lower end of Knocknamaddree; it would have been a perfect sound board for Bronze Age horns calling the surrounding tribes to their annual or seasonal gatherings. This natural stone escarpment rings around the northern side of the enclosure. However, a house has been built on the ceremonial ground and the stones have been placed along the edges of the garden. From here, one has a fine view of Barley Cove.

Another man with strange ears, Labraid Loingsech, has a connection further east along the coast at Lough Hyne [89]. Labraid was banished overseas after his nephew murdered his brother Loegaire, King of Ireland, thus securing the kingship at Dind Ríg [61]. He eventually returned from exile to avenge his brother and win back the kingship at the Battle of Dind Ríg. One version of the story says that Labraid never left Ireland at all but simply went to the *Fir Morca* in west Munster, where he later returned to marry Moriath, daughter of the local king, thus explaining his connection with west Cork and Lough Hyne. As in the myth attendant on all kings, he was said to have been a great

FIGURE 28. Illustration of Labraid Loingsech – the king with horses' ears (James Dorgan).

progenitor and thus had the ears of a horse. To show how this belief survived in folklore, we need only to relate the following tale, collected by S. Ó Dálaigh in 1942, from Lough Hyne:

> Labhar Ó Loinsigh used to sit on top of Cnoc Camtha and wash his feet in Lough Ine. Labhar was a giant who had horse's ears. He used to employ barbers to shave him, but he killed each of them in turn because he feared the secret would become known to the public. He allowed one barber to live but he pledged him to secrecy. The barber retained the secret but it began to weigh heavily on his mind. His health began to give way. A travelling woman understood his ailment; she said he had a secret and advised him to dig a sod and whisper the secret into a hole, then to replace the sod. He did so. Some kind of *eileastrom* grew there. Somebody cut it, and blew on it and the reed began to speak:
>
> *Tá scéal agamsa agus is deacair é innsint, go bhfuil dhá chluais chapaill ar Labar Ó Loinsigh!*—I have a story and it is difficult to say, that Labraid Loinsigh has two horse's ears.
>
> Thus did the secret become known to the public. Labhar then disappeared and was heard of no more. He had a castle on the island of Lough Ine. The ruins of this castle are still there.

An Irish-language version of this tale, collected by S. Ó Cróinín in 1938 from M. Ní Iarfhlaith, Cúil Aodha, is as follows:

> *Ar an oileán i Loch Oighean a bhí Labhar Ó Loinsigh na chomnuidhe. Do thagadh sé amach gach aon Lá Bealthaine chun é bhearradh, agus do chuireadh sé chun báis an té bhearradh é i gcomhnuidhe. Is amlaidh a chuireadh sé fé gheasaibh iad ná féadaidís an rún a insint d'éine agus do chuireadh san chun báis iad. Do bhí cloch mhór amuigh ar an dtalamh agus an fear a bhearradh Labhar do sheasuígheadh sé ar a gcloch, bhí Labhar chómh hard san.*
>
> *Do bhí seanduine ar an dtaobh thiar do Loch Oighean, agus do bhí duine aca taréis Labhar abhearradh, agus bhí an rún aige. Dubhairt an seanduine leis poll a dhéanamh sa talamh agus an rún a insint isteach ann. Dhein sé an poll ar agaidh an chaisleáin thiar, sa choill, agus d'fhás sralladóir san áit.*
>
> *Do ghéarr duine éigin é agus do dhein sé fliúit de, agus an chéad rud a sheinn sé-*

> *Tá sgéal agam-sa agus is deacair liom insint,*
> *Go bfhuil dhá chluais chapall ar Labhar Ó Loingsigh.*

> *Siné a chuir Labhar as an áit mar d'airigh sé cad dubhairt an sralladóir agus d'airig gach éine chómh maith leis. D'imigh sé as an oileán síos an Bhárlóg agus ní fheacaidh éine ó shoin é.*

Labraid Loingsech lived on Lough Hyne. He presented himself each Mayday in order to be shaved and all who shaved him were put to death. Anyone who knew his secret was put to death. There was a large stone on the ground and it was necessary for the man shaving Labraid to stand on this stone as Labraid was very tall.

There was an old person on the east side of Lough Hyne and a person close to him who had shaved Labraid and who knew the secret; this person was told by the old man to dig a hole and to tell his secret into it. He dug a hole in front of the castle east of the wood and a reed grew there. Someone cut it down and made a flute of it and the first tune it played was:

'I have a story difficult to tell; Labraid Loinsigh has horse's ears.'

When Labraid became aware of this and noticing that everyone knew his secret he left Lough Hyne on a long plank of wood and was never seen again.

[Translated by the author]

I conclude the story of Labraid Loingsech with a piece of verse recited by Neily Bohane from the area of Lough Hyne:

Death seized him and they laid him to rest
In that lone little island his heart loved the best.
Strange sounds were heard in the castle each night
And the servants withdrew from its precincts in fright,
'Til at length a great bard to that island came,
Who was longing for glory and panting for fame,
He cut off a branch from King Labra's oak tree
And he polished and pared it a nice harp to be,
But the only tune ever that his instrument played,
'Twas with horse's ears, King Labra was laid.

William O'Brien in *Prehistory of Cork* says 'only one hillfort in Cork can be identified as Bronze Age with any certainty. This is located in Clashanimud townland, Knockavilla'. This unique hillfort [87] is about three-and-a-half miles north from Bandon. O'Brien further states that 'the hillfort is strategically sited on a spur off the southern side of the main east-west ridge crossing the landscape of west Cork to the west. The site has panoramic views of the mid-Cork landscape, extending east to the Nagle Mountains, north of the Boggeragh Mountains, with the Killarney Mountains visible to the north-west'. Several thousand oak posts were used in constructing the palisades and, given that oak trees take 100 years before they mature, one can only assume that west Cork was well lined with oak woods. The last of that ancient line can be found today across Muckross by Killarney in Co. Kerry.

The hillfort at Clashanimud is carbon-dated at 1100 BC or Late Bronze Age. The hill on which it stands is *cnoc an bhile*, 'the hill of the sacred tree', present-day Knockavilla.

Thomas J. Westropp, a noted antiquarian, wrote in 1904 that 'the history of the veneration of the Irish for ancient trees has yet to be written'. This 'veneration' finds its zenith in the *bile*, and as such '*cnoc an bhile*' is well named. Trees in ancient Ireland were a common feature associated with ceremonies and used as places of inauguration, and later, in Early Medieval times, with ecclesiastical sites; fundamentally the *bile* was at the centre of all major gatherings. The fort, although built as a fortress, was essentially a meeting place for the people of the locality, and the sacred tree was the epicentre for their gatherings. It was also at the centre of ritual meetings. From Knockavilla, the rising and setting sun could be seen. O'Brien mentions the burning of the fort here would likely have started with the destruction of the *bile*, and its destruction would have brought to an end the ritual significance of the site and thus its abandonment. Also in the parish of Knockavilla is the townland of Kill, an earlier spelling of which was Kilwylie (*Cill a' Bhile*, 'the church of the sacred tree'). Having two sacred trees so close to each other is indicative of the strength of the sacred tree, and although the trees would have been lost to time and the rivalry of opposing tribes, as well as to zealous Christian clergy who destroyed them as symbolic of pagan Ireland, they still exist in many place names and thus the names act as mirrors to a rich past.

The Bronze Age appears to have been a period of harmony between the sexes before the arrival of monotheism and a strict male godhead. It is characterised by an attachment to all things natural, wherein was seen a connection with the supernatural. The metal used for many of the ornate metal objects that survive from the Late Bronze Age came from various mines such as Mount Gabriel [88] north of Schull and Ross Island near Killarney, Co. Kerry, as well as mines at *Carraigacat*, Millen, Callaross Oughter and Ballyrisode, the latter three being close to the ceremonial centre at *Carrigacat*. The Bronze Age extended throughout Europe, but on the west coast of Ireland it literally faced its golden deity, namely the sun.

According to William O'Brien in *Bronze Age Copper Mines of the Goleen Area, Co. Cork*, 'a site on the western slopes of Ballyrisode Hill [88] 200 m north of the main Schull road and 3 km north-east of Goleen village … a mine site is located on rough ground between two major fold ridges, looking west to a small lake'. The Royal Cork Institution in a meeting in 1880 gave evidence of a primitive copper mine in this area. At an earlier stage, in 1854, Richard Hungerford discovered twelve celts (a *celt* is a prehistoric edged implement of bronze or stone), which pointed to the mining operations carried on at Ballyrisode, and to the use of copper. The centre of mining in Cork was possibly at Mount Gabriel, where there was extensive mining of surface copper beds during the Early Bronze Age.

One of the aims of this book is to attempt to surmise how certain of these artefacts were used in Bronze Age rites. Thus, the hoard of gold, bronze and amber objects from Mountrivers, Coachford [80] together with gold lunulae and sun discs found throughout the island may have been part of the ceremonial dress worn during the gatherings for these sun and moon festivities. Gold objects either for ceremonial occasions or for attire were handmade by goldsmiths from 2000 to 1000 BC. At Cloyne [81] a pair of gold discs were found dating to between 2000 and 1800 BC. It is possible that these discs indicated sun worship and that the hermitage here founded by St Colman in the sixth century may be an example of a Christianising of what was formerly an Early Bronze Age pagan site.

In the sixth century a nunnery was founded at Ballyvourney (*Baile Bhoirne*, 'place of rocky or stoney terrain') [79] by St Gobnat. As St Colman was the guardian saint of the Mac Coilles, Gobnat was the guardian of the Mac Dermots. Like Brigit, Gobnat's origins are pre-Christian, and the discovery of a gold disc and pin here together with two bracelets from the Early Bronze Age may show that the ritual origins of Ballyvourney lie deep in the pre-Christian past. For example, the excavation of St Gobnat's house or kitchen showed debris which included iron tools, bronze wire, crucibles and whetstones. Around St Gobnat's grave are three bullaun stones and the abandoned crutches of hopeful pilgrims. The medieval church here includes a *síle na gig*.

At Knockane, two miles south-east of Castlemartyr [81], a gold plaque and amber bead were found, both from the Early Bronze Age, about 2000 BC. At Ballyhalwick [86], one mile east of Dunmanway, a gold bracelet was discovered in 1844. At Coppeen [86], five miles north of Ballineen, a hoard of three gold bracelets was found together with a gold rod and a gold ring. Alas, many of these golden ornaments were in the collection of a Mr Crofton Croker and were sold in London in 1850. The richness of the Late Bronze Age can be assessed by the fact that there are over one hundred different examples of lunulae found in Ireland. The recent discovery of four gold rings weighing one kilo each at Tullydonnell [6], south of Letterkenny, is a further example of the richness of this age. The heaviness of the rings would preclude them as ornaments, and they would more likely have been used for ceremonial occasions.

KERRY

Ciarraí, 'the Ciarraige people'

The Ciarraige are descended from Cíar, son of Medb,* Iron Age Queen of Connacht, and Fergus mac Roech, who left the court of the King of Ulster and became her lover. Literally Ciarraige means the descendants of the tribe of Cíar. The many septs of the Ciarraige are traceable to the sept which settled in Ciarraige Luachra, which comprises the baronies of Trughenacmy, Clanmorris and Irachticonnor in north Kerry. The Ciarraige Muman also trace their ancestry to Cíar.

The Book of Invasions states that the first invasion of Ireland after the Flood was led by Partholón who, created the first division of Ireland when he divided the island between his four sons. Partholón is said to have come from 'middle Greece', where legend says he murdered his parents. He sailed into Kenmare Bay with his wife Dealgnad and 1,000 followers. *The Book of Invasions* says that he arrived at *esca I nInbiur Scéne*, 'the waters at the mouth of Kenmare river'.

Partholón landed at Rath Strand [84], beyond Lamb's Head on the Kenmare River, and settled at Glanbeg Cove, which may be the present White Strand east of Rath Strand.

Other accounts say he arrived on *Inis Saimer*, a small island on the River Erne [16] near Ballyshannon, Co. Donegal. This could possibly be explained by saying that after landing in Kerry, Partholón* and his people went further up the coast, eventually settling by the Erne. To my knowledge, no memorial has ever been erected to Partholón or his people either along the River Kenmare or on the Erne. Partholón and his people died of the plague and were buried at *Tamhleachta Muinntiré Phartolain* or present-day Tallaght in west Dublin. Four lines from a poem about the harp by the Kerry poet Pierce Ferriter of Ferriter's Cove are as follows:

Maith a hoírchéard eile ruin,
Partholón Mór mac Cathuil,
clairseach an óir sna nallán,
dóig na praisneach Parthalán.

Excellent indeed was its other adorner in gold,
Partholón Mór mac Cathail,
The harp of the gold and of the gems,
The prince of decorators is Partholón.

Around 2000 BC, the Bell-Beaker people arrived in Ireland, from the continent through Britain. The first Celtic settlements of the Britain or Ireland are identified with their arrival. In the year 2000, a team of archaeologists working under the auspices of Kerry County Council excavated ten pits and unearthed Beaker pottery material. This work was done at Gortatlea (*Gort a'tSléibhe*, 'the field of the mountain') [71], thirteen miles north of Killarney on the N22. The excavations in one pit contained over thirty shards of Beaker pottery and a portion of a stone axe-head. The pottery was dated to about 1800 BC.

At a far later time, Ireland was invaded by a people who are credited with giving us our pre-Christian mythology, namely the Tuatha Dé Danand, more popularly known as the Tuatha Dé Danann.* Anand is also known as Ana, Dana, Anu and Áine. The Tuatha Dé Danann are said by some to have come from Greece, by others to belong to the Cimbri, a race from Denmark, and by O'Curry to have been a Germanic people. A more general assumption is that they never existed at all and are the result of a *ceo draiochta* or 'druidic mist'. Nevertheless, they have bequeathed us a pantheon of gods and goddesses which form the foundation of our mythology. Anu or Anand is a mother goddess and is magnificently represented by the two mountains named *An Dá Chích Anand* or 'The Paps of Anand', locally referred to as simply 'the Paps' [79]. Considering that Ireland is named from a goddess, Ériu, it is easy to see that the female body should be mythologised into the landscape. In Babylonian mythology, Anu begot the wind.

A little over five miles north-west from 'the Paps' is Lisbabe (*Lis badbha*, the 'fort of Badb') [79]. Badb is one of a triad of war-fertility goddesses together with Macha and the Mórrígan. She prophesied the end of the world and oncoming chaos:

Son will enter his father's bed,
father will enter his son's bed,
everyone his brother's brother-in-law.

There is a ring fort standing in the townland of Lisbabe and nearby are two standing stones.

A reference to Badb in folklore is as follows: 'Be in before dark or the Babow will catch you', 'Babow' being a local name for Badb. In other references Badb is referred to as the *badb caointe* or the 'bocheentha', namely the banshee.

From Lisbabe one can go down the road to Barraduff and continue along the N72 to Rathmore [79]. The fort here is associated with St Moshillán, a pupil of St Finnbarr. As many ring forts were homes or centres of human habitation from the sixth to the eleventh century, it is possible that St Moshillán was a native of here. There is a ring fort close to Rathmore [79] in the townland of Shinnagh, but whether this is the fort in question is uncertain. There are two further forts closeby in Shinnagh and in the townland of Rathbeg.

Caherdaniel (*Cathair Domhnaill*, 'the caher or seat of Donall'), which still remains, is a remarkable fort and would perhaps get greater recognition if it were not close to an even more remarkable fort nearby. Five miles north-east from Caherdaniel [84] is one of the most perfect cashels or forts in Ireland – Staigue Fort. There are two possible sources for

FIGURE 29. Staigue Fort.

this name. One is the Irish word *stéidhg*, which denotes 'a strip of land', but there is also an Anglo-Saxon word, *stig*, from the verb *steigan* (to ascend), and in Lancashire a ladder is still called a *stee*, or *steigh*. O'Curry suggests that the Lancashire followers of Sir Valentine Browne, the founder of the Kenmare family, may have given Staigue its name. This may explain the reason why many antiquarians in the past regarded the fort as Danish or Norse in origin. The building contains no evidence of tools being used, and thus has no cut stone. The fort simply consists of stones taken from the adjoining mountain, being built of schistose slate and the spaces between the blocks filled with coarse pieces of the same rock.

This fort has been the subject of much speculation. General Vallancey in the eighteenth century thought it was a stone theatre, and the engineer Alexander Nimmo thought it was an astronomical observatory. There are no direct historical or literary references to Staigue, although John O'Donovan says that *Cathair Meathais* is in fact Staigue. If one accepts Estyn Evans in *Prehistoric and Early Christian Ireland*, that the fort is Early Iron Age, then one could see a connection with the arrival of the Gaels or (Gauls) at Waterville [84] at around 100–200 AD. The fort faces almost due south, and this would mean that the Gaels would have been on the lookout for further invasions from their defensive fortification. As a fort at the head of a valley between two small streams opening south to the sea, it further belies the military experience of its builders. The idea that it was intended as a place of defence and security is supported by the moat with which it is surrounded. This magnificent fort is one of a number of stone forts, including Cahergal and Caherdaniel, which presumably acted as defences for invasions arriving from the south-west.

Estyn Evans gives the following measured description of the fort:

> the lintelled doorway, on the south is 6 ft. high, narrow upwards and inwards. The inner face of the walls has ten flights of steps arranged X-wise in 2 tiers, and the whole conception displays a degree of architectural sophistication which far exceeds the practical needs of defence. In the base of the wall on the north and west are two cells reached by traverse passages. They are 4 and a half ft. wide and 7 and a half and 12 ft. long. The corbelled roofs are over 7 ft. high.

The site of the fort is 500 feet above sea level and distant from the sea by about a mile-and-a-half. It is almost circular, measuring 89 by 88 feet, and the masonry is of excellent quality. A small 'cut' in the mountain to the east may be associated with sunrise on certain days; there is also a holy well in this vicinity so the area may be connected to rites of fire and water. The fort at Staigue has been compared to *Dún Aengus* on the Aran Islands and to *Grianan Ailech* west of Derry city.

A mile south of Staigue Fort and close to Staigue Bridge is what is commonly known as rock art, discovered under three feet of bog in the 1830s. The rock is inscribed with circles, single and concentric; shallow circular hollows; small dots; and lines. The rock itself is of coarse slate. At a distance, more inscribed rocks were found. According to Charles Graves, writing in 1873, an obvious interpretation of these symbols is that they were designed to represent astronomical phenomena such as the sun and the moon; the importance of sun and moon worship to the pagan Irish would possibly reflect this view.

A local man at Staigue Bridge suggested to Graves that these circles were intended to serve as moulds in which metal rings might be cast. Others thought they were part of some game, but the disparity which exists between the figures makes this unlikely.

Graves himself thought that they were maps showing the different positions of neighbouring forts. This initiated his effort to solve what might be termed as an antiquarian puzzle, which to this day remains enigmatic. 'The idea which occurred to my own mind,' he said, 'was, that the incised circles were intended to represent the circular buildings of earth or stone, of which traces still exist in every part of Ireland.' He regarded the following considerations supported his case:

> 1. The circles are of different sizes, and some are disposed in concentric groups. The ancient dwellings and fortified seats of the ancient Irish were circular; they were of various sizes, from the small cloghan, or stone house of ten feet in diameter to the great camp including an area of some acres; and the principal forts had several concentric *valla* (stockades). 2. The openings in the inscribed circles may have been intended to denote the entrances. 3. The other inscribed lines may have represented passing by or leading up to the forts.

This theory met with a certain amount of scepticism, and Graves let it lie for a number of years before coming back to it, saying that further examination confirmed his original position. He wrote:

> The centres of the circles and the neighbouring cups and dots arrange themselves generally three by three in straight lines. If then the circles represent forts and are disposed three by three in straight lines on the inscribed stones, I saw that we might expect to find the forts disposed in like manner over the surface of the country; and I think that I have succeeded in verifying this inference. The ancient raths have fortunately been laid down on the six-inch Ordnance Survey maps of Ireland; and unless I am deceived by fortuitous collineations, I find that the forts are actually arranged three by three in straight lines. The discovery of this fact, if it be a fact would be of much more consequence than the explanation of the inscriptions of which I have just given an account. But this further inquiry must be conducted with care. Large portions of the country must be examined, and those difficulties must be confronted which the disappearance of ancient remains must inevitably give rise to.

The map theory of Graves has failed to get much, if any, traction, and it more represents the leisure activities of many of the upper classes who found a fascinating pastime in the pursuit of Irish antiquities; this in no way means that their efforts were in vain, as in many cases they laid the basis for future research.

Professor R.A.S. Macalister of University College Dublin asked why anyone would have expended enormous labour in hammering out these figures. He addressed his own question by saying:

> We find a reasonable answer to this question at the other end of the world. When the time comes to initiate the boys of an aboriginal Australian community into manhood, one of the least dreadful of the ceremonies which they have to undergo is their instruction in tribal traditions, which till then have been kept a secret from them.
>
> To that end diagrams are prepared with pipeclay upon surfaces of ground smoothed for the purpose – diagrams which convey nothing to an uninstructed stranger, but which for the initiated are full of meaning. The resemblance between these diagrams and the rock-scribings found in various places in Ireland is amazing.

Macalister mentions that some of these symbols, such as certain groups of concentric circles, are said to represent a tree, while others represent a well, another an egg and so on. The survival in stone was to ensure that the ritual aspect of these figures survived, and indeed they have in some cases in Ireland for thousands of years.

A significant explorer of rock art in recent times has been the late Dr Blaze O'Connor who named 100 basic design elements used by the original creators. In 2003, she wrote, 'There has been little evidence collected on which to base current theories regarding the types of activities that might have occurred around the rock art, and the chronological range for the active use of these locations.' And speaking of Drumirril in Co. Monaghan, she says: 'The presence of a palimpsest of archaeological features across the townland of Drumirril lends support to the idea that the rock art here represents a ritual component embedded in a complex living landscape.'

A little over ten miles south-west from Tralee is a village named Camp [71], and a mile from here is a minor or third-class road which leads to a ford known as *Ath a nGealtán* or 'the ford of the madmen'. Near here is a ring fort and two standing stones known as *Cloiche na Geilt* ('the stones of the deranged woman') in a glen anciently known as Glannagalt or *Glenn na nGealt* ('the glen of the madmen'). In folklore the glen is associated with quasi-mystical people or disembodied spirits or ghosts known as *glinne geilt*. A tradition connected with Glannagalt stated that people suffering from insanity would be cured if they spent a continuous year in the glen. Another tradition connected with the glen states: 'From all decay and death the afflicted will arise if the glen is reached within twenty-four hours (*Agus as meath nó éag d'aoingheilt éirochas a nÉirinn muna soiche sí an glean sin faoi cheann cheithre n-uaire bhfithched*)'. According to John O'Donovan, 'It is still believed in many parts of Ireland that all the lunatics of Ireland would make their way, if unrestrained, to a valley in the County of Kerry called Gleann na nGealt and remain there feeding on the herbs and watercresses of the valley until they should recover their former sanity.' This glen is still used to cure people of depression, among other things.

A well here, *Tobar na nGealt* ('the well of the madmen') was also supposed to afford relief. A warrior named Gall from Ulster and a member of the Fianna,* although victorious in the Battle of Ventry (see below) had worked himself into such a fury fighting that he lost his senses and fled to Glannagalt. Here his sanity was restored by drinking water from the well and eating the watercress growing in its waters. Another notable to seek refuge in the glen was Bolcán, the King of France, who needed some respite after the rigours of warfare on Ventry Strand. The most famous character to retreat here was Suibhne Geilt or 'Mad Sweeney',* who had been driven insane by the horrors of battle. Although Glannagalt is not mentioned in the 'Adventures of Sweeny', the editor and translator J. G. O'Keeffe says that there is some confusion between *Glen Bolcáin* and *Gleann na nGealt*, and that *Glen Bolcáin* was in Kerry. If so, 'then Glen Bolcáin may well be Bolcán's Glen or present day Glannagalt'. This is further supported by *Cath Finn Trágha* or the Battle of Ventry. In discussing the glen in question, O'Donovan says that 'it is still believed in many parts of Ireland that all the lunatics of Ireland would make their way if unrestrained, to a valley in the County of Kerry called Gleann na nGealt'.

Throughout the saga known as 'The Frenzy of Suibhne' (*Buile Suibhne*), *Glen Bolcáin* is frequently mentioned, and this leaves us with a conundrum as to where *Glen Bolcáin* is actually situated. Hogan mentions that it may be near Ardee in Co. Meath, but J.G. O'Keeffe in the footnotes to his book on *The Adventures of Suibhne Geilt* (I.T.S. Vol. 12) writes, 'It seems to me that it is more likely to be in north Antrim,' and he refers to a ridge called Dunbolcain or Drumbolcain just north of Rasharkin [8]; he mentions that the place derives its name from St Olcain, sometimes called Bolcain. Sweeny* or Suibhne has a strong connection with Rasharkin: 'Suibhne of Ros Earcain (Rasharkin) is my name.'

Gearóid S. Mac Eoin, writing in *Béaloideas* in 1962, tells the following story:

A curious fact happened in the case of one of these madmen, who came down from the North. He was passing by Faha Court quite naked and having been followed by a Mr Falvey, with gun in hand, the fright of being shot down actually restored him to his senses. Years later this Mr Falvey, travelling to the North of Ireland, accidently met this man, who knew his deliverer, and very hospitably entertained him, as he was a wealthy landowner who had accidently lost his mind, and like all mad people of Ireland, had run down to Kerry to this glen as the only means of a cure.

Sweeny* is said to have preferred this glen of sanctuary to any other place:

Glen mBolcáin mo bhithárus
fior fuarus a greim,
mor n-oidhchi rofriothálus
rioth roithrén re beinn.

Glen Bolcain my constant abode,
'twas a boon to me,

many a night have I attempted
a stern race against the peak.

Good its clear blue water,
good its clean, fierce wind,
good its cress-green watercress,
best its tall brooklime.

Good its enduring ivy-trees,
good its bright, cheerful willow,
good its yewy yews,
best its melodious birch.

About twenty miles west from Glannagalt is the strand associated with a famous legendary battle that took place at Ventry Harbour [70], situated on the north side of Dingle. 'The Battle of Ventry' (*Cath Finntrágha*, 'the battle of the white strand') tells of an encounter between Finn and his Fianna* and an invading force from southern Europe. The oldest version of the *Cath Finntrágha* is preserved in the Bodleian Library in Oxford and dates from the fifteenth century. It is the result of a tradition of storytelling that lasted for millennia and of a culture which saw history as an event to be used as much for entertainment as edification, always keeping to the fore the storyteller's motto: never let truth get in the way of a good story.

The beginning of this multi-layered tale is as follows: As Finn mac Cumhail* was looking out to sea at invasion forces, Oscar his grandson spoke to Lugach and Caoilte mac Ronáin: 'Come with me warriors,' he said, 'to visit the good hero who is watching the harbours, and that we may have leisure to redden our hands in the blood of the foreigners, before the Fianna of Érinn join us tomorrow.' Then they went to the cairn of the watch and fell asleep.

Meanwhile the King of the World and his warriors went ashore on Ventry Strand and raised a great shout. The tale then takes on the embellishment of the storyteller: 'Oscar, at this shout leapt in his sleep nine furrows from the cairn … and it was said that never before or after was there one double blow through which more men fell than the powerful Oscar dealt among the hosts of the powerful King of the World, and there lay nine times nine in their blood from it.'

Finn then follows with his warriors to fight the battle of Ventry; on their way, at Ardpatrick, Co. Limerick, they meet Cael ua Nemainn, who is travelling south to woo Créde, the daughter of Cairbre, King of Ciarraige Luachra. They continued their journey with Cael until they reached Loch Cuire, ('the lake of the troop or hosts') north-east of the Paps, the present-day Lough Glannafreaghaun ('the lake of the bilberries'). This was where the court or summer quarters of the princess was. And she was so proud of her residence here that she requested that Cael have a poem for her praising her dwelling. He recited a poem, *Turas acam Dia Aine*: 'I journey to the goddess Anu.' Given that Créide's dwelling was beside a lake in the lea of the Paps of Anu, it is an opening line which shows Cael's awareness of the sanctity of the area. The wedding took place without further ado, the *crann dord* – the rhythmic sounds of the warrior spears – adding to the occasion (the *crann dord* could possibly be compared to the drumming of the Japanese *taiko*). The wedding feast lasted for seven days, and after that the Fianna* set out for Ventry accompanied by Cael and Créide. At the last day of this battle, Cael was drowned and carried out to sea. The warriors with Créide recovered the body of Cael and brought him to the southern end of present-day Ventry Harbour. Afterwards, this part of the strand was called the Strand of Cael or the Grave of Cael. Créide then stood beside the body and lamented her husband with the keening known as *géisid cúan* ('the shrieking by the harbour').

Cath Finntrágha is one of the great sagas of the Fenian Cycle, to which folklore has added different details not found in the literary tale, as well as giving it a different shape in some instances. As in stories from *Emain Macha* in Armagh, the folktale follows the literary saga, and in retelling it both embellishes the tale and embroiders it with fragments of local lore. Folklore often sees the battle as an everlasting one, involving a *cailleach* who brings the enemy dead back to life every night – an aspect not mentioned in the literary version. The retelling of the story in different forms is perhaps due to the rich bardic tradition of Munster. In some stories the invaders are led by Daraigh Donn or *rí an domhain*, 'the king of the world'. This Daraigh Donn comes to impose a tax on the inhabitants of Kerry, and he brings with him a vast army from France and Spain together with soldiers from many nations and continents. A reason for the invasion is that Finn eloped with the wife and daughter of the King of France, and this king appealed to the King of Spain and to the King of the world for aid. Later, twenty kings in all arrive at the Skelligs and from there sail to Ventry, west of Dingle. They were guided by a Killarney man called Glas mac Dreamhain, who later changed sides. According to the tale, 'their fleet was so great that it choked the wide bay'. The Fianna* fought for 'a year and a day', and then only managed to keep the defenders at bay.

The King of Spain was killed early in the battle and the King of France, suffering from battle fatigue, fled to Glannagalt. Dolar Dorbha, the champion warrior of the King of the World, like Cú Chulainn* killed many in single combat. With the help of the King of Ireland, Finn used his poisoned weapons to Darach Donn. His grave is said to be in Kilvickadownig (*Cill Mic Uí Donnain* or *Cill Mhic a Domhnaigh* on the *Discovery* map, 'the chapel of the son of the king of the world') [70], two miles south-west from Ventry on the R559. After two miles, one should find a school on one's left and on one's right the start of the Pilgrims Way to Gallarus's oratory; after a short walk one should find to the left a *gallán*, a *leac na ré* and a *clocháin*.' *Leac na ré* means the 'tombstone of the king', presumably that of Darach Donn.

From the mid-eighteenth century to the middle of the nineteenth, the centre of manuscript copying was in Munster, particularly in Cork city and south Clare. According to Bruford in *Gaelic Folktales and Medieval Romances*, the 'vast majority of surviving Irish

MSS. belong to the late Munster school'. As witness to this, there are fifty-three Munster manuscripts from the eighteenth century recording this battle.

A story from *Cill Rialaig* (mapped as Kilchaelig between Ballinskeligs and Bolus Head) [83] tells of a man who took thorn bushes to build his house from the local churchyard and was then visited by fairies every night until he brought them back. Fairies occur in folklore connected with the feast of St John, or more specifically St John the Bapist, which was commemorated throughout the country but most often throughout the west coast of Ireland. The Irish Folklore Commission collected many stories from schools and locals in the 1930s, and many of these relating to Kerry were published by *Béaloideas* in 2008, the author being Patricia O'Hare who, under the title 'St John's Eve Traditions in Co. Kerry c. 1850–1950', drew a composite picture of this festival in various parts of the county.

In 1939, a Mrs Lane from Finuge [63] recalled: 'On St. John's Eve we used to light the bonfires in Islandanny, and they'd have porter and wine and dance around the fire till morning.' Another informant from Lixnaw [71] stated: 'They boil water in gallons and one girl makes tea. The crowd then sits down and they have a good meal which they well enjoy. After the meal they sing and dance and play music.'

Many recordings from the National Folklore Commission tell of the practice of jumping over the St John's Eve bonfire. In 1938, Seámus Ó hAiniféin in Lisdargan close to Cloghane [70] noted that married women also jumped over the fire:

Nuair a bhíodh an tine dóite go dtí an ghríosach, baineadh na fír óga a gcasóg díobh agus téimidis siar agus aniar thairstí go minic agus an té is sia a sheasódh ag gabháil den obair sin, bheadh an chraobh aige, agus annsan ní bheadh eagla air roimis sprid ná púca I gcaitheamh na bliana.

Nuair a bhíodh an tine nach mór in éag léimeadh na cailiní thairstí, agus an duine acu a léimeadh siar agus aniar trí huaire, phósfaí í sara bheadh an bhliain caite, agus bheadh an rath saolta uirthi féin agus a cúramh. Théadh na mná pósta thar an tine annsan.

When the fire used to be burnt down to the embers, the young men used to take off their coats and they used to jump back and forth many times. And the person who would tolerate this the longest, would be regarded as the winner and as a result he would not be afraid of a spirit or a pooka during the year.

When the fire is almost dead the girls jump over it, and the one who would jump back and forth three times would be married before the year was out. And would have the luck of the world for herself and her care; the married women go over the fire then …

Recently my sister sent me a birthday card from Clairinbridge in Galway and happened to mention that she and her husband were celebrating the feast of St John in a ring fort with a bonfire, and she hoped that the fairies would not be upset; as to whether she was going to jump over the fire I cannot tell.

In the *English Festivals* by Laurence Whistler it is noted that, 'many centuries ago', a dozen bonfires could be seen in the countryside 'blazing in the villages, and round them there were figures moving in rhythm, young men and garlanded girls, dancing and tossing violets and verbena into the flames ... but now the men were seizing the girls and vaulting them over the embers for good luck or else they were driving the cattle through with pitchforks'. Apart from acknowledging the sun, which in the pre-Christian context was not only a source of life but a god who was revered and commemorated at its high and low points, the purpose of a custom like this was a practical one: to rid the cattle of lice and parasites.

Kevin Danagher in his book *The Year in Ireland* records an 'old schoolmaster' from Athea [64], two miles on the other side of the Kerry-Limerick border, who in 1943 wrote the following: 'There were certain things connected with *piseóga* that people considered they were well rid of by throwing them into the bonfire. As far as I am aware, nothing like that is done in our day although *piseóga* and the harm they do are a strong belief in west Limerick in Athea.' Danagher then continues:

As an illustration, permit me to recount a peculiar incident of former days here. On the 23rd of June 1904 I was seated in a farmhouse in Athea among a few old friends. The man of the house John O'Connor (1816–1916), then an old hale hearty man, had just come in, passing the local bonfire on the road-side near the house. He had taken a few drinks in town and was in good form for conversation and spoke about St John's Eve. He recalled how an old fellow of the place had on a former occasion thrown something into the midsummer fire. I asked him what was the nature of the thing he burned as I noticed that two old men present seemed highly amused; he explained the whole business in fluent Irish as he did not wish some of those present to understand him. It seems that over one hundred years ago a girl of the parish gave birth to a child–a baby girl. The father of this girl was said to be a priest–an unheard of thing.

Popular superstition attributed strange powers to this girl's inner garment–the *léine céile shagairt*. Thus while the girl lived this inner garment was ever getting lost or torn. If left on a hedge it was either stolen or had a large piece torn out of it.

If there happened to be a couple in the parish married for quite a long time without any child forthcoming it was advisable then to procure by stealth a patch of that girl's chemise and stitch it on to the *léine mná* "the woman's shift" of the childless wife. Children were then supposed to arrive as a matter of course.

When childless couples had children as a result of this *piseóg*, the superstition was thus reinforced; at some time throwing the patch into the fire brought an end to the power of the *piseóg*. The midsummer fire acted as a magnet for a variety of old customs and as such acted to preserve an ancient way of life and its ceremonies. Throwing the lighted sods into the air was a way of acknowledging the sun at its height, though it is unlikely that this symbolic act was fully understood by the revellers. This act was captured by Jack Yeats in his painting, *Midsummer Eve in Belmullet*. It was subtitled 'fireplay with sods of turf soaked in paraffin'.

A cave in this valley of Gleann Beithe ('the glen of the birches') [78] is said to be the first hiding place of Diarmuid* and Gráinne* but was unfortunately destroyed in the making of the railway line. The glen gives its name to the village of Glenbeigh, which is about seven miles south-west of the town of Lough Gur. At the north-west end of Smerwick Harbour is a perch known as *Binn Diarmada*, yet another of the hundreds of places associated with the eloping couple. Less than two miles from Glenbeigh is a peninsula known as Rossbehy, and to the west of this peninsula is a long beach known as White Strand or Rossbeigh Beach; it is here that Oisín,* the eponymous figure of the Ossianic Cycle of Irish mythology, left Ireland on horseback with the goddess Niamh to cross the sea to *Tír na nÓg* or 'the land of eternal youth'. Oísin first encountered Niamh at Loch Léin just to the west of Killarney [78]. Oisín had two sons and a daughter by Niamh.

The first Gaelic King of Munster, Eógan Mór, the eponymous ancestor of the Eóganachta (including the O'Sullivans, MacCarthys and O'Donoghues), is said to have arrived in Ireland in the second century at the estuary of the Kenmare River [78, 84]. Another version tells us that he was here all the time but fought and lost a battle at Carn Buidhe, which some say is at the mouth of the River Roughty (*An Ruachtach*, 'the routing') which flows into Kenmare, while others with more conviction say it is at Carran in the parish of Kilmacomoge, north of Glengarriff [84] in west Cork. After this route, he fled to Beare Island [85] in Bantry Bay, where he was rescued by his lover Étaín, who helped him escape to Spain. They sailed from *Dún na mBárc*, which may be equated with Dunnamark, a mile-and-a-half north of Bantry and sited in a natural harbour. On his return from Spain, he sailed into Kenmare and deposed the two kings of the Érainn, Conaire mac Moga Láma and Maicia mac Lugdech, both of whom eventually found refuge at Tara. Some accounts say that Eógan was killed at the battle of *Magh Mucrama* in Connacht in 195 AD, but others state that he was slain at the Battle of *Magh Léna* in the parish of Kilbride close to Tullamore, Co. Offaly.

Skellig Michael is one of two rocky islands located off the Iveragh peninsula in Co. Kerry. It is eight miles out into the Atlantic from the village of Portmagee. Standing about 700 feet above sea level, it is one of the most impressive monastic sites in the world. The names of St Finan and St Suibhne are given as the monks who founded a monastery on this inspired site, which was probably built in the sixth century. A hermetic community of Christians lived here, possibly influenced by the anchorites of northern Syria. The rock consists of forty-four acres, although the amount of arable soil is scarce indeed. There are six *clocháns* or beehive huts and two oratories, and these form the monastic settlement. They are in a good state of preservation, which is quite remarkable considering the battering they get from the wind and waves. To get to them, one has to walk up a flight of 670 hand-hewn steps, then pass under a stone lintel to enter the monastery proper. Here one finds the beehive huts; the first on one's left is the largest and may have been a meeting place. The cells are similar to the remains of those at Dingle. Above the monastic settlement is the Needle's Eye, situated at 714 feet on the western pinnacle. This fearsome climb may well

FIGURE 30. Cross and beehive hut on the Skelligs.

have been part of an initiation for young monks. Here, one could be said to be between both heaven and earth.

It was from the Skelligs that St Michael the Archangel is said to have appeared to St Patrick and helped him to banish the snakes from Ireland. Thus, it may well be that this double peak of red sandstone got its name from the archangel.

The way of life of the monks is not recorded, but it requires no great leap of imagination to see that it was the life of the ascetic. Presumably, sheep or goats grazed the limited pastures. Fishing was possible, but it would have been necessary to descend the 670 steps and ascend them again in order to to return to the monastic cells and the oratory. The monks channelled rainwater into storage wells, and one can see these wells today. Surely the most obvious form of food was gannets' eggs and the occasional gannet; however, after September the gannets leave, and unless the monks were lucky and caught a seal, times could be frugal indeed!

From the sixth to the end of the eighth century, the monks lived a life very much resembling the example of St Simeon Stylites (390–459), who lived for thirty years on top of a pillar near Antioch. However, a rude awakening came in 795 in the form of the Vikings. They arrived again in 812 and sacked the monastery. The abbot Etgal was taken away in a raid in 823 and died of hunger and thirst. The monastery survived the Northmen

FIGURE 31. The rock on the Skelligs known as 'The Hag of Beara'.

and some rebuilding commenced. *The Annals of the Four Masters* say that in 950 Blathmac 'of the *sgeillice*' died, and that in 1044 Aodh 'of *sccelicc michil*' died.

In 993, Olav, who was to become King of Norway, was baptised by a hermit from the Skelligs. Olav later became patron saint of Norway. The Skellig community moved to Ballinskelligs in the twelfth century, though some hermits remained on. A tax of twenty shillings is mentioned in 1300 as the ecclesiastical taxation for the Church of St Michael's Rock.

From the sixteenth century, the island became a penitential station. The fact that the Gregorian calendar of 1782 was not followed in detail on the Skelligs meant that Lent arrived later there than on the mainland. This also meant that marriages could be contracted on the Skelligs during this period. This unusual custom has been mentioned in many a verse as the 'Skelligs Lists'.

> *The Hegarty lad*
> *From the strand street bohaun,*
> *Is there with his Mary tonight.*
> *The Abbot of Skellig*
> *Will wed them at dawn-*
> *A wedding that cannot be white ...*

These 'lists' lasted for over a hundred years and only died out in the middle of the last century.

Within the six islands that comprise the Blasket archipelago, the Great Blasket [70] is the largest and most important. About two miles west of Slea Head at the tip of the Dingle peninsula, it is four miles long by half-a-mile wide and rises to 930 feet.

The origins of the word 'Blasket' is open to conjecture. It may be *brasker*, from the Norse, meaning a sharp reef; *blaosc*, from the Irish, meaning a shell or skull; or *bloach*, a sea monster or whale. One can sail from *An Fhaill Mór*, the harbour at *Dún Chaoin*, to *Caladh an Oileáin*, the harbour at the Great Blasket, a distance of three miles. Although the island is deserted now, it had over 170 people in 1916 living on it and 150 in 1925. Over the next few decades, the population dwindled, until in 1953 the final twenty inhabitants left the island and were resettled on the mainland.

The hard life of the Blaskets was well documented by Tomas O'Crohan, Peig Sayers and Maurice O'Sullivan, whose books have been translated into many languages.

Because of the purity of the Irish language, and due to the confined nature of the community, the Great Blasket became a mecca for scholars. One such scholar was Kenneth Hurlstone Jackson, who learnt Irish from Peig and who published her folktales under the heading of *Scéalta ón mBlascaod* ('Stories from the Blasket') in 1938. Peig could neither read nor write, and thus her spoken word is untrammelled by these refinements. Her autobiography was written down by her son Michael in 1936 and is titled *Peig*. Michael was known locally as 'the poet', and strongly believed in the supernatural and in fairies.

Valentia Island [83] is sometimes spelt Valencia, which gives it a Spanish ring, but the name in fact comes from *Béal Inse*, meaning 'the mouth of or approach to the island'. It is named as the 'haven of Bealinch' on a map from the year 1600. The Irish name usually used for the island is *Oilean Dairbhre* or 'the island of the oak forest'. The island is seven miles in length and two in width. It is situated on the western end of the Iveragh peninsula in Kerry, a little more than three miles as the crow flies from Caherciveen to Knightstown on the north-east side of the island.

The island is noted for its red sandstone with its fine-grained purplish rocks. Large slabs of slate from this rock, quarried at Geokaun beside the present grotto, were widely used in the nineteenth century for roofing and flooring. Noted examples of its use can be seen in the Paris Opera House and on the roof of the House of Commons in London. The kitchen and corridors of Muckross House, Killarney, consist of the same slate, and more spectacularly the billiard table in the same house consists of a six-inch slab of this fine stone, not to mention the billiard table of the Duke of Wellington. At a more mundane level, the slate was used for butchers' counters, paving slabs and garden seats. In the nineteenth century, as many as 200 men were employed in the quarry, but its closure in 1884 led to widespread emigration.

At *Carraig na gCrub*, west of Knightstown, are about 200 footprints of a four-legged amphibian who left its imprint about 400 million years ago. These were discovered by a Swiss geologist, Iwan Stossel, on the north coast of the island in 1993. This amphibian is known as a Devonian tetrapod, according to the geological time from which these footprints come.

There are only about six of these Devonian trackways known around the world, and the Irish example is a record of one of the first tetrapods to have evolved. It is to be hoped that this remarkable site will be protected and that the county council will provide close access and viewing facilities.

In more 'modern' times, Valentia has a large number of prehistoric sites, including megalithic tombs, standing stones and ogam stones, as well as some some pre-Christian and early Christian sites such as *fulacht fias* (early cooking places, usually indicated by a mound of burnt stones), *clocháns* (beehive huts), *cillíns* (small chapels), crosses and many holy wells, one of which is dedicated to St Brendan. This well can be found close to the crosses on the road to Beennakryraka Head on the north-west side of the island. Another well, at the foothills of Kilbeg Mountain, is dedicated to St Derarca.

At Bray Head on the south-west end of the island, archaeological excavations have discovered some early habitation sites. There are two star-shaped forts on the island. There are a number of clefts or inlets along the north-western coast known as *cuaisíní*, such as *Cuaisín na Láire Báine* ('the creek of the white mare') close to Beennakryraka Head and *Cuas na hEorna* ('the creek by the wheat field') close to the Valentia Coast Radio Station. The heritage centre at Knightstown, in which many of these places are mentioned, is worth a visit before exploring the island.

Valentia is noted for the fact that the first transatlantic shore-to-shore message by submarine cable was sent from there in 1858 to Heart's Content, Newfoundland. Unfortunately, after 400 messages were sent, the insulation failed, but it resumed in 1866 and was successful thereafter. The cable station closed in 1965.

The Valentia Fitzgeralds were the Knights of Kerry and gave their titular name to Knightstown. This became the social centre on the island, with its hotel, which changed its name from Young's Hotel to the Royal Hotel after Prince Arthur of Connacht stayed there in 1869. By the end of the nineteenth century, Knightstown had an Anglican Church, a hospital, a lifeboat station and a Mason's Hall. Over a mile west of Knightstown is Glanleam where the Fitzgeralds, the co-owners of the island, lived. The other owner was Trinity College, Dublin.

LIMERICK

Luimneach, 'bare area'

Nearly a 100 years ago a paper was read in Dublin to members of the Royal Irish Academy by Thomas Johnson Westropp on the 'Mound of the Fianna,*' better known as Cromwell Hill (*Crom Choill*, 'stooped or slooping wood' [65]). However, Westropp names it *cromglinne* or 'manifestly slooping'. Locally it is called *Crom-aill* or 'sloping cliff', and this is how it was referred to by the local Irish speakers. But given that the land surrounding the hill is known as *Caslán Chruim Dubh* and that Crom, the harvest idol, has many associations with Limerick, such as at Ballyneety, Croom and Askeaton, it is reasonable to speculate that the original meaning of Cromwell is 'the cliff of Crom'. As well as being a harvest god, Crom* was also the god of hilltops and sacrifice. Throughout Europe, many local gods of the harvest were identified with Mercury. Crom is sometimes associated with the sun god Lug,* who is also associated with the harvest and the harvest festival known as Lughnasa. Lughnasa is also the Irish word for the month of August, when the harvest season begins.

Cromwell Hill [65] is a conspicuous hill, 585 feet in height, about four miles north-east from Knockainey and five miles just south-east of Lough Gur. It is called *Crom-aill* ('sloping cliff') by local Irish speakers, but it is reasonable to speculate that the original meaning was 'the cliff of Crom', given that the surrounding land is known as *Cashlán Chruim Dubh* and that Crom,* the harvest idol, has many associations with Limerick, such as at Ballyneety, Croom and Askeaton. According to Westropp, the district around Cromwell was pre-Milesian or more commonly pre-Gaelic. The tribe most represented in this area was the Érainn, who were from east Ulster; they were known in this part of Limerick as the Corcu Loígde.

There are two ring forts on the hill, one to the north-east and the other to the south, and there is a megalithic tomb to the south-west of the hill. This tomb was recorded by Westropp as a long dolmen, but in the 1940s was described by Seán P. Ó Ríordáin as a platform-type earthwork. The platform measures about 100 feet north and south and eighty-five feet east and west. According to Westropp, 'there is a terrace or "set back" ten to twelve feet wide around the edge, and the centre is occupied by a rude, unfinished mound, in parts ten feet above the terrace and twenty-seven feet above the field'. This in turn gives rise to the possibility that this platform earthwork was a meeting place for harvest festivals and possibly sacrifices to ensure a good harvest. *Magh Sleacht* in Cavan is similar but far better known.

Westropp describes the earthwork on top of Cromwell Hill as a *sideán*, which translates as 'fairy mound or knoll'. This was locally known as *Sideán na Feine* or 'the mound of the Fianna'.* The *sideán* was carved out of a natural ridge of red earth and carefully shaped and raised. It was described by a historian named Fitzgerald in 1826 as 'a large mound, like an inverted basin, composed of earth and stones'.

Five miles north-west of Cromwell Hill as the crow flies is Lough Gur (*Loch Gair*, 'the lake of shouting or crying') [65], where there is another strong association with Crom.* The large stone circle is known as the Great Stone Circle at Grange. A large, fifteen-foot-high standing stone in the north-east of the circle is known as *Rannach Croim Duibh* (possibly 'the feasting centre of Crom Duibh'). This is regarded as the most impressive of the Lough Gur sites and is one of the finest stone circles in Ireland, consisting of a ring of contiguous standing stones about fifty yards in diameter. M.J. and C. O'Kelly in their guide to Lough Gur write that 'the entrance to the circle is on the east side, a slab-faced cobbled passage through the bank giving access to the enclosure between two large orthostats'. They say that this is unusual for Irish stone circles and represents a strong ritual significance as well as a high degree of social organisation.

In keeping with Crom,* there were bones found here, but there was no evidence that they formed part of a formal burial. One may suppose that the screeching and screaming from which Lough Gur derives its name may well come from the same primal rites with which Crom was worshipped in Lough Garadise in Co. Leitrim. Although there was no evidence of habitation, many flints were found in the shape of arrowheads, scrapers, blades and so on. Sherds of pottery inside the socket of one of the orthostats near the entrance to the circle are part of a beaker pot similar to one from Wick Barrow in Somerset, England. This pottery would date the community in the area to 2000 BC, or Late Neolithic time into Early Bronze Age. However, it is generally believed that Lough Gur had a thriving community from Neolithic times. According to Ó Ríordáin, 'portions of five entrenched enclosures were uncovered in the excavated area'. Ó Ríordáin goes on to say that these trenches may have surrounded or may have provided foundations for tempory huts or tents. The time lapses for these gatherings is quite vast – from Bronze Age ceremonial rites to the seventeenth century when Lough Gur was garrisioned by Cromwellian forces. During the earlier ceremonial meetings, the circle, according to Áine Barry from the Lough Gur Heritage Centre, could hold up to 3,000 people with 1,000 on the surrounding bank. This bank is very regular, and the entrance has a long passage through the bank which is lined with uprights. The passage ends with portal stones on either side of the entrance.

Three bronze objects were found in the area of the circle, one being part of a thin bracelet found in the entrance to the south. The second piece is a short length of bronze, and it was suggested that this was part of a small tool for boring, more commonly known as an awl. Several examples of this type of tool were excavated at nearby Knockadoon. The last find is of sheet bronze which Ó Ríordáin suggested was an end mounting for a possible dagger sheath.

A striking circular bronze shield, possibly from the Bronze Age, was found in a bog near Lough Gur, between Ballinamona and Herbertstown [65]; it was purchased from a Mr Lenihan of Limerick by the Royal Irish Academy and can now be seen in the National Museum. It was discovered by a boy who drew it out of the bog with a gaff and in so doing punctured several holes in the shield. It is two feet, four inches in diameter. There are about 200 bosses on the shield. Two shields in the National Museum at Edinburgh are somewhat similar but are not so large or so fine; some have connected the shield to Brian Boru, saying that it may have been left there when he strengthened a fort near Lough Gur. Or it may have been left by one of the soldiers of Domhnall Mac Loughlin, King of Ireland, when he plundered the 'Plain of Munster' as far as Emly, Bruree and Lough Gur. The latest occasions in which shields of this type were made was in the time of the Earls of Desmond in the sixteenth and seventeenth centuries.

Another artefact with an even more chequered history is a bronze spear with a gold ferule and a shaft of bog oak found in a peat bog adjoining Lough Gur. This was presented to the Ethnological Society of London in 1869 by a Colonel A. Lane Fox. The spear was

FIGURE 32. The Bronze Age shield found near Lough Gur.

found in the townland of Cahirguillamore about a mile west from Lough Gur. It was taken to Lord Guillamore, as it was on his land that it was found, and he held it for ten years when it was purchased by a Rev. Dr Neligan. It later was sold at an auction at Sotheby's when Colonel Lane Fox acquired it. The spear, according to Lane Fox, is six feet, one inch in length from the point to the butt-end of the shaft. The bronze head is one foot, four inches from the point to the base of the socket. The blade is one foot, two inches long with a leaf-shaped form.

Gearóid, Earl of Desmond, is woven into the legend of Lough Gur, and he is supposed to come cantering on his white horse over the lake every seven years until the time that his silver shoes are worn out. He is an example of a member of the Anglo-Norman settlers becoming fully integrated into the mythology of the area and stimulating and keeping alive the ancient lore associated with the area. The traditional tale of the earl, locally known as Gearóid Iarla, has been recorded by Tom McNamara both on tape and on video. Tom's story is that the earl 'caused an enchantment to fall on the lake'. His mother was Áine, a goddess from nearby Knockainey, or, as Tom says, 'the enchantress Áine of Knockainey'. While practising magic one day, the earl changed himself into a raven. He pleaded with his mother to bring him back to human form, which she did, but she banished both him and his castle under the lake from where he returns every seven years on his white horse. According to Tom McNamara, when the earl eventually overcomes the spell, he will return to lead Ireland as its natural chief.

Folklore maintains the underlying myths in a non-critical form and thus preserves a purity of narrative. The ancient myths are preserved in what apparently was a strong personage in the form of the third Earl of the Fitzgeralds. Áine, his mythical mother was the wife or mother of Manannán mac Lir,* who travels by horse as does Gearóid. I have seen near Lough Gur a sign outside a pub depicting Gearóid Iarla travelling through the heavens on a white horse. Thus, the myth is kept alive by the lore.

A small island in Lough Gur is named after the earl and is known as Gearóid Island. This is a wooded islet near the shore of Knockadoon, and it became of interest to archaeologists after flint flakes were found underwater along its shores in 1948. As the site was given a Mesolithic dating – that is, between 7000 and 4000 BC – it was judged to be important, and further excavations were carried out. The central feature of the islet is a large, circular platform of stones; a wall which by 1956 had almost completely fallen follows the circumference of the stone platform. The site was described locally as 'Desmonds Castle', but no medieval remains have been found. It is now generally agreed that the inhabitants of Gearóid Island lived in a *crannóog*.

David Liversage and Frank Mitchell carried out a detailed exploration here for two weeks in 1956. Sherds of vessels found correspond to the finds at Crom's Circle at Grange, and they say that 'it seems reasonable to suppose that Gearóid Island shows a particularly pure example of one of the groups of pottery in use at Grange before the stone circle was constructed'.

Nearly half the bones found on Gearóid Island were of pig, and as Neolithic peoples depended on cattle more than pig it has been surmised that the inhabitants had lost their cattle in war. Ó Ríordáin contended that due to the similarity of the pottery the *crannóg* dwellers here only occupied the site for a short time. During their time on the island, they became involved in Neolithic gardening; Frank Mitchell mentions that forest clearance had begun prior to settlement and that the fall in the elm tree population was followed by a rise in the number of oak trees. He mentions that the pollen of *Plantago lanceolata* or Ribwort Plantain was present in the area before settlement had begun. Plantain is widespread and abundant in grassy and waste places, and if the evidence supplied by Mitchell is correct then this neolithic group should have found land on the island ready for the cultivation of crops. A piece of wood taken from one of the oak stumps would place this community at the beginning of the Bronze Age or at the end of the Neolithic.

Lough Gur was inhabited during Neolithic times, as is evidenced by the discovery of houses from that era. Charcoal from the base of the post holes gave a date of about 2500 BC. These houses would have had a hearth and a refuse pit inside them. The seeds for their corn would have been stored close to the hearth for the possible reason that this was a well-attended area. Seedlings had to be guarded against birds and larger plants against deer, wild boar and hares.

About twelve miles south-west from Lough Gur is a hill known as Knockfierna (*Cnoc Fírinne*, 'righteous or holy hill') [65] with an altitude of almost 1,000 feet and a commanding view of the local countryside. A thumbnail sketch of the hill is provided by Estyn Evans in his guide to *Prehistoric and Early Christian Ireland*, and reads as follows:

Hill-top Cairn in the townland of Killoughty, two-and-a-half miles east of Ballingarry, occupying a summit (950ft.) of the northernmost ridge of the fold mountains which run across the south of the country, this cairn commands long views over the plain to the north. The site is steeped in lore and legend. It was formerly visited at the August festival, when fruit and flowers were strewn around the cairn and visitors were expected to add a stone to the heap.

A story from this hill is told by the Norwegian folklorist Reidar Thom Christiansen concerning the faith in the fairies: an old Limerick man in his last illness looked out of the window towards Knockfierna, a well-known residence of 'the Little People', and said that it would not be long before he was there with all the others. Joyce in *Irish Names of Places* writes:

> There is a conspicuous isolated hill near Ballingarry in Limerick, called Knockfierna, a noted fairy haunt. It serves as a *weather glass* to the people of the circumjacent plains, who can predict with certainty whether the day will be wet or dry, by the appearance of the summit in the morning; and hence the mountain is called *cnoc-fírinne*, the hill of truth, i.e. of truthful prediction.

An old name for the hill is *Donn Fírinne*. Donn has been equated by O'Rahilly with the Dagda,* the 'Great Father', or Irish Zeus. It was suggested by Kuno Meyer that *Tech Duinn* or the House of Donn is on one of the great rocks to the west of Dursey Island, Co. Cork. However, Clare has also an interest in Donn, where he is known as *Donn Dumhach* or 'Donn of the Sandhills', which is now a golf links.

Máire MacNeill in *The Festival of Lughnasa* writes that 'no place in Ireland has maintained a livelier impression of a fairy-king than the wide region around his hill has of Donn Fírinne'. She also includes an eighteenth-century poem wherein a fairy queen relates the waning influence of the fairy people. A relevant part is as follows:

> *Sé ar fágadh aca d'fhearann a's d'oédhreacht*
> *Acht Cnoc Fírinne amháin, Cnoc Áine a's Gréine.*

> It is all that is left to them of land and heritage
> Save Cnoc Fírinne, Cnoc Áine and Cnoc Gréine.

An annual battle instanced by MacNeill was supposed to take place every autumn between the fairies of *Cnoc Áine* [65] led by Áine Cliach and those of Knockfierna led by Donn Fírinne. The battle took the form of a cross-country hurling match, and the victors took the potato crop to their side of the country. It is not for nothing that Limerick has the oldest hurling club in the country, namely *Fág an Bealach* ('clear the way'), locally known as the Fághs (pronounced 'faughs').

MacNeill also mentions that local people used to see a likeness to Donn in the shape of clouds during stormy weather. His 'appearance' usually heralded bad weather. The folklorist Liam Ó Danachair recalled a conversation he had in 1943 with a local woman from Knockfierna and her son-in-law while sitting around the fire one October night as follows:

> *Abair go bhfuil Donn ag dul ar cos anáirde sa sgamalla anocht!* 'You may say that Donn is riding high in the clouds tonight!' His mother-in-law answered: '*An airigheann tú anois é ag liúighreach go hard insa ghaoith, agus bior nimhneach sa ghlór ghruaimeach? Éist leis sin! Éist leis sin! Sin é é, pus a's púicuí air! Dia idir sinn agus an t-olc! Tá sé ag lasadh le feirg!* 'Do you hear him now screaming in the wind and a festering edge on his gloomy voice! Hark! Hark! What a rage he's in! God between us and harm! He is flaming with anger!'

Kate Müller-Lisowski writing in *Béaloideas* in 1948 states the following regarding Donn:

> He is the gloomy Lord of the Dead in some (folklore traditions) in others a kind of helpful spirt; he is an imposing warrior and a little fairy king; he is fateful and terrible to people, and is said to fetch them after their death to his palace for eternal banquets; he protects crops and cattle and causes storms and shipwrecks; he is a black magician, a wicked demon akin to and confused with the devil, and he plays pleasant little tricks which show his good humour; he is quoted as an arbiter in disputes, and his name is used in curses.

Müller-Lisowski assembled more than 140 folktales relating to Donn, and many relate to Knockfierna. Liam Ó Danachair, mentioned above, is quoted by Müller-Lisowski as follows: 'The day before old C------- died, just after the priest had a last interview with him, and as he looked through the low open window on Knockfierna, he told me he would be up there soon on, on the whaleback "Black Hill," east of the cone where Donn was supposed to marshal his men.' Ó Danachair added the comment: 'I was stuck by the strong hold this stark paganism still held over minds which after fifty generations of Christian baptism still clung to older beliefs.'

Dr Henry Molony writing in the *JRSAI* in 1905 on the topography of Ballingarry Parish says that 'geologically it [Knockfierna] is interesting, as it is of volcanic origin, the plutonic rock of which it is composed having erupted through the red sandstone of the rest of the range'. By the 'rest of the range' he means the hills between the River Deel [64] to the west and the River Maigue to the east. On the summit, to the dismay of the locals, a cairn of stones was removed in order to find the triangulation mark at its base. However, the local neighbours came together and piled up the stones again. This cairn, a testimony to tradition fighting for survival against science, is locally known as *An Buachaill Bréagach* ('the lying boy'), perhaps in memory of the need to constantly 'top up' the cairn after its initial destruction at the hands of the Ordnance Survey unit. However, according to Sheet 65 of the *Discovery* series, there is now a triangular pillar stone atop Donn's cairn, and this accurately measures the State's ignorance to our living past.

On the northern slope of the hill there is a dolmen known as the Giant's Grave. West from the hill is an area known as the 'Strickeens' (*Struicín*, 'jutting ridge'). Here there is a fort known as *Lios na bhFian* or 'the fort of the Fianna'.* Donn was said to live in the centre of the hill, and an entrance to his dwelling was named *Poll na Bruidhne* or 'the cave to the hostel'. The *bruidne* were Otherworld centres for feasting; in keeping with this, the glen below the hill was known as Glownanérha ('the glen of broth'). Donn is said to have often appeared on horseback and, like Gearóid Iarla from Lough Gur, was sometimes seen at night riding through the air.

During the feast of Lughnasa, the local people would celebrate by dancing on the top of the hill and afterwards would leave flowers and fruit for Donn Fírinne and his company. In nearby Ballingarry, it was a custom to visit the hill at least once a year and to bring a stone and place it on the hilltop cairn.

Five miles north-east from Knockfierna and a mile north-east from the village of Croom is Tory Hill, a hill also associated with Donn. Its original name was *Cnoc-droma-Assail* ('the hill of the ridge of Assal') – Assal being the old name of the territory lying around the hill. The word *tóraidhe* translates as a tory, an outlaw or a highwayman.

On this hill is a fort on a limestone hillock 500 feet above sea level and with a summit area of 100 acres. On a clear day one can see large tracts of Cork, Clare and Tipperary, and part of the course of the Shannon. E.J. Bennett writing in the *JRSAI* in 1934 states:

> There are two terraces on the hillside, the lower one partly natural partly artificial, is on the west side; it is about 30 yards in breadth and runs from north to south. The upper terrace is the more important. It is midway between the lower terrace and the summit of the hill and appears to be artificial. It surrounds the whole hill except for 100 yards on the eastern side, where the hill is steepest: at the north and south sides it broadens out, giving standing room whereby a small force could easily defend the hill from an assault. A gold lunula was found on the hill here in 1852. It is now in the National History Museum. There is a local legend among the people of the place that some warrior was buried on the summit, but no further particulars are remembered.

A lake a mile north-west from Tory Hill is Lough na Guira [65] or the 'lake of shouting', given its proximity to Lough Gur, a famous assembly point with a similar name. Tory Hill may well also have been an assembly point at certain times of the year. Lough Gur, like Garadice lake on the Leitrim–Cavan border, also has strong connections with Crom Cruach,* the harvest god. The lunula with its moon symbolism and its Bronze Age dating would further point in this direction.

As to Assal, after whom the fort is named, Bennett has the following to say:

Asal, son of Úmór, sat one day on his *tulach* [a hill or an assembly point], 'Munster's central point,' the ancient Dromassell, now Tory Hill. Fergus mac Roig came to see him and found him very sad, anticipating death. The Red branch hero determined, if possible, to save his friend, so he bade his charioteer drive him first eastward then southward, and reach 'the ford of the chariot of Fergus.' Close to this the hero lay in wait, and soon 'a host from Spain' crossed the river. Thirty spearmen attacked him, but, though badly wounded, he killed them all. His resistance was, however, useless to his friend, for, under cover of the attacking band, the main army crossed, slew Asal, and placed his head on Drom nAsail, whence its name.

Thus, the local lore that 'some warrior was buried on the summit' would seem to have been accurate; they simply forgot that it was Assal.

Áine Cliach mentioned above in the hurling contest between her people and those of Donn of Knockfierna was a sun goddess, and her fairy mound or *síd* can still be seen at Knockainey (*Cnoc Áine*, 'Áine's hill') on 24 June, the eve of the Feast of St John, when men and women used to go in procession in a clockwise direction around Knockainey carrying flaming *cliars* (bunches of hay and straw tied upon poles). This was a rite to honour the goddess at the time of year when the sun was at its highest. She is often represented as a member of the many Milesian or Gaelic tribes that came to Ireland via Spain, but she is far far older than that.

Knockainey and Pallas Green are two low hills, both within a twenty-mile radius of Knockfierna; like Knockainey, Pallas Green is also connected with sun worship, thus the name *Cnoc Gréine* or the 'hill of the sun'. There was a fair held at Knockainey every 11 August up until the early twentieth century.

The burial place for the Érainn or Fir Bolg* is said to be on the north-west corner of Slievereagh [73], where a number of tumuli can be seen to the present day, including a number of ring forts whose building and occupation extended over a long period and which, according to Ó Ríordáin, contain the 'earliest evidence for the fully developed earthen type'.

The Corcu Loígde, according to O'Rahilly, are the foremost representatives of the Érainn. The Fir Bolg* or Érainn were a pre-Gaelic race who came from Britain and who worshipped a goddess and god of lightning, also connected to thunder bolts and the fire of the sun. This deity was known as Bolg, and the *gaí Bolga* was the spear of the lightning god. The sun god is also associated with the well at Ballinvreena (*Baile Bruidhne*, 'the townland of the fairy palace') [73]. The well here, at the northern foothills of Slievereagh and east of the *samair* or Morning Star River, was known as Mug Ruith's well. Mug Ruith was a wonder-working druid who, as O'Rahilly says, was originally a sun god with *roth*, meaning a wheel which circles Ireland every day. Like Balor, he lost one of his eyes, leaving him with one eye as striking as the sun itself. He was, according to O'Rahilly, 'the sun god who was regarded as the champion of paganism and the enemy of Christianity'.

The burial place of the Érainn is at Cush (*Cois*, 'at the foot [of the mountain]') [73], two miles north-east of Kilfinnane and a half mile south-east of Cush Crossroads. The tumuli are between 700 and 850 feet high and, as mentioned above, the foothills also contain several small ring forts, conjoined to form two main groups. Ó Ríordáin notes that 'one of the forts was found to have been utilised as a cemetery when it had gone out of use as a habitation site'. The ring forts at Cush consist of six small conjoined forts with an attached rectangular enclosure. The raths or ring forts at Cush are small, averaging sixty-five feet in internal diameter. There were souterrains here as well, some roofed with stone and some in part with timber. Some of these may have been used as underground granaries. The Cush site was in occupation from the Late Bronze Age until the first century BC.

There are three circular tumuli close together. In one tumulus an encrusted urn was found about a foot below the surface. During Ó Ríordáin's excavation in 1940, traces of a fosse or ditch were found. Ornamented bone flakes of the La Tène type were found in one of the tumuli, and Barry Raftery in *Pagan Celtic Ireland* writes that he believes that the bone objects were gaming pieces. If these tumuli are the burial mounds of the Érainn or Fir Bolg,* it is probable that Ailill or Oilill Olum is buried and cremated here.

Five miles north-west of Slievereagh and nine miles south-west from Tipperary town is Duntryleague Hill [73], where, according to John O'Donovan, Oilill Olum, the ancestor of the Eóganacht and King of Munster (c. 180–234 AD) is buried. On this hill in the townland of Deerpark is perhaps the most westerly passage grave in Ireland, containing a long passage roofed by flagstones. Evans says that a partly burned Brigit's Cross of rushes found in the chamber in 1935 suggests secret practices at the site, though he is vague as to what these were and why they should have taken place here.

Part of a poem by Fland mac Raith composed between 980 and 1010 about *Cend Febrat*, north-west of Slieveragh, is as follows:

Cend Febrat, álaind slíab sen,
adba robúan na ríg-Fer,
atchíu, is adba fír-fhíl hé,
d'éis na ríg-fían co rogné.

Tánac-sa lá co moch moch
tar Cand Febrat na n-úar-scoth:
ní dál do dermat dúane,
tar Cend Febrat folt-úane.

Domrimart gáir na gáithe
im chotlud co cíall-báithe,
ba dál fri gáise glaine,
eter láime láechraide.

Mar rocotlas, come in mod,
and fofúaras m'airfiteod:

tarfas dam co fír I nfat
cach síd fail I Cind Febrat.

Cend Febrat, a beautiful mountain it is,
enduring home of the royal men;
I see it is a home right hospitable
since the days of the royal warriors, noble of form.

I came on a day in early morning
over *Cend Febrat* of the cool flowers,
(no occasion to cause forgetfulness of song)
over *Cend Febrat* of the verdant tresses.

The sound of the wind thrust me,
sleeping with vacant mind,
amid the hands of warriors;
it was a gathering with purity of wisdom.

As I slept (pleasant the manner)
therein I met with the theme of my song:
there was shown me truly and in full
every fairy-mound that is at *Cend Febrat*.

TIPPERARY

Tiobraid Árann, 'Ara's well'

The people of Ara were descended from Fergus mac Roech, King of the horse people from Ulster in the first century BC. These people were driven out of the territory by Eógan, son of Ailill Olum, and from then the territory was known as *Eóganacht Áine Cliach*. The chief of this territory paid the following tribute to the King of Munster: 200 wethers (castrated rams), 100 hogs, 100 milch cows and 100 green mantles. The river *Gaotach* or 'windy river' formed the boundary between Ara and Muskerry; it is now more commonly known as the Nenagh R. It rises south-east of the town of Nenagh [59], flows past the east side of Nenagh and enters Lough Derg at Dromineer. *Sliabh Ara*, or the Arra Mountains, are within the territory of Ara and may well derive their name from the original territory.

The Plain of Femen is known anciently as *Magh Femen*; according to Hogan, it is situated within the baronies of Iffa and Offa which Hennessy says were transferred to the North Déise in the fifth century. The Plain extends from Cashel to Clonmel and from the walls of Cashel [66], one can apparently see all of it, including Knockgraffon, one of the ancient seats of the Kings of Munster. The Irish name is *Cnoc Rathfonn* or *Rath Naoi*; Rathfonn was the foster mother of a King of Munster, Fiachaidh Muilleathan.

An origin tale of the Eóganachta, the dynasty that held sway over Munster from the fifth to the tenth century, relates to when Fiachaidh's father, Eógan Mór, went to seek druidic advice before a battle. The druid knew that Eógan would die in combat the following day and arranged for his daughter Moncha to sleep with him so that she could bear the progenitor of the Eóganacht. Later, when she was about to give birth, the father asked Moncha to wait for a day. The reason for postponing the birth was a druidic prophecy which said that a child born on that day would be the child of a druid and that a child born on the following day would be the son of a king. Moncha sat on a stone on the River Suir for a day and then gave birth. The child's head was flattened on the stone and was thus given the name Fiachaidh Muilleathan (Fiachaidh meaning 'flat-head').

Located on the River Suir four miles west of Cashel is Athassal-Ath Aisiol ('the ford at the division of the territory') [66], one of several places in Tipperary associated with Fiachaidh Muilleathan. Fiachaidh was killed while swimming here by a warrior named Connla, a sufferer from leprosy who had been told that he could be cured of his ailment if he swam in the blood of a king. Thus, at the age of forty, Fiachaidh died a victim of medical superstition – unless, of course, Connla was miraculously cured. The area contains a ring fort, an old church, the ruins of a priory and the River Suir, which winds its way five miles south towards Knockgraffon [66, 74].

Knockgraffon, anciently known as *Cnoc Rafann* ('Rafann's Hill') but more likely to be *Cnoc rath Finn* ('the hill of the rath of Finn'), and known as *Rath Naí* or 'Noé's Hill', was the centre of Fiachaidh's kingdom. Who Rafann was remains a mystery; as to Naí, all one can say is that Naoi was of the race of Cairbre Nia Fear, a king of Leinster.

As King of Munster, Fiachaidh would seem to have been a generous man, as legend has it that he gave the poet Cairbre Músc land stretching from Bellaghmore, east of Roscrea [60] in Tipperary, to Knockainey, twelve miles south from Limerick city, as a reward for a poem. Further generosity ensued when Fiachaidh defeated Cormac Uí Cuinn, King of Tara, at the battle of *Druim Damgaire*, present-day Knocklong in Co. Limerick. Fiachaidh had the assistance of Mug Ruith, a great magician, and Fiachaidh granted Mug Ruith and his descendants the territory of *Magh Féne* in north Cork extending from the Nagles Mountains northwards to the Ballyhoura Hills. Many families in this area, including the O'Dugans, claimed title to this land from Mug Ruith. As well as the land, hostages were sent to Fiachaidh as a compensation for all the injury which his kingdom in Munster had incurred. Thus, in the early fourth century, Munster had declared its independence from Tara, as implied in the following verse:

Fiachaid Muilleathan, maith rí,
A hiath Aibhle I leitribh Craoi;
Tugadh géill dó a Teamhraigh thréim
Go Ráthfoinn réil go Ráith Naoi.

Fiachaidh Muilleathan, good the king,
From the land of Aibhle in Leitre Craoi,
Hostages from great Tara were sent him
To bright Rathfonn to Raith Naoi.

Leitre Craoi is more commonly known as *An Chraig Liath*, Craglea or 'grey crag' [58]. It is little more than a mile north of Killaloe. The crag is associated with Aibhle, or Aoibhell, the familiar banshee or 'fairy-woman', of the *Dál gCais*.

Knockgraffon was an inaugural site for the Kings of Munster; there are several ring forts here and a motte, and a within a mile south-east there is a mound. The motte is presumably a Norman construction from the twelfth century, and as there has been no excavation here, the fourth-century inaugural site of King Fiachaidh has not been established. The motte could have been built on an earlier site, but this is speculative; the summit of the motte would have included a wooden structure. It was a possible inauguration for the Kings of Munster before Cashel became prominent. Macalister stated that the 'enormous mound at Knockgraffon was erected from the first as the foundation for a Norman *bretesche* [a fortified palisade on top of a mound] although in outline it conforms to the motte model'. Prior to the Normans, it was the centre for the chiefs of the O'Sullivan clan.

As a coronation site, it would have given the king a 360-degree vision as he moved *deas sol* ('right to the sun') about the inaugural stone, with vistas of the Galtees, the Knockmealdowns and the Comeraghs as well as the mythic mountain of Slievenamon. The nearby mound is interesting, but again one is left to wonder as to its significance when sufficient information is not forthcoming.

Fiachaidh's murder was possibly the result of instructions given to Connla by Cormac mac Airt, King of Tara. Cormac had at one stage run out of victuals, as he had spent the rents from the provinces feeding his very large household staff, so he was advised to go to Munster and levy further rent on the basis that there were two provinces there. Cormac accordingly demanded rent from Fiachaidh for the second province, who refused to pay. Cormac then advanced on Munster and arrived at *Druim Dámhghaire*, which is now known as Knocklong (*Cnoc Luinge*, 'hill of the ship') [65], in Limerick. A battle ensued and Fiachaidh was victorious; as a result, Cormac had to send hostages to Fiachaidh's fortress at Knockgraffon as a guarantee that he would compensate for all the destruction which he had caused in Munster. This agreement was confirmed by the king's *file* in the following stanza:

Fiachaidh Muilleathan, good the king,
from the land of Aibhle in *Leitre Craoi*,
hostages from great Tara were sent to him
to bright *Rathfonn* to *Raith Naoi*.

Fiachaidh Muilleathan had two sons, Oilill Flann Mór and Oilill Flann Beag; all who survive of the race of Fiachaidh are said to be descended from Oilill Flann Beag. Thus, the poet writes:

> The sons of great Fiachaidh Muilleathan
> were Oilill Flann Mór of the mead-drinking,
> and Oilill Flann Beag of the hosts;
> his progeny are great in Munster.

The 'progeny' are the present-day Mullahans or Molohans and Mulligans. The Psalter of Cashel preserves the genealogy of Fiachaidh.

The place name Carnahalla or Cahernahallia comes from *Ceathamhradh-na-haille*, 'the land-quarter of the cliff', *ceathramh* signifying a quarter division of a townland that was also known as a *baile biadhtaigh* or 'hospitaller's land'. Those who farmed such an area had a position in early Ireland in which they provided food to the king for a certain time every year. Carnahalla [66] is in west Tipperary, and for several miles the River Cahernahallia acts as the border with Limerick. This ancient site has been rediscovered recently, and its significance is mostly due to Tom Coffey, a farmer on whose land the site is located. Tom has built a museum and visitor centre at the entrance to the farm. According to him, Tea, the wife of Eremon, a Milesian king and progenitor of the Eóganachta, who is generally supposed to have been buried at Tara is in fact buried here at Carnahalla. He bases this on his reading of the description of her burial place in ancient records.

The area at Carnahalla is about seventy acres and includes a large dolmen aligned east-west. Dolmens are megalithic tombs with a capstone resting on upright stones; the dolmen or cromlech at Carnahalla is as many as eighty tons in weight. As a megalithic tomb, this tomb is more than 5,000 years old. There is a stone mould for casting a spade from the Early Bronze Age; after this time, clay moulds were used. There is a large assembly area of ten acres shaped like a heart; above this is a ceremonial platform which, like the platform at Dún Aengus on the Aran Islands, was used for Bronze Age fertility rites. On the farm there is a fertility lake in the shape of a pregnant woman.

There is a great diversity of flora on the site, helped by the fact that Tom is an organic farmer. Flowers, trees, shrubs and herbs are a delightful way to learn about folklore, herbal cures and mythology. The orchid found on Tom's land in Irish is *magairlín* a diminutive of *magairle* or 'testicle', as the shape of the orchid is like the male genitalia. The plant has been used for love potions and to increase fecundity, and young girls used to make a powder out of the roots to give to the man whom they fancied. Ragged robin, which flowers from May to July, can also be found here; it has many deep-pink lanceolate flowers on a slender stem up to three feet in height. It is said to get its Irish name *Plúr na cuaiche* or 'cuckoo flower' because it is in flower when that bird is calling. It was considered unlucky to pick the flowers and bring them indoors.

FIGURE 33. Fertility lake at Carnahalla.

Another plant which one can find on the walk around Carnahalla is mint, known in Irish as *mismín arbhair* ('corn mint'). William Wilde's *Irish Popular Superstitions* mentions the use of mint as a love charm. A man held a sprig of mint in his hand until it became warm, then took hold of the hand of his girlfriend and made sure that their two hands were closed tight over the herb. They then had to remain silent for ten minutes. After this she would remain with him forever. Mint was said to protect against as well as relieve sickness; it was also a protection against the 'evil eye' and was held sacred by the druids. Sorrel, whose Latin name is *rumex acetosa,* is known as *samhadh bó* ('cow sorrel') in Irish. It was used as a cure for jaundice and as a cure for dispelling kidney stones. Meadowsweet, *filipendula ulmaria,* in Irish is *airgead luachra* ('shining in the rushes' or meadowsweet); its leaves were strewn on floors to give a pleasant odour, and the plant was put under a person's bed if they were under the influence of fairies. It was used to scrub milk churns and the root yielded a black dye. The goddess Áine of Munster was said to have given meadowsweet its scent. This beautiful, common wildflower blooms between June and September.

Slievenamuck (*Sliabh Muice,* 'the mountain of the pig') is situated north of the Glen of Aherlow [66]. It is buried deep in legend. The mountain gets its name from the slaying of a sow by Finn mac Cumhail.* Finn is said to have spent his childhood in the Glen of Aherlow in the vicinity of Slievenamuck. The sow that Finn killed was called Beo (Irish for 'life'), which had devastated much of Munster. Finn had a pair of spears forged by the local smith named Lón Lochlin. He killed the sow and took its head to Cruithne, the smith's daughter, as a bridal gift. Cruithne preserves the racial name of the Cruithin* or Picts, and the ritual eating of the pig was an integral part of both warrior and wedding ceremonies.

The tales of the Fianna* and their chief Finn include many episodes of the hunting of pigs, the most famous of which concerns the death of Diarmuid* Ó Duibhne,* the lover of Gráinne* who was betrothed to Finn, who was disembowelled by a wild pig. On one occasion, Finn failed to kill a famous boar, which was eventually killed by a peasant. A verse collected by Kuno Meyer remarks on this event:

> It is not well that we fed our hounds,
> it is not well that we rode our horses,
> since a little peasant from a kiln
> has killed the boar of Druimm Leithe [Drumlea, Co. Tyrone].

According to Giraldus Cambrensis writing in the twelfth century, wild swine did not last long after the arrival of the Normans. Their appearance after the destruction of the oak woods in the seventeenth century was presumably minimal, as they largely depended on the oak woods for their food.

Slievenamuck lies on the lower ridge of the Galtee Mountains, and in between these mountains lies the Glen of Aherlow (*Eatharlach*, 'low land between two high lands'). High up in the Galtees [74] is Lough Diheen (*Loch Dabhachín*, 'a vat, large tub or well'), and legend has it that St Patrick banished a snake to the lake and used a curse to keep it there. The Galtees (*Sliabh na gCoillteadh*, 'mountain of the woods') would as their name implies have been a great feeding ground for wild pigs.

Finn is also connected to the two megalithic tombs on the ridge of Slievenamuck. These are locally known as the 'beds of Diarmuid* and Gráinne*'. They are but two of the 366 beds attributed to these eloping lovers. One of these tombs, at the westerly extension of Slievenamuck Hill [66] is known as the Duntryleague Passage Grave.

Less than twenty miles north-east of Slievenamuck is the town of Cashel [66], from *caiseal* or 'stone fort'. There are up to eighty *caiseals* in Ireland, mostly in the west and north-west. Of these forts, Cashel in Tipperary is by far the most important. It is known both as *Caiseal Mumhan*, 'Cashel of Munster' and as *Caiseal na Ríogh*, 'Cashel of the Kings', as it was the royal seat of the Kings of Munster. A local name is *Carraig Phádraig* or 'St Patrick's Rock'. Legend states that St Patrick in clearing out satanic practices threw part of the mountain known as the Devil's Bit [59] as far as Cashel, thus forming the Rock of Cashel. A gold vessel of the Hallstatt type was found on the Devil's Bit in 1692; the Celts brought the Hallstatt culture to Ireland in the third century BC, and the gold vessel may have been used for ceremonial purposes and eventually buried with a noted king or queen. Alas, the object was taken to France in the eighteenth century and has vanished. The Devil's Bit in Irish is known as *Bearnán Éli* ('the gap of incantation'), but it may simply mean 'the gap of the Éile or Ely'. The Éile are a very old tribe, tracing their origins to Cian, son of Ailill Olum, father of Eógan Mór, the ancestor of the Eóganacht. The hogs of the King of Éile fed among the woods of Cashel when the place was known as *Druim Fiodhbhuidhe* or 'the woody ridge'. A poem composed by the poet Ua Dubhagáin relating to Cashel at this time begins as follows:

> Corc, son of Lugaid, warrior-like man, first man who sat in Cashel;
> Under a thick mist was the place, till the two herdsmen found it.
>
> The swineherd of the king of Muskerry of the gold, Duirdre his name;
> And Ciolarn through the plain of evergreen rue, swineherd of the worthy king of Éile.
>
> It is they who got knowledge of the place at first in Druim Fiodhbhuidhe.
> Druim Fiodhbhuidhe; without fault with you, most dear to Corc of Cashel.

[Translated by Myles Dillon]

The origin legend of the kingship of Cashel claimed that Cashel was founded by Conall Corc, son of a British mother and distant relation of Eógan of the Eóganacht. He had spent time as an exile with the Cruithin* or Picts in either north Wales or in western Scotland where tribute-paying kingdoms had been established. An older legend, mentioned in the verses above, is that the swineherds to both the Kings of Éli and Múscraige saw Cashel in a vision and were told by an angel of all the kings who would reside there. The swineherd Duirdre told this to his master and was granted the land by him, and in time Conall Corc bought the land from Duirdre. The return of Conall Corc to Ireland may have been as a result of the expulsion of some Irish chiefs from the kingdoms established in north Wales in the beginning of the fifth century. The kingdom of Cashel may thus extend back to this time.

The oldest name for the Devil's Bit is *Berna Mera ingine Trega* or 'the gap of Mera, daughter of Trega'. Mera is a name associated with a goddess and means 'spirited', 'lively' or 'nimble'. According to the *Book of Leinster*, Trega or Trogaidhe, her father, was the original teacher of military art in Ireland.

> *Trogaidhe, aitte óc nhErend,*
> *ocus Fomorach tall tra.*
>
> Trega was the teacher of the young warriors of Ireland,
> and even of the Fomorians too.

[Translated by Eugene O'Curry]

The oldest name for Cashel was *Síd Druim* or 'the fairy ridge'; early inhabitants here were the Corca Echach or 'the horse people' according to Hogan. Cashel and the Devil's Bit are linked together as ancient spiritual centres. To understand pre-Christian Ireland in Tipperary, one should appreciate what both of these places have in common. The territory of the Éli included Cashel, and the name is related to a word found in such expressions as *iptha agus éle agus ortha* – 'spells, incantations and charms'. It finds its mythic base in the Ellen Trecenn or three-headed Ellen, a destructive deity from the Otherworld, which may have taken the form of a bird.

The Rock of Cashel rising out of the Tipperary plain is the most remarkable of all Irish landmarks. 'Cashel' is the name of about fifty townlands in Ireland, all of which were called after this form of circular stone fort. Most 'cashels' were built between the sixth and the ninth centuries AD, using surface stone as a means of clearing the land, and many of them are situated at the top of a hill or on the lea side of hills and mountains. The majority have internal diameters of less 100 feet. Cashel, however, does not fit into the standard description of a *caiseal* as its 'wall' does not fit into the circular pattern and its date is not clear. It is essentially an extrusion of rock about which several impressive medieval buildings have been built; possibly during the fifth century when it was the capital of the Eóganachta of Munster it resembled a *caiseal*, but today it encompasses a number of monuments which define Ireland from its prehistory to its late medieval history.

During the fifth century St Patrick converted Aengus son of Nadfraoch while he was king and baptised him at Cashel. A story much told about the initiation of Aengus into Christianity is included in the following verse from Keating's History of Ireland:

Tré bhonn Aonghuis anba an bhroid,
Do chuaidh rinn bhaichle bPádroig;
Gur líon an t-urlár da fhuil,
An gníomh ní cómhrádh coguir.

Through the foot of Aengus, great the discomfort,
Went the point of Patrick's crozier;
So that the floor was covered with his blood,
The deed is no whispered gossip.

[Translated by P.S. Dinneen]

It is generally thought now that the above injury was an error, and that Aengus remained quiet as he thought it was part of the ritual. That Cashel was the inaugural centre for the kings of Munster is evidenced by its possession of an inaugural stone and the presence of a goddess represented by a *Síle na Gig*, a fertility figure in stone that is associated with pagan cults. Part of the inaugural ceremony was the symbolic mating of the king with the goddess as represented by the *Síle*. This part of the rite is supported by a verse from the *Dindshenchas** as follows:

> *Atbér-sa, a mac mín:*
> *limas fóit na hair-ríg:*
> *is mé ind ingen seta seng,*
> *flaithius Alban is hÉrend.*

> I will tell you gentle boy,
> with me the high kings sleep;
> I am the graceful, slender girl,
> the Sovereignty of Scotland and Ireland.

[Translated by Edward Gwynn]

Cormac's chapel, built in the early twelfth century, is regarded as the most interesting Romanesque church in Ireland; it has an arch of stone heads over the altar, reminiscent of the cult of the head and the pre-Christian veneration of the head over the heart.

In early Christian times, the Kings of Cashel were also bishops so that they possessed both a temporal and a spiritual role. One tenth-century king–bishop, Cormac mac Cullenan, stands out for his Glossary or *Sanas Chormaic*. He wrote that the name *caiseal* derives from *cis-ail*, a 'tribute-rent', while others say that the name derived from *cios ail*, or 'rent-rock' – the rock on which the Kings of Munster received their rents. Another name was *Lecc na cét* or the 'flagstone of the hundreds'; whether this refers to money or warriors is a moot point; if the former, it would tie in with the 'rent rock'.

Slievenamon (*Sliabh na mBan*, 'mountain of the women') [67, 75] is a mountain 2,364 feet above sea level, seven miles north-east of Clonmel. Its early literary spelling was *Sliab na mban finn* or 'the mountain of the white women', who were presumably goddesses. Unlike Croagh Patrick, the mountain has preserved its prehistoric sanctity to the present day. The conical outline resembles another sacred mountain in France, Puy de Dôme, the ancient sacred mountain of the Auvergne, about sixty miles west of Lyon.

The prehistoric sanctity of Slievenamon is mentioned in an elegy written on the death of Rev. Edmond Kavanagh of Ballyragget in 1764 by Rev. James O' Lawlor:

> *Do chodhluis sgatha ar Pharnnassus Éireann,*
> *Seo é sliadh na m-bann fionn na rann a's na m-béithedh,*
> *'Sé ar fágadh aca d'fearann a's d'oédhreacht*
> *Acht Cnoc fírinne amháin, Cnoc Áine a's Gréine.*

> I have slept for some time on Erin's Parnassus –
> This is Slieve na mBan – fionn, of poems and damsels;

FIGURE 34. Entrance to Cormac's Chapel.

'Tis all that has been left to us of land and inheritance,
Except Knockfeerin, Knockainey and Knockgreany.

[Translated by John O'Donovan]

The poem infers that the kingdom of the 'fairy queens', the *ban sídhe*, has been limited to these four sanctuaries of the goddesses. Footnotes to this elegy state that this state of affairs was due to the rise of the Gaels. It fails to mention that the rise of Christianity played its part in diminishing the influence of the female spirit; however, as well as these places mentioned above, the island of Ireland is still named from one of a triad of goddesses, namely Éire or, more properly, Ériu.

A folktale referring to Slievenamon tells of a race from the base to the summit by a number of women. The story as related by James Fogarty was part of the folklore of the Irish-speaking local population from Iverk (*Uí Eirc*), that section of people who lived in the 1840s on the bountiful sandy shores of the River Suir in south-west Kilkenny [75]:

From amongst the numerous princesses and beautiful young women to whom Finn mac Cumhail had paid attention both in Ireland and foreign nations, he selected twenty-one women, either for their superior personal attractions or for the influence of family connexion, from which to choose his wife, and they were thus to compete for his hand: On an appointed day the twenty-one young women were to stand in a row at the foot of Sliabh na mBan, and upon a given signal to run up the mountain, the first who should arrive at *Mullach-suide-Finn* [the present cairn at the top of the mountain], to become the wife of the king of the Fenians. Finn stood at the summit of the mountain and having blown a loud blast upon his trumpet, the racers set off at full speed.

The above is the essence of the story but the race was not entirely fair as Finn favoured Gráinne and Gráinne* won the race and became Finn's wife. This relationship resulted in the birth of Oisín,* the poet of the Fianna.* Unfortunately, a local man named Diarmuid Uí Duibhne* had a *ball searc* or 'love spot' on his breast, and having seen this Gráinne was smitten. This resulted in their famous elopement. John O'Donovan considered the tale of the race to be a comparatively modern one, as it does not exist in the early Irish manuscript romances.

Another story concerning the women from *Sliabh na mBan* has been compared to the mystic tales of Germany and was part of the folklore of the local people of Gortnapisha (*Gort na pise*, 'the field of Otherworld beings') [67], a townland in the Vale of Compsey at the base of the mountain on its north-west side. The folktale is as follows.

One night many years ago, two industrious women were engaged in spinning flax in a cabin at Gortnapisha. The rest of the family were in bed, but the women continued working except occasionally when they would rake the turf fire in order to obtain 'a soft spark' to kindle their *dudeens* or small clay pipes. It was during one of these intervals that the smokers were disturbed by an unusual knocking at the door. Knock succeeded knock, with dull and heavy sounds for some minutes. The frightened women made no reply. At length, a shrill, hoarse voice asked loudly, '*An bhfuil tú a stig, a uisge na g-cos?*' ('Are you within, feet-water')? '*Táim! Táim!*' ('I am! I am!') came a response from an old pot in the corner of the kitchen in which the family had washed their feet before retiring to rest. '*A g-cloisir? éisd! go dé an diabhal tá sa phota?*' ('Do you hear? list! what the devil's in the pot?'), whispered one of the spinners in a tremulous tone. '*Ó! ní fheadar-tá mo croidhe a bualadh!*' ('Oh! I don't know, my heart is beating!') was the faint reply.

A dabbling noise was next heard from the pot, and some supernatural being in an eel-like form began to uncoil itself and stretch forward in the direction of the door, which it immediately opened, and in a second several women, strangely attired and of extraordinary aspect, stood before the trembling spinners. Without apology for the intrusion, some of the unbidden visitors began to amuse themselves with the spinning wheels, cards and the like. The women of the house were quite dismayed by this visitation, but endeavoured to dissemble their fears; under the pretence of fetching a few sods of turf from a shed in the yard, they walked out, but soon returned in a hurry, exclaiming, '*Tá sliabh na m-ban fionn's an sliabh mór ós a chionn tre theine*' ('*Sliabh na m-ban fionn* and the great mountain over it are on fire'). This exclamation had an extraordinary effect on the unwelcome visitors, who ran out uttering exclamations of alarm.

The two women then lost not a moment in locking the door, and obeying some directions mysteriously conveyed to her who left the house for the turf, as to the precautions to be taken against fairy influence; they thrust the tongs into one of the staples, laid the broom against the door, threw a spark from the fire into the bathing water; plucked a quill from one of the wings of a speckled hen; took the band from the spinning wheel; placed the carded flax or *abhras*, under a weight; raked up the fire; and jumped into bed. Scarcely, however, had they got their heads under the coverlet, when the mysterious females returned, and were heard calling out in Irish as before, 'Let me in, feet-water.' The immediate response was in the same language, 'no, I cannot, for there is a spark in me'; then the requests of the fairy women were addressed to other objects in turn: 'Let me in tongs', 'Let me in broom', 'Let me in speckled hen', 'Let me in, wheel-band', 'Let me in, *abhras*.' Each of the household objects said that it was outside their power to do so as they had taken the precaution made by the owners of the house. The unearthly visitors then raised a yell of disappointment, and departed without their expected victims.

This lively tale was cited around Slievenamon in the early nineteenth century as the origin of the custom of throwing a spark of fire into any vessel in which a person's feet had been bathed. The custom was said to defend a house against the visitation of the 'good people'. One wonders if in the present time 'the whizzing of a red sod in a pot of hot water' is still heard by those living in Gorthnapisha. A similar tale of fairy women arriving from Slievenamon is told in the area between Portnascully and Polroan south of Mooncoin in Kilkenny [75].

The cairn on the top of Slievenaman is known as *Síd Finn* and as *Síd Boidb*; the former refers to Finn mac Cumhail* and the latter to Bodb Derg, a divinity connected with the area and son of the King of the Gods, the Dagda.* Bodb kept supernatural pigs here, which had the ability to reappear after being eaten. The cairn is also referred to as *Síd ar Femen*. *Feimhinn* was an ancient territory co-extensive with the barony of Iffa and Offa East. On a mountain top to the north-east and within the same mountain range is Sheegouna (*Síd Ghamhnaí*, 'the fairy mound of the calf'), and a mountain top north of Sheegouna called Knockahunna may also refer to a calf. The presence of a second *síd* or fairy mound reinforces the belief that Slievenamon was a revered site. A story set on Slievenamon is of Finn mac Cumhail, who speared Cúldub as he was entering *Síd ar Femen* carrying the pig of Slánga.

It was at *Síd ar Femen* that Finn acquired *imbas forosnai*, 'the knowledge that illuminates'. This story connects the Fenian tradition with the pre-Christian goddesses, as Finn's son

Oisín* is connected to the Christian tradition through his discourses at Ardfert with St Patrick. The Fenian sagas thus have a foot in both camps.

At the doorway to the *síd*, Finn met a fairy woman or banshee who had in her hand a dripping vessel from which she had just distributed drink. She closed the door against Finn, and his finger was jammed between the door and the doorpost. He put his finger into his mouth and achieved *fis* or wisdom. An earlier version was that he achieved wisdom from drinking from the vessel that the banshee had in her hand.

A more popular story which I learnt at national school was that Finn acquired wisdom from a salmon. The story is that Finn was with a druid, also named Finn, who asked him to catch a salmon and cook it, but not to eat it; this Finn did, but while cooking it he burnt his thumb and while sucking his hot thumb he acquired the *imbas forasnai*. So, whenever Finn put his finger into his mouth, he acquired this particular insight. Another way to obtain enlightenment was to sleep in the hide of a newly slaughtered bull; this form of invocation was also practised in the Highlands of Scotland.

Slievenamon is where the great lovers Midir and Étaín flew to in the form of swans. Diarmuid* and Gráinne* also spent time here, and its original function may have been as a fertility centre as well as a centre for poetry and illumination. It is an Otherworld dwelling and an epicentre of our pre-Christian culture.

Diagonally across from Slievenamon in a north-west direction is Arra Mountain (*Sliabh Ara*, 'the mountain of slaughter') [59]. To the north-west overlooking Lough Derg is a mountain top known as Tountinna from *Tonn Toinne*, 'wave of waves', or more probably 'the crest of a wave', though this meaning is a little unclear unless Lough Derg is well lashed by the prevailing south-westerlies. It is close in pronunciation to *Tonn Tóime*, which was said to be an entrance to *Tír na nÓg*, but Tonn Tóime is in Kerry. Tountinna may well refer to an onslaught of warfare between the Leinster Vikings and Brian Boru.

There are two sites mentioned in the archaeological inventory for north Tipperary, and both are within half-a-mile of each other. On the north-easterly side in the townland of Cloneybrien [59] is a large natural boulder rising at an angle from the ground known as the 'Tomb Stone of the King of Leinster'. It is locally known as 'Knockaunreelyon', which one can safely infer to be from *Cnoc an Rí Laighean* or 'the stone of the King of Leinster'. Half-a-mile south-east in the townland of Coolbaun and on the north-west facing slope of Tountinna Hill overlooking Lough Derg are a number of small standing stones with a single, large standing stone in the north-east section. This site is known as the 'Graves of the Leinstermen'. Both of these sites fail to conform to any known archaeological site type. The 'Graves of the Leinstermen' are said to be the burial place of Leinster Vikings defeated in battle by Brian Boru, King of Munster, in the early eleventh century. This was but one of the twenty-five battles that Brian Boru is said to have won over the Vikings.

Long before Brian Boru, Tountinna was associated with Fintan, one of three men that Ceasair, the first woman to enter Ireland, brought with her. Fintan is said to have died just before the Flood and was buried at *Fert Fintain* (Fintan's Grave), otherwise known as Tountinna. Legend says that he only pretended to die, for he rose again, having merely fallen into a trance. Over time he was reincarnated in the shape of various animals, until at length he took the shape of a salmon. Eventually, after 2,000 years, he took the appearance of a man again.

At Garryroe (*Gort-an-óir*, 'the field of gold') near Derrygrath (*Deargraith*, 'the red fort') four miles east of Cahir [74], a High King of Ireland, Lugaid Mac Con, was murdered as he stood with his back against a pillar stone; his ashes were later deposited in an urn on Currane Hill, Co. Cork [89]. He was killed by Feircheas, son of Coman Eigeas, at the command of Cormac mac Airt, with a spear called a *ringcne*. Garryroe gets its name from the quantity of gold that Lugaid was distributing to the bards and ollamhs. The reason that Mac Con returned to Munster from Tara was that his druids had warned him that he would not live for another half-year were he to remain there. Unfortunately, Lugaid's kinsmen remembered that Lugaid had slain Eógan Mór in the battle of *Magh Muchruimhe*. Lugaid was returning to Tara when he was slain.

At *Sid ar Femen* mentioned above, the *sídhe* or fairies play a part in the local lore, and at Clonmel (*Cluain Meala*, 'the meadow or pasture of honey') [75] there are stories referring to the *sídhe gaoithe* or 'fairy blast', or whirlwind. The following is a story told by Patrick Condon of Clonmel to Patrick Lyons in the 1940s:

On the night of a 'sheegeeha' a man, living on the mountain, having a large family, ordered his children to stay in the house and to go to bed early, as he had heard from his forefathers that on such nights the fairies would be out hurling. The man's eldest son slept in an outhouse as there was no room for him in the dwelling house. This son did not go to bed but remained sitting in the outhouse. He stole out at eleven o'clock in the night and hid himself in an ivy-covered tree beside the Auch stream. At twelve o' clock he heard the most beautiful music of fifes and drums. He looked out through the ivy, and saw two lovely black ponies, and they were ridden by two little people whom he took to be the King and Queen of the fairies. When they came to the Auch stream, the water stopped flowing, and thousands of little men and women crossed it, and immediately, when the last one was over, the water came on again. He watched from the tree, and they went into a big field and a hurling match began. When the match was over the King and Queen mounted their horses again. The band played and they got into order and they crossed the stream to get home again, and the water dried up when they were crossing the stream, and when the last fairy passed the water came on again. The youth came down from the tree and followed the fairies. They went by the Ragwell to Poulavinuge Hill, and on their arrival the hill opened. They went into the hill in processional order. The King ordered the band to follow into the mountain. The hill closed and they have not been seen since.

The Auch and the Ragwell streams flow down from the foot of the Comeragh Mountains, and Poulavinoge Hill is in the townland of Poulnagunoge, south of Clonmel and in Co. Waterford.

In the north-west of Tipperary, bordering Offaly and Laois, is the town of Roscrea, one of the oldest in Ireland. The town gets its name from *Ros Cré* or 'the wood of Crea'. Crea was the wife of Dála, after whom was named the Slighe Dhála, one of the five ancient roads of Ireland that ran from Tara to north Kerry. Although Roscrea is full of interesting sites, the most enigmatic is five-and-a-half miles south-east from the town; here in the townlands of Timoney Hills and Cullaun [60] exist 292 standing stones and one stone circle of sixteen uprights. This large group of stones does not appear to conform to any known archaeological type and is referred to as an 'anomalous stone feature'. Cullaun contains a graveyard with twenty-one standing stones, three of which have collapsed. The Archaeological Inventory for north Tipperary states that within this complex 'there is a megalithic folly consisting of a rounded boulder ... this megalithic structure was placed within a stone circle; only six of at least thirteen stones of the circle are now standing'.

Ó Ríordáin, in *Antiquities of the Irish Countryside*, writes: 'A concentration of almost three hundred standing stones exists in the townlands of Timoney Hills and Cullaun, near Roscrea. Except for one circle of sixteen uprights, they form no sensible plan at present, but it is possible that they did so before the removal of some of them for road-metalling and other purposes.' Ó Ríordáin goes on to note that a single standing stone may be the remaining part of a larger structure. He says that some stones may have been erected as scratching posts for cattle.

But perhaps the local summation on the mystery of the Timoney site should be given to a local historian, George Cunningham, whose book *Roscrea and District* has an interesting chapter on the stones, in which he states:

> These standing stones did not come to the notice of archaeologists and officialdom until 1933 when Andy Dowling [from] Errill persuaded Helen M. Roe that there really were hundreds scattered over a wide area. She in turn persuaded Dr Joseph Raftery, Keeper of Irish Antiquities at the National Museum, to survey and study the site. The survey revealed, in addition to what was quoted above: 292 stones of varying sizes, of local sandstone and conglomerate; the circle of 16 uprights being 60m [196.9ft] in diameter.

Cunningham then quotes Dr Raferty's description: 'In the centre of the stone circle is a round flatstone about 1m. in diameter, and beside it, forming a three-sided compartment, are three small uprights c. 50 cm high above the ground. No finds on the site are known and no definite indication of date or purpose is present.'

According to Cunningham, expert evidence and opinion point out that this national monument is probably a folly! But then Cunningham asks: 'Can we label all 292 stones as an artificial monument?'

In addition, he mentions the following points:

> There is no mention of the stones in any of the Ordnance Survey material: maps letters or name-books. The surveyors must have been aware of them and even if they were

missed in the original 1838 survey, surely the 1909 revision would have seen their inclusion. Even single standing stones were marked by the Sappers in other areas in this district.

Cunningham further writes that the Timoney stones have left little to no impact on local lore; and if they were an inheritance from the Bronze Age, as some have surmised, one would expect that local legend would have attached to them. The only local response to the stones is that 'the agent's men used to run horses around them'. T.L. Cooke, the Birr local historian and nineteenth-century antiquarian, wrote about many aspects of the past in the district, but he does not mention the boulders or standing stones in his book, the *History of Parsonstown and Surrounding Areas*, nor did he include it in any of the papers he wrote for the journals of his day. Likewise, the Geological Survey of 1862 fails to shed any light on the area.

The landlord of the estate on which the stones were located, John Dawson Hutchinson, wrote in an unpublished diary:

> there are several of these through the land. While the pits are found in the deep soils, the circles are found in the high height parts. Several have been rooted by tenants and some in the course of improvements carried on here; one particularly in Cullaun and another on the Hills; they are just as they were found, nothing either added to or taken from them. I cannot pretend to say what might have been their use.

John Dawson Hutchinson's father, William Hutchinson (1759–1832), carried out a lot of work on the estate; he had, according to his son, 'made all the huge walks now on the land and planted the trees, covering the high and rocky portions of the property, that otherwise would be unsightly, but now ornamented'. The Archaeological Inventory poses the following question: 'Could this "ornamentation" of the estate include the erection of these stones as a landscape folly?' And the Inventory further states that 'none of the standing stones are found in the woodland which skirts around the extent of their distribution and which appears to have been planted c. 1814 by William Hutchinson, though it is possible that the stones were removed prior to planting'. The Inventory also mentions that the stones are set in shallow settings; if one compares standing stones around the island, one is aware that they would not have remained upright for millennia in shallow ground. The final enigma is that William's son does not mention the origin of the stone circles or whether they were placed by his father.

WATERFORD

From the Old Norse Veðrafjorðr, *'ram fjord'; known as* Port Láirge, *'Lárag's Port', in Irish*

The remains of a skeleton found during an excavation at Kilgreany Cave [82] in 1928 was for a while regarded as 'the earliest man who lived and died in Ireland', to quote Professor

R.A.S. Macalister. However, a few years later in 1934, when new evidence was uncovered, the professor revised his earlier statement and stated the the 'most recent researches in this cave have virtually withdrawn from the Kilgreany Man all the scientific importance at first attributed to him'.

The story of Kilgreany Man and Kilgreany Woman, known as Kilgreany B and Kilgreany A, begins with the excavations of 1928 and 1934, which were a joint effort between Bristol University Speleological Society and the Royal Irish Academy. Early findings thought that this couple lived in Ireland during the Late Pleistocene period, as the bones of an Irish giant deer had been found in the same layer. Around this time, as the glaciers began to recede, mammals began to appear. The caves of these islands were inhabited by hyenas, bears and other wild beasts which have left their remains buried in the mud at the bottom of the caves. Older peat bogs can be placed among the later Pleistocene deposits, a period that lasted from 15,000 years before the present. The combination of the late-nineteenth-century drive by archaeologists to discover 'early man' and to associate him with the Pleistocene period provided a stimulus for cave excavation.

Excavations by Hallam Movius at Kilgreany led to the observation that oak and ash were found at the site, and that these were found in the charcoal of the hearth with which Kilgreany Man was associated. The fact that these trees were relatively late arrivals, together with the complete disturbance to the deposits, led Movius to discredit the Pleistocene in favour of a Neolithic period. Kilgreany Man was thus born closer to 5,000 rather than 10,000 years ago; this would have made him a contemporary of the Neolithic Boyne Valley peoples. The finding of an amber bead may have been part of a funeral rite similar to amber beads found on the body of a young man at Tara during corresponding times.

Radiocarbon dating from the British Museum placed the ribs of Kilgreany Woman at approximately 5,000 years before the present. One habit of this early community was to go east to the coast and collect shells such as limpets and mussels in the vicinity of present-day Dungarvan. The walk to the coast was about six miles, so that collecting food could be done in a morning, with large supplies of food being thus collected and stored every so often. As these tribes were hunter–gatherers, they may only have lived in the caves during the mollusc season from autumn to spring, and Kilgreany may simply have been one stop in a wider circle of movement. A final word on the Kilgreany Woman from the Human Remains from Irish Caves Project 2005 states that the woman was over twenty-five years old at the time of her death and that she had suffered a pierced mandible, the possible result of an arrowhead. A juvenile skull also examined showed that the back of the skull had been injured by a sharp weapon. This research gives testament to the presence of violent conflict during Neolithic times.

Kilgreany is six-and-a-half miles west from Dungarvan [82]. Take the road due west from Dungarvan and pass Mapestown and Knockmaon, then go to Lauragh Crossroads and turn right. At the next T-junction turn left, and you are in the townland of Kilgreany. According to Macalister, the cave 'is one of a number of natural watercourses penetrating the limestone west and north of Dungarvan'. He says that the present entrance was originally an opening between two chambers, but that in modern times (the 1920s) quarrying had cut back the rock face, destroying the outer section of the cave.

Whether or not Kilgreany Man and Woman had a pantheon of gods and goddesses is unclear. But the Bronze Age and Iron Age did, and many of their names are preserved in the place names throughout Ireland and in Waterford. Ten miles north-east from Kilgreany is Carrigmoorna [82] or the 'rock of Murna'. This is a fort which backs onto the cliff edge, while the outer fosse, entrance and causeway are situated to its north-east. The site is overlooked by the summit of Carrigmoorna Hill about 165 feet to the north; here there is a conical hill with a four-foot-high, diamond-shaped standing stone thirty-three yards east of its summit. Legend says that the enchantress Murna lives within this rock, and that when the wind blows from certain directions a loud whistling sound comes from its crevices; these sounds can be heard from up to half-a-mile away. Up to the end of the nineteenth century, local people associated this sound with the sound of Murna's spinning wheel. Murna is also said to be associated with Ballyvourney (*Baile Mhuirne*, 'Murna's townland') to the west of Macroom, Co. Cork.

Another location associated with Otherworld beings is Knocknasheega (*Cnoc na sidhe*, 'the hill of the fairies') [74], situated on the south-east end of the Knockmealdown Mountains. Whereas the word *síd* may refer to a man or a woman as in *fear síd* or *bean síd* (and banshee, meaning fairy woman, has become part of standard English), the word *síd* may also refer to a mound or a chambered mound in which the ancient spirits reside. The following verse translated from the *Book of Ballymote* is as follows:

Behold the *Sidh* [*síd*] before your eyes,
It is manifest to you that it is a king's mansion.
Which was built by the firm Dagda [King of the gods];
It was a wonder, a court, an admirable hill.

The presence of the *síd* is virtually connected to all places of residence, and raths or ring forts throughout the country are known as 'fairy forts'. John Colgan, a chief contributor to the *Annals of the Four Masters* and the compiler of *Acta Sanctorum Hiberniae*, who died in 1658 at Louvain where he lived as a Franciscan monk, said the following of the *sidhe:*

Fanastical spirits are by the Irish called men of the *sidh*, because they are seen as it were to come out of beautiful hills to infest men; and hence the vulgar belief that they reside in certain subterranean habitations within these hills; and these habitations, and sometimes the hills themselves, are called by the Irish *sidhe* or *siodha*.

[Translated by P.W. Joyce]

Fifteen miles south-west from Knocknasheega is Knocknalooricaun [74] or 'the hill of the leprechaun'. The word means *lú corpán* or 'small-bodied'. The leprechaun is similar to

the Scandinavian elf; in the pantheon of the *aes síde* he is regarded as a 'merry sprite …
whom maids at night, oft meet in glen that's haunted'. He possesses a *sparán scillinge* or an
'inexhaustible purse', which he will give you if you can hold him spellbound by an unflinching
gaze. Like the local people, leprechauns play hurling, sing, dance, drink and make merry;
in other words, they have always been part of the rural community, and those who respect
them also respect the 'fairy forts', the cashels, the mountains, rivers and the glens.

According to Joyce, by the early seventeenth century the more ancient faith remained
with the peasantry while the middle classes had absorbed education, leading them to see
the ways of the *aes síde* as a remnant of superstition. The destruction of 'fairy forts' in our
own time is in some cases a way of showing that we are better off without these memories
and superstitions.

Another place named after the *síd* is *Pointe na síge* or Cheek Point, where the River
Barrow meets the Suir at the meeting of the waters five miles east of Waterford city [76].
The meeting of the rivers would seem a good assembly point for the *aes síde*.

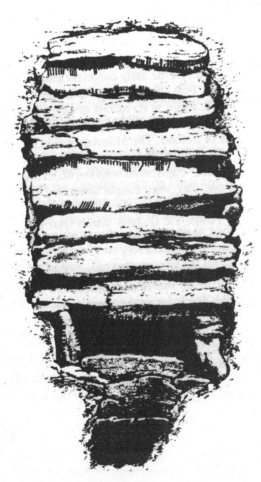

FIGURE 35. Cave entrance at Drumloghan, Co. Waterford, showing ogam stones in place.

An ogam stone with possible connections to the deity Lug* is the Kilcomeragh Stone [75]. In 1896, Professor Rhys was informed that an inscribed stone was lying in the grass at Comeragh Lodge about six miles west from Kilmacthomas. The stone had been used as a gatepost in Knockalafalla in the parish of Rathgormuck. Although Rhys made a reading from the ogam, the reading I am using is from Macalister and is as follows: LUGUDI MAQI L…D…QA MOCOI DONM(A). I have found it difficult to find a translation, and thus give one from the website megalithicmonumentsofireland.com, which is as follows: 'Lugu, son of Lug of the tribe of the Domnonil'. Lug appears on several inscriptions on ogam stones in Waterford. Generally, he is seen as a sun god, but many chiefs or kings took his name in order to show that they were descended in direct line from this deity; a parallel of this practice is the fact that many saints took their name from earlier goddesses, to cite Gobnait and Brigit as but two. To get to the stone, go to Comeragh Lodge and take the road north from Kilmacthomas to the village of Fews. Turn left here, and Kilcomeragh is three miles straight along the road. One should ask permission from the owners, as the stone is on private land.

Another ogam stone relating to Lug* is close to Dromore [81] and within an enclosure known as Kiltera, mentioned in the Archaeological Inventory for Waterford as *Cill Tire*, but is more likely *Cill Teora* or the 'graveyard at the boundary'. It is likely that the River Gooish formed a division of territories in this area. The townland of Dromore (*Drom mór*, 'great ridge') is one mile south of Villiarstown and about eight miles north-west from Dungarvan.

An early recording of the site was by a Richard Rolt Brash who visited the spot in 1869. According to Brash, the ogam stone was four feet, five inches in length and one foot, nine inches in breadth at the centre, having an average thickness of five inches. His reading of the ogam was: COLLABOT MUCOILO. The name 'Collabot' was found on two other monuments in the townland of Laharan [71] and the parish of Kilbonane, Co. Kerry. At the time of Brash's writing, they were in the grounds of Adare Manor and in the possession of Lord Dunraven.

Nearly sixty-five years later in 1934, Professor Macalister began excavating the site at Kiltera. He says that there are 'some lingering but moribund traces of superstition connected with it', but as to what these might be, he does not say. However, he states that the ogam writing on the stones showed that those buried there traced their descent from Lug* and that the cemetery was consequently pre-Christian. He reads the ogam as COLLABOT MUCOI LUGA, which he translates as 'Collobat scion of Lu'. On the opposite angle of the ogam stone is MAQI LOBACCONA, or 'son of Lobchu'. Macalister says that Collabot had another son named Nadchu, and Nadchu's ogam stone is over the border in Tipperary at Priestown [74], where it is marked on the map. Another stone in this graveyard reads MEDUSI MUCOI LUGA ('Medusos the descendant of Lug').

Lug* continues to make his stamp in Waterford with the remarkable ogam stone at Ardmore [82], which reads LUGUDECCAS MAQUI MUCOI NETASEGAMONAS, translated in 1898 by Professor Rhys as 'Lugaid the son of the descendant of Nia Segamon'.

The annalists say that Nia Segamon ruled over Ireland for a period of fifteen years from 183 BC. Unfortunately, it is hard to be certain of dates during the pre-Christian period, and this uncertainty spreads to a scepticism relating to the pre-Christian characters. In other words, one might ask: how do we know such and such a person lived if we do not know when they lived? Pre-Christian history in Ireland thus becomes prehistory or pseudo-history. One should also consider the bias against pagan Ireland, which reduces all pre-Christian characters to the stuff of tales or sagas rather than history.

A lake dwelling was found under the sea at Ardmore in the eighteenth century. According to Macalister, it was not a 'marine crannog' but rather a lacustrine or lake dwelling structure and, as he explains, 'an inroad of the sea has here absorbed an ancient inland lake, on which the dwelling had originally been built'.

On the lawn of Monea House, in the townland of Monea [82] close to the church and round tower lies a remarkable stone, according to Westropp in his 'Notes on the Antiquities of Ardmore'. This stone resembles a cross base and is a little over three feet long, one-and-a-half feet high and two feet wide. It known as the *Cloch Daha*, or more precisely the *Cloch Daghdha* or the Dagda's Stone; the Dagda,* according to the Late Medieval spelling, would have been pronounced Daha. It was also known as the 'good stone', and the Dagda was known as the 'Good God'. It is hollowed into an oval, trough-like shape and looks like a *bullán* or rock basin. According to Wood-Martin, 'Its centre was pierced by a hole, in which on Ash Wednesday, the young unmarried men of the village inserted a wattle [a rod or pole] on the top of which they tied a quantity of tow [rope or possibly uncleansed flax].' The youth then brought the maidens from the village and adjoining townlands and made them dance around the *Cloch Daha*, 'holding the tow or flax and spinning it while dancing. After the dancing the young men dragged the maidens through the village seated on logs of wood'.

This ritual has strong comparisons with the May Pole rite of May Day, and coming on Ash Wednesday it may have been an extension of Shrove Tuesday festivals coming before the forty days of Lent. After the Uprising of the United Irishmen of 1798, all gatherings were suppressed for fear of festivities leading to riots. The pole or rod used for these rites has been equated with the *Bod an Dagdha* or the Dagda's Penis situated near Ballymote. A fertility rite in the name of the Dagda* lasting into the eighteenth century shows how persistent were some pagan customs.

A famous stone at Ardmore is known as *Cloch naoim Deaglain* or 'St Declan's Stone' and is central to the rounds on St Declan's patron day. After their 'rounds', the pilgrims, as part of the rituals, were obliged to squeeze themselves under St Declan's stone three times. This stone is noted for certain cures and especially for pains in the back.

Given the importance of stone heads as evidence for the cult of the head in Iron Age and the Early Medieval Ireland, it is surprising to find that they are rarely mentioned in the archaeological inventories for the different counties. The Waterford Inventory is fortunately an exception. The stone heads at Curraghmore and Clonagam, close to Portlaw [75] and ten miles north-west from Waterford, are evidence of Celtic veneration of the severed head throughout Europe. The Waterford heads may be seen as part of a group that includes the Piltown [75] heads, five miles north from Curraghmore, which the archaeologist Etienne Rynne saw as Iron Age. However, the Irish heads have been always difficult to date, whereas in Britain the heads are often termed Roman or pre-Roman; in Ireland, some have been regarded as pre-Celtic. Either way, the cult of the head would seem to signify an ancient ritual connected both to spiritual veneration of the severed head and to the greatest trophy of war, the severed head of one's enemy. This custom was not peculiar to Ireland; the Scandinavians as well as the Huns and Slavs cut off the heads of their slain enemies and fastened them to their stirrups. They followed this custom as late as the eleventh century.

O'Curry states that 'one use of a *cairn* was probably to protect the heads of fallen warriors'. Thus, by cutting off the head of a fallen warrior before the enemy could get it, the honour of the head was secured. O'Curry also writes that the brain was sometimes removed from the skull and mixed with earth to form a brain or missive ball. This, he says, is known as a *tathlum*; however, the RIA dictionary simply defines *tathlum* as cement, with no reference to the skull. The skull was often used as a drinking cup, as was the custom in other northern nations in Europe. This author knows of a village in Ireland where a skull is still used as a cure for illnesses, the liquid drunk from the skull being said to have beneficial effects.

The stone head at Curraghmore (*Currach mór*, 'a large marshy area') [75] is locally known as 'Mother Brown'. It is cemented onto a conglomerate boulder at the top of a south-west-facing slope on Tower Hill. It is a sandstone head with features incised into a flat face. It is half-a-mile due west from the ring fort on the southern slope of the hill and half-a-mile north from the River Clodagh, which could either mean the 'twisting river' or 'the river of skulls'. West from Tower Hill and a mile north from Curraghmore is the Clonagam stone head carved in sandstone, the facial features partially destroyed and only the ears and hairline visible.

Sliab Cua ('mountain of the hollow') [74] is part of the Knockmealdowns but originally referred to the whole mountain range. Fintan was one of three men who came with Ceasair, the first woman to enter Ireland. The legend is that Noah refused them entry to the Ark so that Ceasair with three men and fifty women set sail and eventually landed in Ireland. When the fifty women sought out Fintan, he escaped from them, crossed *Sliab Cua* and went to Lough Derg on the Shannon. At a much later date, Aonghus Olmochaidh ('Aonghus of the great hogs'), King of Ireland for eighteen years, died at the Battle of *Sliab Cua* when he was slain by Eanna, son of Neachtain, a Munsterman.

Sliab Cua is also connected to a plague that killed all but the bull of the glen and his heifer. This event is commemorated in a poem from the Metrical *Dindshencas*:

Tanic tam, truag ind airle,
do buar Banba barr-aidble,
rosmarb cen timne na teist,
acht tarb Glinni's a samaisc.

Ser mac Rudraigi rigda
Bresal bladach bo-dibda
ba flaith os chuan cach curaich
fobái slúag in bo-chumaid ...

Luid lasin seilb co saine
in fer meirb cen min-gaire
conostuc I mbrothlaig buair
forsin tshleib chochlaig cith-ruaid

Desin atá in caem-sliab Cua,
nocon é in saeb-niam sar nua:
fair fogní fulacht n-ambal
diarbhí in muducht mor-adbal.

Rodelbus gleri cen gua
do shenchus sen Chua,
drong rand raglan im gnim nglice:
oll in t-adbar trias' tanic.

There fell a sickness – sad the news – on the kine of wide stretching Banba [Ireland]: it killed them, without exception or survivor, all but the bull of the Glen and his heifer.

The noble son of royal Rudraige, famous Breasal of the Murrain, was lord over every boat's haven and ruled the people in the cow-plague ...

This undutiful sluggard [Rudraige's druid, Buadach mac Birchlui] went with his master's beasts secretly and put them in a cooking pit for kine on the shady red-showered mountain.

Hence comes the fair Sliab Cua – it is no brand – new specious splendour; upon it he builds a darksome pit, where he wrought the monstrous slaughter.

I have fashioned a choice truth-telling tale from the story of old Cua's Mountain, a muster of polished stanzas in my cunning work: great is the cause whereof it came.

[Translated by Edward Gwynn]

The word *cua* means 'hollow or pit', and this may well be where the above poem finds its origins. *Cua* was also a pet name for Cú Chulainn,* who was of Rudraige's tribe, but the former explanation seems more credible.

Breasal, son of Rudraige, was King of Ireland for eleven years and was known as Breasal Bo-didba, meaning Breasal 'of the great cow-plague', which occurred during his reign. Breasal fell by the hand of Lugaid Luaigne, who reigned for five years until he too was brought down by Breasal's brother Congal Clairingnech. After a fifteen-year rule, Congal too met a similar fate. This ongoing bloodletting would seem to indicate a lasting feud between the Milesians as invaders and the Cruithin* or members of a more indigenous race. As the Milesians or Gaels became dominant, everyone's ancestry was given a Milesian root.

Sliab Cua is also associated with tales from the Fianna* such as 'The Death of Aodh mac Garaidh', who went in pursuit of the *Clan Duibh Dithraibh* until he reached *Caoille na Curadh* or the 'Heroes' Wood' in *Sliab Cua*. However, in this story the mountain range seems to be close to the sea, which adds to the number of topographical inconsistencies quite prevalent in the Fenian Sagas.

Another version has Aodh refusing to play chess with the women, who then insult him by saying that he has lost his vigour and power to throw a spear. This story is related to several places, including Drumcree, Co. Meath, and the Banqueting Hall at Tara. Aodh had a quarrel with Muc Smaile, who had killed Aodh's uncle, Goll mac Morna, and had refused to give an *eric*, a 'blood fine', that Aodh considered sufficient. Aodh then sought out Muc Smaile at Sliab Cua and killed him in single combat. With only a handful of the Clan Morna coming to his aid, Aodh is surrounded by 600 of Muc Smaile's men, all of whom are slain except their leader Finn mac Cumhail.* This may well have been one of the many battles between the followers of Finn and the Clan Morna for control of the Fianna.* In the battle, Aodh suffered several wounds which resulted in 'clouds of weakeness' falling on him.

Aodh died when the waves of the tide came over him and rescue was impossible. Finn mac Cumhail* was not in Ireland at the time, but his son Oisín* recited the following stanzas which are contained in two eighteenth-century manuscripts.

> As aoibhinn Sliabh Cua ro-d-clos,
> faoilinn for a fheur nua anoss;
> tuile fairrge cona fhios,
> is re slios na cairrge ad-clos.

> Sliabh sin da nadhradh an fhian,
> tearc fir fa rian no fa reim;
> adbha firbheach agus fiadh,
> sliabh ciar at-chitear do chein.

> Sliabh a mbidis Aicme Smoil,
> aicme robudh toir do shluagh,
> gusan laithe a torchair Flann
> le hAodh na narm rinnghear ruadh.

> Sliabh sin a torchair Aodh ard,
> ba fear a mbeirdis baird ba,

th'athair dead sholuis, a Dhuinn,
ionsamhail Guill ba gorm ga.

Pleasant is Sliabh Cua, it is famed;
seagulls hover upon its bright sward.
The ocean flood visits it, and it is heard
against the side of the rock.

That is a mount to which the Fianna
were attached; it was the path or the course
of few men; dwelling of the bee and of the
wild stag; a dark height, conspicuous from afar.

That is the mountain on which the Tribe
of Smoil dwelt, a quarry for a host
was that tribe, until the day that Flann
fell Aodh of the ruddy, keen-edged weapons.

That is the mountain upon which noble
Aodh fell, a man from whom bards used
to bring away cattle; even thy white-
toothed father, O Donn, he was comparable
to Goll of the blue spear.

Hogan says that *Sliab Cua* was the old name for the Knockmealdown Mountains, and the Knockmealdown Mountains became associated with the more elevated part of this range. In the nineteenth century, it was in the parish of Tooraneena just south of Ballynamult just east beyond the foothills of the Knockmealdowns. At Ballynamult (*Béal na molt*, 'ford of the ram') [74], just east beyond the foothills of the Knockmealdowns, there was a pit burial in which was found an inverted vase food vessel and a cremated bone. The tumulus was excavated by Vallancey in 1786 but its precise location is unknown today. However, its general location is given in the Archeological Inventory for Waterford and on the *Discovery* map as being about a mile south-west from the village of Ballynamult. Another pit burial at Corradoon is about a mile south-west from Ballynamult, where an inverted urn over the cremated remains of a child with fragments of a possible food bowl were found. Unfortunately, neither of these pits are on the *Discovery* map, and even if one uses the inventory for Waterford, without accurate local knowledge they may be hard to find.

As to the pit where the cattle were buried during the plague, that is unknown, at least to my knowledge, but this general area is a likely place, as the land here at the foot of the mountains is good grazing land, well drained by a number of rivers. *Caoille na Curadh* may mean 'the narrow stretch of the heroes' or 'the heroes' shout' – the place on *Slieve Cua* from where the Fianna* summoned each other. Dyrick Hill on the edge of *Sliab Cua* would be a good assembly point, especially with its cliff and platform cut out from red sandstone; it would have been a natural meeting point for the Fianna in transit. But one should also recognise Scart Mountain or 'the mountain of shouting', just south of Knocknasheega mentioned above. All of this is highly speculative, and the 'clamour' on Scart Mountain may simply have been the result of the fairies partying on Knocknasheega.

ULSTER

ANTRIM

Aontroim, from Old Irish oin treb, *'one tribe'*

The most north-easterly county in Ireland, Antrim is in the province of Ulster, an ancient division which took its name from a tribe known as the Ulaid. The earliest form of this name is quoted by the Greek geographer Ptolemy as *Uoluntii*, and a later name, *Uladstir*, is a combination of the tribal name plus the Norse suffix 's' and the Irish word *tír* ('land').

Antrim has the greatest claim to Lough Neagh [14, 19 and 20], the largest lake in Ireland and Britain, as most of it is within the borders of the county. In fact, an ancient name for Antrim is *Entrum Neagh* or the 'turbulent water by the lake of the horse'. The earliest historical notice of the lough was in 495 AD when Aodh, a disciple of St Patrick, founded a monastery there.

A motif running through the story of the lake is of a great flood which left buildings and many of the Uí Echach tribe ravaged as a result. The Uí Echach tribe were the horse (*ech*) people from whom the lake is named. Their leader was Eochaid or Echaid mac Mairid. The after-effect of the flood is referred to in one of Moore's *Irish Melodies* as follows:

> On Lough Neagh's banks as the fisherman strays
> when the clear cold eve's declining,
> he sees the round towers of other days,
> in the waves beneath him shining.

A legend giving an account of the lake's origins concerns the sons of Mairid mac Caireda, Eochu (or Eochaid) and Rib. The 'u' ending in Eochu signifies a god; Eochu, Echach and Eochaid are interchangeable, and all derive from the word 'horse', whether horseman, horse god or horse chief. Rib gave his name to Lough Ree on the Shannon, from where Eochaid and his followers set out to eventually reach *Liathmuine* ('the plain of the grey copse'), which legend says was the name of the plain now covered by Lough Neagh. Eochaid and his clan lived by an enchanted well which, through the neglect of its keeper, burst forth one morning and covered *Liathmuine*, its waters thus forming Lough Neagh. All were drowned except one member of Eochaid's household, Liban, along with her dog. She had observed salmon playing in the depths of the lake and wished that she could be turned into one of them; this wish was granted, but her head remained human and her dog was turned into an otter. Like the Children of Lir,* she remained in a non-human state for 300 years. At the end of this time, she was netted by a saint named Beoan in the Bay of Larne, Co. Antrim. She was baptised by St Comgall at Bangor, Co. Down, after which she was known as Muirgein ('sea-birth'). As with the Children of Lir, she died after baptism and was buried at *Tech Dabeoc mac Luain*, which has associations with St Beoan and was later named *Tamlachta Menand*, which is in the townland of Meenan, in the parish of of Ahaderg, Loughbrickland, Co. Down. The townland of Meenan [29] is four miles south of Loughbrickland where there is a crossroads, north-west of which is a ring fort said to have contained the house of St Beoan and been the burial place of Liban. After Beoan caught Liban in his net, she chanted the following:

Fo loch Echach adba dam,
Ard in sceng dron dringed graig:
Erdalta fo bruinnib bárc,
Tond mo tugi tracht mo fraig.

Bása inón bíasta n-oll,
Ro snadius muir medrach, mend:
Domfuc tond ós letha lind
I richt íaich acht mo chend.

[*Aided Echach Meic Maireda* from *Lebor na hUidre*]

Beneath Eocho's lake [Lough Neagh] an abode for me,
On protection of strong tents, a flock used to ascend;
Appointed beneath the breasts of barques,
Wave my roof, strand my side-wall …

I was the likeness of mighty monsters,
I swam the merry shining sea:
Wave carried me over Letha's flood,
In salmon's shape save my head.

[Translated by J. O'Beirne Crowe and S.H.O'Grady]

A more popular story concerning the origin of the lough has the horse of Aengus Mac ind Óc (son of the Dagda,* the Irish Zeus) passing so much water on the *Liathmuine* that it filled the spot where the present lake is; this story introduces the eponymous horse (*ech*) of the lake.

Another legend says that Finn mac Cumhail* threw a large chunk of earth from here to form the Isle of Man, and the resulting depression eventually formed the great Lough Neagh. Geology tells a similar story, but from a scientific viewpoint – that a large mass of basalt dropped down and created a basin in which a lake was formed. The deposits under the waters of Lough Neagh extend back over millions of years.

An early medieval tale of the lake is the story of *Tomaidm Locha nEchach* or 'The Eruption of Lough Neagh'. This tale is told in the twelfth-century manuscript *Lebor na hUidre* under the title *Aided Echach meic Maireda* or 'The Tragic Death of Eochaid Son of Mairid'. An older version, based on eighth-century materials, is as follows:

> Hence the coming of the Corco Che [or the Corco Oche, Oiche or Fochai, all of which were a clan in south-west Limerick]; they came to a pool known as Linn Muine or the 'Pool of the Thicket,' this pool flooded Liath Muine or the 'Grey Thicket' and formed Lough Neagh. The floods exterminated the race of Dubthech Doelthengath and only two tribes survived namely the above mentioned Corco Che as well as well as the Cruithne in Farney [*Fernmaig*] Co. Monaghan and in Mordoind, a mountain of the Fews. Eochaid's druid Midend his hound Conbroc and his daughter Uiriu all perished at Liath Muine. It is said that their three cairns are at the edge of the lake to the east.

There is a mound [20] three miles north of Lurgan in Castor Bay just beyond the waterworks which is said to be the burial place of Conbroc, the hound of Eochaid. Whether this has any connection with the above story we cannot be certain. A great number of people are said to have died when the lake was formed; some of these are said to be buried in the many mounds and cairns to the east of Lough Neagh.

There has been a tradition in Ireland of naming megalithic tombs after notables from legends; an example of this is the neolithic court cairn two miles west-north-west of Cushendall (*Cois abhann Dalla*, 'foot of the river Dall') [5], known as 'Ossian's Grave'. Oisín* was a warrior–poet from early Christian times and was a son of Finn mac Cumhail,* the famous leader of the Fianna...* Scotland can be seen from the cairn, and it may be through the revival of the 'Ossianic Tales' by Macpherson in the eighteenth century that the cairn got its romantic name. Oisín is in good company, as the poet Paul Hewett is buried closeby.

A Bronze Age wedge grave three miles south-west of Bushmills [4], or four miles south of Portrush on the Ballymoney Road, derives its name, Gigmagog's Grave, from well before the Fenian Cycle. The name is a localism for Gog and Magog. All the races who occupied Ireland after the Flood are said to have traced their ancestry back to Magog, including Nemed who undertook the second conquest of Ireland. Gog and Magog, which represent a pagan element in Judeo-Christian mythology and are mentioned in the Old Testament and in the Book of Revelation, later entered folklore as a pair of giants. Magog is considered by some to be the ancestor deity of the Scythians and Tartars. Closer to home, the giant statues of Gog and Magog can be seen in Guildhall, London. They are said to have been found in Britain by Brutus, who, legend says, founded the city of London 3,000 years ago. Thus, the name for this chambered grave in Antrim may have been given by a Londoner!

About a mile north of Bushmills [4] is Bushfoot Strand, overlooking which to the west is an earthwork named Lissanduff (*Liosán-dubh*, 'little black fort').

J.D.C. Marshall in his book *Forgotten Places of the North Coast* mentions this earthwork as a ritual site. He says that it is 'an important site which is still largely intact'. It consists of two closely banked enclosures. Marshall also says that a central enclosure may have had a pavement which led out to what may have been a large pond or artificial lake. He regards the ritual aspect of the site to have been connected to the veneration of water, or more specifically to 'water worship rituals'.

Undoubtedly the rite of the *piseóg* or *píosa óg*, a 'roll of cloth of a virgin', was connected to a significant Iron Age or pre-Iron Age rite. When a girl reached puberty and menstruated, the cloth she used to contain her blood was displayed on a whitethorn tree and after a while washed in a local well or pond. It is still quite common to find a well close to a *piseóg* tree. The young woman then walked three times around the tree in a clockwise direction or *deas sol*, 'right to the sun'. The young girl was clearly showing that she had come of age. She did not leave her cloth on the tree for long. Wishes are still made by placing *piseóga* on trees (I have seen in recent times a row of trees covered with all sorts of things at Carrowmore, Co. Sligo), but unfortunately those displaying them have lost the knowledge to clear the tree of their 'wishes' after a short period of time.

Piseóg is translated as 'sorcery' or 'witchcraft', and the expression *lucht piseóga* has come to mean 'sorcerers'. However, the word *piseóga* as 'charms' or 'spells' is still in common use, so that echoes of the original event still survive. What is possibly more common is to hear the reference to all ancient rites as 'just old piseogry', with the underlying inference to pay no attention to all that superstition. However, this is seldom said in a spiteful manner but more often in a mildly humorous way.

As with Gog and Magog, giants play a big part in Irish mythology, and their presence in this part of the island is marked by what is now recognised as one of the wonders of the world, the Giant's Causeway [5], a little more than two miles north of Bushmills. It is known in Irish as *Clochán na bFomharaigh*, or the 'Steppingstones of the Fomorians' (the Fomorians* were magnified into giants by popular legend; they were also known as pirates). Surprisingly, the Causeway is not mentioned in many of the annals; the first drawings and lithographs were done in the late seventeenth century, and part of a poem by Rev. William Hamilton Drummond from early in the nineteenth century is as follows:

The Giant's Causeway

Dark o'er the foam white waves,
The Giant's Pier the war of tempests braves,
A far-projecting, firm basaltic way,
Of clustering columns wedged in dense array;
With skill so like, yet so surpassing art,
With such design, so just in every part,

FIGURE 36. The Giant's Causeway.

> That reason pauses doubtful if it stands
> The work of mortal or immortal hand.

The Causeway derives its name from a legend that it was the beginning of a road to be constructed by giants across the channel to Scotland. In popular folklore still heard in Antrim, Finn mac Cumhail* made the Causeway 'for the honour and glory of Ireland'. Finn is often presented as a giant in folklore. He had a bet with a Scottish giant named Benandonner that he would complete the causeway so that Benandonner could come to Ireland 'without wetting the sole of his shoe'. Benandonner came to Ireland, accepted his defeat and became obedient to the king, Cormac mac Airt.* He then married a local girl, and it is said that the earls of Antrim are descended from them.

The Causeway is a pier or massive structure of columnar basalt projecting from the northern coast of Antrim into the North Channel. It is part of an extensive and overlying mass of basalt from 300 to 500 feet in thickness covering almost the whole of Antrim and the eastern part of Derry. It extends over an area of nearly 1,200 square miles. The columns of Fair Head exceed 200 feet in height. Another pair of remarkable columns rises above the sea at Bengore Head east of the Causeway. The question arises as to how far these columns extend into the sea and in what direction? Under the sea, the Causeway points its main ridge towards Scotland and the Isle of Staffa, eight miles west of the Isle of Mull and geologically similar to the Causeway off the northern coast. On Staffa is the beautiful Fingal's Cave with its associations with Finn mac Cumhail.* The cave is 250 feet in length and the roof is a mass of solid basalt.

Unlike the Giant's Causeway, which has a folkloric connection developed by imagination applied to exceptional geological formations, Crew Hill [14], to the east of Lough Neagh, is full of prehistorical and literary references. The literary evidence is noted in *Agallamh an dá Shuadh* or 'The Dialogue of the Two Poets', a semi-historical tale belonging to the pre-Christian period. The two poets are Ferceirtne and Néide, and their dialogue is about which one is entitled to sit in the poet's seat at Emain Macha.

The reference to Crew Hill or *Craéb Telcha* is in the account of the journey that Néide takes, which was perhaps one of the regular peregrinations taken by poets to certain important places, dating from from the reign of Conchobar mac Nessa* to early medieval times.

Néide, the son of Adna, was the most learned man in Ireland in divination and poetry, and he went to Scotland for training. As Cú Chulainn* went to the Isle of Skye for training in wisdom and military exploits, Néide went to Kintyre to learn the craft of divination (*eolach i écsi*) and poetry, where his teacher was Eochu Echbél.

After a good while there he made for home; he may have started at the Mull of Kintyre and from there to *Rinn Snóc* ('points close to streams) 'somewhere on the rinns of Galloway'. The rinns of Galloway are a number of points south of Corsewall Point (Corsill Point) on the Mull of Galloway.

Néide went out of his way to test his poetic learning with the local king at *Port Righ* ('place of the king'), the same place to which Lugaid Mac Con, second-century High King of Ireland, came to when exiled and where, like Néide, he also received hospitality. This *Port Righ* may be Portpatrick.

From *Port Righ*, Néide and his companions sailed across the Moyle to *Rinn Roiss*, described as Kilroot Point between Carrickfergus and Whitehead [15]. From there they continued to Semne or Island Magee [9], and from there to the territory of Lath, son of Ugaine Mór, who gave his name to Larne; from there to *Moy Line* (Moylinny) south-east of Larne and on to *Ollarba* or Six Mile Water, which enters Lough Neagh past Antrim town. They then crossed the water and went seven miles south to *Tulach Rusc* ('the hill of rousing poetry'), now Tullyrusk [14], four miles due east of Glenavy. So presumably some lively poetry was chanted here, as this would have been a station for the poets.

From Tullyrusk they went south-west to *Ard Sleibhe*, possibly Carn Hill, and from there to Crew Hill. The pausing here was also significant, as Néide wore a silver branch over him, the *craéb airgide*, a decoration received by poets of the second order or *anrads*, which they carried over them.

Crew Hill [14] is generally regarded as an important inaugural centre in Ulster, and perhaps it might be a good idea to consider the various translations of its original name, which is *craéb telca*. *Craéb* literally translates as 'branch' but by extension can also mean a tree; thus, Crew Hill has been translated as 'the spreading tree of the hill', and the 'tree of the mound'. 'The branch of the hill', though literally correct, loses the wider context of the tree as the tribal centre for the community. The word for the tribal tree is *bile*, and this sacred tree, found throughout Europe in times past, was man's connection with those most ancient of gods, the sylvan deities. One of the branches from the *bile* on Crew Hill may have been given to prospective poets; these branches would have been coloured from gold to bronze according to rank. As at Tullyrusk, Néide and his troop would have been required to give some account of themselves here and to have their learning assessed as they recited from the nearby mound; if the poet satisfied the assembly of the Ulaid, not to mention the critical Cruithin,* he may well have been permitted to sit in the coveted stone chair.

Néide and his three brothers embodied the spirit of the horse people (*Ard Echach*) here before the days of St Patrick. With the coming of Christianity, the Church took an active part in the inauguration of a king; *The Tripartite Life of St Patrick* states: *ní rí Caisil curo n-orddnea comarba Patraic* ('no one is King of Cashel until Patrick's successor installs him').

As the *bile* or sacred tree represented the *omphalos* or centre for tribal gatherings, it was natural that the local king or chief was inaugurated here. Since this ceremony occurred out of doors, it is understandable that such events resulted in quite a din, and thus the Irish word for inauguration is *gairm de*, which is to 'call, invoke or shout'. The *bile* was held in veneration, and the ultimate insult to the tribe was to cut it down or uproot it. The sacred tree at Crew Hill was cut down and burned in 1099 by an enemy tribe, possibly the O'Neills; as to how old this tree was or what type of tree it was remains for others to answer. Twelve years after the destruction of their *bile*, the Ulaid raided the inauguration site of the O'Neills at Tullaghoge, Co. Tyrone, and uprooted their trees.

It was not only in Ireland that sacred trees were cut down. St Boniface, the 'Apostle of Germany', destroyed an ancient and sacred oak at Geismar in Hessen in 724; after such an act of abject philistinism, he was made primate of all Germany. According to his mindset, the pre-Christian communion with all of nature was classed as idolatrous and needed to be severely dealt with in favour of an abstract, central deity.

In the sixteenth century, the poet Laoiseach Mac an Bhaird wrote a poem called 'On the Cutting Down of an Ancient Tree'; the poem has echoes of Crew Hill but could refer to any inauguration site in the north. The text and translation of the first four verses as edited and translated by Bergin in his *Irish Bardic Poetry* are as follows:

> *Mo chean duitsi, a thulach thall,*
> *fád thuisleadh ní subhach síonn:*
> *damhna sgíthi do sgeach dhonn,*
> *cleath chorr do-cíthe ós do chionn.*

> *Sgeach na conghára, crádh cáigh;*
> *'na háit comhdhála do chínn;*

buain na craoibhe, mo lá leóin,
daoire 'na dheóidh mar tá an tír.

Dubhach mo chridhisi um chum
fád bhilisi, a thulach thall;
an chleath ó bhfaicinn gach fonn,
do sgeach chorr ní fhaicim ann.

Do bhíoth dhamh ag dénaimh eóil,
an ghégsoin fá gar do mhaoin;
fada siar ón tírsi thuaidh
aniar uaim do-chinnsi an gcraoibh.

Hail to thee, O hill yonder: at thy fall I am not joyous; thy
brown thorn is a cause of woe, the smooth stem that was wont to be seen above
thee.

The thorn of acclamation, a torment to all, I used to see as a
place of assembly: the cutting of the branch, my day of
sorrow! the state of the land is baser thereafter.

My heart in my breast is sad for thy ancient tree, O hill yonder;
the stem from which I was wont to see each tract, thy smooth
thorn I see not there.

That bough was wont to guide my way–it was a transient
possession!–far back from this land in the north I could see in
the distance the branch behind me.

Another feature of royal inaugural sites is the inauguration stone (*lecc na ríogh*). On Crew
Hill a large basalt boulder known as the Crew Stone was used for the inauguration of kings.
Standing on this was an important part of the ceremony conferring kingship, and it could
be seen as a foundation stone in the stability of the tribe. The king stood literally above the
earth and moved in a clockwise direction (*deas sol*), proclaiming his status in all directions.
On some stones a footprint can be seen.

The Crew Stone is a glacial erratic which started its travelling during the end of the Ice
Age before ending up in its current location. The stone had sunk by 1880 to the extent that
little of it was above the ground; it was then raised by local youths who placed supporting
stones underneath. One can thus surmise that the inaugural stone is approximately in the
same place today as it was when the eminent members of the Ulaid stood upon it to broad
acclaim.

Another artefact of the king's investiture was the 'royal seat', known as the 'stone chair'; this was removed by request in 1969 and then placed in its current location in 1970. It is not known, therefore, where its original location was, but local people say that it was not moved more than a couple of yards from its original site.

Philip MacDonald in his archaeological evaluation of Crew Hill recounts a story from a woman who formerly lived in the area as follows: 'In the last battle fought there, the Ulaid were defeated, and as the victors were taking the chair away, they were surprised by another force and dropped it at the place where it remains today.'

Another custom in early medieval Ireland was the use of a sweathouse (*teach an alais*). In the townland of Knockans on Rathlin [5] are the remains of a sweathouse which may have been converted from a *clochán* or beehive hut, a type of structure associated with early monasteries. This conversion would have been easy, as sweathouses were built after the manner of beehive cells. The sweathouse, covered with clay and with a low entrance, may be seen as a primitive sauna in which various forms of ailment were 'sweated out', and was particularly used as a cure for rheumatism since it was believed that the rheumatic poison would be purged by excessive perspiration The sweathouse was filled with turf, and when fully burnt the ashes were swept out and green rushes were placed on the floor. The person intending to take the bath was wrapped in blankets and entered the chamber which was then closed.

In North and South America, 'sweat baths' were used by warriors as a way of keeping their limbs supple and elastic, and were also used as initiation places for young warriors. Whether the Irish sweathouses had a religious significance is an open question, and to what saint a cure was attributed is not known. They were, however, well known throughout Europe, as the term for a 'Turkish bath' was designated *Rŏmische-Irische Bàder*. Such designations were observed in Prague and Nuremberg in 1879 by a Professor Hennessy on his travels.

It is possible that the Vikings were responsible for the introduction of the sweathouses to Ireland; some say that the Danes raiding up the Shannon introduced the custom, which was also known in Finland, but as many recorded houses lie in remote mountain districts it is hard to be specific. To what an extent the sweathouses in Ireland were used for ritual purification purposes is unclear; there is, however, a record of there being 'itinerant bath masters' who officiated at sweathouses, and these may have had a shamanistic role in the curing of local people. The UCD Folklore Collection from Rathlin in 1955 records that 'the last time any woman was in the sweathouse near Brockley some man, for a joke, threw a bucket of cold water down on top of her through a hole in the top'. There are other records of similar tales from the collection, but it is difficult to build up a picture for the use of sweathouses outside medicinal uses. The use of these houses went into decline around the beginning of the twentieth century when the chemist's shop took over from folk medicine.

Six miles from the north-east of Antrim is Rathlin Island [5]. According to O'Rahilly, *Riginia or Ricena* mentioned by Pliny is probably Rathlin; in Irish it is *Rechran*. The island commands the narrowest stretch of the waterway between Ireland and Scotland. Rathlin is the source of porcellanite, the hardest stone in the Britain or Ireland. It is found at Brockley towards the west of the island. Rathlin's first inhabitants, a Mesolithic people, arrived about 8,000 years ago and used this stone to make axes which were exported all over Ireland.

The island is so old that it possesses its own origin myth. The story goes that Finn mac Cumhail's* mother, after her son had drained the north of Ireland dry of whiskey, set out to procure whiskey from Scotland. She carried in her apron 'a mountain with rivers trees and all' to use as a stepping-stone. Less than halfway across the Sea of Moyle, she fell, and the mountain fell on her to form the island of Rathlin. She still exists pinned underneath the island, so that whenever a storm blew up, the locals would say that 'the oul witch is kicking'.

Rathlin Island is noted for its Neolithic axe factory, which was situated in the townland of Brockley [5] close to Church Bay. This factory of stone axes is associated with an outcrop of metamorphosed rock commonly known as porcellanite or bluestone. Given the number of roughed-out axes and waste flakes, this factory must have produced a sizeable amount of weaponry which presumably made its way to the adjoining mainlands. However, a more famous axe factory than the one at Rathlin, and stated by Evans as the 'most famous Neolithic axe factory in Ireland', was based at Tievebulliagh (*taobh bullaidh*, possibly meaning 'the region of the foreigners'). Tievebulliagh, where the porcellanite occurs on the east face of the mountain beneath the summit, is three miles west-south-west of Cushendall. It is 1,346 feet in height and rises from the eastern edge of the Antrim Plateau. Its produce has been identified at Limerick, the Thames Basin and north-east Scotland. Tievebulliagh axes have been found in court graves, confirming the date of the factory to 3000 BC. The hilltop has a cairn of 'possibly Bronze Age' date.

After the Rebellion of 1641, the Campbells, acting on behalf of the English Crown, defeated the local Catholic MacDonalds and drove all the survivors to their deaths over a cliff in a place known as *Slock na Calliagh* ('the roar of the witch'). Other place names that preserve the memory of this event include *Cnoc-a-screedin* ('hill of the screaming') and *Leg-a-vrista-vor* ('hollow of the great defeat'). At one stage, claims by the Scottish crown to Rathlin were successfully dismissed by pointing out that Rathlin had no snakes and therefore must be Irish!

On a clear day from Bruce's Cave, south of the east lighthouse on Rathlin, one can see Murlough Bay [5]. Murlough Bay is about two miles south from Fairhead as the crow flies, but to get there one needs to go to Ballycastle and take the A2 in an easterly direction. Murlough seems to take its original name from *Murbolg*, meaning 'sea inlet' or 'sea swell'. Murlough Bay has a pre-mythological culture, meaning that its early history is simply found in artefacts, the axes and shards speaking for those who made them. On the northern end of Murlough Bay is Drumnakill Point, *Rinn droim na coille*, 'the point at the ridge of the wood', where a stone axe was found in one of the many souterrains. The whole area of Drumnakill has been described by Evans as a 'mass of confused columnar blocks tumbled from the escarpment to the very edge of the sea … riddled with old dwelling places crudely constructed in natural cavities among the tilted columns'.

The Battle of Murlough Bay is the last of the three battles that Nemed, an early conqueror of Ireland, fought against the Fomorians.* And although he won this battle, his son Starn was slain by Conaing of the Fomorians (with whom Tor Conaing on Tory Island, Co. Donegal is associated). The battle was at Leithead Lachtmaighe, which Hogan suggests is the townland and parish of Layd, two miles north of Cushendall on the road to Knocknacarry. Unfortunately, there is nothing to be seen here except a magnificent view from a pair of raths known as the Twin Towers. The ruins of Layd Church are nearby for those who might like to move forward to medieval times.

Nemed's victory is recorded in the following quatrain from *History of Ireland* by G. Keating:

Cath Murbhuilg, é ró chuir,
Go ro-dluigheadh, rob a dúr;
Do mhuidm re Neimheadh na n-arm,
Gion go dtáinig Starn ar gcúl.

The battle of Murbholg–he fought it–
Till it was closed, it was stiff,
It was won by Neimheadh of the arms,
Though Starn came not back (from it).

[Translated by David Comyn]

One of the two royal forts attributed to Nemed was the fort of Rath Cambaeith near Island Magee [9]. Island Magee is *Rinn Seimhne* or 'riveted spearpoint' (referring to its shape) and has also been known as *Oileán Mic Aoidh* or McHugh's Island. No remains of the fort are to be seen today.

At a far later date, one of the many battles between the Dál nAraide or Cruithin* and the Dál Riata took place at Murlough Bay, at which the Dál Riata under *Flaithbhearthach* were victorious. The Dál Riata were an Ulster tribe that had crossed into Scotland. Their territory extended along the west coast of Scotland north of the Antonine Wall in present-day Argyll, and their centre of power was at *Dunadd* near *Crinan*. In Ireland, *Dalriada* was the ancient name of that part of Co. Antrim lying north of Slieve Mis [9], now more popularly named Slemmish. The 'stump' of Slemmish is what remains of a volcanic mountain.

A dividing line between the Dál nAraide and the Dál Riata was the River Bush, which has its source in the foothills of Slieveanee Mountain [9] ten miles north from Ballymena on the A43 and flows into the sea at Bushfoot Strand, one mile north of Bushmills – *ó Buais co Commur Trí nUsce*, 'from the Bush to the meeting of the three waters'. The Glendun, the

Bush and the Skerry Waters all meet south of Eagle Hill within Slieveanorra Forest close to Slieveanee Mountain. The Bush River gets its name from the Gaelic *búas*, meaning 'a stream or gushing water'. It was one of the royal rivers of Ireland – *rígusci Érenn*. From the fifth century it became the dividing line between the Cenél Eógain and the Cenél Conaill, two strands of the northern Uí Néill. The former branch gave their name to Co. Tyrone and the latter to Donegal, which is still sometimes referred to as *Tír Conaill*. The River Bush is said to have been one of the nine rivers founded by Partholón,* the first coloniser of Ireland.

Part of the ancient territory of the Dál nAraide was centred on *Magh Líne* or Moylinny and it extended from Lough Neagh to Carrickfergus. It is therefore understandable that many battles took place here, as the Cruithin* had to increasingly defend their territory against invaders; these defensive attitudes are ingrained and exist to the present day.

An intrinsic part of the culture of the Dál nAraide was the cult of the head, and a story built around it relates to the name Corrievrechan, *Coir Brecain* or the 'whirlpool of Breccan'. The Gulf of Corrievrechan, lying between the islands of Jura and Scarba, is said to exist at the confluence of the seas between Ireland and Scotland. An old poem from the *Book of Ballymote* states that 'the sea of the Orcs (Orkneys) and the cold sea of the Britons meet at Coir Bhreacáin'. At an earlier time, according to legend, the whirlpool was between Antrim and Rathlin and is now known as *Sloc na Mara*, 'the roar of the sea'. Brecan, together with the crew of fifty ships, drowned here. Their deaths were unknown until the blind poet Lugaid came to Bangor [15] and was walking along the strand at *Inver Beg* or Bangor Bay when his companions brought him a 'bare and speckled skull' they had found. Lugaid told them that it was the skull of Brecan's pet dog, 'for all his people have been drowned in yonder whirlpool'. Brecan has been given two possible ancestors, one being Partholón* from the distant past. Another version says that he was the grandson of Niall of the Nine Hostages from the fourth century AD.

Rathmore [14] is situated in Moylinny, in the parish of Donegore, and was the scene of many battles. The Battle of *Rath-Mór-Maighe-Líne*, was, according to O'Curry, 'gained over the Britons' in 680 AD, but this was followed by a Saxon invasion in 683 which was successful. If one sees Rathmore as a surviving outpost of the Cruithin,* then this battle may have ended their power. Keating states: 'Berthus plundered deplorably an inoffensive nation and one ever most friendly to the people or race of Sacsa'. In this battle, Cumascach, King of the Cruithin, was slain. Interestingly, a 'large body of Gaels' were slain at this battle, so it is possible that the invading forces of the Gaels intermarried with the Cruithin and made peace.

If we go back about a further sixty years in time when Rathmore was a capital of Ulster, the king was Mongán. Like Sweeny,* another Ulster king from Moira in Co. Down, Mongán's story, in a time when kings were regarded as divine, is one of early history suffused with the then-prevailing mythology.

The seventh century AD was a time when the poets held great sway in Ulster, as noted above with the peregrinations of the poets from the Mull of Kintyre in Scotland to Crew Hill and to Emain Macha in Armagh. Mongán fell into dispute with the poet or *file* Dallan

Forgaill, the author of an elegy on the death of Columcille. The dispute was about an event which had occurred 300 years prevously, namely, the manner of the death of Fothadh Airgteach, one of a trinity of brothers who had ruled Ireland in the third century. The poet, when challenged as to the veracity of his story, said that he would satirise Mongán's parents and grandparents even though they were long dead. And to quote a twelfth-century description of a seventh-century story, he said: *Docechnad for a n-usciu conná gebtha íasc ina inberaib; docechnad for a fedaib conna tibertaís torad for a maige comtis ambriti chaidchi cacha clainde* ('That he would satirise the waters of the country, so that no fish could live or be caught in them; he would satirise the trees so that no fruit could be borne by them; and the plains, so that they should for ever remain barren'). To make amends for the insult, the poet was paid seven *cumhals* or sixty-three cows. This event is said to have occurred in the vicinity of Rathmore and Rathbeg [14] in the old Cruithin* stronghold, on the plain of Moylinny, north-east of Lough Neagh.

Manannán mac Lir,* both an Irish and a Welsh sea god, is recorded in *Lebor na hUidre* as having visited Rathmore in the shape of a noble, young man. In Welsh mythology he is known as Manawydan, son of Llyr. He gives his name to the Isle of Man. He is most truly the god of the Irish Sea and represents a confluence between Irish and Welsh mythologies. At Rathmore, he told the wife of Fiachna, the local king who was then fighting in Scotland, that her husband would be killed in battle unless she consented to have a son by him, and thus was Mongán sired. When Fiachna returned, his wife told him about the arrival of Manannán and its consequences and her husband thanked her. When Manannán left the queen the following morning, he left a quatrain with her which reads:

Tíag dum daim
dufail in matin bánglain
iss é Monindan mac Lir
ainm ind fhir dutárlid.

[*Compert Mongan* from *Lebor na hUidre*]

I go home,
The pale pure morning draws near:
Manannán son of Lir
Is the name of the man who has come to thee.

[*Translated by Kuno Meyer*]

So, like Cú Chulainn* at an earlier time, Mongán had both an earthly and a spiritual father.

Moylinny is the plain on which Scottish, Welsh and Irish legends converge. Although Mongán was an historical King of Ulster in the late sixth and early seventh centuries, he possessed many of the characteristics of Manannán. Another legend states that Mongán was taken when he was three days old from the royal rath at Rathmore by Manannán* to the 'Land of Promise' or *Tír Tairngire*. He returned home at the age of 16 and took revenge on the killer of his father, and in 622 became King of Ulster at *Rath Mór* in Moylinny.

Rathmore is marked 'Rathmore Trench' on *Discovery* map 14. It is an irregular oval shape, measuring inside 138 feet in the long diameter and 108 in the short. Reeves's *Ecclesiastical Antiquities of Down and Connor and Dromore* states that 'it was formerly surrounded by a deep and wide fosse, which time and agriculture have in part filled in'. Berry, writing in the 1890s, described the embankment as about twelve feet high, 'but when the moat was dug it must have been very much higher'. The age of the rath is less precise than its internal measurements. The Four Masters state: 'Rath-Mor-Muighe Linne, or the Rath of Mor of Moy-linne, an ancient fortress and residence of the Kings of Ulster, was so called according to O'Flaherty and the *Annals of Tigernach*, at 161 AD, from Mor, wife of Breasal, King of Ulster.' Mor is a powerful name with connections to *Mor Muman*, to give Munster its full name. Her connection with the ancient centre of the Cruithin* reinforces its strength. She is said to have died of grief at the supposed death of her husband.

There were a number of glens in Ireland where people went for respite if they felt undue stress; one of these was at Glenbuck near Rasarkin [8]. Glenbuck may be the anglicisation for *Glen Bolcain*; *cenn mbolg* means a state ignorance or not being in one's full faculties. According to Reeves, there is a ridge called Dunbolcain or Drumbolcain about half-a-mile north of Rasharkin. He suggests that Glen Bolcain is in the same district. The person most associated with this glen is *Suibhne Geilt** or 'Mad Sweeny'.*

> *Suibhne mh'ainm o Ros Ercain,*
> *as misi an gealtán gealtach.*

> Suibhne of *Ros Earcain* is my name,
> the wild demented one am I.

Suibhne* was a seventh-century king of ancient Cruithin* stock and was cursed by St Ronán to wander naked for the rest of his life. 'Sweeter indeed were it to me to hear the voices of the cuckoos on the banks of the Bann ... than the grig grag of the church bell.' However, the inspiration of Ulster poets had a tough life, being constantly on the move:

> Sad forever is my cry
> on the summit of Cruachan Aighle
> from Glen Bolcain to Islay
> from Cinn Tire to Boirche.

> *[Translated by J.G.O'Keeffe]*

During penal times, Glenbuck, a glen cutting into Long Mountain for about a mile, was a refuge for Catholics and a place where Mass was celebrated. The Sheskin Burn River runs through it from north-west to south-east. On the south-west side is a hill known as Mass Hill and on the north-east side is an 'old altar'. There is a long lane from the Glenbuck Road [8], and half-a-mile along this track there is a well-formed grotto of stones with a thorn bush above. This, presumably, is the 'old altar'.

The area to the northwest of Glenbuck contains two chambered graves, four raths and three standing stones, so there is a continuity of time here.

The Antrim coast has the distinction of possibly being the site where man first arrived in Ireland. The raised beach gravels at Larne [9] have yielded many implements, giving the name *Larnian* to the people who both made them and used them. The Larnian sites extend from Larne to Cushendun to Newferry north of Lough Neagh on the lower Bann as well as Mountsandel and many other sites as well. The principal findings for our first ancestors are at the Curran in Larne.

After a deep cutting was made during the construction of the railway to Larne Harbour in the 1870s, a scientific investigation of the site was carried out. At a considerable depth in the ground, and over a large area, a number of hand-worked flints were unearthed. Curran Point in Larne Harbour, which was excavated in 1935, produced no fewer than 15,000 pieces of flint that had been struck by man. The absence of charcoal, and by extension fire, at these sites raises the question as to whether these early people were ignorant of the use of fire and of pottery. Finds of oysters, limpets and periwinkles from shell heaps show that these very healthy nutrients were part of the diet of these Mesolithic peoples. We may presume that they also ate fish as well as sea birds and their eggs.

These earliest inhabitants in different parts of Antrim are said to have come from the southern end of the Baltic Sea and from the Cantabrian Mountains of Asturias near Leon in northern Spain. The settlers from the Baltic are identified as part of the Campignian culture and are associated with Curran Point, while those who landed on Island Magee are associated with Asturian culture. These two peoples were identified by the German scholar Dr Walther Bremer in a paper to the Royal Irish Academy as being distinct, owing to the different types of flint from the Curran and Island Magee. Bremer's point is that the flint users came from more than one tradition, making the culture more widely spread than originally thought.

As these peoples left no stories, we must rely on their work tools and the surrounding landscape to tell their tale. Their flint tools were used both to cut and to scrape, while the surrounding area was wooded and bogland, the animals in proximity being deer, wolves and bears. When they moved inland, they did so by boats such as coracles and arrived at sites in such places as Newferry, Lough Beg, Toomebridge and Portglenone. We may assume that they were aware of the clear night skies and thus may have felt part of a larger universe than we do. The unadulterated night sky may have led them to time the seasons and thus over generations lay the foundations for seasonal markers such as Newgrange.

FIGURE 37. Photograph of a coracle, a type of vessel used on the Boyne from early medieval times until the 1940s.

For a Mesolithic outing, it might be a good idea to start at Curran Point, Larne [9], and from there walk to the ferry that goes to Island Magee. The strip of gravel known as the Curran from its sickle-like shape is taken from the Irish *corrán*, meaning a 'sickle', and juts into Larne Lough. Once off the ferry, go on the B90 south to Ballylumford, and here beyond the wood on the left-hand side of the road is a chambered grave known as the Ballylumford Dolmen and locally as the 'Druid's Altar'. From here one can see the peninsula of Curran. Although named as a druidic altar, this dolmen, as most others, well preceded the druids. Three miles south along the B90 is Ballyharry, where excavations have discovered pottery, flint and arrowheads. An early graveyard at Gransa close by will bring one back to more recent times and, to finish, one should join the B150 leading to the B90, ending up at Brown's Bay. A walk north-west from here will lead you to the Rocking Stone, or Loggan Stone, said to have been used in the rites of the druids. The *log* or hollow under the stone meant that that it could give slight vibrations, and from these vibrations came its magical power.

The power of the Cruithin* was beginning to wane in the seventh century AD, and they lost a battle in the peninsula of Curran; this battle was fought at Ard Corrain where the Dál Riata were victors. According to Hogan there is a mound on the hill above the Corran where Fiacha mac Demain, the defeated King of the Dál nAraide, is said to be buried. Carn Duff and Cairndhu are on a hill above the Corran, but these are not marked on the *Discovery* series for Northern Ireland. The Dál Fiatach who defeated Fiachna mac Demain were named the Ulaid, but they were Gaels, and the true Ulaid were the Dál nAraide with their horse people, the Echach.

The Dál Riata, or in modern Irish the Dál Riada, were a tribe who, due to loss of territory, were confined to north Antrim. They later found an important kingdom based in Scotland in Argyllshire at Dunadd. The Dál Riata and the Dál nAraide had close bonds and bloodlines, making one wonder if both tribes constituted the Ulaid. An example of this 'closeness' was that both tribes fought the Dál Fiatach and that in the seventh century the

Dál Riata were commanded by Connad Cerr, son of the King of the Dál Riata, whose sister is reputed to have been the mother of Congal Cáech, King of Dál nAraide.

For a Neolithic outing, one could spend a pleasant afternoon on Lyle's Hill, a Late Neolithic hilltop enclosure and cairn in the townland of Tobernagree, eight miles north-west of Belfast and two miles south-east of Templepatrick [14]. This site was discovered by aerial photography in 1927. This hilltop encloses a pear-shaped area of twelve acres, and there is a single entrance on the north-west which is thirty feet wide. Evans says that 'no other defensive earthworks of Neolithic age are known in Ireland'. There is a cairn on the west side of the hillfort. Evans compares the hillfort at Lyle's Hill with the Camp of Lizop, near Carnac in the Morbihan in Brittany. Tens of thousands of potsherds and worked flints were also recovered. Evans goes on to describe:

'Sunk into the subsoil beneath the pit were eight shallow pits containing offerings in the form of sherds and traces of cremated bone. These were located south of the centre around a thickening of the burnt layer which was interpreted as the site of a funerary pyre.'

ARMAGH

Árd Macha, 'the high ground of Macha'

Macha was one of a triad of war/fertility goddesses along with Badb and the Mórrígan, as can be seen in the *Lebor Gabála Érenn*:

> *Badb is Macha mét indbáis*
> *Morrigan fotla felbáis,*
> *Indlema ind ága ernbais,*
> *Ingena ana Ernmais.*

> Badb and Macha, rich the store,
> Morrigan who dispenses valour,
> Devisers of death by the sword,
> Noble daughters of Irondeath.

[Translated by R.A.S. Macalister]

Armagh is the only county in Ireland to be named after a goddess. As so often happens, there are many human forms to the goddess; in one of these, Macha traced the ritual centre of *Emain Macha* (commonly known as Navan Fort) with her brooch-pin (*emain* is said to be derived from *eó muin*, meaning a 'neck-brooch'), and the sons of Dithorba, a local chief, dug the trench for her. A more popular legend is where her farmer husband Cruind forces Macha to race against a horse. During the Iron Age the god of the horse people was *Echdae*, and these people would then have been the dominant stock at Emain Macha. One may

FIGURE 38. Emain Macha.

see in this race a competition between the goddess and the rising god of the patriarchy. Macha wins the race but consequently dies in childbirth; her twins survive, and according to this tale Navan Fort's other name, *Emain Macha*, refers to the 'Twins of Macha'. The introduction of Cruind shows that this story came from a later time, a time of farming and cultivation. This region is one of the richest agricultural and cattle-raising areas today in Northern Ireland. This ancient capital of Ulster is two miles west of Armagh city [19].

The oldest document for Irish place names is Ptolemy's map of Ireland. Ptolemy may have garnered much of his information from sailors in Alexandria in Egypt, and thus the map is more informed about the coastal areas than the interior, which is fairly blank. Emain Macha is written as *Regia Polis* or 'Royal City', mixing the Latin *regia* with the Greek *polis*. However, Navan Fort was, rather like Tara [42, 43], more a centre for tribal gatherings than a daily communal centre. For the past half-century, it has been the focus of much archaeological study. I first became acquainted with the site while attending a talk by Patrick Collins in Dublin in the 1970s. He was discussing D.M. Waterman's excavations at Navan. My abiding memory is of a vast number of post holes into which oak posts had at some time been inserted.

This site was excavated for eight years from 1965 by Waterman. It is generally regarded as a masterwork in excavation and has led perhaps for the first time to providing a physical context for life and legend in the Late Bronze Age and Early Iron Age. One might say that it earths the myths. The mound known as Site B was probably begun around 700 BC. Briefly, Emain Macha includes a large mound (B) and another of smaller size (A), and both are surrounded by a large earthen enclosure. In the Later Bronze Age, hilltop locations were chosen as places for settlement. At Emain Macha, a round house was built during the Bronze Age next to a circular stockade. Despite a number of reconstructions, the house remained on the same site into the Iron Age when it became a ritual centre and the focus of the Ulster Cycle of legends. The actual buildings at Emain Macha in which the heroes of the Ulster Cycle lived during the Iron Age clearly show the distinction between literary description and archaeological excavation. In *Lebor na hUidre* the banqueting hall (*Tech Mid-chúarta*, 'the house of the circulation of mead'), had

> nine beds from the fire to the wall; thirty feet up was each bronze frontage to the house. There were carvings of red yew there. A frieze along the lower part added to it; above a tiled roof. A frieze of silver surrounded Conchobar's bed at the front of the house; the support posts were of bronze, with lustrous gold upon the head, with inlaid carbuncles of precious stones; there was equal light both day and night there. There was a silver gong above the king's parapet in the royal household. When Conchobar beat the royal rod against the gong, all the Ulaid turned towards him. Twelve beds there, twelve beds for the charioteers and those visiting in their company.

Waterman's excavations at Navan Fort reveal a less romanticised picture; on Site B, or the large mound, as seen from the road, there were two round structures, one on the north and one on the south; these existed prior to the mound's construction. They are archaeologically known as the Southern and Northern Ring-Slot Enclosures. The south side of the enclosure contained nine successive ring slots, inferring that the round structure at the south was reconstructed over time. These slots, which were cut into the subsoil, formed a diameter of about forty feet. Gaps of about five feet on the east of both Site A and Site B indicate east-facing entrances (it was customary for the king to face the rising sun in the morning). Hearths were placed at the centres of the sites; this is supported by the presence of burnt areas and groups of flat stones. Outside the 'royal building', a series of post holes concentric with the slots and a few feet outside them added reinforcement to the habitation. This roundhouse had an opening to a bawn or farmyard. The main entrance for inhabitants and charioteers was in a line with the entrance to Site A. The Ulster Cycle of tales is thus centred on a certain place in a certain time in a definite location.

Through dating by tree rings or dendrochronology, it has been established that the timber used in the large wooden structure at *Emain Macha* was felled in 94 BC. This massive structure stood on the summit of the fort and represents one of the most prominent Iron Age ritual sites in north-western Europe. It began life as a circular timber building consisting of 275 posts standing in five concentric rings and with a large post at the centre. The large post hole at the centre required a ramp about twenty feet long in order to stand the central post, which was about fifty feet tall. All the timber was cut down at the same

FIGURE 39. A student poses as an ancient warrior in *Emain Macha* – taken on the same day as the signing of the Good Friday Agreement on 10 April 1998.

time. The completed structure may have had a roof, though this is uncertain. The interior of the building was filled in with limestone blocks. So, if one can imagine five concentric circles of large timber posts rising out of a limestone cairn, then one has some idea of this phenomenal centre. The temple was nearly forty-four yards in diameter and was ritually burnt some time after being built. This final phase of the building at *Emain Macha* was purely for ceremonial reasons, although what exactly these reasons were is open to speculation. After the ceremony of fire, a sod mound was placed on top of the cairn, and this is what one sees today.

The fire at Navan Fort remains an enigma at the heart of the sun worship tradition. Lug* was the sun god of the Ulaid as Balor was the sun god of the Fomorians.* Immediate associations with this rite spring to mind, such as the Vikings burning their ships, or Irish Traveller families burning their caravans on the death of a member.

Emain Macha is the location for the opening of the great romantic tale of Deirdre and Naoise, known as *Longes mac nUisnig* or 'The Exile of the Sons of Uisnech'. Also known as *Oideadh Chloinne Uisnech* or 'The Death of the Sons of Uisnech', it is a fusion of history, folklore and mythology and existed in oral traditions of Ulster, Connacht and Scotland. The folkloric tradition gives the legend much variation and moves away from the pseudo-historic origins of the story. The original saga is recorded in the *Book of Leinster* as one of the three sorrowful tales of Ireland, the others being 'The Fate of the Children of Lir'* and 'The Fate of the Children of Tuireann'.

The *Book of Leinster* version begins in the house of Feidlimid mac Daill, storyteller to Conchobar mac Nessa,* High King of Ireland. Conchobar came to a feast at the house where Feidlimid's wife was pregnant, and as she passed the Ulster warriors (the Ulaid) the child cried out in the womb. This motif has been enriched in the telling; in some folk versions the unborn child screams each time the visiting king sticks a fork into his meat, while other versions state that the scream comes from the *Lia Fáil* under the king's chair.

Cathbad, the king's druid, was asked to explain this. He put his hand on the woman's womb and said, 'Truly it is a woman child who is here. Deirdre shall be her name, and evil woe shall be upon her.' Or in the original: '*Fír ar se ingen fil and. Agus bid Derdriu a hainm, agus biaid olc impe.*'

After the child's birth, Cathbad again prophesied that she would bring ruin. The Ulaid called for her death, but Conchobar said that he would have her reared and when she was grown, he would take her for a wife.

When she had grown up, she saw a warrior that satisfied her three requirements in a man – skin as white as snow, hair as black as the raven's and cheeks red like blood. It was the warrior Naoise walking on the plain at Emain. Deirdre spoke to him and said that she would prefer him to the king. As with the tale of Diarmuid and Gráinne, the heroine chooses a younger man rather than the king. This is the story of many sagas in Europe and is still pertinent today in many cultures.

Like Gráinne, Deirdre uses the direct approach to get her intended love and the following dialogue ensues: 'I would take myself a younger bull,' Deirdre said. Naoise tried to avoid her advances, as he feared the prophecy of Cathbad. 'Sayest thou this to refuse me?' said she. 'Yea indeed,' he said; and she sprang upon him, and seized him by his two ears (it is important to note that ears are symbolically related to testicles, and this is seen in the story of Labraid Loingsech who had 'horse's ears', or 'large ears', necessary for a fecund king). 'Two ears of shame and mockery shalt thou have,' she cried, 'if you do not take me with thee.' 'Release me, O my wife!', said he. 'That will I,' said she.

A place full of mythic and folkloric significance is Slieve Gullion (*Sliabh Cuilinn*) [29, 36], about six miles west of Newry. The name of the sun goddess Anu here was preserved in the name Áine or Aighne, who was the sister of Milucradh of Slieve Gullion. Here she was commonly known as the *Cailleach Biorar*, or the 'old woman who frequents the water'. The lake associated with her is known as *Calliagh Berras Lough* and can be seen on top of Slieve Gullion. The lough was anciently known as *Loch Dagruadh* or the 'fiery lake'. This Áine was said to be the daughter of Cualann mac an Gabhann, the smith from whom the mountain gets its name. Cualann is more usually known as Cualann Cerd or 'Cualann the artificer'.

Cualann at one time is said to have lived on the Isle of Man at the same time as Conchobar mac Nessa,* the legendary king of the Ulster Cycle, when Conchobar was but a humble warrior. Conchobar consulted the oracle of Clochar, who was possibly a druid from Clogher, and asked him where he might acquire a reputable sword and shield which would possess the *buadha* or power to help him gain the sovereignty of Ulster. He was advised to go to the Isle of Man and get Cualann to make a sword, shield and spear for him. Cualann agreed to make these armaments for Conchobar, and while Conchobar was awaiting their completion he met a mermaid named Tiobal who claimed that she was the 'princess of the ocean'.

Conchobar's shield had the following inscription: *Tiobal bean-fhlaith na mara* or 'Tiobal, princess of the ocean'. Her figure was also inscribed on the shield, and she told Conchobar that whenever he was in battle her figure would possess such power (*buadha*) that, when looked upon by the enemy, it would instantly diminish their strength. The legend says that when Conchobar returned to Ireland he won the kingship of Ulster. In gratitude to Cualann, he gave him lands in Ulster from *Gleann Righe* or the Vale of the River Newry on the north to *Glas Neasa* or the river of Annagasson, near Dunany [36] in Co. Louth, which at that time were the boundaries of ancient Cuailgne or Cooley.

A famous tale from the *Book of Leinster* that bore the brunt of time is the story of Cualann's banquet and his invitation to Conchobar to attend:

> *Cuillean Ceard a ainm, agus do rinneadh fleadh lais do Conchobar, agus do curaidh do thocaradh go h-Eamhain; agus adúbhairt le Conchobar gan do breith leis ach uathadh fíor-laech, oir ní raibh críche no ferand aicce ach toradh a óird, agus ainneona, agus a thancaire.*
>
> Cuillean Ceard was his name; and having prepared a banquet for Conchobar, he went to Emain to invite him. He requested Conchobar to fetch none with him but a few warlike men; because he had neither land nor patrimony nor lands to support him, and solely relied on the produce of his hammer, anvil and vice.

Cualann resided according to tradition in a cave near Slieve Gullion, but where that is or was varies according to local historians; perhaps his spirit simply dwelt in the passage grave on the hill at Slieve Gullion. It is interesting to note that the *Discovery* map [29] from the Ordnance Survey of Northern Ireland notes two cairns on the hill, while the *Discovery Series* [36] from the Ordnance Survey Ireland notes neither.

Slieve Gullion was a pre-Christian centre, and Cualann's adherents were known in Gaelic as *giolla Guillin* or 'the servant of the devil'. His daughter was the *Cailleach Bhéara* or the 'old hag of Beare' as she is also known, named after Beare Island in west Cork. The *Cailleach* is also supposed to dwell in the cave or 'artificial vault', namely the passage grave inhabited by her father. The south cairn features in folk tales and is known as the Cailleach Bhéara House. The lake on the mountain top which she frequents is also named after her; legend says that it was formed by the Tuatha Dé Danann* at her request. It is said to possess many *buadha*, which in this case would mean many occult or mysterious properties.

At 1,894 feet the passage-grave cairn on the southern summit of Slieve Gullion [29] is the highest surviving passage grave in Britain and Ireland, and in the words of A.E.P. Collins, who surveyed it in 1961, 'this passage grave cairn is by far the finest example of this type of monument in Northern Ireland'. Evans, in his book *Prehistoric and Early Christian Ireland*, writes that 'the careful excavation of this exposed and difficult site, in 1961, was one of the triumphs of modern archaeology in Ireland, although it was unrewarding in that very few grave goods were recovered, and we are still left in doubt as to its place in the sequence of passage-grave construction'.

Charlotte Brooke, our earliest female antiquarian whose famous work is the *Reliques of Irish Poetry* (1789), records the entry of local peasants into the chamber with the discovery of 'only a few human bones', inside. The chamber was cleared of stones and other debris by the County Louth Archaeological Society in 1906.

Findings, though limited, were as follows: some blocks of stone with a shallow basin-shaped depression on one side; a lighter basin cracked in two with artificial dressing which were hidden for safety by Estyn Evans; some fine, black soil within a fissure on the floor, which supplied the only traces of burial deposit: a half-dozen tiny fragments of cremated bone, pointing to cremation as the original burial rite. Several pieces of worked flint were also found; these included an arrowhead and a round scraper. Collins completes his study with the following words: 'There are some grounds for believing that our cairn, magnificently sited and splendidly built as it is, can in addition claim pride of place at the head of the whole series of such tombs in Ireland'. As such, it is a suitable resting place for the great smith Cualann.

CAVAN

An cabhán, 'the hollow'

Described as the 'pulse of pagan Ireland' by Dr Anne Ross, author of *Pagan Celtic Britain*, to Tom Barron, a local historian, Cavan is the crucible in which many of our pre-Christian deities found their origin. Walking nearly forty years ago with Tom Barron to Corleck Hill

FIGURE 40. The three-sided stone head found at Corleck.

(described by him as 'the Highland of the Gods') [35], I felt an affinity with early Ireland that I never had before. Tom said that Corleck Hill, which is 588 feet above sea level, was also known as *Sliab na dTrí nDeé* or the 'hill of the three gods' – Brian, Inchoaba and Iuchair, three gods of the Tuatha Dé Danaan.* According to him, many stone heads were found here, and each contained a hole in the base of the head so that at certain times of the year it was placed atop a stone pillar on Corleck Hill where it could be venerated. The most famous stone head from Corleck Hill, which is sometimes called Conn, is a three-headed or tricephalos head, and possibly dates from the Iron Age. This superb example of the cult of the head was at some point taken from its original site and eventually ended up built into a wall at Woodlands near Raphoe, Co. Donegal. It can now be seen, but not touched, at the National Museum of Ireland, Dublin.

In the early nineteenth century, Corleck Hill was located on a farm owned by John Mahood and contained a passage grave mound, a circular embankment and a circle of flagstones. The circle of flagstones, according to Barron, was smashed by the Longmore family to build a house on the Mahood farm in 1836.

The Plain of Moybolgue is not marked on the *Discovery* map but is three miles south from Bailieborough [35] on the Meath border and just north of Lough Lenanavragh. At the ancient cemetery here are said to be buried more kings than anywhere else in Ireland.

FIGURE 41. The Killinkere stone head known as the *Cailleach Gearagain*, 'the wailing witch' (Carole Cullen).

It was at Moybolgue that St Patrick is said to have overcome the local goddess or *cailleach*. Less than five miles north-west from Moybolgue is Killinkere, and here on the outside wall of a Catholic church is the Killinkere stone head known as the *Cailleach Gearagain*, 'the wailing witch'. The lips of this stone head are shaped as if to represent the *Cailleach* blowing with her breath, a feature which may be compared to that of Boreas, the Greek god of the North Wind. Until the lovely stone church was neglected in favour of a more 'hip' design, she remained for all to see unmolested and undefiled. Local lore mentions that the local priest removed the head and placed it under his bed – a marriage of the Christian and the pre-Christian!

Close to Virginia (*Achadh an Iúir*, 'the field of the yew tree') is Lough Ramor, which takes its name from Munremur ('fat neck') mac Gerrcind, who was a tribal god of the

Mugdornai. This tribe had connections with Yorkshire in England. The Mugdornai were protectors of sacred stone heads in Cavan.

In the north-western corner of Co. Cavan, five miles south-west from Ballyconnell [27A] and one mile north from Ballymagauran, is Derryragh Hill in the townland of Derryragh. Here, Crom* Cruach was worshipped, a god of the harvest and the principal idol of all those who colonised the island from earliest times to the final domination of Christianity. The ancient territory where he was propitiated was known as *Magh Slecht* or the 'plain of prostration', from the Irish *sléchtad* meaning 'bending' or 'bowing'. The following is an extract from a poem from the *Dindshenchas:**

> *Sund nobíd*
> *idal ard, co n-immud fhich,*
> *diarbo chomainm in Cromm Crúaich:*
> *tuc in cach thúaith beith cen síd …*

> *Do cen búaid*
> *marbtais a claind toísig trúaig*
> *con-immud guil ocus gáid*
> *a fuil do dáil 'mon Cromm Crúaich …*

> *Blicht is ith*
> *uaid nochuingitis for rith*
> *dar cend trín a sotha slain:*
> *ba mór a grain is a grith …*

Here used to stand a lofty idol, that saw many a fight, whose name was Crom Cruach; it caused every tribe to live without peace …

For him ingloriously they slew their hapless firstborn with much wailing and peril, to pour their blood round Crom Cruach …

Milk and corn they asked of him speedily in return for a third part of all their progeny: great was the horror and outcry about him.

[Translated by Kuno Meyer]

Crom* was worshipped throughout Ireland anywhere a harvest festival was held. The origin of the Festival of Lughnasa begins with Crom. In Cavan, I was told by Tom Barron that his head is to the side, as he was carrying a bag of corn over his shoulder, and thus he was bent or stooped, which is the meaning of *crom*. The Festival of Lughnasa also included horse swimming and possibly racing in the water at Milltown Lough [35], south of Shercock or *Searcóg*, 'beloved', on the R178. At Cornalaragh, a townland two miles east of Milltown

Lough, there is a river where horses were brought to be washed; whether this is connected with the horse swimming at Milltown Lough is uncertain.

Generally, Lughnasa was known as *Domnach Chrom Dubh*, 'the Sunday festival of Dark Crom' or the festival of the 'Dark Bent One'. The present names, Garland Sunday or Reek Sunday, represent a commemoration of the victory of Christianity over paganism. Reek Sunday is held on the second Sunday in July and coincides with the pilgrimage to Croagh Patrick in Co. Mayo, also known as the 'Reek'. It survives as the Fraughan (Irish *fraochán* or bilberry) Festival in Glencullen, Co. Dublin.

Many other harvest festivals are held on the last Sunday in July and some are held in August; thus, the Irish for August is *Mí Lughnasa*, meaning the month of the festival of Lug,* the sun god. *Lá Lughnasa* is 1 August or Lammas Day. The name 'Lammas' is derived from the Anglo-Saxon *hláfmaesse*, which means 'loaf mass' – a religious festival in which loaves of bread made from the first ripe corn were consecrated. In England, the gathering of the harvest remained a pagan feast, and the poet Thomas Hardy wrote that 'women, whose chief companions are the forms and faces of outdoor Nature, retain in their souls far more of the pagan fantasy of their remote forefathers than of the systematised religion taught their race at a later date'. This celebration came to an end with the Reformation. In Ireland, even to the present day, the Festival of Lughnasa remains vibrant and strong.

Close to the ritual centre at Darraugh, *Domnach Crom* Dubh* was celebrated up to the 1850s on the last Sunday in July at Kilnavart (*cill na bhfeart*, 'church of the graves'). However, even during the early twentieth century, 'some old individuals in the locality still make the station on the last Sunday in July'. These pious people kept up the traditional practice of moving on their knees after the example of St Patrick and reciting prayers along the connecting pathway between the well (*Tobar Patraic*) and the ring fort (*Fossa Slecht*). The well and ring fort connected to this station are south of the church which is east of Kilnavert.

John P. Dalton whose work on 'Crom Cruaich of Magh Sleacht', published in 1922 in the *Proceedings of the Royal Irish Academy*, remains a testament to the research of the committed scholar, writes that towards the end of the 1920s

> Domnach Sunday carnivals, at the end of July, are decaying; the numbers who frequent them are diminishing and getting restricted to the juvenile population; the race of blind minstrels has died out, and music is rarely heard on these occasions. The assembly stations hide, in a continuous line, within the long chain of mountains that overlook Magh Sleacht from the west, in retreats or at elevations difficult of access. From Darraugh fort the full extent of this range to both of its extremities can be surveyed at ease, its course throughout being clearly discernible.

Domnach Crom Dubh* is mentioned on a number of occasions by the *Annals of the Four Masters* as a date mark when recording specific events such as the murderous attack by Hugh O'Rourke and O'Brien on the bishop and people of Kells in 1117 AD.

A Christian legend from the *Book of Fermoy* associated with Crom* Dubh is as follows: A demon related to St Cainnech of Roscrea that on the day that Crom died

> the evil powers whom Crom had served so well sought to carry off his body so that they could possess his spirit; but that suddenly St. Patrick with a host of saints and angels appeared, who assailed us with fiery darts, one of which struck me in the leg and left me lame for ever. It seems that Crom's charities and good works were more than a balance for his sins; so that the saints took possession of his soul and put us to flight.

This legend reiterates the story of St Patrick invading *Magh Slecht* with his angels and saints and replacing paganism with Christianity. Various saints such as Brigit and Brendan became the guardians of Crom's* spirit.

The territory of *Magh Slecht* was under the control of the Tuath Masraighe, who were members of the Aithech Tuatha, the rent-paying or vassal tribes of ancient Ireland. The Aithech Tuatha revolted in 56 AD but were defeated, and half a millenium later, in the sixth century, the Masraighe rose up but were defeated by the Uí Briuin. *Magh Slecht* may be seen stretching from south of Bawnboy in a south-easterly direction as far as Garadice Lough to include Killycluggin and Derryragh, locally known as Darraugh. Within this area there are more than twenty prehistoric monuments, including megalithic tombs, cairns, standing stones, a stone row and a stone circle, as well as ring barrows and holy wells. This is the area where the corn god was supreme and where it was believed that a brutal deity held the fruits of the harvest under his control.

If *Magh Slecht* is the centre for these harvest ceremonies, then the ring fort atop of Derryragh (Darraugh) Hill is the epicentre. A description by Dalton is as follows:

> The crest of this hill is crowned by an elliptically shaped rath, whose major axis points directly south. The rath commands beautiful prospects in every direction, but the most picturesque view opens to the south, where the panorama is adorned by a series of lakes that stretch away to right and left out of range of sight. Darraugh stands medially over the circuit of this water system, and looks straight down, along a gentle slope, on its midmost basin underneath.

The tribes controlling this fertile tract were the Horse people or *Uí Echach* and the MacGoverns or Maguarans (*Magh Shamhráin*, 'the plain of summer', or as it is known today, Ballymagauran), but the dominant tribe during the time of Crom* were the Masraighe. Although vassals for a long time, the Masraighe Magh Slecht eventually became *ollamhs* or professors to the Kings of Breffni in Leitrim.

Garadice Lough on the boundary of *Magh Slecht* was known as Loch Guthard or *Guth Ard*, 'high pitched voices', attributable to the wretched sounds of those being sacrificed on Darraugh Hill and later to the loud voice of St Patrick as he brought these practices to an end. Dalton, quoted above, says that Guthard was in early times a vast, continuous water-sheet which broke into two branches and which met at *Tuam Seanchaidh* [27A]. Although *Tuam Seanchaidh* is just inside Leitrim, I have left it under Cavan as it is part of the *Magh Slecht* story. *Tuam Seanchaidh* means the 'grave of the storyteller', and this was the point between the two loughs – Garadice and Ballymagauran – where the southern pilgrims embarked on their way to worship at *Magh Slecht*. A road is said to have gone from Tara to *Magh Slecht*, which the High King Loegaire is said to have taken many times when he set out to worship at Darraugh Hill. It was from *Tuam Seanchaidh* that St Patrick crossed when he sailed over 'the water named Guthard'.

The hill at Darraugh [27A] was in the time of Crom* covered by oak wood, and thus the name Derryragh or *Doire rath*, 'the ring fort by the oak wood'. The hill is almost 400 feet above sea level and 200 feet above the lake underneath. Porturlan, north of the hill has an interesting older name, Portnerlinchilinchy, which in Irish is *Port-na-h-Urlaidhe-h-Innsi*, 'the slaughter bank of the island'. Apparently older maps show Garadice extending around the side of the hill; thus, Derryragh was once an island.

As Darraugh was a centre of pilgrimage from at least the Iron Age until the onset of Christianity, it is only natural that it had, like all assembly points, its fairs and it served as a centre for a great social occasion. A horse-racing meeting was held there from time immemorial and only came to an end during the First World War. The road going east from Ballymagauran served as the racecourse for the annual meetings.

The stone representing Crom* at Darraugh was said to have been gilded with gold and surrounded by twelve subordinate deities of stone. St Patrick was supposed to have destroyed this monument, and as a result a large hole was dug and Crom was buried in it. But a part of the stone idol stuck out from the ground, and later tales tell of it being dynamited around 1900 by a local farmer. Fortunately, he was not fully successful, as the remains of this stone now can be found resting quietly in a corner of the National Museum of Ireland in Dublin, where it is known as the Killycluggin Stone. Killycluggin is less than two miles north-east from Darraugh on the R205. However, as there were reputedly twelve stones, more than one has been identified as the Killycluggin Stone, such as that in the museum at Ballyjamesduff. A replica of this stone stands at a crossroads near Killycluggin, and it contains rich artwork associated with the Late Iron Age.

The worship of Crom* occurred at *Samain* or Hallowe'en. *Samain* means 'summer's end', a time that would have corresponded with the beginning of the harvest. A noted worshipper of Crom was Tigernmas, King of Ireland about 150 BC. He died with three-quarters of the men of Ireland about him while worshipping at *Magh Slecht*. A plague was said to have been responsible for both his death and the deaths of many of his people.

According to the early *Tripartite Life of St Patrick*, the saint erected a church at Kilnavart, which is situated about one mile north-east from Darraugh on the R205. Kilnavart was originally *Cill na bhfeart* or the 'church of the graves'. The *feart* was a pre-Christian circular grave, and there is a barrow grave at Kilnavart today. There is or was a cromlech close to the church, which, according to Dalton, was surrounded by a small ring fort. He writes:

'The tenant occupier (Mr Murray) informed me that the interior was dug up many years since by searchers for treasure trove, when a stone cist containing ashes and human bones was exposed. A tall pillar stone stands just outside the fort, and another inside, at the end of the grave.'

The rath or ring fort at Kilnavert was, Dalton wrote, the homeplace of the Masraighe, the protectors and overseers of the sanctuary grounds who were thus a priestly caste with ample lands and provision.

Five miles west from Kilnavert and within the plain of Magh Slecht is Bellaleenan, a townland north of the river Blackwater, and here the last Sunday of July still attracts a number of people for *Domnach Crom* Dubh*. The gathering takes place at St Patrick's Well.

Moving about ten miles north-west from Killycluggin and passing Bawnboy on the N87 and turning towards the Cuilgagh Mountains ('chalky mountains') on the R200, one comes to Bellavally [27A], and there on the right-hand side of the road is a mass of rock known as the 'Black Rocks'. This crag is also known as 'Maguire's Chair' and is regarded by some as the inauguration site and tribal meeting place of the Maguires. It was also where 'stations' were held on the last Sunday in July as part of the celebration of *Domnach Crom* Dubh*. On a fine day one can see from there the spire of the cathedral in Cavan town.

Cavan is shaped like a fish, with its tail in Blacklion [26] and its head in Virginia [35], running in a north-west direction from Virginia, and its north-western area contains possibly the largest collection of sweathouses in Ulster apart from groups around Carrickmore in Co. Tyrone.

Sweathouses were discussed under Antrim, but as there are far more in north-western Cavan, a more detailed picture will be developed here. P. Richardson, writing in the *Ulster Journal of Archaeology* in 1939, stated that many people he talked with remembered the houses in existence up to the end of the nineteenth century. North-west of Dowra [27] in the foothills of a low mountain range, there are two townlands named Corrakeeldrum and Moneen, and here are several sweathouses. Women were responsible for tending the fire and bringing the turf to the houses. When the houses had become fully heated, the ashes were swept out and green rushes were thickly spread over the floor. Those entering removed their clothes and used them to block the doorway. At Moneen, sweathouses were used in autumn for their healing powers. As many as six people entered the houses at the same time, and after about an hour they went and plunged into a nearby stream; after this 'sweat bath', they went to bed.

Corrakeeldrum, which is adjacent to a stream, is described by Richardson (1939) as 'a small circular, beehive-shaped, drystone-built structure'. The interior diameter is approximately six feet in width and the height is just six feet. The entrance is roofed by two lintels, and there is a chimney at the west side of the house. The cures for many ailments were attributed to the sweathouse, among them gout, skin disorders and rheumatism. In the 1930s, many people in this region of west Cavan remembered a time when each townland had its sweathouse. At Moneen, an informant told Richardson of observing 'drifts of women going to the sweathouses'. Richardson recorded twenty-five sweathouses in the west Cavan area, and in the neighbouring county of Leitrim the same number exists to the present day.

With the coming of dispensaries, sweathouses were consigned to superstition and history. None of these markers of our medicinal history are protected as a national monument in the Republic, while only two are protected in Northern Ireland. Their numbers, according to two Ordnance Survey maps, halved over fifty years. The Archaeological Inventory of Co. Cavan published in 1995 records twenty-six sweathouses, with four cited as having 'no visible remains'. A sweathouse known locally as a 'duck house' is in the townland of Moneensauran, which is close to Glangevlin [27]. It is not marked on the *Discovery* map although it still exists and is a very good example. One wonders why such a unique reminder of our past can be treated in such a slovenly manner; if monuments to our history are ever to mean anything, let's start with the humble sweathouse.

DERRY

Doire Calgaich *or* Doire Cholm Cille, *'the oak grove of Calgach' or 'Columcille'*

Derry has been associated with Columcille since the saint established a church there in 546 AD. Oak trees, which first arrived on the island about 7,000 years ago, were sacred in prehistoric Ireland, and oak groves were used by the druids in many of their rites. It was an offence to interfere with them, and the *Annals of Ulster* record in 1083 AD how one violation led to the killing of Domnall Ó Cananáin, King of the Cenél Conaill, by his own people.

The county's main river is the Bann (from the Old Irish *ben dia* or *ban día*, a goddess, which is also found in *Bandae*, the Bandon River in Co. Cork). The Bann begins its journey out of Lough Neagh between the town of Toome in Antrim and The Creagh, a townland in Derry. It passes under the old railway bridge known as the Carlisle Bridge, then enters Lough Beg or 'small lake' before finally entering the Atlantic between Portstewart Strand and Castlerock.

The Bann, which legend says was first discovered by Partholón,* is one of nine rivers between Lí and Eille, territories lying east and west of the Bann, south of Coleraine. Legend says that Partholón led the first colony to Ireland more than 200 years after the Flood. *The Annals of Clonmacnoise* synchronised the arrival of Partholón with the twenty-first year of the Patriach Abraham, and the twelfth year of the reign of Semiramis, Empress of Assyria.

The ancient name in Irish for the mouth of the Bann is Túag Inbir, 'the bow-like river-mouth' [4]. The name has also long been associated with a daughter of a local chief named Conall Collamair. Túag was wooed by many kings and chiefly by the sea god Manannán mac Lir.*

A poem of forty verses titled 'Túag Inber' is attributed to a poet named Bard Maile who, according to Gwynn, 'must have borrowed it from the original on which his poem is based'. The original, like so many tales, has perished, but a similar tale may be found in the *Book of Leinster* where it is mentioned as *Tomaidm Locha Echach* – 'the eruption of Lough Neagh' – in a list of the Irish epic tales.

Some of the opening verses are as follows:

Túag Inber álaind, gáeth glass,
in eól dúib a dindshenchas?
in cualabair cen chaire
senchas Túaige tond-glaine?

Túag, ba taitnemach a dath,
ingen Chonaill Chollomrach:
rosalt asa ligi shiúil
Conaire mac Etersciúil.

Ó rogabsat rig rige
tochmarc Túaige tond-gile,
ro chúala Manannán mass,
co roscar hi cét-shercas.

Cartais Manannán mac Lir
techta úad dia hindsaigid
otá tech Manannán múaid
fri Túaig Inbir anairthuaid.

Ainm in techtairi 'ca thig
ba Fer Fí mac Eogabail,
dalta do mac Lir na lann
druí de thúathaib Dé Danann.

Túag Inber, lovely, grey-watered, do you know its legend? Have you heard clearly the story of Túag, bright of skin?

Túag (dazzling was her colour) was daughter to Conall of Collamair: Conaire son of Eterscél reared her from her birth-bed …

When the wide-ruling kings began to woo Túag, bright of skin, comely Manannán heard of it and loved her with his first love.

Manannán son of Lir despatched messengers to seek her from where mighty Manannán dwelt northeastward of Túag Inber.

The messenger's name, in his home, was Fer Fí, son of Eogabal, fosterling to Mac Lir of the blades: he was a druid of the Tuatha Dé Danann.

As harbingers of significant events, the Three Waves of Ériu were said to tremble and roar; they were the Wave of Clidna, at Glandore Harbour, Co. Cork, the Wave of Rudraige, at Dundrum Bay, Co. Down and the Wave of Túag Inbir.

[Translated by Edward Gwynn]

A battle between an Ulster king, Fergus mac Lede, and a former Ulster king, Conghal Cláiringhseach or 'flat-faced Conghal', was fought at *Aonach Inber Tuaighe* ('the assembly ground at Inbir Tuaighe'). The battle is included in the story of *Caithréim Conghal Cláiringhneach* ('The Martial Career of Conghal Cláiringhneach'). The tale belongs to the Heroic Period, although it is based around the mac Rory clan – the Ro-ech or 'great horse people' – in the pre-Cú Chulainn* stage of the Red Branch Knights. Insofar as it has a date, it would be about 20 BC in the early historical period. To illustrate this, it is worth noting that Congal's full name is Conghal Cláiringhneach mac Rudhraighe, or simply Conghal mac Rory.

The background to the tale is that the High King at Tara, Lugaid Luaigne, fearing the growing power of Ulster, decided to use the old political strategy of 'divide and conquer'. As a result, Conghal lost his kingship and Fergus mac Lede became sole King of Ulster. Conghal felt that his only option then was to do battle for this injustice, and he sought the help of the King of Meath and several disaffected chiefs. He then marched north, urging revolt throughout the province.

At this time, Fergus mac Roich was in Tara where nuptials were being celebrated between Fergus and the daughter of Lugaid Luaigne. After the wedding, Fergus left Tara to defend his territory against Conghal, but he fell out with Fergus mac Lede and sided with Conghal. Conghal then went on with Fergus mac Roich to destroy the ancient fortress of *Dún da Beann* ('the fort of the two peaks'), at Mountsandel [4], near Coleraine. At this rout, they took away Craob, the wife of the local king Niall Niamhglonnach. Rather than captivity, Craob threw herself into the Bann.

Mountsandel is believed to be the oldest inhabited site in Ireland, with radiocarbon dating showing the presence of people here 9,000 years ago. The original inhabitants, who were hunter–gatherers and had no knowledge of farming, arrived during the Mesolithic Age. They used flint points for cutting and small flint axes for chopping and killing. As many of these hunting tools were found in Denmark, it is not inconceivable that these people came from there. Excavations have shown Mountsandel to have been inhabited during the Neolithic and Bronze Ages as well as the Mesolithic. Local ploughing has turned up many small flint points or 'microliths', which were used in spears and arrows.

At a much later date, the fort there became the residence of a chief of the Ulaid, Niall Néamglonnach. The tale of the attack on *Dún Dá Beann* is told in 'The Martial Career of Conghal Cláiringhneach' and is included among the tales of the *craeb ruad* or Red Branch Knights. Here the eponymous Conghal says:

Let us move against the Dun of Niall
in battle array, sternly marching;
seize Niall himself in battle,
and Craobh daughter of Durthacht.

We shall harry his people,
multitudes, and hosts.
Bring hither his female retinue
to Aonach Tuaidhe.

[Translated by P.M. MacSweeney]

The attack on *Dún Dá Beann* included kings from Leinster, Connacht and the son of the King of Scotland. The attacking army first arrived at *Fertas Camsa*, 'the ford at Camus', on the river Bann near the old church of Camus, and from there proceeded two miles along the eastern shore of the Bann. They attacked the fort and broke down the wall, so that the whole place was reduced 'to dust and smoke'.

Five miles south-west of Coleraine on the B201 is a hill known as Sconce Hill [4], on the top of which are the remains of a stone citadel or a cyclopean stone fort known as the Giant's Sconce ('sconce' means a small stone or earthen fort). Its old name was *Dún Ceithirnn* ('the fort of Cethern'), and it is a hilltop cashel. Much of it is destroyed today, but it originally measured 495 feet by 288 feet. At the north-eastern end was a passageway or souterrain, the walls of which were nineteen and-a-half feet thick. It was demolished by looters in 1837. Cethern was the grandson of Niall of the Nine Hostages (*Niall Noíghiallach*). The northern Uí Néill (originally a Leinster tribe) were frequently in arms against the original inhabitants or the Picts, then known as the Cruithin.* It is possible the Uí Néill built this fort as a testament to their growing superiority, and to control the mountain range lying between north-eastern and north-western Ulster.

In 681 AD, according to the annals, Dungal, King of the Picts (Dál nAraide) and Cennfaelad mac Suibhne, King of the Ciannachta, were both burned to death here by Máel Dúin mac Máel Fithrich, King of the Cenél nEógain. Máel Dúin was consequently free to assert his line throughout the land, and the Cenél nEógain were High Kings of Ireland until the next inevitable slaughter – which, as it happened, took place in the same year at *Blá Sléibe*, where Máel Dúin was slain. There is an excellent trivallate fort, Dunglady or *Dún gCláidi* overlooking the Clady River, three miles north-east of Maghera.

Four miles south-west from Bushmills on the B17 lies Dunmull ('fort on the hilltop') promontory fort [4]. Dunmull is sited on a basalt plateau, and it has a rock-cup entrance. The table of the fort is about 327 feet by 654 feet. The place may have been an inaugural site, but nowadays it is in ruin; it does, however, possess a chair-like rock which would have been used for inaugural rites. This chair has also been called a 'witch's chair' but this would appear fanciful. Another stone has a footprint, and this was used in the kingly rites. An example of this type of stone can also be found at Clonalis House in Co. Roscommon, having originally been at the inauguration site at Carnfree, near Tulsk, Co. Roscommon. Dunmull also has a fine bullaun stone. A massacre of rebels occurred here in 1641 after they were captured by Crown forces under General Munro. The place has been used for get-togethers by locals during the May and Harvest festivals. Permission to visit the site must be sought at the local farmhouse.

Two miles north-west of Draperstown on the B40 motorway is the townland of Drumderg (*droim dearg*, 'the red ridge') [13]. Here in the south-east of the townland is a grave known as Dergmore's grave. As is common with the sagas of the Fianna,* there are a number of folktales associated with this grave. One such is that a son of Finn mac Cumhail* with the odd name of Derg mac an Draoigneain (from *draigen*, 'blackthorn') is buried here. He is said to have fought in Scotland against the Romans in the fourth century AD. Another tale relating to Derg is that he fought against Goll mac Morna and that Goll was victorious after a long and unremitting contest. Goll mac Morna was chief of the Connacht Fianna. According to yet another story, Derg was a giant from Scandinavia and was killed by Cú Chulainn.* The word *derg* when related to a person's name may refer to a red stripe on the face or body which serves as a form of identification with or membership of a particular tribe or sept. Thus we come across Lugaid Réoderg – 'Lugaid of the red stripe' – and Eochaid leth Derg, among others with this designation.

Leaving Draperstown on the B47, after seven miles south-west one should arrive at Glengomna, *Glen Gamna* ('the glen of the calf') [13]. The Glengomna Water runs through this glen and at its western end is bisected by the Ulster Way. The glen gets its name from the famous *Glas Gaibhleann* ('the grey white forked cow of the smith'), a cow recorded in the mythology and lore of many counties. The famous cow belonging to the smith god Goibniu,* or the Gabha, was noted for its inexhaustible supply of milk, and it was said that wherever she slept would be luxuriant and milk-producing. An old Irish saying refers to rich pastures thus: *Chodail an ghlas Ghaibhneach ann* ('the Glas Gaibhleann slept there'). In Glengomna the *Glas Gaibhleann* had one of her many calves, and thus the glen is named. According to a local legend here collected by O'Donovan, the glen was flooded by torrents of milk after the *Glas Gaibhleann* had calved. The *Glas Gaibhleann* has further connections with an adjoining townland named Labby just east of the Moyola River and two miles south-west from Draperstown on the B47 [13]. The local people stated to O'Donovan that the townland got its name from *leaba* ('bed'), and that this was the place where the mythic cow had slept. They claimed that the original name was *Leabaidh na Glaise* ('the bed of the grey cow').

Two miles south-west of Labby and on the south side of the Moyola River is a townland named Tullybrick or *Baile na Tulaí Brice* ('townland of the speckled hill') [13]. Here a stone column stood, known as Brackan Naglisha (*Breacán na Glaise*, 'speckled hill of the cow'). The *Glas Gaibhleann* was said to have been tethered to this stone, which locally was known as the 'the grey cow's tether'. This stone seems to have disappeared or to have been broken up. However, these townlands all share an association with the cow of the smith god, though in Tullybrick the stone column is said to have belonged to St Columcille.

About a mile east of Tullybrick is a townland known as Boley (*Buaile Cholm Cille*, 'Columcille's pasturage') [13]. In a general sense *buaile* means a 'milking place', but in a more specialised sense it refers to the custom of bringing cattle to the uplands to graze in summer, a practice known as transhumance or 'booleying'. The word *buaile* is represented in anglicised form by place names beginning with Booley, Boley, Boola, Bouly and Boula. 'Booleying' has been described as nomadism, but this is incorrect as the practice involves movement from a *permanent* home to a seasonal pasturage. Transhumance was practised along the mountain stretches of southern Asia, north-western Africa and southern Europe, especially in Switzerland, and as far north as Scandinavia. In Ireland it died out in the early nineteenth century. The Boley in question here has been described by O'Donovan as 'a green spot in the mountain' immediately above Lough Patrick. It was said to have been chosen by St Columcille 'as a place of meditation and prayer'. Situated just above Cow Lough, it would have been a natural place for watering cattle during the 'booley' season. A stone here was also known as the 'grey cow's tether stake'; this cow belonged to Columcille, and in this story it appears that the *Glas Gaibhleann* tale has been subsumed into the broader life of the saint. Less than half-a-mile above Cow Lough is a chambered grave, which could have acted as a marker for those summering with their flocks.

A gathering was held each year at Lough Patrick on St John's Eve, 23 June, and a few miles south-east on the Slieve Gallion range, fires were lit on 1 May for the feast of Bealtaine or Beltane. A mountain in this range is named Tintagh, as is a nearby townland, the name deriving from *tinteach*, meaning 'fire'. According to a John Mac Closkey, writing in 1821: 'Numerous crowds of both sexes assemble, and while the neighbouring hills and the plain below are blazing with the midsummer bonfires, indulge themselves in rustic amusements, dances, and thus pass the evening in harmless pleasures. But the priests seem to think it has ceased to be harmless: now they exert themselves to prohibit such meetings.'

Perhaps many of those attending the midsummer festivities were already pasturing their flocks at nearby Boley. They would have been familiar with the stone circle a half-mile west of Lough Patrick and the cairn a third of a mile north-west of the lake.

After travelling two miles north-east of Draperstown on the B41, one arrives at a point on the road from where one can see the Black Hill [13]. The hill, which is encircled by three ring forts, is on the right-hand side as one faces south. Its name in Irish is *Cnoc na Daróige Duibhne* ('hill of the black oak'). It was thus called after an ancient oak which once stood there, known as *Daróg an Oireachtais* ('the oak of the assembly'). The oak is a symbol of strength, kingship and endurance, and assemblies around the oak would have had significance in early Irish society, especially in May when the Beltane fire was 'kindled by rubbing a drill made of oak in a bore hole of an oak plank' (Cotter). A local farm is known as the Oak Farm. The Roman historian Pliny associated the oak with the druids, but its veneration in Ireland would seem to predate them.

Two miles north of Cookstown on the B162 is the parish of Lissan, which spans parts of Co. Derry and Co. Tyrone. *Liss Áine* means 'the fort of Áine' or, according to some, 'the marshy fort' or *liss enach*, anglicised as Lissananny. The latter would be the most normal interpretation, but in this case, as *Áine* is so connected with neighbouring Co. Tyrone, it is tempting to suggest that she may override the common topographical definition. The local river is also named the Lissan Water, and as Áine is a fertility goddess associated with water, it is in keeping that the river would be named after her.

In this area [13] there are three ring forts and a chambered grave. *Tober Áine* ('the well of Áine'), which had dried up by the nineteenth century, may well be in the present townland of Toberlane, which is a little over a mile south-west from Lissan. Along the river is a ravine named *Alt na Síon* ('the high creek of the whistling or keening'). It is said that when an O'Corra (Corr) is about to die, Áine is heard wailing in a plaintive tone there. According to local folklore, she was taken away from her husband's side at night by the *aes síde*, more commonly known as the 'wee folk'. Another hill associated with Áine is Crockanney or *Cnoc Áine*, two miles north from Lissan on the B162. It is situated between Lissan Water and a stream. Above Crockanney, there is a standing stone.

The famous convention of *Drom Ceat*, which ended the power of the poets or *filid*, was held on Mullagh Hill in the present-day Roe Valley Park, close to the River Roe and just west of Limavady [7], on the third weekday and the fourth day of the moon in the month of January 574 AD, according to the *Annals of Ulster*. The *Annals* here are very brief and simply note that Columcille and Aed mac Ainmire were present. The *filí* essentially performed a priestly role in pre-Christian Ireland and were also seen as seers or diviners. The higher class of *filí* practised *éicse*, or divination, and was part of a highly organised class whose functions were like that of the druids. They were classed among the *saernemed* or privileged classes. As St Patrick had either banned or limited many of their practices, it was only a matter of time before they would become a downgraded profession. In earlier times, the *filí* would act as judges and historians. They were charged at the convention of *Drom Ceat* with charging too much for their services and with being too populous. It was said by the historian Keating that one in three of all Irishmen were members of the *filí* class, a possible exaggeration, but suggestive that their ranks were becoming overcrowded. There were seven grades of *filí*, the highest of which was the *ollom filed* or master poet.

The banishment of the *filí* had already been proposed five centuries before in the reign of Conchobar mac Nessa, also due to the poets' unjust demands, but because of their protests they were kept on for seven years. Five hundred years later, they were still around. They would seem to have been most appreciated in Ulster. In the sixth century, Maolcobha, King of Ulster, retained them after they were banished, and their number amounted to 1,200 under Dallán Forgall, who wrote:

Feacht do Mhaolchoba na gcliar,
Ré hIobhar Chinn Tráchta aniar;

Dá chéad déag file fosfuair
Fris an Iobhar aniar-dthuaidh …

[*History of Ireland* by G. Keating]

When Maolcobha of the companions was once
At Iobhar Cinn Trachta [Newry] on the west side,
Twelve hundred filés he found
Behind the yew to the north-west.

Maolcobha, the chief gave them
Maintenance for three fair years.
It shall live to the day of pale judgment
For the well shaped race of Deaman [father of Maolcobha].

[*Translated by P.S. Dinneen*]

As the Irish Church developed, there was an overlap, with some *filí* appearing among churchmen. One such was Colman of Cloyne, who died in 604 AD and was known in his lifetime as the 'royal poet of Munster'. In time, the *filí* were replaced by bards whose verse quite often consisted of public speaking and writing for kings, patrons and benefactors; they thus sprang from a different well than that of our early *filí*. As a result of the overlap between the *filí* and the churchmen, the early monks introduced a Christian discourse into Irish literature and through the manuscript tradition preserved the foundation of the ancient literary culture.

Drom Ceat (575) as a local name has ceased to exist, and 'Daisy Hill' or the Mullagh is now regarded as the site where this famous convention was held. This loss of the original name has given rise to disputes about the actual site of the great convention. The Rev. Dr O'Doherty has written that in his opinion the convention was held not on the Mullagh but on the hill of Enagh on the opposite or eastern bank of the Roe. I cannot find O'Doherty's argument for Enagh being the site for *Drom Ceat*, and can only say that it is the site of an excavated Neolithic house and has an early Christian history. The possible answer is that, given the size of the gathering, both hills were presumably in use, as the eastern hill, now part of Limavady, is less than half-a-mile from the Mullagh.

The convention was attended by 10,000 persons called together by Aed mac Ainmirech, King of all Ireland, who came from Ailech in Donegal. The assembly consisted of kings, nobles, bards, clergy and a great following on horse and foot. As it is said to have lasted for almost a year, it is likely that not only the two hills were fully encamped but all along the banks and the site of the ancient town of Limavady as well.

The Mullagh is 182 feet high and gives its name to the local townland. The *drom*, or ridge, which is part of an esker drift, coincides with the ridge which runs north–south through the demesne of Roe Park for 460 yards. The mound at the Mullagh is part of the esker drift which has been cut off and levelled, according to Robert Cochrane, writing in the *JRSAI* in 1902. Cochrane also noted that 'a plateau of irregular oval shape, measuring about 200 feet by 100 feet, has been artificially formed'. Thus, Mullagh Hill would seem to have been constructed to allow a large number of persons to assemble at the level platform. This would have been impossible on the natural ridge. One might then surmise that the 'Ridge of Cette' was constructed to become the Mullagh, and that this was done to facilitate the great convention.

The River Roe runs six miles from the Mullagh to the sea and is navigable by boat. The chief of the *filí*, Dallán Forgall, in *Amra Choluim Chille* described the ecclesiastical aspect of the meeting as led by Columcille as follows:

> *Dá fhichid sagart a lion,*
> *Fiche easpog uasal bríogh,*
> *Fri gabháil psalm, clú gan acht,*
> *Caoga deochan tríochad mac.*

> Two score priests was their number,
> Twenty bishops of excellence and worth,
> To chant psalms, a practice without blame;
> Fifty deacons and thirty minor clerics.

[Translated by P.S. Dinneen]

Colgan, one of the scribes of the *Annals of the Four Masters*, wrote that Columcille attended the convention uninvited, and was accompanied by Aedan, King of the Scots, and his followers. He sailed from Iona, was nearly shipwrecked in Lough Foyle near the mouth of the River Roe, and by a miracle his frail barque was brought in a flood up the river, thus allowing him to attend the convention and take 'an important part in the proceedings'. He arrived close to *Drom Ceat* at a place which was named *Cabhain an Churaidh* or 'hills of the boat'. However, O'Curry in *Manners and Customs of the Ancient Irish* writes that Columcille came from I or Hy, now named Iona, and 'quite unexpectedly arrived at the meeting'.

The poets under their chief, Dallán Forgall, were no doubt full of anxiety as they assembled in the vicinity of Mullagh Hill. However, as Dallán Forgall was held in great respect by Aed mac Ainmire, an understanding was achieved. We do not know the specifics of this 'understanding'; suffice to say that regardless of the social changes occurring, there was sufficient recognition of the role of the *filí* to allow them to retain sufficient status as to appease them. As a result of this good news, all the poets rose and performed an *aidbsi* or chant in praise of Columcille. This is recorded in the twelfth-century *Lebor na hUidre* as *Amra Choluim Chille* ('Eulogy of St Columcille'), which is attributed to Dallán Forgall and is as follows:

Luin o cheolaib uingi o dirnaib
crotha ban náethech óc crothaib rígna.
ríg ic Domnall dord ic aidbsi
adand oc cainnill colc oc mo choilcse.

[*Lebor na hUidre*]

As the blackbird to the swans;
As the ounce to the *dirna* [a large mass of metal]
As the shapes of vassal women to the shapes of queens
As any king is to king Domnall
As all music is inferior to the *aidbsi*
As a rushlight to a candle
So is any sword compared to my sword.

[Translated by J. O'Beirne Crowe]

Besides curbing the power of the *filí*, there were two other reasons for the convention. The first was to arbitrate between the respective claims of Aed, King of Ireland, and Aedan, King of the Scots, to the kingdom of Dalriada, in Ireland. Aed wanted to impose a tribute on the Dál Riata of Scotland, as no tribute had been paid by them except that they were bound to raise an army by land and sea and pay an *eiric* or 'blood fine' in the case of murder. The second reason was to oust Scannlan Mór from the kingdom of Ossory, as he also had not paid tribute to Aed.

The three reasons for the convention at Drom Ceat were summed up by the chief poet at the meeting, Dallán Forgall, as follows:

Trí fátha fríotha don dáil,
Ar tí aithríoghtha Scannláin,
Um Dhál Riada, ríodhgha an treas,
Is um dhíochur na n-éi eas.

[*History of Ireland* by G. Keating]

There were three reasons for the convention:
In order to depose Scannlan from kingship,
The case of the Dál Riada, kingly the battle;
And the extermination of the bards.

[Translated by P.S. Dinneen]

When the convention concluded, votive offerings were made to acknowledge the safe deliverance of the saint and the king. Given that they arrived safely by boat, it has been suggested that the votive offering of a 'boat of gold' found at the neighbouring church of Broighter was in gratitude for the safe arrival of Columcille.

Broighter [7] is a mile west of the Ballymacran Bank of Lough Foyle. The Broighter gold find, dating from the Iron Age and from the beginning of the Christian era, consists of a collar, a torc, a necklace and a little boat complete with oars, all beautifully worked in gold. They were ploughed up in a field by the tidal River Roe close to the southern shore of Lough Foyle. Robert Lloyd Praeger in *The Way That I Went*, published in 1937, describes how the discovery was made:

> A Thomas Nicholl ploughing at Broighter, situated on the flat ground near the tidal Roe, in a field the surface of which was about four feet above high-water, turned up some rare and beautiful objects of gold – a collar richly ornamented with repoussé [raised or beaten into relief] designs of the Celtic Period; including a bowl, a torc and a necklace.

FIGURE 42. The gold boat from the Broighter Hoard.

The ploughman gave the objects to his employer, a Joseph Gibson, for a few pounds. Gibson then sold them at a great profit to a Robert Day of Cork, and he in turn sold the find to the British Museum for £600. When the Royal Irish Academy heard of the find, they contacted the state solicitor and claimed them as a treasure trove. However, the Trustees of the British Museum refused to part with the objects, claiming they were not a treasure trove because they were abandoned at sea and not buried on land. The Irish government then requested the English law officers take action so that the objects could be recovered. The British Museum contended that when the objects were deposited in the ground, approximately 1,500 years previously, the waters of Lough Foyle flowed over the land in question so that the objects were deposited with no plan of recovery, as they were possibly cast overboard as a votive offering and therefore abandoned.

Praeger then became involved when he was asked by the solicitor to the Treasury to demonstrate whether the land was dry or submerged at the time of the deposit. This led Praeger and another antiquarian named Coffey to excavate at a similar raised beach at Portstewart, Co. Antrim. Both of the above were then examined by Edward Carson, the Dublin-born lawyer of Oscar Wilde fame, but not before the ploughman who unearthed the gold hoard had stated that the hoard was about fifteen inches below the surface, and 'one part catched on the nose of the plough and it turned out of line'. After that, two classical scholars, Myers of Oxford and Jennings of the Ashmolean Museum, gave an in-depth account of votive offerings from the time of the Persian Xerxes to Finland to the Malay Archipelago, and even our shared sea god with Wales, Manannán mac Lir* was dragged in. All of this mythic aspect of the hoard made the judge restive, and he protested with the following words: 'I must express my opinion that the Court has been occupied for a considerable time in listening to fanciful suggestions more suited to the poem of a Celtic bard than the prose of an English Law Report.'

The result of all this was that the gold hoard was returned to Ireland and was for a while in the possession of the Royal Irish Academy. This collection remains to the present day in the National Museum of Ireland in Dublin. One must remember that the boat was well crushed by the plough or, according to the Law report, 'crumbled up', and what we have in the museum is a goldsmith's reconstruction. One could surmise that this type of craft is like the skin-covered currach still in use in parts of the west and north-west coasts.

Unfortunately, the date of the burial of the hoard has never been established, but is generally regarded as being at the beginning of the Christian era or more likely the beginning of the Christian era in Ireland if it was a votive offering celebrating the safe arrival of Columcille to Drom Ceat.

Another notable find in the county is the Bann Disc, a decorated bronze disc about four inches in diameter which was dredged from the River Bann at Loughan Island [4] near Coleraine in 1939. It is dated from the Iron Age between the first and second century AD. The relief patterns on the disc contain bird heads. The disc has been described by E.M. Jope and B.C.S. Wilson in an article published by the Ulster Archaeological Society in 1957 as follows:

The ornament consists of a swirling three-fold whirligig pattern generated by three fine raised lines flying out tangentially from a small central circle, which spin out to give the impression of a larger concentric circular area ... its whole restless swirling movement is stabilised and made a taut rigid structure by the binding lines in tension and suggests an interplay of rotational forces caught in a moment of time.

Its Early Iron Age decoration suggests both a British and a European influence. Its decoration in fine cast lines with individually modelled bird-head finials are regarded as masterpieces. Jope and Wilson say that the purpose of this disc is not clear, though the fact that chains were attached to three holes on the disc, with one bronze link still in place, suggests that it may have been used as a breast ornament or the central member of a ceremonial headdress. They conclude their appraisal of the disc with the following words:

Here we have in the products of this thin casting another group of objects connecting south Britain and Ireland in the 1st and 2nd centuries AD ... and showing how the Irish craftsmen took up, and made their own, the technical accomplishments of the workshops in just pre-Roman Britain and those of early Roman Britain which themselves had a strong native background even after the Roman conquest.

In 1949, a similar disc to the Loughan Island disc was found at Lambay Island, and this was classified by Macalister as from the La Tène period. It was dated by Dr Joseph Raftery at about 300 AD. The purpose of these ornaments remains somewhat vague, though presumably they were used in dressing for ceremonial customs. The Bann Disc is the logo of the Ulster Museum.

The drainage of the River Bann in the nineteenth and twentieth centuries led to the discovery of thousands of artefacts. The dredged material was taken by barge and placed in dumps from Toome, north-east of Lough Neagh [14], to Coleraine. Thus, the Bann has the potential to give archaeologists centuries' worth of artefacts, allowing them to assemble from these a picture of various ages in the history of the river. Examples of the finds are 700 or so axe heads and numerous flints used as tools during the Stone Age. The smaller and sharper flints were used as scraping tools in the processing of animal hides for clothing and for tent roofing.

One large artefact of the Bronze Age was the dug-out boat which survived on the Bann from the Bronze Age to the seventeenth century, to be replaced by the flat-bottomed cot, propelled by a single pole, which served the eel-fishers of the Bann. The tradition of eel-fishing on the Bann may well go back millennia, and today the fisheries are probably the largest of their kind in western Europe. Both salmon and eels are now exported, though salt salmon was exported to America in the eighteenth century. The ice-houses in which the salmon were preserved can often be seen in ruins in the county houses; the ice-house on the Bann close to Ulster University was sadly destroyed despite resistance from archaeological groups.

At Newferry north of Lough Beg [14], a Neolithic site was discovered after excavation in 1934. The Diatomite Co. Ltd. of Manchester, which had rights to diatomite deposits in the area, granted permission to the archaeologists to carry out an excavation on a site 500 feet west of the Bann and 700 feet north of Lough Beg. (Diatomite or diatomaceous clay is clay laid down in fresh water and formed from the silicified bodies of minute algae called diatoms. It is used as a filter or absorbent, among other uses.)

As the area was liable to flooding, the site could only have been used during the dry period of the year. The discovery of hearths led the team to believe that they were used for smoking and drying fish, which was the major occupation of the people responsible for the Bann Culture. A possible date for the site was placed at the beginning of the second millennium BC, the time of the Late Neolithic culture.

There is a possibility that the stone implements from the Bann are derived from the older coastal sites of Larne, Island Magee [9] and elsewhere on the north-east coast. In a monograph entitled *A Neolithic Site on the River Bann*, H.L. Movius writes:

> In the present state of our knowledge regarding the Stone Age of Ireland, the evidence points to the conclusion that the Bann culture, with its blade implements, is basically an indigenous North Irish development. It was probably derived from earlier coastal elements which had come in contact with a fully developed Neolithic civilization with *Campignian* affinities.

The raised beach at Larne has for many years been the focus of the Campignian culture, while close by on Island Magee have been found the remains of the Asturian culture. These two cultures represent the transition between the Old Stone Age and the New. To quote Macalister, 'They fill in the time, so to speak, that intervened between the final disappearance of the glaciers of the Ice Age and the establishment of modern climatic conditions.' He further writes that the Campignian culture

> seems to have originated in the lands bordering on the southern end of the Baltic Sea. Implements similar to those yielded by the Antrim raised beach have been found at Nöstvet in the south of Norway, in the famous shell heaps of the Danish coast, and then spreading westward through Northern Europe, and as far as the hill called Le Campigny (Seine-Inférieure) in France. The typical implements are the 'Campignian pick', a roughly chipped bar of flint, some four to six inches in length, with a blunt point at each end; and the 'kitchen-midden axe' or *tranchet* – a sort of chisel, having a straight sharp edge, intercepted between two plane faces. Both types of tool appear among the shore debris of the Antrim Raised Beach; they are sufficient to identify the dwellers on that beach as settlers from an area of Campignian culture–presumably from the Baltic area, whether they arrived by a direct or an indirect route.

The Asturian culture is associated with the north of Spain. Excavations in the caves of Asturias have revealed implements of a Mesolithic civilisation more or less contemporary with that of Campigny. The conically fashioned flint there is found in sufficient numbers at Island Magee to justify the assumption that an Asturian colony settled there.

It was on the north-eastern coast that the first people arrived in Ireland, and, like that of the later monks on the Skelligs [83], their diet consisted of fish, shellfish, seabirds and their eggs. As to the fate of our earliest ancestors, we have no knowledge: whether they fell to invaders or perished by plague or whether we today have some drops of their blood in our veins is difficult to determine.

One-and-a-half miles north of Derry in the garden of Belmont House, in the townland of Shantallow, is an inauguration stone known as St Columb's Stone. The stone originally stood in St Columb's Wells Street and then in the old cathedral. The stone, which is said to have been the inauguration stone of the O'Dohertys, is seven-and-a-half feet square and is embedded in the ground; it has two deep depressions ten inches long, placed side by side. Each depression is composed of two large, linked cup marks with a small one attached for the big toe. According to the inauguration rite, the chief of the O'Dohertys placed his feet in the footprints and gained strength from the stone.

DONEGAL

Dún na nGall, 'fort of the foreigners', a name first documented in 1447; prior to that the name used was Tír Conaill, 'Conall's territory'

Our exploration of Ireland's most north-western county begins on Tory Island (*Oileán Thoraí*) [1], nine miles off the coast and the most remote inhabited island of the country.

The island has a rich pre-Christian tradition and is also strongly associated with St Columcille, who travelled there to convert the people. However, the chief there, called Oillil, refused to allow Columcille to bless the island, after which the saint asked if he would be allowed the width of his cloak for his monastery. This was granted, and the cloak spread out until it covered the island. As a result of this piece of trickery, Oillil set his hound on the saint, but Columcille made a sign of the cross in front of the dog so that it flew into the air and landed on a stone where the marks of its paws are still visible. As it turned out, no one on the island wished for the new faith except an O'Duggan, and because of this the monastery was built on O'Duggan's land. This monastery existed until 1595 when the Elizabethan governor of Connacht, George Bingham, destroyed it.

Because of the conversion, the O'Duggan clan was given the sole right to the sacred clay on Tory. Apparently, the King of India, upon hearing of Columcille's good works, sent his six sons and daughters to hear him preach. However, after the long voyage they all died and were buried within the grounds of the monastery chapel. The corpse of the daughter constantly came to the surface of the grave, and eventually she was buried separately; it is from her grave that Tory clay is dug by the most senior member of the O'Duggan clan. The O'Duggan at the time of my visit in 2005 was Philip; his father was Dennis, and before him were Patrick, Anthony John and Dan. The grave from which the sacred clay comes is known as *Mór Shesúr* ('one [woman] more than six men'). The clay is highly prized, as it is said to ward off rats and protect fishermen. When giving it to anyone who has requested it, the O'Duggan says:

> *From age to age … from*
> *Generation to generation*
> *May you carry this gift.*

Also associated with Columcille are the remains of a round tower, which can be seen as one enters the harbour, a remnant of the monastery founded in the sixth century. It once possessed a brass bell, but this was stolen in the eighteenth century. Close by is the Tau Cross made from heavy mica slate. It is T-shaped with no section above the arms; some see connections with the Coptic Church of Egypt in this cross. It may be pre-Christian in origin.

An interesting custom on Tory was the use of 'cursing stones', which were carried anti-clockwise around the island while running barefoot as a curse was pronounced. This custom was known as *Turas Mór* or 'the long journey'. The most famous case involving the use of these stones was the sinking of HMS *Wasp* in 1884, with the loss of fifty-two men. The *Wasp* had been carrying out evictions along the west coast and was on its way to Tory to collect back taxes and rent; in the event of a failure to collect these, the young men were to be conscripted and the islanders evicted. Although the curse of the stones was said to have been responsible for the sinking of the *Wasp*, other reasons given were the rough seas or a conflict between the officers, policemen and sailors aboard. Six of the crew survived, and those taken from the sea were buried on the island. A local man, Seamas Uilliam Mac Ruairi, is said to have informed a Fr Eóghan O'Colm that the *Turas Mór* never existed but was merely a rumour spread by people from Malin and Inishtrahull. A vivid painting of the sinking of the *Wasp*, *No Cries of Seagulls*, was executed by one of the Tory primitive painters, Antoin Meenan, in the 1980s.

Perhaps Tory's strongest pre-Christian association is with the Fomorian* sun god Balor. As a sun god, he earned the epithet *súil Bhalair* or 'the eye of Balor', more commonly translated as 'Balor of the Evil Eye'. The spot where his shining tower was said to be sited is still known as Balor's Tower. As a mythical personage he was known as Balor mac Doit. It may be more than coincidental that the Dagda,* the sun god of the Tuatha Dé Danann,* was also known as Dagda Doit; in both cases the word *doit* means bright.

The Fomorians,* *lit.* a race from 'under the sea', are often regarded as being synonymous with the Phoenicians; this conjecture is reinforced by the similarities between Balor and their god Ba'al. Another name for Balor is Bel, which is also synonymous with Ba'al. Belteine, 'the fire of Bel' is also associated with Balor and is commonly translated as the month of May (in modern Irish *Bealtaine*). Ba'al was the title conferred on several gods by the Phoenicians; his mother was Asherat – 'of the Sea', who is reputed to have borne seventy children; she is also 'Creator of the Gods'. Mythological texts in cuneiform script written on clay tablets describing the Phoenician gods were discovered at Ras Shamra in Lebanon, and at Jebeil, a village north of Beirut. These texts date back to 1400 BC.

This writer saw a statue of Ba'al in the church of Our Lady of Tortosa in Syria; for those who do not wish to travel so far, there are at least two representations of Ba'al in the Louvre in Paris. Both are from Ras Shamra, one a statuette of Ba'al as the god of the tempest and wielding a lightning spear, the other a representation on a stela or stone slab of Ba'al with a club in one hand and a tree plant in the other.

An apocryphal story from the Book of Daniel in the Old Testament about Bel and the Dragon was in times past read out on Ash Wednesday and on 23 November in Anglo-Catholic churches. In the seventeenth century, Catholics were often called *Ba'alists* or *Ba'alites*.

When the Fomorians* or the Phoenicians arrived in Ireland more than 3,000 years ago, they commanded the waters between the Donegal coast and Tory Island. They were pirates yet also settled and intermarried with the local tribes. Their chief took the name of their god Bel or Ba'al. This was a common practice at the time, and it gave status to the chief as being in a direct line to the godhead. Thus, in folklore, rather than in mythology, Balor is recorded as a pirate as often as a god.

In one mythological story, Balor was told by a druid that his only daughter would have a son named Lug,* who would kill him. To avoid this, Balor imprisoned his daughter in a fort known as *Dún Balair*, a promontory fort at the eastern extremity of Tory Island. The story relates that there was a chief called Mac Kineely from Rath Finan (also associated with Dunkineely, five miles east of Killybegs) who owned a generous cow known as the *Glas Gaibhleann*. It was Balor's ambition to get possession of this animal; and this he did, and then sailed from Portnablahy ('the landing place of the buttermilk') across Tory Sound and into Port na Glaise, which is named after the *Glas Gaibhleann*, 'the grey cow of Goibniu',* the god of the smiths.

As a result of this, Mac Kineely sought the advice of a *leanán síde*, a familiar sprite, who dressed Mac Kineely as a woman, and he then crossed over to Port na Glaise on Tory. From there he went to Balor's daughter at *Dún Balair*, left her pregnant and returned to the mainland, where he was captured by Balor and beheaded at a place called after Kineely, namely Cloghaneely – *Cloch Chionnaola*, 'the stone of Kineely'; here there is a massive stone of quartz raised on top of a plinth, and on this stone Mac Kineely is said to have been beheaded. This stone can be seen today at Fort town, one mile north from Falcarragh, Co. Donegal [1].

Mac Kineely's son, Lug, avenged his father by thrusting a glowing rod from the smith's furnace through the eye in the back of Balor's head. This epic battle took place at Dunlewy, about five miles south-east of Bunbeg on the Gweedore road, or directly south of Errigal Mountain [1]. The Irish for Dunlewy is *Dún Lughaidh* or *Dún Lúiche*, both meaning 'the Fort of Lug'. Also found in the area are Dunlewy Lough and two glens both named Dunlewy Far, meaning 'beyond Dunlewy'. These glens are named *Dún Lúiche Íochtarach* or 'low-lying glens'. However, an older name for the glen is revealed in the name of the river running through it, *Abhainn Chró Nimhe* or 'the River of the Poisoned Glen'. Dunlewy Far to the west has a river running through it named the Devlin, which is a contraction of *Dubhlinne* or 'black pool', which runs into a lake known as *Loch na mBreac Méith* ('the lake of the plump trout').

Other accounts say that Lug* used a sling consisting of a missile containing conglomerate stone to kill Balor. This sling missive was called a *Tathlum*.

A *Tathlum*, heavy, fiery, firm,
Which the *Tuatha Dé Danann* had with them,
It was that broke the fierce Balor's eye,
of old, in the battle of the great armies.

[Eugene O'Curry, *Manners and Customs of the Ancient Irish*]

Balor's divinity was centred on his eye, which shattered all those who saw it. It was hidden behind a massive structure, which presumably protected a large glass mirror and faced the sun, so that when it was opened it had a blinding effect. Legend states that Balor's tower on Tory was made of glass. Lug,* who defeated Balor by smashing his 'eye', also carried the position of the sun god of his people. Thus, the name of the god changed to that of the dominant tribe, but the sun god remained at the core of the tribal mythology.

A number of places throughout Ireland are called after Bel, showing that the fire ritual of Belteine on the first of May, noted above, was observed throughout the country. In Donegal there are at least two places called Beltany: one [6] roughly two miles south of Raphoe and close to the Deele River, about a mile from which in a north-west direction there is a stone circle and standing stones; the other a mile south of Gortahork. It was customary to climb Beltany and the larger hill of Carn Treena, *Carn Traonach* ('the carn of the corncrake'), three miles south-west of Beltany and a mile west of Aspick Bridge on the N56. This local gathering was held on the feast of Lug* on 1 August until it died out in the early twentieth century. An account of the custom was given by an old woman in 1942, who had heard it from her mother. She related how the people brought 'flat cakes of oatmeal and milk' and would spend the day there picnicking. The boys gathered bilberries and with these made bracelets for the girls, competing to make the best and prettiest, for 'his own girl'. They would sing, tell stories, recite verses and dance. Before going home, the girls would take off their bilberry bracelets and leave them behind on the hillside. Given the name of the place, the custom presumably was held originally on 1 May but later moved to 1 August. Perhaps it was the lure of the bilberries that caused the switch.

FIGURE 43. The Grianán of Ailech.

Possibly older than Balor is the presence of Anu or Áine, the sun goddess, who is mentioned throughout Ireland. In south-west Donegal [10], a hill, Crockany, is associated with her. Crockany is one of the lesser-known sites associated with the goddess, but is as good as any of the others for viewing the sun as it sets on the Atlantic Ocean. To the north-west of Crockany are megalithic tombs and one also to the north-east.

According to legend, Partholón,* who led the first invasion of Ireland, is said to have settled just before the present town of Ballyshannon on *Inis Saimer* on the River Erne [16] (which corresponds to the River Ravios mentioned by Ptolemy) after sailing up the west coast from his original landing place at Rath Strand on the Kenmare River in Co. Kerry. On Assaroe lake east of Ballyshannon, there is another *Inis Saimer* (more commonly known as Sam's Island), the Irish word *saim* meaning 'a pair'. According to legend, the first battle fought in Ireland was fought on the plain of *Magh Itha* between the Fomorians* and Partholón, who was victorious. *Magh Itha* is one of the large, ancient plains of Ulster and extends south-west of the Foyle and between the rivers Deele and Finn.

According to Keating, Partholón* divided Ireland into four parts among his sons. He gave the first part to Er – that is, all the territory from *Ailech Néid* in the north of Ulster to

Ath Cliath (Dublin) in Leinster. *Ailech Néid* is today more popularly known as the Grianán of Aileach (*Grianán Ailigh*, 'the sun chamber of Ailech'); it is situated on the Inishowen peninsula [3] three miles west of Derry city and features a stone-built hilltop fort. At a later stage, Ailech was the name for the kingdom of the northern Uí Néill who in the fourth century AD controlled the present counties of Tyrone and Donegal. Dagda,* the King of the gods, and the later chieftains who were descended from him are said to have had their castle there. Legend also says that the builder Frigrinn was the architect of Ailech in the fourth century. Frigrinn was a young Scottish chief who eloped with Ailech, the daughter of Fubtairé, the King of Scotland, and brought her to Ireland where they were put under the protection of Fiacha, a local king who gave them an ancient fortress. He built a residence close by and called it Ailech. The Munster poet Fland Mainistrech wrote a poem about Ailech in the eleventh century, which begins:

> *Cia triallaid neċ aisneis*
> *senċais ailiġ e altaiġ*
> *d'eis eaċtach áin,*
> *is gait a cloidib allaim Hectáir.*

> Should anyone attempt to relate
> the history of host-crowded Ailech,
> after Eochaidh the illustrious,
> It would be wresting the sword out
> of Hector's hand.

> *[Translated by Edward Gwynn]*

An earlier poem about Ailech is attributed to Cuaradh, a tenth-century poet and possibly an Ó Néill. The poem consists of twenty-eight stanzas and is titled *Décid Ailech nImchill nÚaib*. It begins:

> *Décid Ailech nImchill n-úaib*
> *sosad slúaig sírthenn síl Néil*
> *fert fo dáenai Banbai mhbáin.*
> *Aída áin meic Dagdai déin.*

> Behold Ailech from all sides
> home of the hosts of Niall's vigorous race,
> mound of the assemblies of noble Ireland,
> and the grave of Aedh, son of the powerful Dagda.

The twelfth verse is as follows:

Ailech nImchill os cech áit
dia do báirc birchinn frí ét
la Tuatha De dremuin dúairc.
Cuaird I mbaí Nemain is Nét.

Behold Ailech above all places
the sharp crested strong hold
jealously guarded by the vigorous Tuatha Dé,
which was on the circuit of Nemain and Nét.

[Translated by Edward Gwynn]

Nuadu, an ancient king of Ireland, is said to have been buried at the Grianán of Aileach. A small statue of him is to be seen in the Anglican Cathedral on Armagh Hill in Armagh city.

A second legend regarding the naming of Ailech concerns Aedh, mentioned in the verse above as the son of the Dagda.* He had an illicit affair with Tethra, the wife of a friend of the Dagda's named Corrgenn, a chief from Connacht. After Corrgenn killed Aedh during a feast at Tara where the Dagda was the host, the Dagda forced Corrgenn to carry the dead Aedh on his back until he had found a stone to fit him exactly in length and breadth, and sufficient to form a tombstone for him. Corrgenn found such a stone close to the shore of Loch Foyle, and his moans and groans after all his exertions led to his death and to the naming of Ailech from the *achs* of the groans combined with the *ail* for the stone. On a more mundane level, *ailech* simply means 'stony' or a place made of stone.

The name Aedh is also associated with a waterfall that existed at Ballyshannon before it became a hydroelectric power station. It is known as the Assaroe Falls or *Ess Ruad*, 'the waterfall of Aed Ruad', another name for Aedh. Aed means 'fire' and he is a sun god and a god of thunder and lightning; according to legend, he was drowned in the water beneath the waterfall where he is said to still reside. There are two recorded mounds associated with Aedh at Ballyshannon: *Síd nAeda* at Assaroe or Mullashee and *Síd Aeda Esa Ruaid*.

Assaroe also features in a tale from the Fenian sagas. It concerns Cailte, a cousin of Finn mac Cumhail* and a member of his warrior party, who was staying at the fort of Ilbreac at the Falls during the *Samain*, three days before and three days after Hallowe'en, during which time the spirits of the dead arose. Assaroe also plays a part in perhaps the great love story of early Ireland, 'The Exile of the Sons of Uisnech' (*Longes mac nUisnig*), which is said to have inspired the Romantic movement in Germany. Deirdre was loved by Naoise, one of the sons of Uisnech, but the High King Conchobar mac Nessa* had a right to her and this he was determined to pursue. When Naoise and Deirdre eloped, they set out for Assaroe, so this ancient waterfall associated with the god Aed must have been a noted place as far back as the first century AD. After being

FIGURE 44. The statue of Nuadu in St Patrick's Cathedral, Armagh (Anne Cassidy).

pursued there, they fled to Howth in Dublin and eventually went to Scotland, where they settled for a while.

The River Finn flows into Lough Finn (*Loch Finne*) just below Fintown, fifteen miles south-west from Letterkenny [11]. A story from the Fenian cycle is based here and tells of a woman named Finda or Finne, after whom the lake is called. When Finn mac Cumhail* had a feast in the Finn Valley close by, he asked two of his warriors, Gaul and Fergoman, to bring him a fierce bull who grazed on the borders of the lake. On their way they came across a litter of pigs at Lough Muck ('the lake of the Pig'), about half-a-mile south-east of Lough Finn, which they slaughtered and left, intending to call for them on their way back and bring them to the feast. Finn, sensing some impending evil, ascended a hill and called to his heroes to return by a different route. Gaul followed Finn's instructions but Fergoman returned to the spot where the pigs were. On arriving, he saw a large sow standing over the bodies of her piglets. The sow sought vengeance and attacked Fergoman, and in the furious fight that ensued Fergoman called to his sister Finne, who happened to be standing at the same side of the lake. However, hearing the echo (*macalla*) from the cliffs on the opposite side, she immediately plunged in and swam across. As she reached the shore, the voice came from the side she had left, and when she returned the voice came again from the opposite cliffs. Thus, she swam back and forth until she eventually drowned in the middle of the lake. (When I was there with a friend in the early 1990s, we met a couple who had built a new house and were wondering what to call it; a few days later we met them again and they told us that they had decided to name it 'Macalla' on account of their proximity to the lake.)

Two other places which may be associated with the story are *Mínte Mórgail* ('the smooth plains of great fury') and *Mín na Scróna* ('the flat-topped place of the snouts'). A megalithic tomb stands right between Lough Muck and Lough Finn at Crockannaragoun and existed long before the events at the two lakes occurred or the story was conceived.

During the reign of Fergal mac Maoiledúin, King of Ireland in the seventh century AD, three unusual showers fell throughout Ireland, two of them in the vicinity of Fahan, a village three miles south from Buncrana overlooking Lough Swilly [2]. A shower of honey fell on *Fahan Beag* and a shower of silver on *Fahan Mór*. Also during the reign of Fergal, a shower of blood fell on the Plain of the Liffey in Leinster. Fergal was King of Ireland for seventeen years and was eventually defeated at the Battle of Allen beside the Hill of Allen in Co. Kildare. He was a descendant of Niall of the Nine Hostages and died in the eighth century.

On the Inishowen Peninsula just south of Inishowen Head is *Srúib Brain* or Stroove [3], which translates as 'the snout (or headland) of Bran' and is one of the three *oirrderca* or famous places of Ireland. The story of Bran is known as *Imram Brain*, the *imram* being a voyage to the Otherworld, which was also known as *Magh Mell* or 'the plain of honey'. *Imram* literally means 'rowing about'. The *imram* stories are among the oldest tales preserved today. Bran is said to have set out from *Srúib Brain* on the entrance to Lough Foyle and voyaged until he arrived in Kerry at a place also known as *Srúib Brain* or Stroove. It is assumed that the voyage was from Donegal to Kerry, as *Magh Mell* was in the south-west. The sea was believed to 'fall down' at the horizon of the 'flat earth'; the Otherworld was therefore not too far off, and one entered it quickly. The *imram* could have been an ancient rite practised before death. The later tale of the voyage of St Brendan may well have fallen into this category, but, rather than a sudden entrance to the Otherworld, St Brendan went on to discover the 'New World'.

Srúib Brain is also associated with Éremón, the son of Míl, the progenitor of the Gaels. Éremón and his brother Éber divided Ireland between them, and Éremón's half extended from the Boyne River in Co. Meath to *Srúib Brain* at the entrance to Lough Foyle in Donegal. A quatrain from the *Dinnseanchas* of *Magh Slecht* alludes to Éremón and his time:

Since the rule
of Éremón, the noble man of grace,
there was worshipping of stones,
until the coming of Good Patrick of Macha.

[Translated by Kuno Meyer]

The Inishowen peninsula is connected with an early meteorological event in Ireland, an event which occurred at *Ard Uilinne* at the end of a drought in 764 AD:

Tri frosa Aird Uilinne
ar gradh Neill do nim:
fros argait, fros tuirinne,
ocus fros do mhil.

[Ruaidhrí Ó Luinín, 1489 Annals of Ulster]

Three showers at Ard Uilinne
[Fell] from heaven for love of Niall:
A shower of silver, a shower of wheat,
and a shower of honey.

[Translated by Seán mac Airt and Gearóid mac Niocaill]

A tale from *Agallamh na Senorach* or 'The Discourse of the Old Men' relates how Finn mac Cumhail* was hunting with six companions in Donegal and sat down on the mountain of *Bearnas Mór* (Barnesmore), twenty-two miles south-west of Letterkenny [6]. His party startled a wild boar and sent their dogs after him, but the boar killed them all except Bran, Finn's hound, which captured the boar. The boar let out a roar, and soon a giant of a man appeared from the hill and requested that the hog should be set free.

The companions of Finn attacked the man, but he overcame them and tied them up. He then invited Finn to his *síd* or fairy mound at *Glenndeirgdeis*, an invitation both Finn and the Fianna* accepted. At the door of the *síd*, the giant struck the boar with a stick and the animal turned into a beautiful young woman. Finn and his friends then entered the fairy hill and sat down to a feast. At the feast Finn fell in love with the young woman, whose name was Scathach ('shadowy one'). Finn asked her father, the giant, for her hand in marriage and her father assented. After much music and merriment, Finn retired to his rooms, expecting his bride to follow, and this she did. But before joining him she asked for the loan of a musician's harp:

Cruit baoi istigh ar thrí téad,
dar liom fa sulcharr in séud;

téad diarann, teud dumha an,
an ceadna darccod iomlán.

Anúair do éirigh grian osfiodh,
dhoibriomh níor bhadhbhal ancion;
ann robhádor imbéarnuis,
ger lugha leo a ttigernus.

The household harp was one of three strings,
methinks it was a pleasant jewel:
a string of iron, a string of noble bronze,
and a string of entire silver.

When the sun had risen over the woods,
to them it was no mighty loss;
where they found themselves was at *Bearnas*,
which showed their diminished power.

[Translation by Eugene O'Curry from a twelfth-century manuscript]

Malin Head [3] is the headland at the top of the Inishowen peninsula and the most northern point on the island of Ireland. It is also known as 'Banba's Crown', Banba being one of a triad of godesses associated with Ireland along with Ériu (or Éire) and Fódla. They represented different aspects of the island: Ériu the territory, Fódla the intellectual, and Banba the warrior aspect. Banba was a queen of the Tuatha Dé Danann* and was slain by Caicher at the battle of Telltown in Co. Meath. She was buried at Cruachain in Connacht. She may have taken her name from an older Banba who is said to have been the first woman to enter Ireland and thus rightly claimed sovereignty.

Inis Keel near the mouth of Gweebarra Bay [10] is where the poet Dallán Forgall, who wrote *Amra Cholmchoille*, the famous elegy on St Columcille, was killed about the year 594 AD. He is buried in the church founded by St Conal.

An Mam Mór, the 'Gap of Mamor' [3], is situated on the Inishowen peninsula, and the 'five fingers of Finn' are said to be in this area. However, no stones are to be seen on the *Discovery* map. There is a small loch nearby and a hill named Mam Mór Hill.

Another place associated with Columcille is at *Ceall mhac nÉanáin*, or Kilmacrenan [6], east from the Rock of Doon, the inauguration site of the princes of *Tír Conaill*. Keating in his *History of Ireland* says:

I gCill mic Creannáin do gairthí Ó Domhnall; agus Ó Fiorghail do ghaireadh é, agus Ó Gallchubhair a mharuscál sluaigh.

In Kilmacrenan, O'Donnell was inaugurated, and it was O'Farrell who inaugurated him, and O'Gallagher was the marshal of the hosts.

An account of the ritual inauguration of the Ó Domhnall chiefs of *Tír Conaill* was written in Latin by Philip O'Sullivan Beare in 1625 when he was living in Spain, where he had joined his uncle, The O'Sullivan Beare. According to O'Sullivan, the rite at the time had become fully Christianised and included 'a Mass … celebrated with great solemnity'. A rod was consecrated to be used as a sceptre for investing the prince. He professed his faith on a book of the Gospels copied by the hand of St Columcille. At the end of the ceremony he left the church and went to the secular and possibly pre-Christian site at *Carraig Dúin* or Doon, two miles west from Kilmacrenan, where he mounted a horse and was proclaimed King of *Tír Conaill*. The word *ascendo* in O'Sullivan's record in Latin has been translated as 'to get upon [the female] for the purpose of copulation, mount'.

O'Sullivan's version gives a more sanitised account than that of Gerald of Wales, who wrote towards the end of the twelfth century that the inauguration rite consisted of a symbolic mating with a mare, eating its flesh and drinking the broth in which its flesh has been cooked and bathing in its blood. The king sought fertility for himself and his people by performing this rite. This rite is also found in the Gaulish cult of Epona, the horse goddess found on statuettes and reliefs in France and Germany. She was also held in high regard among the cavalry of the Roman army. Her cult extended from Spain to eastern Europe and from northern Italy to Britain and Ireland. Closer to home is the horse goddess Macha, who is the eponymous goddess of Armagh (*Ard Macha*).

The last king installed at Doon was Aodh Ruadh Ó Domhnall in 1592; after the defeat at Kinsale he went to Spain and was poisoned and died at Simancas in 1602. The poet to The O'Donnell (an anglicised way of referring to the chief of the clan) was Ferghal Óg mac an Bhaird, and part of a poem he wrote for this last inauguration at the Rock of Doon [6] is as follows:

D'fhior Dúine nach dáigh as a chuirmthighibh
Turnfidhir glúine cáigh mar as chomh-chubhaid
flaitheas na Banbha re theas tuill-fidhir
cuirfidhir na habhla theas fa throm-chumhaidh.

To the prince of Dún who has no rival in banquet-halls
the knees of all men shall bend, as is proper;
rule over Banba shall be merited by the warm weather [he brings]
and fruit trees shall be planted in the South beneath his strong rule.

[Translated by Osborn Bergin]

Another inauguration site is at Doonan Rock (*Carraig an Dúnáin*) on Doonan Hill just to the west of Donegal town [11] and thirty-five miles south from Kilmacrenan. This is said to have been the inauguration site of the *Ua Canannáin*, who were chiefs of south Donegal. Their name derives from the Irish *cano*, meaning 'wolf cub', and the English version is O'Cannon or simply Cannon. The rock rises to a height of about 197 feet and is composed of greenstone, which consists of basalt and feldspar. Basalt comes from lava which has cooled under the sea, and its unusual green colour led people to believe that it had magical properties. St Columcille was presented with a round, green stone which he used to ward off demons. Green was also indicative of royalty, and kings or chiefs wore green cloaks as a symbol of their position.

The site consists of a series of terraces known as the Green Stone Dyke or Greenstone Crag. The ceremony included the killing of a white ox and the making of a broth from the animal in a large cauldron, which the chief sat in up to his chin and drank; only members of his clan could partake of this ritual drink. As with the rite at Kilmacrenan, Gerald the Welshman is fairly explicit about the ritualistic details:

> When the whole people of that land [Donegal] has been gathered in one place, a white mare is brought forward into the middle of the assembly. He who is to be inaugurated, not as a chief, but as a beast, not as a king, but as an outlaw, has bestial intercourse with her before all, professing himself to be a beast also. The mare is then killed immediately, cut up in pieces, and boiled in water. A bath is then prepared for the man in the same water. He sits in the bath surrounded by all his people, and all, he and they, eat of the meat of the mare which is brought to them. He quaffs and drinks of the broth in which he is bathed, not in any cup or using his hand, but just dipping his mouth into it about him. When this unrighteous rite has been carried out, his kingship and dominion have been conferred.

This real or symbolic mating of a new king with a mare represents the fertility of earth. This rite has similarities to the Bull Feast (*tarb fes*) at Tara, where the broth of a bull was drunk. The latter rite also involved the inauguration of a king.

Ten miles south from Doonan Hill on the N15 is another inauguration site, namely *Árd Fothaid* or 'the foundation site' (for kings) [11]. This important place is located at present day Ardpattan Hill. In the *Annals of Clonmacnoise* it is termed Ardfahie, and the *Annals* also say that Donell mac Aedh or later MacHugh died here in 641 AD. According to the *Book of Lecan*, he was slain here after returning from Rome:

> *Bás Domhnaill mic Aodha mic Ainmireach ri Éireann in Árd Fothaigh.*

> Donell mac Hugh, King of Ireland, died at *Árd Fothaid.*

This territory is known as the barony of *Tirhugh*, or the land of Mac Hugh. As well as being an inauguration site, *Árd Fothaid* was a royal fort. As Glasbolie Hill has also been suggested as the 'foundation site', the actual location of the centre of the Mac Hugh kingdom is open to speculation. *Árd Fothaid* is four miles north from Ballyshannon [16] or, more precisely, turn left at the crossroads after four miles and take the road for Coolmore, and Ardpattan Hill can be seen a mile down this road on the left-hand side. On the right of this road is Ardpattan Lake.

Loch Derg (*Loch Dearg*, 'the red lake') [11] is situated about ten miles north-east from Ballyshannon; it does not get a very favourable review from R. Lloyd Praeger in *The Way That I Went* (1937), in which he states: 'Out to bleak peat covered hills to the eastward lies Lough Derg, dreariest of Donegal waters, one of the most famous places of pilgrimage in the country.' The monastery on what is known as Station Island was said to have been founded by St Daveog, a disciple of St Patrick, and Patrick himself was said to have purged himself of sin here – thus the association of the island with 'St Patrick's Purgatory', though St Brigit also gets a look in here with a large block of stone known as St Brigit's Chair. According to Christian belief for a long time, only saints had direct access to Heaven, while everyone else, if they were not damned to Hell, had to purge themselves in the fires of Purgatory. Thus arose the practice in medieval Christianity of earning 'indulgences' to shorten Purgatorial torture by donating money to the Church or by making a pilgrimage to a place like Lough Derg, where the rigours undergone, such as fasting and other self-inflicted abuse, guaranteed extra bonus points. It remains a popular destination for pilgrims.

Referring to the 'pagan origins', one wonders why the cave on the island is seldom discussed, as this was the entrance to the Isles of the Blest in the pre-Christian tales and the exit for Purgatory in the Christian context. But let us begin our pre-Christian story with the Voyage of Connla, the son of Conn Cét Chathach, who is invited to *Magh Mell* by a goddess and requested to go there with her on a *noi glana* or a 'currach of pearl'.

The currach of Connla and the goddess move in the direction which 'drowns down the white sun', and according to J. Beirne Crowe in *The Adventures of Condla Ruad*,

> this [direction] is in accordance with the general tradition of pagan nations; the point of departure from the world as well as the entrance to the next, whether for pain, bliss or business was always on the west, and the route westwards. For the ancient Irish belief on this point we can appeal to the Vision of Adamnán, which gives 'the angels of the west' the guardianship to the entrance to the region of punishment, as well as to the cave of Loch Derg, which is most decidedly a pagan relic. The cave of Loch Derg is situated in the west of Ireland as the corresponding cave of Avernus is situated in the west of Italy.

We shall end with one pre-Christian view of the land beyond the west and part of a poem on Loch Derg by Patrick Kavanagh:

Is ed a tír subatar
Menmain cáich dodomchele:
Ní fil cenél and nammá,
Acht mná ocus ingen.

It is the land which delights
The mind of everyone who turns to me:
In it no living race is found
Save women and maidens only

And from Kavanagh:

Lough Derg, St. Patrick's purgatory in Donegal.
Christendom's purge. Heretical
Around the edges: the centre's hard
As the commonplace of a flamboyant bard.
The twentieth century blows across it now
But deeply it has kept an ancient vow.

DOWN

An Dún, 'the fort'

The largest ring fort in Ireland is the Giant's Ring [15], a great, banked ritual enclosure with a circumference of a third of a mile overlooking the River Lagan. It is in the townland of Ballynahatty, four miles south from the centre of Belfast. The ring-bank is 60–70 feet wide at the base and twelve feet high, enclosing a circular area 650 feet across and seven acres in extent. According to Estyn Evans, the bank is composed of 'fluvio-glacial gravel and small boulders'. At the centre of the ring is a dolmen or single-chambered grave consisting of five uprights with a capstone seven feet across. Cremated bones have been found in this chamber. The monument or dolmen is an example of a stone grave which is to be found all along the western Bronze Age trade route from the east Mediterranean to the regions of England and Ireland, producing the metals of copper, gold and tin.

Down to the eighteenth century the ring was used as a racecourse. Excavation work on the Giant's Ring was carried out in 1917 by Henry Lawlor on behalf of the Belfast Natural History and Philosophical Society. Later, Pat Collins did three weeks of excavation in 1954.

According to Lawlor in *Ulster: Its Archaeology and Antiquities*, the best example in Ireland of a great circular or oval wall is the Giant's Ring.

The enclosing-wall around this cromlech is made entirely of small stones carried from all the surrounding country; the sacred area enclosed by the wall is about ten

FIGURE 45. The dolmen at the centre of the Giant's Ring.

acres; the almost circular wall originally of small stones, has in the course of 4,000 years, been overspread with a thin covering of soil so that from a superficial glance it appears to be made of earth.

Lawlor surmises that the earthen bank of fifteen feet arises from two causes: the common earthworm piling up the earth over the millennia, followed by birds nesting and dropping their seeds which grew into plants and gradually decayed into soil. Barrie Hartwell writing in *Archaeology Ireland in* 1995 seems to have another theory which states that 'the bank was created from a shallow internal scoop and may originally have been revetted on the inner face'.

Yet its original significance was as a gathering place for Late Neolithic and Early Bronze Age burial rites. As the Giant's Ring was the assembly point, the next field north known as BNH5 or Ballynahatty 5 was the ritual centre for Late Neolithic ceremonies. Here Barrie Hartwell from Queen's University did significant work both in excavating the site and using postholes to recreate its original appearance as a ceremonial centre. Part of these rites may have involved placing certain notable skulls here, and as if to support this theory, an ancient sepulchral chamber was discovered in 1855. The local farmer had taken the skulls found here and locked them up in his house to protect them from injury. It is important to note that at least two of these heads were female.

The skull in pre-Christian mythology was where the spirit was placed, as opposed to the Christian tradition, where the heart symbolising love was central to belief. Thus, the separation of the head after death was not unusual; for instance, we can find such examples as the skull of the female Eitech, from whom the village of Kinnity in Offaly gets its name. The temporary burial of Cú Chulainn's* head in Tara and the triple-headed god Conn from Cavan, known as the Corleck Head, shows the reverence to the cult of the head. Thus, among the other rites performed at BNH5, the ceremonial burial of the head was significant if not central. To reinforce the above, I will quote the following from John O'Donovan's footnotes to the *Annals of the Four Masters*: 'The practice of removing the head from the trunk in order to bury it in some celebrated locality must have been one of not unusual occurrence among the early Irish.'

Belfast Lough in Co. Down is credited by some with being the site of the invasion into Ireland from Britain by the Érainn, a pre-Gaelic race. Originally, this tribe was known as the Iverni according to the Egyptian geographer Ptolemy, writing about 100 AD but drawing on sources from at least 300 years prior. The Érainn are also known as the Fir Bolg* or Belgae of the Continent and of Britain. The invasion legend of the Érainn says that they were of the same stock as the Britons and their leader was Lugaid mac Dáire. Prior to the invasion, the indigenous people of Ireland were the Cruithin* or Picts. The Érainn took their name from the god Érann, who was a sun god. The female equivalent of Érann was the goddess Ériu, who gave her name to the whole island.

Lugaid has a number of names, among them being Lugaid Mál, Lugaid Mac Con and, as mentioned, Lugaid mac Dáire. These are possibly one and the same person, as legend states that Dáire the father of Lugaid was told by a *cailleach* or wise woman that one of his sons named Lugaid would be King of Ireland – so he named them all Lugaid. Lugaid came to Ireland and conquered the indigenous Cruithin.* Lugaid arrived with seven ships and landed at *Carn Máil* on the south side of Belfast Lough, east of Grey Point [15]. The question is, where is *Carn Máil*? Also known as *Carn Lugdach* from the aforementioned Lugaid, it has been linked to the townland of Carnaleagh, *carn laoich*, 'the carn of the hero', two miles west from the town of Bangor. Vol. 1 of the *Ulster Journal of Archaeology* (1853) states that *Carn Máil* or Carnaleagh 'is a rock projecting out from the coast between Grey Point and Crawford's Burn [on the shores of Belfast Lough] and gives its name to the lands adjoining'. According to this source, there is a small rath or tumulus near the spot. The Rock of Carnaleagh was often mentioned in some late legal trials at Belfast as a boundary in several patents. It was regarded as the spot near high-water mark where it was usual to bury suicides.

It is said that prior to the battle at *Carn Máil* each man carried a stone, and thus the cairn was formed on which Lugaid stood on as the battle was being fought. A small mound was said to exist near the point of the rock, but this is not mentioned in the *Discovery* map, nor anywhere that I can find. Maybe it is a small hillock on the thriving golf club at Carnalea.

Lugaid's victory at Carn Máil is recorded in the *Dindshenchas*.* Here are three verses describing this victory:

Iarsin tic anuas co lúath,
do chur chatha fo chomúat
cloch cach óen-fhir tuc 'sin cath
de do ringned carn Lughdach.

Is and roboí Lugaid mál
isin charn chloch-throm chnes-bán,
cor-róemid in cath mór mend
for firu áille hÉrend.

Rogab Lugaid il-Lius Breg
gíallu Gall ocus Gáedel;
rí ris' torgbad in carn cruind
fail ar maig Ulad óebind.

Then down he comes with speed to offer battle, even matched; a stone for each fighter he brought to battle, with these was built Lugaid's cairn.

There stood Lugaid Mal, on the massy white sided cairn, till he brake the great and famous fight against the goodly men of Erin.

Lugaid received at Less Breg hostages from Gall and Gael: he was the king that rearted the round cairn which stands above fair Magh Ulad.

[Translated by Edward Gwynn]

As in so many myths, one myth is countered by another one. The countering myth is that Lugaid Mál was descended from Íth who was of Milesian or Gaelic stock, and that he was here all the time ever since his return from having been banished to Scotland. As throughout history, the myths of the oppressors become the dominant ones, so the narrative of Lugaid Mál being of Gaelic stock has been preserved in the above poem from the *Dindshenchas..*.* Even today, it is said and written that Ireland was first invaded by the Milesians from Spain rather than Britons. In the Gaelic version of the story the reappearance of Mac Con results in internecine battle among the Gaels, whereas in the earlier version it is a battle between the Érainn and the Cruithin* or Picts.

A famous battle between the Cruithin* or the Dál nAraide and the Laigin or the Uí Néill was fought at *Magh Rath* or present-day Moira [20] between Lurgan and Lisburn. There are two raths or ring forts, one known as 'rough fort' and the other as 'Pretty Mary's fort', both situated south of the village. However, the battle fought in 637 AD was possibly fought north of the River Lagin about the townlands of Maghahinch and Magheralin, just south of Moira. This is regarded as a significant battle and is recorded in the *Annals of Ulster*, the *Chronicon Scotorum*, and the *Annals of the Four Masters*. The annalist Tigernach writes about it as follows:

> A.D. 637. The Battle of Magh Rath was fought by Domhnall, son of Aedh, and by the sons of Aedh Slaine (but Domhnall at this time ruled Tara), in which fell Congal Cáech mac Scannail, King of Uladh, and Faelan, with many nobles; and in which fell Suibhne, son of Colman Cuar.

The old name for *Magh Rath* was *Magh Comair*, and the battle is said to have lasted on this plain for six days.

Despite the dry, minimalist accounts given in the various annals, the battle is the focus of a whirligig of various tales, each telling its story in terms of classical literature rife with bardic embellishment and clear, poetic verse. The battle, which aided by the cult of Patrick ended the power of the Ulaid as well as their aspirations to the High Kingship of Tara, has survived in many tales such as *Cath Muighe Rath* or 'The Battle of Magh Rath', and *Buile Suibhne* or 'The Frenzy of Sweeny',* more popularly known as the 'Adventures of *Suibhne Geilt*', *geilt* meaning 'mad'. Both these tales may be termed Middle Irish romances.

Suibhne,* or more popularly Sweeny, was a prince of the Dál nAraide or the Cruithin,* and he fled from the Battle of *Magh Rath* in a state of shock and roved about Ireland until he was murdered at Tigh Moling, the present St Mullin's in Carlow. In the vicinity of the River Lagan and south of Moira, among the many hills of assembly such as Carney Hill [20], poets and bards would recite the tale of this decisive battle in order to display their knowledge and poetry. These open-air meetings were not just limited to the *seanchaide* or historians, but were also assembly points where the *breithem* or judge held court. Gatherings on these *airdibh oireachtais* ('heights or hills of assembly') were outlawed in Elizabethan times by statute. To quote from the Privy Council Book, 'Item, he shall not assemble the Queen's people upon hills or use any traghtes or parles upon hills.' Perhaps this law brought about a change in the approach to how history was communicated, shifting from an open-air, inclusive experience to an indoor recording by solitary academics.

As mentioned above, the story is often told in verse. In 'The Battle of *Magh Rath*', Domhnall's thoughts about his adversary Congal Caech or Claen are as follows:

> *Cid do gén re Congal Claen*
> *a ruire nime na naem?*
> *Ní uil dam beith im betháid,*
> *ic mac Scannlain Sciath-Leathain.*

> What shall we do with Congal Claen,
> O Lord of heaven of saints?

I cannot remain in life
With the son of Scanlann of the Broad Shield.

[Translated by John O'Donovan]

Then Domhnall exhorted his men to rise up against Congal:

Arise, arise, O youths [*Ergid, ergid, a ogu*], said the monarch, 'quickly and unanimously, fairly and prudently, vigorously and fearlessly to meet this attack of the Ulaid and foreigners; so that the evening of the reign and the destruction of the dominion of the Ulaid and foreigners shall be brought about, who are on this occasion joined and implicated in this iniquitous insurrection of Congal against you.

Domhnall then entreats the Munster men of the race of Olioll Olum, a third-century King of Munster, and the Dáirfhine or the *Corca Loígde* of Cork and the *Muscraighe Breogain* from the present barony of Clanwilliam in Co. Tipperary. The resulting battle apparently lasted for six days, and the emerging Uí Néill defeated the Ulaid, led by the Clann mac Rury and their relations from the western kingdom of Scotland. One could summarise this conflict as the final victory of the Milesians or Gaels over the indigenous Cruithin.* The great possibility of a kingdom of Ireland and western Scotland forming from the kingdom of *Dál Riata* was lost at this battle. The Scottish background to the battle lay in the fact that Congal's father Scandal was defeated in the battle of *Dún Ceithirnn* in 629 AD between the victorious Uí Néill and the Cruithin. As a result, Scandal was banished to Scotland where he levied a great army and arrived back in Ireland for further defeat at *Magh Rath*. After Scandal's defeat Congal was fostered to Domhnall.

In 1856, an antiquarian named J.W. Hanna set out in a paper presented to the *Ulster Journal of Archaeology* to show that the Battle of *Magh Rath* did not occur at Moira [20] but rather a mile north-east of the town of Newry near the Crown Rath [29]. Crown Rath is just north-west of the old Crown Bridge and south of the new Crown Bridge. Both bridges cross the Clanrye River less than a mile from the town of Newry. This paper shows the importance of place when discussing historical events and the importance that topography has in giving meaning to the historical and prehistorical stories. As the work of this book is an attempt to understand place and relate it to events, it is worth looking in detail at Hanna's pioneering work in this area.

Hanna says that Charles O'Conor of Belanagare, Co. Roscommon, was the first to associate *Magh Rath* with Moira, and this opinion was held by subsequent writers on the subject. The plain of *Magh Comair* is given in most references as being synonymous with *Magh Rath*. *Magh Comair* means the 'plain at the confluence of rivers', which is consistent with Hanna's placing of the battle at the Crown Rath, as there is a confluence of rivers to the west of Derryleckagh Bridge. To reconnoitre the position of King Domhnall's forces,

Congal sent his druid Dubhdiadh to *Ard na h-imaircsi* ('the hill of espying)' where his attention was absorbed by his own people, the Ulaid, with their 'proud tufted beards reaching midways, and prominent eyebrows, arrayed in glossy, half length, wide folded shirts, and gold embroidered tunics, with black woollen sheepskins folded about them'. As for 'the hill of espying', it has, says Hanna, remained unidentified. An even more important site not identified is *Cnocan an choscair* ('the hillock of the slaughter'), so called because it was where Congal was 'cut down by the men of Erin'. The battle was fought on 'the very middle of the wooded Magh Comair'. This wood has been identified by Hanna as Derryleckagh Wood, and an oak wood is still there.

The arrival of Congal to the battle is described by the poet as follows:

Mightily advance the battalions of Congal
To us over Ath an Ornaim, (the ford of Ornamh)
When they come to the content of the men,
They require not to be harangued.

The token of the great warrior of Macha,
Variegated satin, on warlike poles,
The banner of each bright king with prosperity
Over his own head conspicuously displayed.

The banner of Scanlann, an ornament with prosperity,
And of Fiachna Mór, the son of Baedan,
Great symbol of plunder floating from its staff,
Is over the head of Congal advancing towards us.

A yellow lion, on green satin,
The insignia of the Craeb Ruad,
Such as the noble Conchobhar bore,
Is now held up by Congal.

[Translated by John O'Donovan]

As a result of the battle, Ulster was left without a chief and Emain Macha fell into decline, as did the great Mac Rory clan or the Rudhraighe, the 'horse people' (*ro ech*), the tribe from whom the Ards Peninsula (*Ard Echach*) gets its name, along with the great warrior caste of Ulster, the *Craeb Ruad* or Red Branch Knights.

There is a need to distinguish as far as possible the various tribes that were present in Down at the turn of the first millennium and down to the Christian mission in Ireland. The Ulaid are often regarded as being of the Dál Fiatach race, but the real Ulaid were the

the Dál nAraide or the Cruithin* and their blood-brothers the Ard Echach and the Uí Echach Coba from the Ards Peninsula; thus, the Cruithin and the Echach or horse people were closely integrated. Margaret Dobbs has described the Dál nAraide as 'the oldest and most famous stock in Northern Éire'. Her colleague Professor Eoin Mc Neill wrote, 'the true Ulaid are Dál Araidi who spring from Conall Cernach …'

The Dál Fiatach were centred around Downpatrick; a few miles north-west from here at Saul [21], St Patrick arrived, having crossed the North Channel. According to the *Cáin Adamnáin*, or the Law of Adamnan, Bécc Boirchi of the Dál Fiatach was King of the Ulaid. Thus, the Ulaid are to be distinguished from the Cruithin or Dál nAraide and from the Uí Echach or the horse people who are remembered as the Mac Rorys, and whose name remains in the Ards Peninsula as Ard Echach.

The Mound at Downpatrick was known as *Síd air Celtrai*, and in O.S. maps it is marked *Rathceltchair*; it is also marked as *Dundalethghlas* and has associations with Ogma, the god of eloquence. Also known as the Mound of Down, it is just down the hill from Down Cathedral.

The strong belief that St Patrick was buried there was supported in *The Tripartite Life of St Patrick* by the seventh-century monk Muirchú, who writes:

An angel came to Patrick (on his deathbed) and gave his advice as to the manner of his burial: Let two unbroken bullocks be chosen and let them go whithersoever they will, and in whatever place they lie down, let a church be built in honour of thy poor body. And as the angel said, restive bullocks were chosen, and they drew a wagon with a litter firmly fixed on it in which the holy body was yoked to their shoulders … and they went forth, the will of God guiding them, to Dundalethghlas, where Patrick was buried.

There is, however, no direct evidence of the saint being buried here, but in 1900 the Belfast Naturalist's Field Club put down a stone at the spot believed to be his grave.

Due to high tides at Strangford Lough, the mound became an island on occasion. The River Quoile (*An Caol*, 'the narrow') water barrier prevented this after it was constructed in 1957. The elevated causeways leading to the mound are still visible in the Quoile marshes. The earthworks on top of the mound have been hard to distinguish, except for a motte and bailey which would show Norman habitation around the thirteenth century.

Legend also says that Oisín* was buried in one of the two burial sites here. The traces of a large, earthen enclosure on the Cathedral Hill and the tradition of the site being occupied by pre-Christian Kings of Ulster makes for an interesting association with Oisín, son of Finn mac Cumhail* and a member of the Fianna,* who are not generally associated with the Ulaid.

In 1953, excavation on the site of a graveyard at the centre of the enclosure yielded twelve gold penannular bracelets. Two more were unearthed in 1956 together with a fragment of another one as well as a neck ring. The hoard has been dated to the Late Bronze Age or the seventh century BC. Two circular houses from the middle Bronze Age had 'an

FIGURE 46. *Dún Rudraige.*

assemblage of remains dominated by a cordoned urn'. Finds of pottery and stone axes show also that the site was inhabited during the Neolithic Age.

According to Evans, when the cathedral was restored about 1800 many of the relics of the monastery of the Irish Church were destroyed. A round tower which stood here at sixty-six feet was destroyed because of a conflict between two rival landlords.

A little over two miles east of Downpatrick, and less than a mile south of Lough Money [21] and a half-mile east-north-east of Ballyalton village, is a chambered grave. When the excavation of this 'Druidical Ring' was begun in 1933, it was done without damaging the thorn tree growing on the cairn. The preservation of the tree was because the archaeologists were told that when an earlier digger had interfered with the tree, 'the plates that night danced on the dresser in his kitchen'. In the chambers, among Neolithic sherds, a decorated bowl was found, which has given its name to the 'Ballyalton Bowl' type. The Ballyalton bowl is like the type known in Scotland as Beacharra, having a rim diameter less than that of the shoulder.

The mythological heart of the Iron Age in Ulster is *Dún Rudraige* [21], as it was from here that the horse people settled, having arrived in Millin Bay from Papua New Guinea across Europe, with a mixture of aboriginal pre-Celtic blood. The 'Echaid', whose god was Echdae, the horse god, travelled throughout Ireland, and from them are named the Ards Peninsula (*Ard Echach*) and Lough Neagh (*Loch nEchach*, 'the lake of the horse'), as well as many other places throughout the island. The present Dundrum Castle, a Norman dungeon and twelfth-century circular castle, was built either on the site of *Dún Rudraige* or close to it.

Fled Bricrend, 'The Feast of Bricriu', a tale whose text we have from the ninth century, is based at *Dún Rudraige*. Although excellent in every other way, George Henderson, the text's editor and translator, fails to mention *Dún Rudraige* in his notes on geographical names. However, Edmund Hogan in his *Onomasticum Goidelicum* refers to *Dún Rudraige* as the site where Bricriu had his house and writes that it was on the 'site of Dundrum Castle'. The story relates that Bricriu erected his house 'after the likeness of [of the palace] of the Red Branch in Emain'. It was here that a council of Ulaid was assembled. The story is built around a rite or custom from Iron Age Ulster. The rite is known as the 'Champion's Covenant' or the 'Beheading Game', in which the winner got the first cut (called the *curad mir* or 'champion's portion') of the pig prepared for the feast. This story is paralleled in the Romance of Sir Gawayne and the Green Knight in the Arthurian legends. The rite may be a rite of passage. The hero of the tale is Cú Chulainn,* the foster son of Sualtaim mac Roech and probable son of Conchobar mac Nessa, King of the Ulaid and of Ulster.

As there was no apparent archaeological work done on the original *dún* or fort, all we must go on are stories and tales, such as 'The Feast of Bricriu'.

FIGURE 47. *Sheela na Gig* at doorway to old church at White Island.

FERMANAGH

Contae Fhear Manach, 'county of the Manachs (Manapii)'

In keeping with the naming of the county, a journey to White Island on Lower Lough Erne [18] would satisfy both Christian and pre-Christian interest. On this island is a little ruined rectangular church from the twelfth century, which possesses a fine example of a Hiberno-Romanesque doorway. This doorway collapsed about 1900 and was restored in 1928 by the archaeological section of the Belfast Natural History and Philosophical Society; the discovery of a photograph taken in 1896 ensured that the restoration was accurate. During the restoration, seven stone carvings were found, which were at the time described as 'grotesque', 'extraordinary' and 'remarkable'. Some of these carvings are *síle na gigs*, a group of female sculptures also found in Britain and France. They serve as fertility symbols and as wards against evil. Of the seven figures, three had previously been known to exist, having been found lying loose on the ground by the owner of the land, after which he incorporated them into the wall of the church. Incorporating pre-Christian stone figures into a church is not unknown, as was practised at the church of Killinkere in Co. Cavan as well as at Holy Cross Abbey in Co. Tipperary and St Patrick's Anglican Cathedral in Armagh city. The seven carved stone figures now stand in a row and face visitors as they enter the church. The largest of these carvings is forty-two inches by twelve inches and the smallest is twenty-two inches by sixteen inches. According to Françoise Henry in *Irish Art 800–1020* AD, the island once had a workshop which produced stone figures. Some, especially the unfinished works, may have been the remains of a stonecutter's workshop.

The island may well have related to a cult of the goddess or *cailleach* over a long period, as some of the heads look late medieval while others look as old as what is known as St Adamnán's Cross, at Tara, Co. Meath. Some of the figures appear pre-Christian, at least in their symbolism, and some are Christian. An example of the latter is the figure of a monk or bishop with a crozier in one hand and a small bell in the other. The shape of the crozier, says Henry, dates the Christian figures to the ninth or tenth century. Some of the figures were caryatids, or column supports. One figure measuring twenty-four inches by six inches is definitely a *síle na gig*; it is represented face on, with the lower part fully naked with legs splayed and the hands placed behind the thighs with fingers opening the vulva.

White Island is in Castle Archdale Bay, near the eastern shore of Lower Lough Erne, and is five miles north-west on the B82 from Enniskillen. There is no regular ferry, but a boat can sometimes be found to ferry one across at the marina in Castle Archdale Country Park. To the north of White Island is a rock known as Finn mac Cool's* Stone, one of many spots associated with the legendary hero.

At the northern end of Lower Lough Erne is Boa Island, described on map 17 as a carved stone; it is accessible by road. Here in the graveyard known as Caldragh (*cealltrach*, 'a burial place for unbaptised infants') is what some have termed a Janus-faced head, though the back of the figure may have been defaced. The original name in Irish is *Inis Badhbhannr* ('the island of the goddess Badb'), who along with Macha and the Mórrígan is part of a war-fertility triad of goddesses. Locals on the island pronounce the island Bo – with a short 'o' – and this is closer to the island's original name. The name is also pronounced similarly in Wexford.

Before entering into the various interpretations of these heads, it might be good to have an introduction from a Fermanagh poet from Enniskillen, Francis Harvey, whose poem was published in 1997 under the title of 'The Boa Island Janus':

> a squat twin-headed stone idol
> that was looking two ways long before
> I knew there were two ways of looking
> upstream to a source and downstream to the sea.

On one visit, as my wife Alison and I turned off the road at the point where a signpost directed us to 'Caldragh Cemetery', we met four people leaving the entrance to the graveyard who stopped us to ask if we knew where the stone figures were. We said, 'Follow us.' The joy of seeing the stone figures *in situ* was so great that I hope I imparted some of our excitement to them. They were from Belfast, and it was nice to share the site with four Ulster people and appreciate their directness and sense of humour. As we were in a cemetery, the conversation turned to graveyards and Belfast City Cemetery in particular, which one of the group said contained both Catholic and Protestant graves. He described how at one time the Catholic bishop had built an eight-foot wall underneath the ground for what I surmise was a way of avoiding 'spiritual contagion'.

It has been suggested by Dillon and Chadwick in *The Celtic Realms* that the double statue on Boa Island was a cultic stone introduced to Ireland by Gauls fleeing the Roman invasions. This would give them a pre-Christian date in Ireland. There may well be a connection between this carved stone and subsequent carved stones on other islands in Lough Erne. I have also seen a similar carved stone at Dam Yang in south-western Korea. A letter to *Archaeology Ireland* in 2003 shows an illustration of a stone in the Diego Rivera Museum in Mexico resembling the Boa Island figure. However, there is the possibility that such similarities exist throughout very many countries.

Lady Dorothy Lowry-Corry, though not the first to describe this stone, was the first to do so in detail in a paper read to the Royal Irish Academy in 1933 in Dublin. She mentions that George Du Noyer had drawn sketches of the stone in 1841. Du Noyer described the stone as

> the carving of the rudest description, the size of the head of the male and of the female figure being out of all proportion, and the features of both brought out by flat narrow bands. The male head is distinguished by a forked and pointed beard of the Saxon type, and the figure on the opposite side of the stone is that of a female is

suggested by a waist-belt. The arms of both effigies are crossed on the chest and more resemble flat bars than anything else.

Du Noyer further mentions that at the cemetery he met a man who said that there was a piece of stone set in the groove on the top of the stone, and that this was probably a cross.

Lowry-Corry disagrees with Du Noyer regarding the female figure and says, 'I am convinced that both these effigies are undoubtedly intended to represent male figures.' However, she says that she does not know what the original object of the stone was or whether it was connected to rites of the grave. The Boa Island effigy has a companion from nearby Lustymore Island, which was taken to Caldragh in 1939 and is a single figure with no socket or slot in which to place an object.

Professor Estyn Evans, a noted collector of Irish folk life, was a friend of Dorothy Lowry-Corry, and his description of the stone figure at Caldragh is like hers. He writes that it

> is an unusual carved stone, which has been referred to as a two-headed god, but there are in fact two separate male figures, back to back, each with a grotesquely pointed face, crossed arms and a diminutive body. The features are not carved in relief, but merely outlined with narrow grooves. The stone stands two and a half feet high and has a socket on top, like the nearby White Island figures, with which the stone has some affinities … presumably early Christian in date, but they betray pagan ideas.

The preliminary survey of the ancient monuments of Northern Ireland (PSAMNI) was published in Belfast in 1940 and states about Boa Island:

> On Boa Island (*Oileán Badhbha* – Badb's island, 'Island of the Raven goddess of War and Death'), in the townland of Dreenan (*Draighneán*, 'blackthorn place'), towards the southern shore of the island, one enters the Caldragh, an old graveyard, which is the only clue that there was once an early Christian foundation here. In 1940 the unusual old stone figure sited here was described as a 'stone carved with two human effigies, with crossed arms, back to back. Has a certain affinity to Gaullish sculpture, but may date from the 5th or 6th century A.D. Also, in the townland of Dreenan, according to the above survey of the ancient monuments, are the ruined foundations of an ancient burial place of pagan times, described in 1940 as 'a ruined cairn, about thirty-five feet in diameter'. This ruined cairn is close to Inishkeeragh Bridge at the southern tip of the island. Was this the sacred mound associated with the goddess Badb who gave her name to the island? These ancient mounds or *side* according to ancient belief contained the spirits of the dead and are kept alive in folklore to the present day where they are referred to as fairies or the little people, '*luchorpán*,' meaning, leprechaun or 'small person.' They are also

referred to as *na daoine maithe,* 'the good people.' This ruined cairn at Dreenan therefore should be the beginning of a tour of this ancient townland on the island of the goddess Badb.

A further addition to the Boa effigy was discovered by the archaeologist Richard Warner, who found a large stone which showed a hand on its left side. Laser imaging revealed that the hands 'go around onto the side of the stone, one belonging to "each person"'.

What is the significance of all these effigies?

A problem with analysing artefacts associated with our mythology is that nearly all the work is carried out by archaeologists. The problem with this is that they are limited as to the dictates of their science and often fail to see the underlying story that these artefacts are telling us. Badb, the eponymous deity of the island, is often described as *Badb Catha* or 'battle raven', and she is also frequently described as a goddess associated with death. A suggestion that the groove between the Janus-headed figure may have been filled with blood fits into this perspective. What is left out is that Badb is a war/fertility goddess and a goddess of sovereignty; thus, the rite to which these effigies give testament to are more connected to regeneration rather than death. The Lustymore figure was described by a Major Trevelean in 1911 as a *síle na gig* and later by the archaeologist John Murphy as an early form of the figure; the entwinement of the Boa figures would also fit a ritual mating. Also on Lough Erne is a *síle na gig* from White Island, which Edith M. Guest described in a 1936 article in the *JRSAI*: 'In 1864 the figure lay horizontally in a course low down near the south door of the Irish Romanesque church. It is now built into the north wall of the church with other figures from an older church.' She describes it as having crossed legs and a close-fitting garment around the shoulders and arms.

These figures are near Church Archdale in the remains of a twelfth-century church and are evidence of a continuous record of early religious figures from the seventh century to the late medieval period. *Síle na gig* thus finds herself in the company of two ecclesiastics bearing croziers. These ecclesiastics have been dated to between the eighth and the twelfth centuries. The figures on White Island have, according to Evans and others, affinities to Gaulish work. The *síle na gig* figure, although aged as a seventh-century artefact, does represent a strong symbol from our pre-Christian culture, and this later date afforded to it may be evidence of the survival of pre-Christian rites into the eighth century.

Slieve Beagh [18] in south-eastern Fermanagh and within a stone's throw of Monaghan, reputedly contains the burial site of the first man to arrive in Ireland, Bith, or Bioth, and in Irish Beatha, who was the fourth son of Noah. The south-western slopes of Slieve Beagh, which is named after Bith, lie in the townland of Carnmore (*carn mór,* 'a great cairn') and were once topped by a massive burial cairn which was taken to be Bith's final resting place. It is locally known as Carnrock. The cairn is mentioned by P.W. Joyce in *Irish Names of Places* as existing in 1878. He described it as 'a conspicuous monument on top of a hill, in the townland of Carnmore (to which it gives name) and may be seen from the top of the moat of Clones [and is] distant about seven miles north-west'.

A monument preserving the myth of the first man buried in Ireland, a man from when the Canaanite religion was still strong and when monotheism was waging war against polytheism, is itself a priceless cultural possession. The story of how he came to Ireland is as follows:

After agreeing to the number permitted to enter the Ark, Noah refused entry to Bith, who was accompanied by his daughter Ceasair, on account of their being polytheists. Noah told them to build a fleet of ships and to go to the western borders of the earth in the hope that the flood would not reach them. They took off in three ships, only one of which survived and managed to land in Co. Kerry. This ship included Bith and Ceasair, the first woman to land in Ireland, Bith's grandson Fintan and a man named Ladra. There were also fifty unnamed women, all of whom became the first inhabitants of Ireland.

Their departure is recorded in the *Book of Leinster* as follows:

Ro gab ém Cessair ingen Betha meic Noe .xl. láa ria ndilind.

True indeed Cesair, daughter of Bith son of Noah [departed] forty days before the flood.

And again, from the *Book of Leinster*:

Dolluid aniar Cessair
ingen Betha in ben
cona coicait ingen
cona triur fer.

Cesair went west
daughter of Bith
with fifty women
and with three men.

[Translated by David Comyn]

As to Ceasair's burial place, it is disputed as being between Knockma Hill in Co. Galway and Carn Ceasra on the banks of the River Boyle in Co. Roscommon.

Enniskillen (*Inis Ceithlenn*, 'Kathleen's Island') [18] lies between upper and lower Lough Erne. The Kathleen from whom it gets its name is somewhat lost in the mists of legend, though there is mention that she threw a fatal missile at the King of the Gods – the Dagda,* also known as Eochaid Ollathar or Eochaid the 'father of all'. As a result of these bloody missiles, the Dagda died at Brug in the Boyne Valley, Co. Meath. These fatal injuries occurred during the epic battle of *Magh Tuiredh*.

MONAGHAN

Muineachán, 'place of thickets, thorns or briars'

According to the *Annals of the Four Masters*, towards the end of the second millennium BC and during the reign of Aengus Ollmugaid ('Aengus the Great Destroyer'), Belahoe Lough (*Loch béil átha hoa*, 'the mouth of the ford on the lake of the two ears') on the borders of Monaghan and Meath burst forth. This lake is less than five miles south of Carrickmacross [35]. The *Annals* also say that another name for the lake is *Loch oen beithe* ('the lake of the one birch tree') which may be a simple topographical description or a memory of when the birch provided a communal centre as a *bile* or 'sacred tree'.

The German archaeologist Mahr in an article on a wooden cauldron found at Altartate Glebe, north-east of Clones [28A], says that it may be of Bronze Age date and that these cauldrons were generally used for storing butter. A wooden cauldron was also found at Clogh bog, on the mountain between Lisbellow and Enniskillen, Co. Fermanagh, as well as in Gartagowan bog, Co. Tyrone. A sheet-iron cauldron from Drumbane, Co. Cavan, was found in a bog, bringing the number of such finds to about twenty in Ireland as well as about ten in Britain.

As to the underlying custom of this form of storage, O'Curry says:

> Butter, while abundant in summer, was preserved in small firkins or barrels for winter use, and for expeditions or feasts. Many of these vessels filled with butter are found in peat bogs, the butter being altered into a hard, crystalline fat, free from salt. If salt was used in the curing of the original butter, it must have been gradually removed along with the products of the alteration of the glycerine. As butter is still made without salt in some parts of Ireland, it is probable that it was sometimes similarly prepared in ancient times. The term *Saland*, applied to salted meat and butter, show that the method of curing provisions with salt was practised at a comparatively early period in Ireland.

Linear earthworks are a feature of the southern areas of Ulster and the north midlands, and the surviving stretches of these are found in south Down, south Armagh, Cavan, Fermanagh, Longford, Leitrim, Roscommon and Monaghan. The earthwork with the most common name is the Black Pig's Dyke, which is also known as the Worm Ditch. In 1835, the antiquarian John O'Donovan wrote that 'it must have been a tremendous *Ollphéist* ['huge worm'] that ran across the country when she formed so deep a track, but her coils, voluminous and vast, cannot have been more terrible than the tusks of the huge boar that rooted the Valley of the Black Pig'.

Unfortunately, since 1835 the linear banks have somewhat contracted due to agricultural activity. A length stretching east–west across Monaghan runs for a few miles, but its future is in doubt as the tendency is for ignorance and practicality to obliterate our early history.

Barry Raftery, writing in *Pagan Celtic Ireland*, notes that 'excavations on the Black Pig's Dyke in Co. Monaghan have revealed that a substantial timber palisade once stood on the inner edge of the inner ditch, and such structures doubtless existed elsewhere. Indeed, older investigations on other sections of dyke indicate the probability that timber palisading was a significant element in their construction'.

With the rise of the Tudors, the end was in sight for the Irish chieftains, and their many rites, including the inauguration of kings, came to an end shortly after the battle of Kinsale in 1601. At Leac (*leac na ríog*, 'the kings flagstone'), now the townland of Ballyleck just north of Ballyleck Lake, two miles south-west of Monaghan town [28A], is where the inauguration of the McMahons took place.

Hamilton, writing in 1912, states that portions of the maps made in 1609 for the purpose of the Plantation of Ulster allow us to identify the site of the inauguration of the McMahon (*Mac Mathghamhain*, 'the son of the bear'). The McMahon Stone, according to the *Memorial Atlas of Ireland*, is marked in the parish of Kilmore and barony of Monaghan, a little to the east of Ballyleck.

Hamilton writes: 'A careful comparison of the maps locates this stone in the centre of the small townland of Leck (O.S. 13). The Ordnance map of 1836 marks an unnamed object in the middle of the townland. From this evidence it appears that the townland of Leck derived its name from the *leac* or flagstone on which Mac Mahon was inaugurated, and that the hill on which it is situated is named *Mullach Lice* or 'summit of the flagstone'.

There is a hill in the townland of Ballyleck just south-west of Ballyleck Lake, but it is unmarked in the *Discovery* map [28A]; this may be the *Mullach Lice* that Hamilton is referring to. However, a discrepancy arises as to the former location of the stone, as the *Memorial Atlas of Ireland* puts the stone to the east of the lake but the hill within the townland is to the south-west. It would also appear that the hill is a more appropriate place for an inauguration, as it was on top of a burial mound, possibly over the tomb of the original founder of the family. It was over tombs in Carnfree in Roscommon and *Magh Adhair* in Clare that the O'Conors and the Kings of *Dál gCais** were inaugurated; also, the hill or hillock is the place from where the king-to-be could see his people and his kingdom.

Edmund Spenser, author of *The Faerie Queene*, writes in *A View of the State of Ireland*:

> the Irish used to place him [the king-to-be] on a stone always reserved for that purpose and placed commonly upon a hill; in which I have seen formed and engraven a foot, which they say was the measure of their first captain's foot, whereon he standing received an oath to preserve all the ancient former customs inviolable.

At least three other inaugural places were denominated '*leac*', and they are *Leac na Ríogh* at Tara,* *Lecc Cothraidi* in Cormac's Chapel on the Rock of Cashel* and *Leac mic Eochadha* (Kehoe), where mac Eochadha inaugurated the Lord Uí Ceinnsealaigh (Kinsella).

The last inauguration of a High King in Ireland was of Rory O'Connor in 1166. He came north through Monaghan to claim hostages from the nobles of Ulster prior to his inauguration.

> *Sluaidheadh Érenn la Roidri mac Toirdealbhaigh Concubuir gu machaire Arda Macha, agus as sin go Bealach Gréine agus go Tigh Damnatan agus tríd an bhfotair tar Sliabh Beatha agus a Madh Leamhra agus go Fearrna go Meabhla Toghad. Tangadar maithi an tuarscirt ana coinne agus tugadar ceathra bráidi dó, a dó ó Sliabh ó tuaigh agus a dó ó Sliabh ó geas co n-abuir tí rí Éireann re Ruaidri ann sin.*
>
> A hosting of Ireland by Ruaidhri son of Toirdhealbhach Ó Conchobhair to Machaire Arda Macha, from there to Bealach Gréine to Tigh Damhnatan through the road over Sliabh Beatha [Slieve Beagh] to Magh Leamhna and to Fearnach na Meabhla or Toad. The nobles of the north came to meet him and gave him four hostages: two from the north of the Mountain and two from the south of the Mountain, so that Ruaidri was then named King of Ireland [Ó hInnse, *Miscellaneous Irish Annals*. Dublin 1947–8].

Tigh Damhnatan ('the house of Dympna'), now Tedavnet [28a], mentioned above in the extract from the annals was formerly the burial place of the princes of Oirgialla. Colgan in his *Acta Sanctorum* writes that Dympna was the daughter of Damen son of Cairbre, surnamed Damh-Airgid, son of Feign of the Colla-da-Crioch race who founded the kingdom of Oriel about 332 AD.

Dympna was the local saint of the area, and her church was in Tedavnet; during the Reformation, the stones of St Dympna's Church were taken to Bellanode, a few miles south, and used in the erection of the Protestant church, but her bust was installed in the gable wall of a house owned by a Mr Mitchell in Tedavnet. This house was burned down in 1832 and then taken over by a Mr Skelton who intended to have the bust restored. But a workman named McRory, a Presbyterian, said he would have no graven images and smashed the head with his hammer.

A legend about St Dympna is that she founded a church and a home for those troubled by mental illness at Gheel (Geel) in Belgium. This is supported by Colgan, and while lecturing Erasmus students in Dublin I mentioned this, only to be told by a Belgian student that that mental institution was still in existence. However, subsequent research would seem to dissociate the Dympna in Belgium from the Dympna in Monaghan. The belief that they are one and the same saint is possibly due to the large number of Irish saints who arrived in Europe in the sixth century. Legend says that Dympna was escaping the sexual advances of her father, but the likelihood of a fifteen-year-old girl leaving Ireland and sailing to Antwerp in the sixth century seems doubtful.

The only existing relic of St Dympna is the crozier in the National Museum of Ireland in Dublin. Known as the *bachall Damnait*, it was in the Lamb family in Monaghan and was hired out for purposes of swearing the truth; if the truth was not told, the liar's mouth would move towards their ears. According to the antiquarian John O'Donovan, writing in 1835, when demand for the crozier fell, the Lamb family were happy to sell it.

The feast day of St Dympna of *Tigh Damhnatan* is 13 June, and the feast day of St Dympna of Geel is 15 May on which day a fair is held in her honour. Dympna was known as *Damhnat ogh ó Sliabh Betha* ('virgin of Slieve Beagh').

An old saying in connection with St Dympna and Slieve Beagh was:

Sé do bheatha go Sliabh Beatha.

Bless your journey to Slieve Beatha.

TYRONE

Tír Eoghain, 'the territory of Eóghan'

Tír Eoghain, according to Geoffrey Keating in *Fora Feasa ar Éirinn*, comprised Co. Tyrone and Co. Derry, the baronies of Inishowen and Raphoe in Donegal and a portion of Co. Armagh. Eógan was one of the ancestor deities among the Érainn; it may be that the Eógan in question was Eógan Mór, though it is more likely that the name refers to the Eóganacht, but this again is dubious as the Eóganacht were a tribe associated with west Munster.

FIGURE 48. Bronze Age cauldron found at Castlederg, Co. Tyrone.

Anu or Áine, the sun goddess and wife or daughter of Manannán mac Lir,* the Irish Neptune or sea god, is found in the Paps of Anu on the Cork–Kerry border, and in Limerick at Knockainey, while in Tyrone she is commemorated by a chambered cairn and decorated stones at Knockmany – *Cnoc Áine*, just two miles north-west of Augher [18]. In 1959, in order to safeguard the engraved stones, the grave was enclosed in a protective enclosure which is lit from the roof.

Anu, who has many associations in Ireland, is also a river goddess with many rivers named after her in Europe – the Danube; the Rhône (Celtic, *Rodános*); the Russian Don, anciently Tanais; the Dniester (Danu Nazdya, 'river to the front' and Dnieper 'river to the back'); the Don in Co. Durham and the Doon in Ayrshire, Scotland; and the Donwy in Wales.

Anu is the sister of Fer Í, 'man of yew', and is also synonymous with Danu, from whom the Tuatha Dé Danann* are named. She is also connected to Donn, a god of the Tuatha Dé Danann, all of which names may signify the same deity. Anu's three sons are *na trí dee danann*, the masters of crafts, and these are the Goibniu,* the smith god; Luchta, the wheelwright or brazier; and Credne, the worker in bronze. These are the original *aes dána*, unlike the present Aosdána, a government-subsidised branch of the arts not noted for manual skills.

Lissan, meaning the 'Fort of Áine', is situated two miles north of Cookstown on the B162. In this area [13] there are three ring forts and a chambered grave. The nearby river known as the Lissan Water is also associated with Anu. *Tobar Áine* or the 'well of Áine' may well be the present townland of Toberlane, which is a little over a mile south-west from Lissan. Along the river is a ravine named as *Alt na Síon*, meaning the 'cliff or glenside of the fairies'; a less accurate though interesting translation is the 'high creek of the whistling or keening'. It is said that when an O'Corra (Corr) is about to die, Áine is heard wailing in a plaintive tone in the glen. Local folklore says that in this district she is regarded as a woman who was taken away from her husband's side at night by the *aes síde*, more commonly known as the 'wee folk'.

As a sun goddess it is no wonder that Anu was called upon to bless fruit, crops and vegetables. One wonders if her influence stretches back to Neolithic times when Beaghmore (*beitheach*, 'birchland'), eight miles north-west of Cookstown in the foothills of the Sperrin Mountains [13], was occupied and when part of the culture of these early farmers stretched into the Early Bronze Age with their ceremonial structures and burial cairns. The birch is one of our oldest native trees, and Beaghmore may simply mean a great birch in the land of birches, or a significant birch like a sacred tree or *bile* among the plain of birches.

When I first arrived at Beaghmore in the 1970s, I was excited by the abundant number of small stone circles. The area was unearthed by chance by turf-cutters in the 1940s, and shortly afterwards the site was acquired by the Ministry of Finance in Northern Ireland. This rapid investment in Beaghmore shows a consistency in Northern Ireland in acknowledging and respecting the richness of our early heritage.

The site contains seven circles, nine alignments and many small cairns. Estyn Evans in his *Prehistoric and Early Christian Ireland* writes that 'at some stage peat began to grow over the site, and it is tempting to see in the decreasing fertility of the soil a factor in the erection of monuments whose purpose was perhaps propitiatory. Some students have seen a lunar calendrical, significance in the circles and alignments, but there is no simple explanation'. If there were propitiatory offerings to the gods, one would hope that they did not include human sacrifice.

The actual extent of Beaghmore may well be more than what has at present been excavated, as the surrounding area comprises blanket bog. Seán Ó Ríordáin in *Antiquities of the Irish Countryside* says the following of Beaghmore:

> The most remarkable stone-circle site in Co. Tyrone is that at Beaghmore, north-west of Cookstown. The remains here were only very incompletely appreciated before the turf was removed in the course of excavation. It is now known that they extend over several acres, and the area already uncovered has revealed a complex system of circles, small cairns, and alignments. One of the circles contains a close setting of small uprights resembling, in appearance, though on a very diminutive scale, the *chevaux de fries* of the Aran Forts.

Two miles south-east of Cookstown is the Tullaghoge (*Tullach Óg*, 'the inviolate hillock') a bivallate ring fort and inauguration site [13]. Traditionally this was the inauguration site of the O'Neills and the capital of medieval Tyrone.

Edmund Campion, writing in his *Historie of Ireland* in 1571, has in his chapter on old custom the following passage:

> In Ulster thus they used to crown their king: a white cow was brought forth, which the king must kill, and seeth in water whole, and bathe himself therein starke naked; then sitting in the same caldron, his people about him, together with them he must eat the flesh and drink the broath, wherein he sitteth, without cuppe or dish or use of his hand.

According to Keating,

> *I dTulaig Óg do gairthí Ó Néill; agus Ó Catháin is Ó hÁgáin do ghaireadh é. Ó Donnghaile a mharuscál sluaigh is muinntear Bhrisléin is clann Bhiorthagra breitheamhain fhéineachais Uladh uile.*
>
> It was at Tulach Og that O'Neill was inaugurated, and it was O' Cathain and O'Hagain who inaugurated him; O'Donnghaile was his marshal of the hosts and muinntir Bhrislein and clan Biorthagra were the brehons of feineachas of all Ulster ['the brehons of feineachas' – those in charge of jurisprudence].

The O'Cahans and the O'Hagans were titled the *ur-ríoghta* or uraights, and as subsidiary kings or lords were in charge of the inauguration of the king.

Leabhar na gCeart or 'The Book of Rights' stated that the King of *Tullach Óg* was entitled to 'fifty serviceable foreign bondmen, fifty swords, fifty steeds, fifty white mantles and fifty coats of mail'.

In an inauguration rite as in any other ritual it is important to discover what were the actual artefacts used and what was the influence of natural things such as rocks, trees and water. Thus, when investigating a particular place such as *Tullach Óg*, it is imperative to find out what exists at present *in situ*, what according to historical evidence did exist and what according to lore was said to exist.

If we start at the end and attempt to find out what was said to exist, we can quote J. Hogan, who writes: 'There is evidence to suggest that the hill [Tullach Óg] was originally the site of a sacred tree, *bile*, under which initiation to kingship took place.'

Hayes-McCoy, writing in 1970, mentions the presence of another artefact, the inaugural chair of the O'Neills, referenced in 1602 by Richard Bartlett, a cartographer with Mountjoy, the Lord Deputy and leader of the victorious English army at the Battle of Kinsale in 1601: Tulloghog on this hill were four stones in the manner of a charre, wherein th' Oneales this manie yeres have bin made. The same are now taken away by his lordship [Mountjoy].' Hayes-McCoy continues: 'So this royal seat comprised four large stones and set as to make a royal seat. If one could assume a great tree or *bile* enveloping it, then one has the setting for the rite which would ensue when the rightful king to be was in place. These stones or *Leac na Rí* were claimed to have been blessed by St Patrick.'

A map attributed to Bartlett shows a picture of the inauguration of an O'Neill. The map, which also shows the broken chair outside the rath, consisting of a boulder framed by three slabs, was executed just before the destruction of the chair by Mountjoy, an act that apparently brought him even greater satisfaction than his burning of the season's corn, which caused a local famine.

James Stuart's *History of Armagh* states:

> In August 1602, Sir Arthur Chichester (during the war with Tyrone, namely Hugh O'Neill) spent some time at Tullaghoge, and here broke into pieces the stone chair of state in which, from remote antiquity, the sovereigns of Ulster had been inaugurated into the regal title and authority of the O'Nial. Several stones, said to have been fragments of this chair, were in the glebe-land belonging to the Rev. James Lowry, rector of Desert Creaght, about the year 1768.

I was shown around the inauguration site and bivallate rath by Professor Mac Erlaine of Coleraine University at a time when this capital of medieval Tyrone was no longer overgrown with trees and, apart from the loss of the *bile* and the destruction to the royal seat, still preserved an atmosphere in which one could easily conjure the past. The great Hugh O'Neill was said to have been the last king to be installed here; a map drawn by Richard Bartlett shortly after 1600 shows the broken chair outside the rath, consisting of a boulder framed by three slabs.

H.F. Hore, writing about the inauguration, says:

The *Leac na Riogh*, literally the flagstone of the kings, upon which the chieftains of the northern Uí Neill race used to be inaugurated, stood in a large circular rath, on a tullagh or low hill, near the present village of Tullaghoe, a name which signifies 'the hill of the youths.' The *Leac na Rí* or the 'kings stone', which is one of many inauguration stones in Ulster was seen as the stone of destiny. Legend has it that the stone at Tara was taken from there to Scotland in the sixth century and moved to London by Edward the First in 1296.

If this is true, then the stone forms part of the coronation chair in Westminster, Abbey and Elizabeth I was presumably crowned on this stone in January 1559. However, the stone of destiny remains at Tara,* so what stone found its way to Scotland in the seventh century?

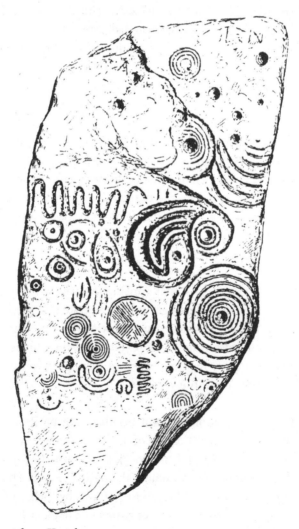

FIGURE 49. Rock art from Knockmany.

A third material element in the rite was the shoe that symbolised the hope that the new king would walk in the footsteps of his predecessors and continue to honour their achievements. During the ceremony at Tullaghoge, the king, seated at the centre, was surrounded by a group of eight, and the person directly to his left, an O'Cahan or an O'Hagan, one of the *uraights*, placed a shoe upon his head. The other *uraight* directly to his right placed his left hand on the coronation chair. This appears to have been the significant part of the ritual. Whether or not the king then placed his foot in a foot-engraved stone is unknown.

Inaugural foot stones still exist at Listoghil in Sligo and close to Carn Fraoich in Roscommon, so that this stone marked the conclusion of a rite at Tullaghoe which only ended after Hugh O'Neill in the sixteenth century. Another famed stone bearing a carved imprint of a foot, allegedly the inauguration stone of the Clan Donald, Lords of the Isles, was at Loch Finlaggan in Islay. The Finlaggan Stone was smashed by the Earl of Argyll in 1615, when the old Gaelic order both in Ireland and Scotland was drawing to a close.

Two miles north-west of Ballygawley is Sess Kilgreen [18]; it is one of a number of chambered graves in the area, the most prominent being Knockmany, mentioned above. Like Knockmany, Sess Kilgreen is associated with a decorated stone which now lies in an adjoining field. Unfortunately, these so-called 'decorated stones' remain obscure and to my knowledge we only have the interpretation of N.L. Thomas, whose book *Irish Symbols of 3500* BC attempts to comprehend the symbols depicted and show that their meaning is more indicative of their originating culture than mere decoration. The decorated stone at Sess Kilgreen is divided into two parts by a line of dots in a north-east–south-west axis. Is this a division of the year into two parts? If so, it was an attempt to configure the year in the Neolithic era, when people turned from being hunter-gatherers to farmers.

George Coffey, in the *JRSAI* in 1911, described the 'decorated stone' at Sess Kilgreen as

> a remarkable incised stone, containing cups and rings and several stars and to the left some large groups of cups. The most striking feature of the markings is, however, a line of over twenty cups which go regularly and evenly diagonally across the stone. Below these lines to the right are several cups and rings and some good stars with cup centres. Some of the stars have lines going from them, giving them the appearance of flowers.

Coffey measured the stone at four feet, four inches in height and five feet, four inches in width and the stone was six inches thick.

A shard of Neolithic pottery was discovered here in 1996 by Sinéad McCartan from the Department of Archaeology and Ethnography at the Ulster Museum. A Father J. Rapmund, excavating the tomb in 1911, found cremated bones and a fine specimen of a hammer, which has since been lost. Prior to Rapmund's excavation, the tomb had been left undisturbed for nearly 4,000 years.

NOTES ON PICT-LAND
AND SCOT-LAND

'Take a blessing from me eastward to Alba; good is the sight of her bays and valleys; pleasant was it to sit on the slopes of her hills when the sons of Uisnech used to be hunting.' –Deirdre from *Oideadh Chloinne Uisnech* (The Fate of the Children of Uisnech).

Before we move to Scotland, it is as well to point out that the term Britannic Isles included Britain and Ireland, whereas the term Albion was used for the larger island. The name 'Britannic' (or Pretanic in an older form) has its origin in the Welsh *Prydain* or *Prydyn*, the Old Irish equivalent being *Cruithin*.* The origins of these words, according to W.J. Watson in his *Celtic Placenames of Scotland*, come from the Indo-European root *qrt* meaning 'a cut', and hence the Latin *curtus* and the Gaelic *cruth*, meaning 'form or shape';

FIGURE 50. Clootie Well in Munlochy, Scotland, north of Inverness, showing evidence of the *piseoga* ritual common to Scotland and Ireland (Dace Conner).

344

this then leads to Pretani, meaning the 'figured folk', referring to their custom of painting the skin, as mentioned by Caesar, thus giving rise to the name 'Picts' (Latin *picti*, 'painted people').

Later the island of Britain took the latinised name of Britannia, while Albion has remained as the name of Scotland in Gaelic (*Alba*). The name *Cruithin* and *Cruithin-tuath* or 'Pictland' also applied to the Cruithin territory in Ireland. *Cruithin-tuath* or 'Pictland' is thus, according to Watson, a name for a district in Scotland and in Co. Meath, Ireland. The area of Scotland he refers to is north of the Forth in eastern Scotland, but I am unaware of an area in Meath with this name. *Cruithinchlár* ('the plain of Cruithin'), an old name for Scotland, acknowledges the Cruithin, while the modern name recognises the Gaelic influence, as it is named after Scota, whose children from Galicia in Spain became the standard-bearers of the Gaelic conquest of Ireland. Legend also says, however, that both the Picts and the Gaels came from Scythia, north of the Black Sea in present-day Ukraine. Scotia is thus said to be a version of Scvthia.

The sixteenth-century French historian Nicholas Serarius wrote:

> Scotia was also a name for Ireland. However, since there came from the same land of Ireland a certain race to the east of Britain, where the Picti were dwelling, and there they settled down with them, and at first were called Dalrheudini (that is, Dál Riada), from their leader Rheuda (that is, Cairbre Rioghfhada), as Bede affirms. But after this they routed the Picti themselves; and they occupied the entire northern portion of that country; and they gave it the old name of their race, so that there is but one Scotic race. There are however two, two Scotias: one of them, the elder and proper Scotia, is Ireland, and the other, which is recent, is the northern part of Britain.

In *Historia Brittonum*, Nennius, writing in the ninth century, said that the Picts occupied the Orkney Islands. Their influence passed through France and they founded the city of Pictavis or Poitier.

St Columcille,* who visited the Pictish King Brude at Inverness in 585, when they both apparently conversed in Gaelic, gave the foundation myth of the Picts as follows:

They divided the land into seven divisions:

> Seven children of Cruithne
> Divided Alban into seven divisions:
> Cait, Ce, Cirig, a warlike clan,
> Fib, Fidach, Fotla, Fortrenn.

And the name of each man is given to their territories.

Five of these names are recognisable in the province kingdom north of the Forth. Cait ruled over Caithness, Cirig over Angus, Fib over Fife and Kinross (the people of Fife were known as *cu sídhe* or 'fairy hounds'), Fotla over Atholl and Gowrie (it should also be noted that Fotla or Fodla, together with Banba and Ériu, is one of a triad of goddesses from whom Ireland is named) and Fortrenn over Strathearn and Menteith, the central district between the Forth and the Tay. *Fortrenn* in Gaelic means 'very strong'; it may also be an early name for the River Forth.

In the names Cait and Caithness and Cait, meaning the 'cat people', we can detect a strong connection to the Cruithin's* identification with animals. They saw a spiritual relationship between themselves and certain animals; thus, the Cruithin in Ireland had an ancestor deity and king named Cairbre Cinn Cait or Cairbre 'cat-head' who ruled Ireland north and south. This cult of the animal deity also extended to Wales, where in Caerleon many cat-eared heads have been found in stone.

> *Amhail do bhí Cairbre cruaidh,*
> *Do gabh Éire theas is thuaidh:*
> *Dá chluas chait um a cheann cain,*
> *Fionnfadh cait tré n-a chluasaibh.*

> Thus was Cairbre the hardy
> who ruled Ireland south and north:
> Two cat's ears on his fair head,
> Cat's fur upon his ears.

[Translated by P.S. Dinneen]

Cairbre also wore the snout of a cat over his nose. Presumably the 'cat people' from Caithness had similar customs.

Cairbre and his tribe were Irish 'Picts', and in Galloway the Irish 'Picts' were known as 'Creenies'; according to Watson, 'they lived in the south western coastal regions of Galloway known as the Rinns'. The Rinns of Galloway is a peninsula with Loch Ryan to the north-east, Luce Bay to the east and the Irish Sea to the west. 'Creenie' clearly derives from *Cruithnigh*, the plural of *Cruithneach*, and they came from the Cruithin* part of Ulster facing Galloway; thus, the original 'Ulster-Scots' were Ulster-Picts. In Galloway, the 'Creenies' were also known as 'Gossacks'. In Welsh, the common noun *gwasog* means 'a servile person'. This is apparently what they became after the *Scotti* or Gaelic invasion, or they may simply have been rent-paying vassals to the established Picts from 'Pictland' in much the same way as the Cruithin in Ireland became the *Aithechtuatha* or servile class to the Gaels.

In an article published in *The Celtic Review* (1906), Watson writes: 'Seven hundred years after Ptolemy's time, the invading Norsemen found in eastern Sutherland and Caithness a tribe who called themselves the Cats – Catti, "wild cats"'. Thus, the Picto–Norse hybrid, Katanes, 'cat-promontory', now Caithness. That these folks were regarded as Picts is sufficiently proved by the name Pentland Firth applied to the sea that washes their northern coast, which certainly means Pictland Firth. According to medieval Gaelic legend, Cat was one of the seven sons of Cruithne the Pict who divided Scotland into seven provinces, of which the most northerly is referred to as *Crich Chat* or 'bounds of the cats'. Watson doesn't mention Cairbre Cinn Cait and thus misses the tribal and ritualistic aspects of the Cruithin* or Dál nAraide and the powerful Irish connection.

Taking a leap back in time, evidence in Caithness of the astronomical observations of Late Neolithic societies may be seen on the Hill of Clyth, behind the village of Mid Clyth, close to the North Sea and ten miles south of Wick. Here are twenty-two fan-shaped rows running north to south, set on a south-facing slope beneath a cairn. Professor Alexander Thom has suggested that the site may have had an astronomical function, with the stones acting as a grid by which observations of the moon were plotted. As Thom suggests 1900 BC as the date of the erection of the stones, we may connect them with the onset of farming, particularly with the growing of emmer and einkorn wheat. Understanding the mechanics of the sky was vital for survival if one were to become dependent on farming. However, once farming became well established, astronomical measuring began to fade, and from medieval times legend took over so that the stones became headstones from an ancient battle.

Watson says that the Kyle of Sutherland is *An Caol Catach*, 'Cat-Kyle'. The Earl of Sutherland was *Morair Chat*, 'Mormaer' or 'Lord of Cats'; the Duke of Sutherland is *An Diúc Catach*; and Sutherland men are *Cataich*. A hundred miles out in the North Sea from Caithness are the Shetlands, the old name for which is *Inse Catt* ('the islands of Catt').

North of Caithness lie the Orkneys, in Gaelic *Inse Orc* ('the isles of the boars'). The respect for cats and boars among the Picts was perhaps because they saw them as ancestral deities. The Cruithin* of Ulster were attached to the hound; thus Conchobar, the King of Ulster, had a name which means 'one who loves hounds', and the great Ulster warrior Cú Chulainn* was known as 'the hound of Ulster'. Animal cults are not peculiar to Britain and Ireland but can be found in times past in many cultures, including Egypt, India and indigenous people in North America.

The Picts of Scotland and Ireland recognised themselves as one people, namely the Cruithin* or Dál nAraide, and later they intermarried with the Gaels or Dál Riata (modern Irish Dál Riada). Thus, the Welsh name for the Picts is *Gwyddil Ffichti*, or Gaelic Picts.

The Picts lived in *brochs*, which were prehistoric structures peculiar to those found in the Orkneys or Shetland Isles and adjacent mainland of Scotland. The *broch* was a tower with outer and inner walls of dry stone. The outer area contained chambers for humans, and the open central area was for cattle. Many ancient structures on Orkney were classified by Petrie as *brochs* and as 'Picts' houses'. The former he mentions as being circular towers of fifty to seventy feet in diameter and sixteen to seventeen feet high. The circular wall around them forms two concentric walls, with a gallery or passage between them. Forty *brochs* at least were known in Orkney, and these were also to be found in the northern counties of Scotland. According to Petrie, the 'Picts' house', on the other hand, is of a conical form,

FIGURE 51. Skara Brae on the Orkneys (Mike McBey).

externally resembling a large, bowl-shaped barrow. Its masonry is solid, and its entrance is by a long, low, narrow passage, the walls converging to the top; no implements are found in them, 'but the bones of domestic animals are plentifully found therein'. Petrie concluded that the houses were tombs, or chambered cairns or barrows. The finest example of a Pictish *broch* can be seen at Mousa Island in the Shetlands, which can be reached by boat from Leebotten on the Sound of Sandwick. This 45-foot-high *broch* survives to approximately its original height.

In the baffling world of the Picts, one is inclined to agree with the Venerable Bede, who saw them as the original inhabitants of the British Isles – more properly the Pictish Isles – and who were, I would suggest, an aboriginal people similar to, if not identical with, those tribes named as Cruithin* and Dál nAraide. In terms of historical documentation, one must mention the *Pictish Chronicle*, written in Latin in the time of Cinead, son of Mael Coluim, King of Scotland, 971–995 AD. The work is divided into three parts: a brief account of the origin of the Picts, founded on the work of Isidore of Seville; a list of the native Pictish kings; and a full account of the Celtic Kings of Scotland after the union of the Celtic invaders with the aboriginal Picts.

According to R.A.S. Macalister, 'some of the early Pictish kings were doubtless mythical; but from 583 to 840 AD we have a certain amount of corroborative evidence afforded to us by the Irish Annals of Ulster; and between these dates we may take the list as authentic'.

The great German scholar Heinrich Zimmer comments in *Das Mutterrecht der Pikten* ('The Matriarchal Laws of the Picts') that there is a limited number of kings' names and they occur over and over again; the kings' fathers' names are given in each case, but none of the kings' fathers appear as kings themselves. Also, the kings' names are all Pictish, but the kings' fathers' names are not necessarily so; some are Irish, some are Welsh, others are Anglian or Saxon. In the case of Conchobar mac Nessa, King of Ulster, we see an example of the matriarchal line with Ness, his mother, whose name, meaning 'a narrow channel', may also be connected with Loch Ness and Inverness.

James Ferguson, writing about the matriarchal nature of the Picts, says that their succession to the throne and indeed to property in land was in practically all cases through the mother. He regarded this custom as a reason for their downfall and the eventual dominance of the patriarchal Scots or Gaels (the present author bows to greater minds to unknot this historical phenomenon). Ferguson further writes:

> In no case does a son succeed his father. As in the Irish Law of Tanistry brother might succeed brother, but beyond that, when, as Bede says, '*ubi res pervenerit in dubium*,' (where a doubt will arise), the succession passed to the sons of sisters, or to the nearest male relation on the female side or through a female. The most common names of the kings never appear as those of fathers and the fathers appear to have been men of another race or of another tribe.

Thus, the father of Brude mac Bile was the British King of Strathclyde, while Talorcan mac Ainfraith was the son of Eanfred, the heir of the kingdom of Northumbria, and Kenneth MacAlpin was the son of Alpin, who is not listed as among the Kings of Scotland.

As with the earlier Neolithic and Bronze Age peoples, the material evidence of the Picts' culture comes in the form of a rich type of sculptured stone; these stones are found in greatest numbers in Aberdeenshire and Angus. At Inverurie, Aberdeen, the ancient Brandsbutt Stone stands just a half-mile to the north-west of the town; it bears Pictish symbols and an ogam inscription. In Inverurie Cemetery, Gordon, there is a fine horse, regarded as a deity by the Dál nAraide and the Picts, inscribed on a stone. Thus, Macha from whom Ard Macha (Armagh) is named was a horse goddess and the Echach were horse people. According to Elizabeth Sutherland in *In Search of the Picts*, 'the phrase "straight from the horse's mouth" is said to be connected to Macha'. At Rhynie, about thirty miles north-east from Aberdeen, is a Pictish stone known as the 'Crow Stone', although one of its symbols appears to be more like a salmon. North of Rhynie is a vitrified fort, and close by is Tap O'Noth, which probably was a central living quarter for the north-eastern Picts. Rhynie Man, incised in stone, consists of a bearded male wearing a belted tunic and carrying an axe; he may be a warning to outsiders or simply a worker or warrior. At Onich, Inverness, near the pier at Loch Linnhe, is a standing stone named *Clach a' Charra* or 'stone of friends'; this perforated monolith may have been the place where business or tribal agreements were made or where tribal disagreements were ended by a handshake.

If so, its equivalent can be found in St Patrick's Cathedral, Dublin, where the door has an oblong hole through which the rival Fitzgeralds and Butlers brought their troubles to an end by shaking hands – thus giving rise to the expression 'chancing your arm', since placing your arm in the hole risked also having it cut off.

On the Isle of Lewis, sixteen miles west of Stornoway at Callanish, is a group of standing stones which are exceeded in importance only by Stonehenge. Dr Aubrey Burl, whose book *The Prehistoric Stone Rows and Avenues of Britain, Ireland and Brittany*, has examined megalithic sites from Carnac to Callanish and regards these stone rows as 'the neglected relics of prehistoric Europe'. Like the stones at Mid Clyth in Caithness, a definite answer to these rows may be hard to find, but some suggestions are that they were pathways to circles, cairns and barrows, or possible markers of time with the sun and moon involved. The remarkable collection at Callanish amounts to nearly fifty stones – a well-marked megalithic avenue comprising nineteen monoliths ending in a circle of thirteen stones. A cairn, forty feet in diameter, stands within the circle.

In Rosemarkie, seven miles south-west from Cromarty on the Moray Firth, there is an interesting Celtic sculptured grave slab with a cross on one side and Pictish symbols on the other. This is a fine example of Pictish and Christian cultures colluding to express themselves. In the Groam House Museum, Ross and Cromarty, there is another fusion of Pictish and Christian art in the Rosemarkie red sandstone cross slab. One can see a connection with this stone and the upright columns of ornate Irish high crosses – so one must ask if the Picts were the original artificers of these stones; the answer appears to be yes.

The animal symbols used by the Picts could easily be transferred to illustrate biblical stories. They may also mark a time when the Picts were being Christianised. Like much of the symbolism of the Neolithic stones, which is simply regarded as 'art work', the artistry of the Pictish craftsmen on the magnificent cross slabs is seldom seen for what it is – namely, a vibrant expression of the Picto–Irish Church. Another fine example of this cultural marriage can be found in Angus at Aberlemno, five miles south-west from Brechin. This splendid cross slab is fronted by a shaft which has three intertwined and interlaced circles at the centre of the cross. According to Sutherland, 'the central motif of spirals is said to represent the "motionless mover" around whom all life revolves'. The reverse side is different, with the Pictish symbols showing a battle scene. There are nine warriors in the stone engravings, including five horses. Some of the Anglian warriors appear to be wearing long-nosed guarded helmets, some seem to be carrying spears and horns and one with an animal headdress seems to be beating a drum. Others attack the Anglians under King Ecgfrid with axes and spears. This battle is said to depict the victory for the Picts at Dunnichen Moss in 685 AD. Sadly, someone has put a hole through the front right circle above the cross; this supreme historical monument is still *in situ*, and a cast of it exists in the National Museum of Scotland.

Sutherland says that a 'relic of old horse ritual magic may have survived in the farms of Pictland up to the early twentieth century':

Initiation took place in the barn where the young farmer was blindfolded and led before a court of older men to an altar formed by inverting a bushel measure over a sack of corn. After certain secret ceremonies, he was given the magic word, though to be 'Both in One', which may have indicated harmony between man and beast.

After initiation, carried out by the society of the Horseman's Word or Horse Whisperers, the ploughman had power over horses and women. Manannán mac Lir,* who was a horse-god as well as a sea-god, is said to have supported the Picts/Scots in battle against the Saxons.

About a mile north of Arbroath Angus is an eleventh-century church known as St Vigean's, which contains a number of inscribed Celtic stones. Outstanding among these is the Drosten Stone, which may contain in its top-left corner a *Síle na Gig*, representing a woman with legs splayed, hands placed behind the thighs and fingers opening the vulva. There are an estimated seventy-five of these in Ireland, twenty-one in England, seven in Wales and three in Scotland. So, if this is a *Síle na Gig* to the west of Carlingheugh Bay, it is a rarity.

Seventeen miles south of Glasgow and seven miles east of Kilmarnock is Darvel in Ayr, and here on Burn Road one can find the prehistoric Dragon Stone, around which processions marking New Year's Day were once held. The stone was seen as a fertility symbol, around which people walked three times *deas sol* ('right to the sun') or in a clockwise direction. It was also a custom to walk three times around it before a wedding. In the nineteenth century, a blacksmith from Darvel welded a stone ball to the top of the stone so that it now looks more like a person.

At Munlochy, six miles from the Fairy Falls at Rosemarkie is Clootie Well ('the well of the rags') where a large tree still holds *piseoga* to the present day. The Old Irish word *pisóc* (modern Irish, *piseog*) means 'the cloth of a virgin', but is more commonly misunderstood as 'magic' or 'superstition'; it is central to an understanding of the rites surrounding certain wells. A young woman after her first menstrual cycle went to a well close to a tree and washed her bloodstained garments in the well, then walked three times clockwise around the tree and placed her cloth on the tree. The older tradition was that after three days family or neighbours would remove the cloth. That tradition has drastically changed both in Ireland and Scotland to the extent that these sacred trees are now blemished by rotting cloth. In Scotland, one is dissuaded from removing the cloth at all. This rite brings us back to both a pre-Gaelic and pre-Christian time when nature was a component part of life's changes. The above rite connected with female puberty acknowledges the well, the tree and the sun as forces with which to share life's changes.

At Dornoch, Sutherland, the Witch's Stone is a testament to how those carrying out pre-Christian rituals were treated. Situated on the links north of Dornoch Firth, it is where the last woman accused of witchcraft was executed in Scotland in 1722. She is said to have turned her daughter into a pony, which was then shod by the devil. The fear and hatred of witches increased to such an extent that in England and Scotland, between the years 1640 and 1661, between 2,000 and 3,000 persons suffered death for witchcraft. Scotland was perhaps the last country in which the interrogation of witches was legally allowed. At Spott Law or Spott Loan in East Lothian and two miles south of Dunbar, the parish register has the following record: 'October, 1705, many witches burnt on the top of Spott Law.' At Tower Hill, Gourock, in Renfrew on the River Clyde, is the ancient Granny Kempock's Stone, which is probably prehistoric. Here, in 1622, Mary Lamont was burnt as a witch on a charge of intending to throw the stone into the sea to cause shipwrecks. One wonders why so many women were tortured, drowned and burned to death in Scotland, when only one was recorded as being burned in Ireland.

The centre of Scotland is marked by a stone known as the Drumgask Stone, which is south-east of Cluny Castle in Inverness and is at an altitude of 950 feet. The stone has some arrow markings and may be compared to the Cat Stone in Westmeath, which is a similar *omphalos* representing the centre of Ireland.

In Sma' Glen in Perthshire between Dunkeld and Crieff is a large stone known as Ossian's Stone, which is said to mark the hero's grave. It is possibly due to the much-maligned Macpherson that elements of the Fenian sagas have entered Scottish folklore. Oisín,* according to legend, is also buried in Cushendall, Co. Antrim, as well as wrapped in the hide of a bull on Curran Mountain, near Manorhamilton, Co. Leitrim, where a standing stone is said to mark the spot, and finally at Síd Airceltrai, Downpatrick, Co. Down. He is commemorated by W.B. Yeats in his poem *The Wanderings of Oisín*, written in 1889:

> I throw down the chain of small stones when life in my body has ceased,
> I will go to Caoilte, and Conan, and Bran, Sceolan, Lomair,
> And dwell in the house of the Fenians, be they in flames or at feast.

Perhaps it is time to quote from 'The Prayer of Ossian' or *Urnigh Ossian*, as it is called in Scotland, where it is preserved in the Advocates' Library, Edinburgh. In Ireland this tale is entitled *Agallamh Oisín agus Phadruig* or 'The Colloquy between St Patrick and Oisín' and is preserved in the library of the University of Dublin. The following verses are the Scots Gaelic version, with James Macpherson's translation of 1760:

Ossian: *Innis sgeul a Phadruic, An n'onair do leibh,*
          Bheil neamh gu aridh
          Aig maithibh Fianibh Eirin?

Patrick: *Bheirimfa dhuit briartha,*
          Ossian na 'n glonn,
          Nach bheil neimh ag t'aithar,
          Aig Oscar na ag Gobhul.

Ossian: *'S olc an sgeul, a Phadruic,*
          A thagad dhamh ri leibhibh,

Com an bithimfe re crabha,
Mar bheil neimh aig Fionnibh Eirin.

Ossian: Tell me Patrick
      With respect to your reading
      Is Heaven barred from celebrating
      The noble Fianna of Ireland.

Patrick: I give you my word,
      Ossian of great deeds,
      That neither your father nor Oscar, nor of Gaul,
      Are celebrated in Heaven.

Ossian: This is a sorry tale, O Patrick
      That you tell me of my ancestors.
      Why should I be religious,
      If the Fianna are not celebrated in Heaven?

While it would be nice to think of Oisín* with his hounds in the Sma' Glen, it would appear that the *Smail* mentioned above refers to Glenasmole on the Wicklow–Dublin border. However, as Oisín has connections with Sma' Glen in Perthshire, his father Finn mac Cumhail* has connections with the Aven River which flows through Glen Aven in Banffshire, its Gaelic origin being *Ath'inn* for *Athfhinn*, 'the very bright one'. According to Watson in *The History of Celtic Placenames of Scotland*, 'Tradition makes Athfhinn to have been the wife of Finn mac Cumhail,* who lived at Inchrory. She was drowned in Aven, which hitherto had been called *Uisge Bàn*, "*fair water*". Then said Finn:

Chaidh mo bhean-sa a bháthadh
Air Uisge Bán nan clach sleamhain;
`S o chaidh mo bhean a bháthadh,
Bheirimid Athfhinn air an abhainn.

'My wife has been drowned in Aven of the slippery stones; and since my wife has been drowned, let us name the river Aven.'

Legend has her connected with *Clach nam Ban*, the Ladies' Stone, a seat upon which she and Finn sat; the seat is close to the precipice of Meall Gainmhich, 'a small hill or knoll of sand', according to Watson, overlooking Loch Aven and may be the marked 'shelter stone' here. A final reference to the Fianna* of Finn mac Cumhail* occurs in Burgie in Moray, west of Banff, where the monks of Kinloss were granted land in 1220 AD. Part of this land included the Picts' Field and Tubernacrumkel (*tober an crombeoil*, 'well of the bent opening') and Tubernafeyne (*tober na Féine*, 'well of the warrior band').

****

Western Scotland is a most underrated part of Irish folklore and mythology, just as Irish myth and legend is an underrated part of Scottish mythology. The reasons for this are many and beyond the scope of this book, but the connections through all the complexities of our history survive. And although the Ulster Cycle of tales is the most predominant in our shared past, the length and breadth of Ireland is in fact full of Scottish connections.

Two Irish High Kings, Lugaid Mac Con and Cormac mac Airt, when in difficulty, went to the isles of west Scotland and received help from the local king. Cú Chulainn* trained under Scáthach, after whom the Isle of Skye is named, and Deirdre and Naoise fled to Glen Etive in Scotland in order to escape the wrath of King Conchobar mac Nessa, King of Ulster.

Lugaid Mac Con, High King from 195 to 225 AD, was banished before he became King to Scotland, where he was welcomed by the king, Béinne Briot, who promised him help from both himself and the Britons. Lugaid is said to have married a daughter of Béinne and to have had three sons by her, who were known as the three Fothads. One of these brothers, Fothad Canann, was a leader of the Fianna* (*rígféinnid*) and is said to have taken

FIGURE 52. The plain on the Isle of Skye where Cú Chulainn did his training under Scáthach.

possession of lands in Argyll. Keating says that the house of Mac Cailín of Argyle derives from Fothad Canann.

After seven years, the king's promise held good, and a large number of ships and galleys and a vast flotilla of currachs were gathered at *Port Rig* ('king's port'), which is now the present Portpatrick on the Rinns of Galloway across the peninsula from Stranraer. From here, Lugaid then embarked with his British army and sailed around Ulster to land in Connacht. Watson writes in his *Celtic Placenames of Scotland* that 'this *Port Rig* must be the one which is now Portpatrick'. This is reinforced by the legend that the number of boats was so great that they formed a continuous bridge between Ireland and Scotland.

However, Irish commentators say that *Port Rig* is really Portree on the Isle of Skye. This harbour is definitely more protected than the harbour on the Rinns of Galloway.

A strong connection with Scotland arose after the uprising of the *Aithechtuatha* or underclass led by Cairbre Cinn Cait, in which three kings of Ireland, namely Feig, Fiachaid and Breasal, were slain. This occurred in the second century AD, and the tale states that the three respective wives of the three kings were Beartha, Eithne and Áine, and that they were carrying in their wombs the three children of the above kings. These women fled to Scotland and possibly landed at *Port Rig* and gave birth to three sons, Tuathal Techtmar, Tiobraide Tirech and Corb Olom. These sons remained in Scotland until they were ready to return to Ireland and take up their respective kingships.

FIGURE 53. *Dún Scáthach* on the Isle of Skye.

The famous lactiferous cow, the *Glas Gaibhleann*, had a bed on the Isle of Skye at somewhere called Glasghoilean, but this place has yet to be located. However, a more famous place on Skye, namely *Dún Scáthach*, can be traced and still exists. It is on Loch Eishort and north of the Bay of Gauscavaig (*Òb Gauscavaig*). The castle sits on an offshore rock that rises forty feet above sea level, and there is a gap of twenty feet between the rock and the mainland. The ruins of the castle that in later times was a Mac Donald stronghold are said to stand on the site of *Dún Scáthach*.

The Cuillin Hills to the west of *Dún Scáthach* are named after Cú Chulainn.* In the tale *Siabur-charpat Con Culainn*, or 'The Ghostly Chariot of Cú Chulainn', this fort is said to have been protected by seven ramparts. The archaeologist Dr Mortimer Wheeler has suggested that this came as a direct consequence of the introduction of the sling, which required a multiplication of defensive ramparts. These ramparts would have had individual entrances, though not necessarily in line. A series of irregular entrances would force the invader to turn his troops to the next entrance, where presumably a defensive force would be awaiting.

The twenty feet between Scáthach's fort and the island include the 'Bridge of the Pupils' (*droichet na ndaltae*), which Cú Chulainn* had to cross before meeting Scáthach. This bridge, according to lore, had 'two low heads or ends and it was high in the middle; and when a person stood on one end of it the other end would rise up and he would be cast off to the bottom'. Cú Chulainn, however, did the hero's 'salmon-leap' and landed on the ground at the end of the island. He went to the fort and pushed the point of his spear against the door so that it went through it. Scáthach sent her daughter Úathach to find out who this man was. Úathach praised the man she saw to her mother, and Scáthach said to her, 'I see that you are pleased by this man.' 'That is true,' said the daughter. 'If your passion is such,' said Scáthach, 'then you should request that he spends the night with you.' As well as warrior feats, sexual initiation would seem to have been part of training under Scáthach.

A great yew tree was a noted part of Scáthach's fortress. It was around this tree that much of the training took place. Cú Chulainn's* friends on Skye included Fer Diad mac Damain, who was eventually slain by Cú Chulainn on the River Ardee in Co. Louth, and Naoise mac Uisneach, the lover of Deirdre, whose story in Scotland is told below.

Against much local protest, a bridge was built to Skye so that access by car is easier. It is regarded as one of the most beautiful islands on earth and its early history, though shrouded in shadow, is now beginning to surface slowly to reveal its rich prehistory and mythology.

Longes mac nUisnig, 'The Exile of the Sons of Uisnech', is recorded in a Scottish manuscript dated 1238 AD and known as the Glenmasan Manuscript. The tale it relates, that of the great love between Deirdre and Naoise, is set in some of the most beautiful landscape in Europe, and it tells the early history of the glens, rivers and mountains from a female and aesthetic perspective rather than being preoccupied with the chronicling of battles, which seems to be a characteristic of the male account of history and myth.

Professor Mackinnon has suggested that the manuscript may have been put together at an early date by an Irish scholar and that a copy found its way to Argyllshire, where the Scottish aspects to the story were expanded. According to him, the tale was well known in the Scottish Highlands 'from time immemorial' and was one of the *primscela* or principal tales that a poet must know.

> Who but the sons of Usnoth, chief of steamy Etha?
> Blessed are the rocks of Etha.

The above is a quote from Macpherson's *Ossian,* which was instrumental in reviving ancient Scottish lore and, though heavily criticised, retains in its wayward way memories of older times. Despite the bitter criticism he received, Macpherson had a strong influence on Thomas Jefferson, Napoleon and Goethe, among others. The above quote refers to the sons of Uisliu, now more generally referred to as the sons of Uisnech. Etha, more correctly *Éit* ('a herd of cattle'), refers to the present-day Glen Etive and Loch Etive. This great romantic tale is in the finest Ulster-Scots tradition, and its heroine Deirdre has been named as the highest type of Celtic womanhood. The love story of Deirdre and her lover Naoise precedes Romeo and Juliet and was an inspiration to the eighteenth-century German Romantic movement.

'Take a blessing from me eastward to Alba; good is the sight of her bays and valleys; pleasant was it to sit on the slopes of her hills when the sons of Uisnech used to be hunting' – So sang Dearshula or Darthula, the name they knew Deirdre by in Scotland on account of her dark-blue eyes. When she spoke the above words, she was homesick for the land of her birth. When she and Naoise and his brothers eloped to Scotland, it was on Loch Ness, south of Inverness (*Inbhear Ness,* 'the mouth or harbour of Loch Ness'), that Deirdre is reputed to have built their first home. Local lore has it that the original fort or *caher* was where the ruins of Urquhart Castle now stand. Urquhart Castle is just south from Urquhart Bay on the northside of Loch Ness, equidistant between Fort Augustus and Inverness. Some say that Loch Ness derives its name from Naoise, but this is fanciful, as almost all names in Gaelic describe the topography of a place. One meaning for *ness* is a hill or a hillfort.

While at Loch Ness Naoise and his brothers hired themselves out to local kings in order to collect taxes and to right wrongs like their cousins Cú Chulainn* and Conall Cernach before them (Cú Chulainn's mother was Deichtine and her sister was the mother of the sons of Uisneach). This type of work consistently led to pressures, at one time from the King of the North who desired Deirdre for himself, so they all moved to Glen Etive, where, according to one writer, the old inhabitants in the early nineteenth century could point out the apple trees of Naoise, of Ainlee and of Ardan. The many other places associated with Deirdre and Naoise include the towering mountains of Glen Etive, namely Ben Ceitlein, Stob Dubh, Coire Dionach, the *Buachaile Beag* and the *Buachaile Mór* and the Grianán, below which stretch the waters of Loch Etive far away into the distance. Ben Ceitlein and the Grianán, also known as Grianán Darthula, may well be the same place; *grianán darthula* means the 'sun chamber of Deirdre', and it is an area on the south side of Glen Etive. Stob Dubh, which possibly comes from *Stuaigh Dubh* and is another form of *Sliabh Dubh* or 'black mountain', is also to the south of Glen Etive. To the north of Glen Etive and on the border with Argyll is a mountain known as *Sgor na hUlaidh*, and this has a possible association with the sons of Uisnech, as it means the 'camp of the Ulstermen'.

Dalness, on the River Etive, or *Dal an Eas*, 'flatland by the waterfall', or more simply the 'field by the waterfall', was the area in which the poet Duncan Bán Macintyre (1724–1812) lived. It is interesting to note that in his lifetime, a James Macintyre from Glencoe, a mere stone's throw from Glen Etive, had the Glenmasan Manuscript in his possession some years before 1782.

Six miles south-east of Dalness is *Beinn Dóbhrain* ('peak of the streamlet'), mentioned in the verses below from a longer work by Duncan Bán. The poem represents a continuous tradition in Gaelic poetry from the fourteenth to the eighteenth century both in its metre and in its simple though strong affinity with nature; it could well have come from the lips of Deirdre herself.

An t-urram thar gach beinn
Aig Beinn Dóbhrain;
De na chunnaic mi fonghréin,
Is I bu bhóidhche leam …

Monadh fada réidh
cúil and faighteadh féidh
soilleireachd an t-sléibh
bha mi sónrachadh.

Doireachan nan geng,
coille anns am bi feur
's foinneasach an shréidh
bhíos a'cómhnaidh ann.

Honour beyond each ben
For Beinn Dorain
Of all I have seen beneath the sun,
The most glorious is Ben Dóbhrain …

Its long moor's level way,
And its nooks whence wild deer stray,
To the lustre on the brae
Oft I've lauded them.

Dear to me its dusky boughs,
In the wood where green grass grows,
And the stately herd repose,
Or there wander, wander slow;

But the troops with bellies white,
When the chase comes into sight,
Then I love to watch their flight,
Going noisily.

[Translated by, among others, Iain Crichton Smith and Tom Thomson]

In the tale of 'Deirdre's Lament', told in the Glenmasan Manuscript, Deirdre is depicted holding the lifeless body of Naoise in her arms as follows:

And Deirdre dishevelled her hair and began kissing Naoise and drinking his blood, and the colour of embers came into her cheeks and she uttered this lay:

Glen Etive!
There I raised my first house,
Delightful its wood! when we rose in the morning
A sunny cattle-fold was Glen Etive.

The drinking of a dead lover's blood is also found in a more recent lament, namely the famous *Caoineadh Airt Uí Laoghaire* ('A Lament for Art O'Leary') in which Eibhlín Dubh Ní Chonaill keens for her murdered husband:

Is do chuid fola leat 'na sraithibh
Is níor fhanas le hí ghlanadh
Ach í ól suas lem basaibh.

Your blood pouring in streams
I did not stay to wipe it
But filled my hands and drank it.

[Translated by Seán Ó Tuama]

A fourteenth-century poem attributed to Deirdre could also describe Glen Etive:

Sweet are the cries of the brown-backed dappled deer under the oak-wood above the bare hill-tops, gentle hinds that are timid lying hidden in the great-treed glen.

There are many 'bare hill-tops' in this enchanted area beloved of Deirdre, and the following are the names of some of them: *Beinn Ceitlein*, 'the mountain-peak of Ceitleen', which is to the east of Glen Etive; *Buachaille Etive Beag*, '[the mountain] of Etive's small shepherds'; and *Buachaille Etive Mór*, '[the mountain] of Etive's large shepherds' – all of which are to the north of the glen. To the north also is Ossian's cave close to the A82, and west of the glen is *Scór na hUlaidh* or 'the encampment of the Ulaid or Ulstermen'. About twelve miles south-east from *Scór na hUlaidh* is *Beinn Ulaidh*, and within this area may be seen the territorial base of the sons of Uisnech while encamped in the region of Glen Etive.

Forty miles south of Glen Etive and north of Holy Loch and Dunoon is Glen Masan or 'Massan's Glen', where Deirdre and the sons of Uisnech stayed for a while before their return to Ireland. In her farewell to Scotland, Deirdre sang:

Glen Masan!
Tall is its wild garlic, white are its stalks:
We used to have a broken sleep
On the grassy river-mouth of Masan.

Glen Urchain!
That was the straight, fair-ridged glen!
Never was a man of his age prouder
Than Naoise in Glen Urchain.

Twelve miles south of Glen Etive on the A82 is Glen Orchy; its river, the Orchy, flows all the way to Loch Awe. Two miles south from Glen Orchy is Glen Lochy, also known as Glen Laidhe or Glen Lay. The A85 follows the glen as far as Loch Awe.

Glen Lay, O Glenlaidhe,
There I used to sleep under a shapely rock.
Fish and venison and badgers fat,
That was my portion in Glen Lay.

Eight miles west from Glen Masan is Glendaruel, and here the lovers spent time in the vicinity of the Kyles of Bute. Of this glen Deirdre said:

Glendaruadh, O Glendaruadh,
I love each man of its inheritance,
Sweet the noise of the cuckoo on bended bough
On the hill above Glendaruadh.

Glendaruadh was the glen's original name, and it presumably means 'the glen of two reds'.

At the close of the fifth century AD, Fergus mac Eirc founded a kingdom known as Dál Riada, which would expand its sway to western Scotland. The kingdom in Ireland came to an end after the Battle of Moira in 634 AD when the Irish and Scottish members of the tribe were defeated in a battle against Domnall mac Aed, King of Tara. However, the Scottish branch lasted until the twelfth century.

The centre of the Dál Riada kingdom in Scotland was Dunadd, also known as *Dun Att* and *Dun Monaid* or 'the fort on peatland'. Dunadd is twenty-five miles south from Oban. To quote the historian Aodh de Blacam: 'At the hill-fort of Dunadd in the purple Moss of Crinan, the rulers of Dál Riada made their seat.' It was here at Dunadd that Columcille* met King Conall, the ruler of Dál Riada; to quote Dorothy Pochin Mould,

> He probably found him on the rock of Dunadd, which still rises, a bluff of rock, from the flat moss of the Móine Mhór. This ancient fortress commands a great outlook, over the little hills of Knapdale and to the sea and out to the island of Jura. Perhaps the king suggested Iona as a good base of operations and arranged for the land to be granted to Columcille.

St Columcille* is known as Columba to Anglicans in Ireland and on Iona, where he founded his monastery in 563 AD. Iona was the centre of the Irish Church in Scotland, which later extended to other islands in the Hebrides and throughout Europe, even to Bobbio in northern Italy. Southend, Argyll, at the southern end of the Mull of Kintyre, is believed to be where Columcille first set foot on Scottish soil, and local legend says that the footprints to be seen near the remains of Dunaverty Castle are his. At Ellary, Argyll, is St Columba's Cave which contains what resembles an altar or a table or a primitive stove. When he died in 594 AD, an Ulster bard wrote: 'A *cruit* [harp] without a *ceis* [peg or key] is like a church without an abbot.'

The centre of the Dál Riada in Scotland appears at first sight to be nothing more than a rocky hill, and this indeed is what it is, yet this rocky outcrop standing nearly 200 feet above the surrounding land contained the great fort of Dunadd. From its summit, one can see the harbour at Crinan and the islands of Jura and Scarba. Apart from the aesthetics, the fort's position was a strategic one, which may explain its persistence over a number of centuries. Its defensive nature is shown by the fact that at one time the walls were more than thirty feet thick.

The inauguration of kings took place here for the Kings of Argyll; at the top of the hill, there is a footprint carved into a rock near the summit, known as the Royal Footprint. It is said to represent the footprint of Fergus Mór mac Eirc, the first King of the Dál Riada, who died about 500 AD. Another tradition says that this was originally the footprint of Oisín,* the hero of Scotland's Ossianic Tales, but this can be seen as folklore added to the early history of Dunadd. Nearby is a faint image of a boar and some writing in ogam, which if translated could yield valuable information. The boar was traditionally associated with feasts wherein the hero had first cut of the animal, which was known as the *curad mir* or the 'champion's portion'. A basin carved into the rock may have been used for water during the many ceremonies held here.

A probable seventh-century design known as the Dunadd motif-piece is said, according to Robert D. Stevick from the University of Washington in Seattle, to represent an example of 'the ancestry of insular designing'. This piece is both compass- and free-hand drawn, and is in the shape of a brooch. The diameter of the sketched form, which is on slate, is about one-and-a-half inches. Workshops producing decorated Irish and Anglo-Saxon style bronzes were located at Dunadd, which was exposed to international ideas and design. Hand-pins, which were originally large for laying out a sacred centre, were reduced in size as they became fashionable objects of choice. Brooches were also reduced in size, and the penannular ring with intricate designs representing animals or deities was produced here as well as in Irish workshops along the Moray Firth.

Archaeological excavations on the hill show that the Dál Riada was trading with people from mainland Europe. Moulds have been unearthed in which valuable objects were made. Many of these objects can be seen in the Kilmartin Museum about five miles north of Dunadd and at the National Museum of Scotland in Edinburgh. Stones carved with Christian symbols and motifs can be found in many local chapels and parish churches; Kilmartin parish church, close to the museum, contains many Christian artefacts. Within a six-mile radius of the museum there are 150 prehistoric monuments; Kilmartin Glen is an entry to prehistoric Scotland, as it contains 350 ancient monuments.

At his inauguration, each successive king placed his foot in the footprint of his royal ancestors. There are as many as twenty and possibly more inauguration sites in Ireland, one such being the Carn Fraoich mound close to Tulsk in Roscommon. During this rite, the king-to-be stood in the footprint of his ancestor and turned a circle right to the sun (*deis sol*); this showed that he was lord of the land in all directions

Another possible inauguration site was Dumbarton on the Clyde River, its earliest name being *Alt Clut* ('rock of the Clyde'). The ruling houses of Dumbarton and Dál Riada came into contention in the seventh century after the death of the Dál Riada King Aedán. Aedán's grandson Domnall Brecc attacked King Owen of Dumbarton and was heavily defeated, leading to the bardic verse of how 'the ravens tore the head of Domnall Brecc'.

Later, Dumbarton became known as *Dún Breatann*, or 'fortress of the Britons', who at that time were the Pretanic people or Cruithin* or Picts, a pre-Gaelic race who had strong connections with both Ulster and the rest of Ireland. According to W.J. Watson in *Celtic Placenames of Scotland*, it was once the acropolis of the ancient British kingdom of Strathclyde. At an earlier time, Dumbarton is supposed to have been the Roman station Theodosia. Legend holds that the prophet and druid Myrddin (later Merlin) stayed here as a guest of King Riderch sometime in the sixth century. In the ninth century, kings Olaf and Ivar arrived from Dublin in 200 longships and carried off slaves and looted treasure.

GLOSSARY

Children of Lir: One of the 'three sorrowful tales of Ireland' belonging to the tradition of medieval Gaelic romances, it tells how the four children are turned into swans by a druid so that they could escape murder at the hands of their stepmother. They remain in this form for 300 years at Loch Derravarragh in Co. Westmeath, then for another 300 years on the Sea of Moyle between Ireland and Scotland, followed by the same amount of time at Erris, Co. Mayo. They eventually meet a Christian missionary who baptises them shortly before they die.

Colmcille, St: Also known as Columba throughout Derry, Scotland and within the Church of Ireland. A prince of the Uí Néill, he founded a monastery on Iona after being exiled after a dispute with another churchman over the ownership of a manuscript led to a battle. He was the first to bring Christianity to Scotland. He returned to Ireland at one point to preside over the Synod of Drum Cett, one purpose of which was to exercise control over the *filí*.

Crom Cruach: According to the *Dindshenchas*,* the principal idol of all the colonies established in Ireland from earliest times to the sweep of Christianity, Crom Cruach is probably synonymous with Crom Dub whose festival celebrating Crom's overthrow by St Patrick, known as *Domhnach Chroim Duibh*, is held in many places throughout Ireland on the last Sunday in July or the first Sunday in August. He was a corn god to whom animal and human sacrifices were offered.

Cruithin: see under Dál nAraide.

Cú Chulainn: Originally named Setanta, he went as a youth to train with the Red Branch Knights at Emain Macha. He killed the hound of Culann, who was a smith to the king. As recompense, Setanta offered himself in place of the slain hound and thus got the name Cú Chulainn or 'the hound of Culann'. His deeds as a warrior are the focus of many tales, but especially that of the *Táin Bó Cúailnge*,* in which he meets his death. As a central figure in mythology, he remains a major force in the Irish imagination.

Dagda: The chief of the Gaelic pantheon, he is the Irish equivalent of Zeus, Jupiter and Odin. He had powers of wizardry and led the Tuatha Dé Danann* into Ireland against the Fir Bolg.* A warrior god in the heroic mould, he is associated with a club so weighty that it had to be borne on wheels. He was killed at the battle of Magh Tuiredh against the Fomorians.*

Dál nAraide: This is the name given to the Cruithin people who survived in Ireland, mostly in Co. Down. They were the earliest inhabitants of Britain and Ireland and were in Ireland before the Fir Bolg* and the Gaels. The kingdom of Dál nAraide stretched from Slemish mountain to Newry. A notable king of the tribe was Suibhne Geilt* or 'Mad Sweeny'.

Diarmuid: see Gráinne.

Dindshenchas: The term means 'lore of places' and is used to describe a body of early Irish literature recounting the origins of place names. The corpus is mainly made up of poems and several prose commentaries. Edward Gwynn compiled and translated *dindshenchas* poems from various manuscripts which were published in five volumes between 1903 and 1934 under the title *The Metrical Dindshenchas*.

Fianna: A band of roving men whose principal occupations were hunting and war and who were the focus of the tales from the Fenian Cycle. They were led by Finn mac Cumhail.*

Finn mac Cumhail: A mythical warrior–hunter of ancient Ireland, though some writers also see him as a historical figure. He also plays a prominent part in the mythologies of Scotland (where he is known as Fingal) and the Isle of Man. Stories about him and his band of followers, the Fianna,* are collected in the *Duanaire Finn*, 'The Lays of Finn'.

Fir Bolg: Pre-Gaelic Invaders of Ireland associated by some historians with the Belgae, a tribe of continental Celts, though this has been disputed. They are regarded as belonging to the lower social order. They worshipped an ancestor god named Bulga, a god of lightning.

Fomorians: A race of pirates from present-day Scandinavia associated with the north-west coast of Ireland, particularly with Tory Island off the Donegal coast. Scholars have suggested that the ancient Irish believed in two divine races: the Tuatha Dé Danann,* lords of life and light, and the Fomorians, lords of darkness and death. Their name is derived from an Irish phrase meaning 'under the sea'. They possibly have their origins in the Middle East where, like the Phoenicians, their god is Ba'al or Balor.

Gabha: see Goibniu.

Goibniu: The Irish smith god and one of the chieftains of the Tuatha Dé Danann.* Placed along with Credne the silversmith and Luchta the carpenter as one of 'the three gods of art', he forged the weapons used in battle against the Fomorians.* His name is derived from the Old Irish word for 'smith' – *gobae* (modern Irish *gabha*). He is also the owner of the *Glas Gaibhleann*, a magical cow of abundance.

Gráinne: The daughter of a high king, she marries Finn mac Cumhail* when he is an old man. She falls in love, however, with Diarmuid* Ó Duibhne, a member of the Fianna.* They elope and are followed by Finn and the Fianna all over Ireland. 'The Pursuit of Diarmuid and Gráinne' is one of the greatest of all the Irish love stories. Dozens of places are called after the famous couple, many cromlechs being described as their 'love beds'.

Lug: One of the principal gods of the Tuatha Dé Danann,* he is both the Gaulish and Gaelic sun god, the god of genius and light. His name is found as an element in many place names throughout Europe, such as London and Lyon. The month of August in Irish, *Lughnasa*, is named after him.

Manannán mac Lir: He may be seen as the Irish Neptune, or sea god, his name meaning 'son of the sea (*lir*)'. He is also regarded as a sun god, often seen as riding through the waves on horseback, and his daughter Áine is a sun goddess.

Medb: A queen of Connacht and a central figure in the great Irish epic, the *Táin Bó Cúailgne.* *Some scholars are of the opinion that she was an historical figure who reigned at the beginning of the Christian era. She is said to be buried under a large cairn in Knocknarea in Co. Sligo, while another resting place associated with her is Knockma in Co. Galway.

Oisín: The great poet of the Fenian Cycle and son of Finn mac Cumhail. He is known as Ossian in Scotland. He is taken to *Tír na nÓg* ('the land of youth') by Niamh, a fairy woman and daughter of Manannán mac Lir,* where he remains for what he thinks is three years. However, when he returns to Ireland he finds 300 years have passed, and he becomes an old man when he dismounts from his horse. He meets St Patrick and the dialogue between them is told in the poem *Agallamh Oisín agus Phátraic*.

Partholón: Said to have led the first colony to Ireland in 2678 BC, 278 years after the Flood. Arriving from Greece with his wife, three sons and a 1,000 followers, he landed in Donegal Bay. The first recorded battle in Irish history was fought between Partholón's people and the Fomorians at *Magh Ith* near Lough Swilly. Four years later, Partholón died at Moynalty in Leinster.

Suibhne: A seventh-century chief of the Dál nAraide* who fled after he was driven mad by the horrors of battle. He spent the rest of his days in the branches of tall trees, living on water and watercress. His adventures are recounted in the romance titled *Buile Suibhne* ('Mad Sweeny').

Sweeny: see Suibhne.

***Táin Bó Cuailgne*:** This epic, which is the central text of the Ulster Cycle tales, concerns a war between Connacht and Ulster, centred around the desire of Medb* for the Brown Bull of Cooley, an animal attributed with great powers of fecundity. A central character in the epic is Cú Chulainn,* who fights single-handed against the forces of Connacht.

Tuatha Dé Danann: The people of the goddess Anu or Danu, a mother of the gods who is associated with fertility and nurture. The Tuatha Dé Danann are said to have been the fourth of the six legendary peoples who invaded Ireland, arriving in 350 BC. Legend says that after they were defeated by new invaders, the Milesians, they entered the underground beneath the hills and vales of Ireland, and thus became known as the *aes síde* or fairies, who played a major part in Irish folklore.

BIBLIOGRAPHY

Aldridge, R.B., 'The Routes Described in the Táin Bó Flidhais', *JRSAI*, 91, 1 (1961).

Andersen, Jorgen, *The Witch on the Wall* (London, 1977).

Annals of Clonmacnoise, edited by Denis S.J. Murphy (Dublin, 1896).

Annals of the Four Masters, edited by John O'Donovan (Dublin, 1851).

Annals of Innisfallen, edited by Mac Airt, S. (Dublin, 1951).

Annals of Ulster, edited by Seán mac Airt and Gearóid mac Niocaill (Dublin, 2004).

Automobile Association, *Illustrated Road Book of Scotland* (Basingstoke, 1974).

Bergin, Osborn, *Irish Bardic Poetry* (Dublin, 1970).

Best, R., and Bergin O. (eds), *Lebor na hUidre* (Dublin, 1929).

Best, R. I., O. Bergin and M.A. O'Brien (eds), *Book of Leinster*, vols 1–5 (Dublin, 1954–67).

Bhreathnach, Edel, *Ireland in the Medieval World* AD *400–1000* (Dublin, 2014).

Boyle, Paddy, *Drumanagh* (Dublin, 2001).

Brookes, Charlotte, *Reliques of Irish Poetry* (Dublin, 1789).

Bruford, Alan, *Gaelic Folk-Tales and Medieval Romances* (Dublin, 1969).

Cameron, A., *Reliquiae Celticae*, vol. I (Inverness, 1892).

Campion, Edmund, *Histories of Ireland* (London, 1571).

Carmichael, Alexander, in Matheson Angus (ed.), *Carmina Gadelica, Hymns and Incantations* … (London, 1968).

Carney, James, *Studies in Irish Literature and History* (Dublin, 1979).

Carney, James, and David Greene, *Celtic Studies: Essays in Memory of Angus Matheson* (London, 1968).

Chadwick, Nora, 'Imbas Forasnai', *Scottish Gaelic Studies*, 4, 2 (1934).

Chadwick, Nora, and Myles Dillon, *The Celtic Realms* (London, 1967).

Cochrane, Robert, 'On Broighter, Limavaddy, Co. Londonderry, and the Find of Gold Ornaments There in 1896', *JRSAI* (1902).

Coffey, George, 'Sess Kilgreen', *JRSAI* (1911).

Condren, Mary, *The Serpent and the Goddess* (Dublin, 2002).

Cooke, John, *Wakeman's Handbook of Irish Antiquities* (Dublin, 1903).

Cooney, Gabriel, and Eoin Grogan, *Irish Prehistory* (Bray, 1999).

Corkery, Daniel, *Hidden Ireland* (Dublin, 1967).

Croker, T.C., *Fairy Legends and Traditions from the South of Ireland* (1825).

Cunningham, George, *Roscrea and District* (Roscrea, 1976).

Cunningham, Noreen, and Pat McGinn, *The Gap of the North* (Dublin, 2004).

D'Aliella, Count, *Migration of Symbols* (London, 1894).

Daly, Eugene, *Leap and Glandore, Fact and Folklore* (Cork, 2005).

Dooley, Ann, and Harry Roe, *Tales of the Elders of Ireland* (New York, 1999).

Dinneen, P.S., *Foclóir Gaedhilge agus Béarla* (Cork, 1927).

Davidson, H.R. Ellis, *Myths and Symbols in Pagan Europe* (Manchester, 1988).

Davies, O., *The Black Pig's Dyke*, Ulster Journal of Archaeology (Belfast, 1955).

Dalton, John, 'Crom Cruaich of Magh Sleacht', *PRIA*, 36 (1922).

Di Martino, Vittorio, *Roman Ireland* (Cork, 2003).

Dillon, Myles, *Early Irish Literature* (Chicago, 1948).

Dillon, Myles, *Early Irish Society* (Cork, 1959).

Dillon, Myles, *Irish Sagas* (Dublin, 1959).

Dobbs, Margaret, 'The Territory and People of Tethba', *JRSAI*, 11, 3 (1938).

Dobbs, Margaret (ed.), *Táin Bó Flidais* (RIA, 1916).

Durell, Penelope, *Discover Dursey* (Cork, 1996).

Evans, D. Delta, *The Ancient Bards of Britain* (Merthyr Tydfil, 1906).

Evans, Estyn, *Irish Folk Ways* (London, 1957).

Evans, Estyn, *Prehistoric and Early Christian Ireland* (London, 1966).

Evans Wentz, W.Y., *Fairy-Faith in Celtic Countries* (Oxford, 1911).

Flanagan, Deirdre, and Laurence Flanagan, *Irish Place Names* (Dublin, 1994).

Flower, Robin, *The Irish Tradition* (London, 1973).

Freud, Sigmund, *The Interpretation of Dreams* (London, 1974).

Gantz, Jeffrey, *Early Irish Myths and Sagas* (London, 1981).

Green, Miranda, J., *Dictionary of Celtic Myth and Legend* (London, 1992).

Gwynn, Edward (ed.), *The Metrical Dindshenchas*, 5 vols (Dublin, 1903–1935).

Hamilton, G.E., 'Two Ulster Inauguration Places', *JRSAI* (1912).

Heany, Paddy, *At the Foot of Slieve Bloom* (Kilcormac Historical Society, 1999).

Henderson, George, *Bricriu's Feast* (London, 1899).

Henry, Francoise, *Irish Art During the Viking Invasions* (London, 1967).

Hogan, Edmund, *Onomasticon Goedelicum* (Dublin, 1910).

Howe, G., and Harrer G.A., *A Handbook of Classical Mythology* (London, 1931).

Jackson, Kenneth, H., *A Celtic Miscellany* (London, 1957).

Jackson, Kenneth, H., *The Oldest Irish Tradition: A Window on the Iron Age* (Cambridge, 1964).

Joyce, P.W., *Irish Names of Places* (3 vols) (Dublin 1869, reprinted Dublin 1995).

Joyce, P.W., *A Smaller Social History of Ancient Ireland* (Dublin, 1906).

Joyce, P.W., *Old Celtic Romances* (London, 1914).

Kearney, Terri, *Lough Hyne, From Prehistory to the Present* (Skibbereen, 2013).

Keating, Geoffrey, *Foras Feasa ar Éirinn* (*History of Ireland*), 4 vols, trs., David Comyn and Patrick Dinneen (London, 1902–14).

Kelly, Fergus, *A Guide to Early Irish Law* (Dublin, 1988).

Kelly, Fergus, *Early Irish Farming* (Dublin, 2000).

Kennedy, Patrick, *Legendary Fictions of the Ancient Celts* (London, 1866).

Kinsella, Thomas, *The Táin* (Dublin, 1969).

Lawlor, H.C., *Ulster: Its Archaeology and Antiquities* (Belfast, 1928).

Liversage, David, 'An Island Site at Lough Gur', *JRSAI*, 88, 1 (1958).

Löffler, C.M, *The Voyage to the Otherworld Island in Early Irish Literature*, 2 vols (Salzburg, 1983).

Lowry-Corry, Dorothy, 'The Stones Carved with Human Effigies on Boa Island and on Lustymore Island on Lower Lough Erne', *PRIA*, 41 (1932–1934).

Lynn, Chris, *Navan Fort* (Bray, Co. Wicklow, 2003).

Lysaght, P., *The Banshee: The Irish Supernatural Death Messenger* (Dublin, 1986).

Macalister, R.A.S. (ed.), *Lebor Gabála Érenn* (Dublin, 1938).

Macalister, R.A.S., *Ancient Ireland* (New York, 1978).

Macalister, R.A.S., *Archaeology of Ireland* (London, 1996).

Mac Cana, Proinsias, *Celtic Mythology* (London, 1970).

Mac Coitir, Niall, *Irish Trees, Myths, Legends and Folklore* (Cork, 2003).

McCone, Kim, *Pagan Past and Christian Present in Early Irish Literature* (Maynooth, 1990).

Mac Culloch, John Arnott, *Religion of the Ancient Celts* (Edinburgh, 1866, 1911).

MacDonald, Philip, 'Archaeological Evaluation of the Inaugural Landscape of Crew Hill' (Co. Antrim. Ulster Journal of Archaeology, 2008).

McGowan, Joe, *Echoes of a Savage Land* (Cork, 2001).

McGowan, Joe, *Inishmurray, Island Voices* (Sligo, 2004).

Macleod, Paice, Sharon, *The Descent of the Gods* (Harvard, 2000–1).

McMahon, Joanne, and Jack Roberts, *The Sheela-na-Gigs of Ireland and Britain* (Cork, 2000).

Mac Neill, Eoin, *Celtic Ireland* (Dublin, 1921).

Mac Neill, Eoin (ed.), *Duanaire Finn*, Part 1 (ITS London, 1908).

Mac Neill, Máire, *Festival of Lughnasa* (Dublin, 1982).

Mac Niocaill, Gearóid, *Ireland Before the Vikings* (Dublin, 1972).

McParlan, James, *Statistical Survey of the County of Mayo: With Observations on the Means of Improvement* (Dublin, 1802).

Macpherson, James, *Ossianic Tales* (London, 1762).

Mac Sweeney, P. M., *The Martial Career of Conghal Cláiringhneach* (London 1904).

Marshall, J.D.C., *Forgotten Places of the North Coast* (Moy, Co. Antrim, 1987).

Meyer, Kuno, *Death Tales of the Ulster Heroes* (Dublin, 1906).

Meyer, Kuno (ed.), *Sanas Cormaic* (Dublin, 1912).

Meyer, Kuno, *Ancient Irish Poetry* (London, 1913).

Meyer, Kuno, *Anecdota from Irish Manuscripts* (Dublin, 1913).

Meyer, Kuno, *Bruchstüche der älteren Lyirk Irland* (Berlin, 1919).

Meyer, Kuno, and Alfred Nutt, *The Voyage of Bran*, 2 vols (London, 1895–97).

Mitchell, Frank, *The Irish Landscape* (Glasgow, 1976).

Morris, Henry, 'Where is Tor Inis, the Island Fortress of the Formorians?', *JRSAI* (1927).

Morris, Henry, 'Where Was Bruidhean Da Derga?', *JRSAI*, 65 (1935).

Morrison, Alex, *Early Man in Britain and Ireland* (London, 1980).

Mulchrone, Kathleen, *Tripartite Life of St. Patrick* (Dublin, 1939).

Murphy, Gerard (ed.), *Duanaire Finn*, Part 2 (ITS London, 1933).

Murphy, Gerard, *Ossianic Lore* (Cork, 1955).

Neary, Michael, 'The True Origins of the Sons of Mil', *County Louth Archaeological and Historical Journal*, 18 (1973).

Ó Cathasaigh, Tomás, *The Heroic Biography of Cormac Mac Airt* (Dublin, 1977).

Ó Cháthain, Séamas, *The Festival of Brigit* (Dublin, 1995).

O'Connell, Michael, Ursula Lyons and Breda Buckley, *Murragh, A Place of Graves* (Ballineen and Enniskeane Heritage Group, 2017).

Ó Crualaoich, Gearóid, *The Book of the Cailleach* (Cork, 2006).

Ó Cuív, Brian, *Cath Muighe Tuireadh – The Second Battle of Magh Tuireadh* (Dublin, 1945).

O'Curry, E., *Lectures on the MS Materials of Ancient Irish History* (Dublin, 1861).

O'Curry, E., *Manners and Customs of the Ancient Irish*, vols 1–3 (Dublin, 1873; 1996).

O'Donoghue, Bruno, *Parish Histories and Place Names of West Cork* (Cork, 1983).

O'Donovan, John, *The Banquet of Dún na n-Gedh and the Battle of Magh Rath* (Dublin, 1842; 1995).

O'Donovan, John, 'Pre-Christian Notices of Ireland', Ulster Journal of Archaeology, 8 (1860).

O'Grady, Standish, *The Coming of Cuculain* (Cork, date not given).

Ó hÓgáin, Dáithí, *Fionn Mac Cumhaill* (Dublin, 1988).

Ó hÓgáin, Dáithí, *The Sacred Isle* (Cork, 1999).

O'Keeffe, J.G., *The Adventures of Suibhne Geilt* (London, 1913).

O'Kelly, Michael J., *Newgrange, Archaeology, Art and Legend* (London, 1982).

O'Kelly, Michael J., *Early Ireland* (Cambridge, 1989).

O'Leary, Daniel, *Kilmeen and Castleventry Parish Co. Cork* (Cork, 1975).

Ó Muirithe, Diarmaid, and Deirdre Nuttall (eds), *Folklore of County Wexford* (Dublin, 1999).

O'Rahilly, Cecile, *Táin Bó Cuailnge* (Dublin, 1978).

O'Rahilly, Thomas F., *Early Irish History and Mythology* (Dublin, 1946).

Ordnance Survey of Ireland, *Discovery Series* (Dublin,).

Ordnance Survey of Northern Ireland, *Discoverer Map Series* (Belfast,).

Ó Ríordáin, Seán, P., and J. Ryan, 'The Excavation of a Large Earthen Ring-Fort at Garranes, Co. Cork', *PRIA*, 47 (1941–2).

Ó Ríordáin, Seán, P., *Antiquities of the Irish Countryside* (London, 1964).

Ó Síocháin, Conchúr, *The Man From Cape Clear* (Cork, 1975).

O'Sullivan, Sean, *Folktales of Ireland* (London, 1966).

Pedersen, Holger, *Scéalta Mháirtín Neile* (Dublin, 1994).

Piggott, Stuart, *Neolithic Cultures of the British Isles* (Cambridge, 1954).

Piggott, Stuart, *The Druids* (London, 1977).

Praeger, Robert Lloyd, *The Way That I Went* (Dublin, 1980).

Raftery, Barry, 'A Late Ogham Inscription From Co. Tipperary', *JRSAI*, 99, 2 (1969).

Raftery, Barry, *Pagan Celtic Ireland* (London, 1994).

Raftery, Joseph, *Prehistoric Ireland* (London, 1951).

Rees, Alwyn, and Brinley Rees, *Celtic Heritage* (London, 1961).

RIA Dictionary, *Dictionary of the Irish Language* (Dublin, 1913–1975).

Richardson, P., 'Sweat Houses between Blacklion and Dowra, County Cavan', *Ulster Journal of Archaeology*, 3, 2 (1939).

Rynne, E., 'A Sheela-na-Gig at Cloonlara, Co. Clare', *North Munster Antiquarian Journal*, (1967).

Ross, Anne, *Pagan Celtic Britain* (London, 1974).

Shee Twogig, Elizabeth, and Margaret Ronayne, *Past Perceptions – The Prehistoric Archaeology of South-West Ireland* (Cork, 1993).

Sjoestedt, Marie-Louise, *Gods and Heroes of the Celts* (Dublin, 1994).

Smith, Robert Angus, *Loch Etive and The Sons of Uisnach* (London, 1879).

Smyth Alfred P., *Celtic Leinster* (Dublin, 1982).

Smyth, D., *A Guide to Irish Mythology* (Dublin, 1996).

Smyth, D., *Cú Chulainn, an Iron Age Hero* (Dublin, 2005).

Stokes, Whitley, 'Second Battle of Moytura', *Revue Celtique*, 12 (1891).

Stout, Matthew, *The Irish Ringfort* (Dublin, 1977).

Sutherland, Elizabeth, *In Search of the Picts* (London, 1994).

Thomas, N.L., *Irish Symbols of 3000 BC* (Cork, 1988).

Thurneysen, R., *Die Irische Helden-und Königsage* (Halle, 1921).

Thurneysen, R., *Studies in Early Irish Law* (Dublin, 1936).

Turner, Alan, *The Glens of Antrim* (Belfast, 2005).

Waddell, John and Elizabeth Shee Twohig, *Ireland in the Bronze Age* (Dublin, 1995).

Waddell, John, *Foundation Myths* (Bray,2005).

Wagner, Heinrich, 'The Origins of Pagan Irish Religion', *Zeitschrift für celtische Philologie*, 38 (1981).

Wainwright, F.T., *The Problem of the Picts* (Edinburgh, 1955).

Warner, Richard, 'Two Pagan Idols', *Archaeology Ireland* (2003).

Waterman, D.M., *Excavations at Navan Fort, 1961–71* (Belfast, 1997).

Watson, W.J. *Celtic Placenames of Scotland* (Dublin, 1986).

Westropp, T.J., *Folklore of Clare* (Co. Clare, 2000).

Westropp, T.J., 'Magh Adhair, Co. Clare, The Place of Inauguration of the Dalcassian Kings', *PRIA*, 4 (1896).

Westropp, T.J., 'The "Mound of the Fianna" at Cromwell Hill, Co. Limerick, and a Note on Temair Luachra', *RIA*, 36 (1921).

Whistler, Laurence, *The English Festivals* (London, 1947).

Wilde, William, *Irish Popular Superstitions* (Dublin, 1852).

Wood-Martin, W.G., *Traces of the Elder Faiths of Ireland*, vols 1–2 (New York, 1970).

ACKNOWLEDGEMENTS

I would like to thank my wife Alison for helping me to complete this book and especially for her research on Western Scotland.

I would like to thank the following for assisting me in my travels throughout Ireland: Loughie McQuillkin from Rathlin Island, Co. Antrim; Stephen Hall from Whitehead, Co. Antrim; John Hall from Belfast; Sally Cox from Castletown, Co. Louth; the late Tom Barron from Virginia, Co. Cavan; the late Dr Dermot Mc Daid from Moynalty, Co. Meath; Paddy Mc Guinness from Dublin; Paddy Boyle from Rush, Co. Dublin; the late Dr Stephen O'Sullivan from Wexford; Daniel O'Leary from Caherkirky, west Cork; Michael O'Connell from Ballineen, west Cork; Michael John Crowley, Letter, Clonakilty; the Ballineen and Enniskeane Area Heritage Group; Áine Barry from Lough Gur, Co. Limerick; the late Colm O'Conghaile from Inishmore, the Aran Islands; the late Professor Etienne Rynne from Athenry, Co. Galway; Padraig Meehan from Carrowmore Centre, Co. Sligo; Anton Meehan from Tory Island, Co. Donegal; Bernie Moran from Co. Offaly; Paddy Heany from Cadamstown, Co. Offaly; the late Paddy Lowry from Co. Offaly; Ulrich Johanningmeier from Darmstadt, Germany; Tom Coffey from Carnahalla, Co. Tipperary; and Grainne Pym from Ballaghmore Castle, Co. Laois.

I would also like to thank Jack Roberts for use of some of his illustrations from his book *The Sacred Mythological Centres of Ireland* and Carole Cullen for her photographs. Finally, thanks to my editor Maurice Sweeney for his invaluable help in preparing my manuscript for publication.

INDEX

Note: Page references in bold refer to maps, illustrations.

Contents

THE RÁS

A DAY BY DAY DIARY
OF IRELANDS GREAT BIKE RACE

BY JIM TRAYNOR

ISBN: 978-1-905451-71-5

A CIP catalogue for this book is available from the National Library.

This book was published in cooperation with
Choice Publishing & Book Services Ltd, Drogheda, Co Louth, Ireland
Tel: 041 9841551 Email: info@choicepublishing.ie
www.choicepublishing.ie

Acknowledgements

Bridie Traynor wishes to thank all those who helped her in bringing Jim's book to fruition. In particular she's pleased to mention the huge contribution from Dermot Dignam, Miceal Campbell and Shane Stokes.

The Late Jim Traynor

1979	9 Day	10 Stages	179
1980	9 Day	9 Stages	187
1981	9 Day	11 Stages	196
1982	9 Day	11 Stages	206
1983	9 Day	9 Stages	223
1984	9 Day	13 Stages	232
1985	9 Day	12 Stages	242
1986	9 Day	13 Stages	250
1987	9 Day	10 Stages	263
1988	10 Day	12 Stages	275
1989	9 Day	11 Stages	284
1990	9 Day	10 Stages	293
1991	9 Day	11 Stages	300
1992	9 Day	9 Stages	307
1993	9 Day	10 Stages	314
1994	9 Day	10 Stages	322
1995	9 Day	11 Stages	330
1996	9 Day	9 Stages	338
1997	9 Day	10 Stages	346
1998	9 Day	9 Stages	356
1999	9 Day	9 Stages	365
2000	9 Day	9 Stages	374
2001	8 Day	8 Stages	383
2002	8 Day	8 Stages	393
2003	8 Day	8 Stages	403
2004	8 Day	8 Stages	413
2005	8 Day	8 Stages	424
2006	8 Day	9 Stages	435
2007	8 Day	8 Stages	449
2008	8 Day	8 Stages	461

FOR JIM

This book tells the story of Ireland's greatest bike race which was formally named "RÁS TAILTEANN" from its beginning in 1953 but has always been informally referred to as 'The RÁS'. It is largely written by one of the sports greatest volunteers, the late Jim Traynor who died in 2003, and is now published by his wife Bridie as her tribute to Jim and their lifelong love of cycle sport.

Jim became fascinated with road racing as a teenager in Newry and joined the Newry Wheelers club. The highlight of his competitive career was his participation in RÁS TAILTEANN during the sixties and seventies. Initially his main involvement was as a competitor in road events but he then became involved in organisation and for many years was the club's main event promoter, with responsibility for the Tour of Ulster during the 1960s. He was still a member at the time of his death.

Jim began his contribution to The RÁS in the early 1970s and performed a range of useful functions until in more recent times he focussed on the position of Chief Judge, in which role his decisions were rarely questioned and hardly ever challenged. Jim's reputation on The RÁS led to him also being in demand by other event organisers all over Ireland and there was nowhere too distant for him to travel to from start to end of the year.

Like most people involved in cycling, Jim also worked for the sport in a variety of capacities. He is credited as being the man who first introduced a computer-based result system to stage racing, using a basic programme written by himself at a Tour of Ulster. He helped to set up and became a member of the Irish Cycling Tripartite Committee, the umbrella body used to first co-ordinate the three separate organisations that used to "control" cycling in Ireland, and he worked towards the eventual unity that followed in the setting up of the Federation of Irish Cyclists, now